Where Have All the Pop Stars Gone?

Volume 1

Marti Smiley Childs
and Jeff March

EditPros LLC, Davis, California, USA • www.editpros.com

Published by EditPros LLC
423 F Street, suite 206
Davis, CA 95616
www.editpros.com

ISBN-10: 1-937317-00-5
ISBN-13: 978-1-937317-00-3

Library of Congress Control Number: 2011932632

Printed in the United States of America

CATALOGING INFORMATION:
Childs, Marti Smiley, and March, Jeff
        Where Have All the Pop Stars Gone? – Volume 1
    Filing categories:
        Biography
        Biography, musicians
        Biography, pop music
        Biography, rock music
        History, musical
        History, pop culture
        Music, popular
        Pop culture

Table of Contents

Acknowledgments

We would not have been able to create this book without the enthusiastic cooperation of the performers about whom we wrote, as well as their family members, producers, managers and musical colleagues, and others with whom we spoke. We offer our gratitude to all of them listed here.

THE ASSOCIATION
Gary "Jules"Alexander
Ted Bluechel Jr.
Jordan Cole
Russ Giguere
Terry Kirkman
Larry Ramos
Jim Yester
Pat Colecchio

HERMAN'S HERMITS
Karl Green
Keith Hopwood
Peter Noone
Barry Whitwam
Jana Eisenberg

THE KINGSTON TRIO
Nick Reynolds
Bob Shane
John Stewart
Frank Werber
Ken Bradshaw
Jim Connor
Henry Diltz
Chip Douglas
Cyrus Faryar
Gretchen Ballard Guard
Tom Guard
Alec Palao
Leslie Reynolds
Allan Shaw
Rick Shaw
Buffy Ford Stewart
Mikael Stewart
Paul Surratt
Jerry Yester

CHRIS MONTEZ
Chris Montez
Jimmy Joe Lee

THE SPIRAL STARECASE
Harvey Kaye
Dick Lopes
Vinnie Panariello
Pat Upton
Carol Fyffe
Johnny Hyde
Candy Kaye
Sunny Jo Petry
Sonny Knight

BOBBY VEE
Robert Velline
Jeff Veline

THE ZOMBIES
Rod Argent
Paul Atkinson
Colin Blunstone
Hugh Grundy
Chris White
Paul Arnold
Helen Atkinson
James Atkinson
Lucy Atkinson
Keith Atkinson
Molly Molloy
Matt Atkinson
Bob Sherwood
Alec Palao
Matthew White

PHOTOGRAPHY
J. Gary Alexander
Alex Anton
Pete Bentley
Totte Bergström
(www.myspace.com/totteberg-strom)
Susi Blunstone

Howard Bruensteiner
(www.sonic.net/roadman)
C.F. Martin Archives
Tracy Coles
Keith Curtis (www.keithcurtis.co.uk)
Henry Diltz (www.morrisonhotelgallery.com)
Amanda Domingues
(http://amandadphoto.com/)
Ann Grenier
Tom Guard (www.tomguard.com/)
Dan Hopwood
Ken Ige
Tom Keck
Craig Kienast
Matt Kellard
Alec Lewis
Dick Lopes
Jeff March
Tony New
Cory Panariello
Paul RyBolt (http://thisoldsong.com/)
Paloma Sendrey
Buffy Ford Stewart
Buddy Taylor

MUSIC CHART DATA
Joel Whitburn's Record Research Inc. (www.recordresearch.com), Menomonee Falls, Wisconsin

Preface

A half-century ago, amid the uneasy tension of the Cold War, millions of young families quietly pursued the American dream, a vision for which they had fought so bitterly in World War II and Korea. The heads of those households were survivors of the Great Depression and children of the hordes of immigrants who had passed through Ellis Island at the beginning of the century. They had become accustomed to extreme hardship, but they were determined to avail their children of opportunities they never had during their own youth.

During the 1950s, their children began attending classes in the thousands of new schools that were built to accommodate them, and after school they watched television programs that catered to the burgeoning "baby boom" population. Parents who may have owned only two pairs of knickers, one pair of shoes and a doll or handmade slingshot in their own childhood bought Davy Crockett caps, Hula Hoops, Keds sneakers, Levis dungarees, saddle shoes and poodle skirts for their fad-conscious offspring.

Encouraged to think for themselves and not burdened by the harsh realities that had placed limits on the lives of their parents, the first of the baby boomers reached adolescence in 1960. They quickly began to exert their influence, first as consumers, then in far more substantive ways. The 76 million baby boomers who ultimately came of age during the 1960s indelibly altered the global economic, political and artistic landscape in a way that no youth generation preceding it had ever done before.

We look back on the '60s as a convulsive era of civil rights and antiwar protests, of civil disobedience, of generational divisiveness, as the decade not only of the miniskirt, the Mustang and the lava lamp but also of LSD, draft card burning and assassinations. However, the 1960s also were characterized by remarkable creativity in popular music. Freed from the conventions of traditional crooning and formulaic big-band tunes, a new breed of composers and musicians drew upon an eclectic sphere of influences encompassing gospel, blues, jazz, folk and country music to evolve a new musical architecture built upon a solid beat and catering to the concerns and interests of young people.

WHATEVER HAPPENED TO THEM?

Where Have All the Pop Stars Gone? - Volume 1 is a window into the lives of 26 recording artists who topped the national record charts during the late 1950s and '60s - performers who were household names. Many of them pursued other interests in the decades that followed and prompted fans to wonder "Whatever happened to…?"

Remember the Kingston Trio, the nation's most popular, trend-setting recording combo of the late 1950s and early 1960s who avoided politics until questioning the morality of the growing American involvement in the war in Vietnam with their poignant rendition of "Where Have All the Flowers Gone"? Where have the members of the Kingston Trio gone? How about the Association, who fused folk and rock into an enormously popular repertoire of beloved songs including "Cherish," "Windy" and "Along Comes Mary"? Whatever became of all the original members of Herman's Hermits who popularized early 1900s dance-hall ditties but also recorded upbeat pop hits and sweet ballads? What about Chris Montez, who drew inspiration from the rockin' style of Ritchie Valens but then matured into a smooth crooner? And what about Bobby Vee, whose career was unexpectedly propelled when he helped the show go on the night after Buddy Holly, Valens and the Big Bopper died in a plane crash while on tour? And what of the Zombies, the first British band after the Beatles to rely on their own songwriting talents to score a number one hit in America with "She's Not There" in 1964? Whatever became of that group's members?

We were curious to know, asked questions and, with the involvement of the performers, family members, managers and producers, we learned the answers. In accurate detail, *Where Have All the Pop Stars Gone? – Volume 1* tells the stories of:

- the 1960s performer who became a licensed counselor deterring young people from drug and alcohol abuse;
- the member of a prominent band whose work as an optical designer and technician included installation of devices in a photo analysis laboratory for the CIA;
- the singer-guitarist who intentionally retreated from the spotlight with one of the world's most popular groups to live in seclusion as a rancher;
- the singer with one of the most distinctive pop music voices who entered the insurance field after his group dissolved, then re-emerged in music under a different name;
- the band leader who went from blowing sax to blow-drying hair;
- the former rock music guitarist who as a record company executive administered the recorded archives of Frank Sinatra, Nat "King" Cole, Peggy Lee, Dean Martin, Vic Damone and other traditional pop vocalists.

Where Have All the Pop Stars Gone? - Volume 1 is a tribute to them and other elite performers. In these pages, we reveal the aspirations, trials, triumphs and life's lessons learned by the musical pied pipers of the remarkable period between the late 1950s and late '60s. The musical creations of these talented individuals helped galvanize a restless youth generation and articulated the confused emotions that young people were experiencing as they came of age in a turbulent world. We explore how serendipitous musical success plucked these individuals from anonymity and thrust them into the spotlight; we describe how fame at such a young age influenced their decisions about how they would lead their lives; and we chronicle the professional and personal pursuits of those performers following the 1960s.

AUTHENTICATED, AUTHORIZED BIOGRAPHIES

Where Have All the Pop Stars Gone? - Volume 1 is the product of five guiding principles:

1. We obtained information about all artists we profiled from conversations we had with the performers themselves (and with family members of some of the deceased performers);

2. We collaborated with the performers, who reviewed and authenticated our manuscripts;

3. All performers profiled were soloists or members of vocal groups or bands whose recordings scored on the national pop music singles and/or album charts during the late 1950s and '60s;

4. We have placed an emphasis on achievement, celebrating the personal and professional triumphs of performers within and outside the music industry following the 1960s;

5. We intentionally selected artists who are representative of the widely divergent musical styles that distinguished the 1960s from all the other decades of the 20th century – musical diversity encompassing and influenced by rockabilly, rhythm and blues, surf music, jazz, folk standards, calypso, pop ballads, the British invasion, novelty tunes, folk-rock, art rock, psychedelia and country music.

This book does not dwell on the sordid or the sad. Although the text does acknowledge significant hardships, including financial and personal problems, our focus was on successful resolution of conflicts and discovery of what individuals learned about life as a result of confronting difficulty. Even though its content is entertaining and it has a nostalgia component, *Where Have All the Pop Stars Gone? - Volume 1* also seeks to teach and inspire by example.

Each chapter encompasses three segments:

- A historical overview of the highlights of each artist's recording career;

- A discography list of prominent hit recordings of each artist; and

- Biographical epilogues chronicling the life experiences of soloists and band members.

Where Have All the Pop Stars Gone? - Volume 1 affords many new insights into the personal lives of these individuals. We look beyond the music and peel away misperceptions and debunk myths about two dozen individuals with the same concerns as ours: establishing a stable household, the challenges of parenthood, paying the mortgage and the phone bill, caring for aging parents. We discover that beneath the public veneer, they are simply people whose jobs have involved creating music and performing in front of thousands of fans.

This is the first in a planned series of books. We hope you enjoy reading it.

—Marti Smiley Childs and Jeff March

1951 Seeburg Model 100C Select-O-Matic jukebox owned by Terry and Cindy Knight. Photo by Amanda Domingues.

The Association in 1969. Front row (from left) Ted Bluechel, Terry Kirkman; back row (from left) Russ Giguere, Brian Cole, Larry Ramos, Jim Yester, Jules Alexander. Photo by Henry Diltz.

1

Cherish

The Association

Impeccable harmonies and brilliant musical arrangements distinguish one of the most talented groups of the '60s, whose flame only flickered during the late '70s but burned bright once again throughout the '80s, '90s and into the new millennium. With three No.1 hit singles of which to boast, the Association earned record sales exceeding 100 million. In 1967 the Association was voted the No. 1 group by the radio Program Directors of America, becoming the first group to unseat the Beatles after three years.

The Association appeared on more than 30 major television shows, including the *Smothers Brothers Comedy Hour*, the *Ed Sullivan Show*, and the *Tonight Show with Johnny Carson*, and were the only group to have an entire *American Bandstand* show in 1969 devoted to their music. This national exposure and their reputation for polished performances brought them concert dates at the Greek Theatre in Los Angeles, the Saratoga Performing Arts Center, Tanglewood (home of the Boston Symphony Orchestra), and Ravinia Park in Chicago – prestigious venues that had catered to mature audiences and had never before hosted a self-contained rock group.

"We really owned Chicago, I think probably because of 'Windy,'" says guitarist Jim Yester. "We were their favorite sons for a lot of years. We used to get situated in a hotel in Chicago and then work in a radius of 400 to 500 miles surrounding Chicago."

Russ Giguere recalls, "We were the first rock and roll band that played the Coconut Grove, where Sinatra, Frank Gorshin, and Martin and Lewis performed. I remember when the lights came up I saw Carol Channing and George Burns at the front table, and I about fell over. It was so cool. And at that time I was the one who spoke to the audience first, so I looked down and said, 'You know, ladies and gentlemen, one doesn't often get the opportunity to do this, but I'd like to thank the man who taught us everything we know about singing – Mr. George Burns.' I was so thrilled. I'm still stoked about it. I'm still so pleased to have met the man and worked with him. He was a fan of the band, weirdly enough, years ago, of course."

The Association's concert tours broke numerous attendance records, including exceeding by 3,000 a 1958 record set by the Kingston Trio at Ravinia Park. On August 2, 1967, an enthusiastic crowd of 17,432 fans jammed into Ravinia to see the Association, who by then held two No. 1 singles – "Cherish" and "Windy."

With a career spanning more than two decades, the Association garnered three No. 1 singles, 15 *Billboard* and *Cashbox* chart records, 10 *Billboard* and *Cashbox* chart albums, three RIAA-certified gold singles, three RIAA-certified gold albums, an RIAA-certified platinum album and an RIAA-certified multi-platinum album.

The Association began as an outgrowth of a 13-member band called the Men, which evolved out of a talented group of folk singers who began folk-jamming together at a weekly hootenanny showcase at Doug Weston's Troubadour night club on Santa Monica Boulevard in West Hollywood.

"The hootenanny group, called the Innertubes, was originally put together as a protest against over-commercialization of the Troubadour showcase night and was open to anyone who wanted to get on stage and participate in a good old-fashioned sing-along of popular folk tunes," says Terry Kirkman. "At one time or another during its short existence, the group consisted of many soon-to-be famous people, including David Crosby, the Dillards, actor Harry Dean Stanton, as well as two remarkable future female stars – Cass Elliot [later of the Mamas and the Papas] and Spanky McFarlane [of Spanky and Our Gang]."

The Innertubes was such a crowd-pleaser that Weston extended an invitation to its participants who wanted to be part of an official organized group to be called the Men that he and the Troubadour would sponsor.

"The Men was just this incredible wall of sound. It really was like an orchestra – very much the inspiration for the Association, although we never thought of it that way," says Kirkman.

Terry was among the contingent to break away from the Men and form the Association. He recalls, "On any given hootenanny night there literally were 25 droppable names, or soon-to-be droppable names in the audience. The Eagles, Buffalo Springfield, the Byrds – originally called the Beefeaters – would be rehearsing in the folk den, which later became the bar of the Troubadour. We were rehearsing the Men in the big room, and we would literally go back and forth. It was really incestuous, creatively incestuous. You'd sort of be in a group for a week, helping them out with an idea, do an arrangement."

The Men was one of the first groups to adapt a folk-rock style, encompassing folk-flavored music set to a rock beat with electric guitars. Toward the end of the Men's sojourn at the Troubadour, Ted Bluechel recalled meeting Bob Dylan for the first time.

"Dylan came up on stage and we threw him a guitar that was electrified. He was grooving on that to the point where he wanted to play a number of songs. The next thing I heard from him was *Bringing It All Back Home*. He had gone electric. He'd gotten out of the 'A Hard Rain's Gonna Fall' bag and into 'Hey, Mr. Tambourine Man.'"

When differences in musical interest among the members arose, Terry Kirkman, Ted Bluechel, Brian Cole, Bob Page, Jules Alexander and Russ Giguere left the Men in the summer of 1965 to form what was to become the Association.

"The name was found by Terry's soon-to-be wife," explains Giguere. We looked up the word "aristocrats," which was the punch line to an off-color joke that everyone in entertainment knew. As she was looking up the precise meaning of that term in the dictionary, she came across the word "association." "And she said, listen to this: 'a group of individuals united toward a common goal,' and we said, 'Cool.' That's exactly who we were. It was that easy."

The six former members of the Men met at Terry Kirkman's West Hollywood apartment to discuss their options when they discovered that among them were two tenors, two baritones and two basses – perfect harmony. The group's blend of jazz and classical harmonies with a heavy influence of sophisticated folk music placed the Association in a musical category of its own.

"We were really doing a lot of experimental music. Very jazz-influenced, classically influenced. We were influenced by all kinds of music," says Giguere. "We all came out of pretty complex backgrounds. Terry was real well-schooled and played a bunch of different instruments. And Jules had always been a master of whatever he touches."

While auditioning at the Ice House nightclub in Pasadena and the Troubadour in Hollywood to become a solo act, Jim Yester learned about the new startup group and asked if they needed another member. Some members of the group had known his brother Jerry from the Modern Folk Quartet and agreed to audition him. "Terry and Jules were in the audience and left me a note to call them," says Yester. "I had also taken a phone number off a bulletin board. It was theirs!" Jim took the place of Bob Page.

The Association approached rehearsals and performances with professionalism. In the beginning, the group practiced eight hours a day and choreographed the entire performance, including what to do if, for example, a guitar string broke.

During its humble beginnings, the Association played at the Ice House in Pasadena and Burbank, the Troubadour, the Mecca in Orange County, coffee houses, junior colleges, colleges and high schools. They also performed demo sessions for songwriters. Yester recalls, "Jules came home one night after playing on a demo session for a friend named Tandyn Almer, who was a jazz pianist – kind of a beatnik, last of the Kerouac guys. He had written the song 'Along Comes Mary.' Jules brought it home and said, 'Wow, you gotta hear this song. It's really great.'" And the song became part of the Association's repertoire.

"We gave ourselves two years," says Giguere. "We figured it would take that long to get maybe a top 30 hit. Within a year, we had a top-10 single, and within 15 months, we had a No. 1 hit. So we considered ourselves real lucky."

Barry DeVorzon, a prolific songwriter, producer and arranger who founded the independent Valiant Records label, saw great potential in the Association. Jim Yester recalls, "Barry DeVorzon had produced 'Rhythm of the Rain' with the Cascades, and he wanted to produce us. So he took us into the studio and produced 'One Too Many Mornings,' which wasn't really great technically. It was a good record, but we were capable of a lot more."

By then the Association had a good fan club base from steadily playing at the Ice Houses – a clever move by the group's then-manager Dean Fredericks with his associate, Joe Koistra. Dean was an actor who was best known for his starring role in *Col. Steve Canyon, United States Air Force*, a 34-episode TV series in the late 50s. "Dean gave us $25,000 so we could rent a house to live and practice in, buy a few items of equipment, and become an act," says Kirkman.

Yester recalls, "Within a few months after starting to perform at the Ice House, we had standing room only lines around the block, and we talked Barry DeVorzon into allowing Curt Boettcher and Steve Clark to produce us. Curt had come out of Eau Claire, Wisconsin, with a group called the Goldbriars. In fact, he was the one who sang lead on 'Along Comes Mary' on the demo record. So he produced us and we went into the recording session with five songs. One of those five was 'Along Comes Mary,' which went right up the charts."

Jules Alexander attributes one of the group's biggest breaks to a managerial change – the hiring of Patrick Colecchio. "Dean Fredericks was with us when the Men were together, and he was with us when we put the Association together. He was a wonderful fellow and a good actor. But he had no idea about managing a rock and roll band. 'Along Comes Mary' was a hit and it was making money. But we were only making $500 a week playing the Golden Bear in Huntington Beach. And that was not cool. So Terry Kirkman knew Pat, and we said 'we've gotta do something.' So we dismissed Dean and hired Pat, and the next gig we made a grand for playing 30 minutes. That's probably the biggest punch that the band ever had."

A few months after "Along Comes Mary" – among the earliest hit songs of the sixties written about drugs – began a steady climb up the *Billboard* Hot 100 chart, a Chicago distributor convinced Valiant to press 60,000 copies of "Cherish" as a single. "This unusually large pre-order was a risky proposition for such a small label, but the release was an unprecedented success and precipitated the sale of Valiant to Warner Bros. Records, which continued to record the Association until 1972," says Kirkman.

With more than 5 million broadcast airplays to its credit, "Cherish" is now in the top 20 most played songs in Broadcast Music Incorporated (BMI) history, and "Never My Love" is the second most airplayed song in BMI history. "Originally, Cherish was too long to be a single release, but when a deejay in Ohio started playing it off the album, we decided to shorten it and release it as a single. We cut one of the repeats off the end and shortened the play-time length on the label. Quickly it became No. 1 and remained on the charts for several months," says Yester.

When Warner Bros. decided it wanted the Association, it bought Valiant Records. "There were three artists on Valiant Records: the Association, Shelby Flint, who had 'Penny In My Pocket And An Angel On My Shoulder,' and Maurice Chevalier, who sang 'Thank Heaven For Little Girls.' An odd combination," says Yester. "About that time Pat Colecchio became our new manager and he was real excited about the Mamas and the Papas' first album [*If You Can Believe Your Eyes and Ears*]. He contacted Bones Howe, who engineered that album. So Bones Howe produced us, and the first song off that album was 'Windy,' which screamed up the charts, and 'Never My Love' followed that."

But "Windy" almost didn't make the cut in the Association's repertoire, because the group initially voted against recording it. "There were seven of us voting on the 20 or 30 demo songs we were listening to," recalls Ted Bluechel. "When we first listened to "Windy' and voted on it, four guys voted against it and three voted for it. But Pat Colecchio knew it was a hit and he was counting the votes, so he took somebody's 'no' vote and made it a 'yes.' We were our own worst enemies for some reason at that time."

Colecchio helped to heighten the Association's presentation, based on what he observed growing up during the big band era. The late Patrick Colecchio recalled during a 2000 interview, "When I started managing the group, rock and roll had a lot of dead air, especially when someone broke a string. I told the guys, 'You bring the audience way up in your presentation and a string breaks or there's dead air so the audience comes down and you have to bring them up again on the next song. So as soon as something happens, someone get on the microphone and start doing some schtick."

Colecchio insisted that stage performance distinguished the Association from other groups. "I'm not saying it because they were my group, I'm saying it very objectively. A lot of people thought that because of their great harmonies the Association was just a vocal group. We played in England with Rod Stewart and Small Faces, Dusty Springfield and the Rolling Stones. After our performance, Mick Jagger walked into the dressing room and actually said, 'I don't believe what I just heard – singing and playing that well at the same time.'"

The group members not only sang and played their instruments with precision, but they also had a great sense of theatrics and comic timing, and would break out into skits and comedy bits to entertain the audience. "We were at the very end of sort of the golden era of Hollywood, and the ethic and the ethos throughout entertainment was one of old-time show biz," says Alexander. "A lot was attitude. We had a professional attitude. That was a big portion of it. We were doing music that was a strange hybrid between folk music and rock and roll. And nobody quite caught that niche. Nobody quite got it except us. We caught it in that perfect little niche; the right place at the right time."

On June 16, 1967, the Association opened California's Monterey Pop Festival with the apropos song "Enter The Young." The three-day lineup of performers included Jimi Hendrix, Janis Joplin, Otis Redding, the Who, the Byrds, the Mamas and the Papas, Buffalo Springfield, Country Joe & the Fish, the Blues Project, Quicksilver Messenger Service, Laura Nyro, Jefferson Airplane, Canned Heat, the Electric Flag, and others.

"Some of the biggest names of rock music shared bills with the Association, but many prominent performers learned that it was preferable to play before rather than after the Association because of the band's ability to energize a crowd," said Colecchio.

By the 1970s the band began to succumb to the effects of stress and fatigue. Jules left in 1968 to spend six months in India, returning to the band until 1974. Russ Giguere left the group in 1971, and bass player Brian Cole died of a drug overdose in 1972. By 1977, Jim Yester and Ted Bluechel were the only remaining original members, and Yester decided to leave the band. About eight months later, Bluechel called it quits and leased the name to Rob Grill of the Grass Roots.

Yester recalls, "We were touring close to 250 days a year. It was insane. That, I think, is part of what caused the mental downfall of the Association. You lose perspective and you're trying to fit recording sessions in between your touring schedules. It was just too crazy, too crazy. I mean, hindsight is 20/20, but had we given ourselves a little bit of a break and taken time, I think it would have continued in a much better vein."

The group was resurrected in late 1980, after filming an HBO special called "Then And Now," for which Kirkman was co-writer and associate producer. The lineup included the Association, the Temptations and the Kingston Trio, and it was held at the Coconut Grove in L.A. with Mort Sahl as the host. "We rehearsed on weekends, and we got together five or six songs and produced them for the show," says Giguere.

After the show, Bluechel said, "This is what the Association should sound like." Everyone seemed to appreciate that thought and agreed to get back together if the business end made sense. In a few weeks, tours were being booked and all of the original members (except the late Brian Cole) finished what they had been doing and enthusiastically got back to performing together again.

The Association continues to perform concerts throughout the country, drawing a nostalgic crowd along with their friends and family members of all ages. Original members Russell Giguere, Larry Ramos and Jim Yester, along with Brian Cole's son Jordan, Larry Ramos' brother, Del, and Bruce Pictor, continue to perform the songs we all cherish.

For more information, visit http://theassociationwebsite.com/

The Association in 2011. Back row (from left) Jordan Cole, Del Ramos, Bruce Pictor; middle row, Russ Giguere, Larry Ramos; front, Jim Yester. Photo by Henry Diltz.

THE ASSOCIATION U.S. HIT SINGLES ON THE NATIONAL CHARTS

Debut	Peak	Gold	Title	Label
6/66	7		Along Comes Mary	Valiant
8/66	1	Δ	Cherish	Valiant
11/66	35		Pandora's Golden Heebie Jeebies	Valiant
2/67	51		No Fair At All	Valiant
5/67	1	Δ	Windy	Warner
8/67	1	Δ	Never My Love	Warner
2/68	10		Everything That Touches You	Warner
5/68	39		Time For Livin'	Warner
8/68	47		Six Man Band	Warner
3/69	80		Goodbye Columbus	Warner
2/73	91		Names, Tags, Numbers & Labels	Mums
1/81	66		Dreamer	Elektra

Δ symbol: RIAA certified gold record (Recording Industry Association of America)

Billboard's pop singles chart data is courtesy of Joel Whitburn's Record Research Inc. (www.recordresearch.com), Menomonee Falls, Wisconsin.

Epilogue: Jules Gary Alexander

Guitarist and singer

Jules Gary Alexander never had any ambitions to become a professional musician. He just wanted to play music. He recalls that his first interest in music began when he was 4 years old. "I remember traveling to my aunt Ondine's house in north Georgia. It's way out in the sticks, almost to Tennessee. She had a piano, and I remember playing 'Buttons and Bows' on it." That's when he discovered he could play by ear. "I tried to take piano lessons and I got kicked out of class for playing by ear, then I tried to take flute lessons, and I passed out in the class from blowing too hard, so that was quashed."

As a child, Jules enjoyed listening to a late-night radio program sponsored by Randy's Record Mart in Gallatin, Tennessee. "At the time, their playlist would include a Jimmy Reed tune right next to Henry Mancini, right next to Tennessee Ernie Ford, right next to Tony Bennett. So I had this really wide, diverse musical input at the time. Mostly pop, except we had a few classical records at my house, so I listened to some classical."

Jules was born September 25, 1943, in Chattanooga, Tennessee, to Jean and Jay Vidal Alexander. "The name Jules was not a great name to grow up with. So my folks called me Gary, or in the South you would say, 'GAY-ree!'" His mother and father divorced when he was very young, so he grew up with an extended family consisting of his grandparents, mom and uncle, all sharing the same house in Chattanooga for 14 years.

Music and art were a natural progression for Jules, whose grandmother was a piano teacher and mother a visual artist. "My mother did, in fact, photo restorations. She was one of the best in the country. She did incredible stuff," says Jules.

Recognizing his talent and early interest in music, Jules' mother supported his endeavors. Not long after

Courtesy of Jules Alexander.

12

his mother remarried and they moved to Pomona, California, in 1959, she bought Jules a Fender Telecaster. "It was a cheap little guitar, but as I look back on it, if I had it now, it would be worth thousands and thousands of dollars."

Jules taught himself how to play the guitar in junior high school, and his first high school rock band was called Terry and the Twisters. "We played pure rock and roll. I still have the promo material. We'd play school functions, and on Saturday nights we'd play for dances at the YMCA, and we played at park events. There were only about two other bands in that entire area at the time I started, so we were working. I mean, if you had a guitar and you had a band, you were in demand. We weren't bad either; we were really pretty good."

Jules attended Pomona High School but left in 1960, short of graduating, to join the Navy at the age of 17. "A friend of mine, Arnie Mount said, 'Are you having a good time?' I said, 'No, I hate school.' He said, 'Let's go join the Navy.' I said, 'OK, let's go.' So we did."

In the Navy he was assigned a specialty as an optical instruments technician. "I was an apprentice at an observatory in Chattanooga when I was a kid. I knew optics and telescope repair and optical instrument repair, having done it for a number of years, so they put me right into optics. And I worked on binoculars and periscopes and other instruments," Jules said.

Jules served in the Navy for three years, eight months and 28 days, earning his high school equivalence certificate during that time. He was stationed at Pearl Harbor when he met Terry Kirkman for the first time. The two were at a party when they discovered a common interest in folk music. "While I was stationed at Pearl Harbor, I didn't have much to do except play music during my off times. So I just played and played, mainly by myself. Just learning. I started playing with a few people – then it was hootenannies, of course, because it was during the very early folk era, '61. And so that's really where I learned a whole lot and found myself performing more, and more, and more, and more."

Jules completed his tour of duty just before the United States began significantly increasing its military presence in Vietnam. "I was real fortunate because I got out in late 1963. Then, to most of us, Vietnam was just a blip – still more or less undercover."

When he got out of the Navy, Jules returned to Pomona. One night he walked into a folk club in nearby Upland and was surprised to discover Terry Kirkman was there. "The folk music thing was peaking. Terry and I played together a lot, and we started hanging out in L.A. at a folk club called the Troubadour. We got an apartment in L.A., and were regulars at the Troubadour, along with Crosby, Stills and Nash, and John Kay [leader of Steppenwolf]. Everybody in the music business in L.A. in the '60s seemed to hang out there. There were actually three clubs – the Troubadour, the Ash Grove, and Randy Sparks' club, Ledbetters. Randy Sparks' club attracted all the white guys, the white jocks. It was a Christy Minstrels kind of a 'Hi! I'm an American short-haired boy. I'm playing folk music.' And then there was the Troubadour, which was a lot funkier. And there was the Ash Grove, which was blues. But we hung at the Troubadour, where we started the band called the Men, which evolved into the Association."

Although Jules had never engaged in any formal music training, he credits singing background with the Association more valuable than any training he could have paid for. "Your pitch has to be dead on, and you really have to have something or develop it. It's extremely difficult to sing background vocals really well. That's where it came from."

Jules admits he didn't cope well with the stardom that accompanied the Association's success on the record charts and on the concert circuit. "I was a terrible, terrible, terrible celebrity, mainly because I didn't like it. I really enjoy my anonymity. It's fun to be high profile, everybody goes, 'ooh-ooh' and that kind of stuff, but I'm just not good at it. I think now it's a bit different, but at that time it was just horrid," Jules told us in 2000.

With more than 1,000 dates in the nearly 20 years Jules remained with the band, many of those years remain a blur. But one particularly memorable event stands out in his mind. "About 1984 or '85, we were doing the 'Legends for Liberty' tour to raise money for the Statue of Liberty restoration. Chrysler sponsored it, and the bill consisted of the Association, Tommy James, the Four Tops, and the Supremes with Mary Wilson. We'd gotten into San Antonio and we had a bus out there. Well, we all got on the bus and we were sort of waiting for the bus driver to show up, and this bunch of tourists decided they were going to get on the bus. And they were getting pissed because they couldn't get on the bus, because it was going to their particular hotel. And so Mary is standing there, and all of this stuff is going on, and she says, 'I know how to take care of this, guys.' She looks around the bus and says, 'I'm going to get rid of these people.' And she just starts screaming and shaking and violently jerking. We all start laughing really hard, and she is going for it. I mean, she is serious! And they walked off the bus. It was really funny."

For about three years during the late 1960s, Jules was married to Christy Eberhart and the couple had two children: a daughter Eden (born in 1967) and son David (born in 1969). Despite all that he had endured in his lifetime, Jules never faced a calamity as devastating as the loss of his son, David, who took his own life at the age of 21 in 1990.

From 1971 to 1986 Jules was married to Cynthia Jo Riedel, whose daughter Kristen Cloke, from a previous marriage, is an Emmy Award-winning actress who has appeared in *The X Files*, *Millennium*, and numerous movies. Jules and Cynthia Riedel have a daughter born in 1971 named Amy Alexander-Palliser, who is a licensed therapist working with people with eating disorders.

With the skills and experience he acquired in precision optical instrumentation during his stint in the Navy, Jules could easily find work in the aerospace industry, building aircraft instruments, and microfilm cameras and viewers. He built small cryonics refrigerators that were used in infrared detectors at a company called Kinergetics Inc., where he worked with Jim Yester for about a year during the '70s.

From Kinergetics, Jules joined McBain Instruments, where he built high-altitude photo viewers. "This was really cool, as I was working with absolute state-of-the-art optical devices," he says. "Once, several of us went to D.C. and installed some of these devices in the CIA photo analysis shops, and we rubbed shoulders with CIA-types. What a kick!"

In the 1980s, Jules developed a keen interest in computers, teaching himself how to operate and program them. He computerized essentially all of the Association's bookkeeping tasks. "I'm a voracious reader and if I become interested in something, I'll burn every book there is about it. I will study it," he said.

Jules left the Association in 1989. "I screwed around for a long time after I left the band. I did a couple of other jobs. A friend of mine had a tree-trimming company in Texas and I managed that for a while, which was great. It was really a cool job."

A couple of years prior to leaving the band, Jules moved from Southern California to a little town in Texas just south of Austin called Wimberley. There, in 1991 he met Cynthia Juniper at the Third International Stone-Skipping Contest. "I swear to God. A friend of mine here named Jerry McGhee is the Guinness World Record holder. And about once every two or three years, he'll put on an international stone skip. And they have the contest," he chuckled. Cynthia grew up in Wisconsin and moved to Texas to work on her master's degree at Texas Woman's University in Denton. When Jules met her, Cynthia was acting director of a rape crisis center in San Marcos, and was previously an investigator for the Austin Child Protective Services. The couple married in 1992, and following the birth of their daughter Hannah Jules Alexander on March 1, 1999, they bought a house and moved to San Marcos, which is halfway between San Antonio and Austin.

"San Marcos is a college town. Southwest Texas State University is here. We live right in town now, in a house that was built in the late 1800s. It has 10-foot ceilings and it's pretty funky, but it's in great shape. The neighborhood is real cool." San Marcos is situated in what's called the hill country of Texas, which has numerous lakes and rivers and has very mild winters compared with the rest of the state. "We're only two hours from the ocean."

Jules worked out of his home as a consultant from 1993 to 1995, installing and configuring computer systems, and setting up local-area networks. In 1996 he joined a large information and systems company as a data analyst. "I interpret manufacturer electronic data, and I have to fix it and massage it and goof with it and make sure it's right."

In 2006, the Association's longtime manager Pat Colecchio called Jules and said he wasn't happy where he was living in New Jersey. The two had always remained close and kept in touch often. "So I said, 'Pat, why don't you come live with me in Texas for awhile? And Pat said, 'Texas, what am I going to do in Texas?' Well, after two days, he fell in love with Texas. What we found out was Pat had a cowboy in his heart trying to get out," Jules told us in April 2011.

"It was hilarious, when Pat got here, he practically took over the town. By the time he left, everyone knew him. He was the godfather of this club we liked to go to. Pat was 82 or 83 when he left here, and he was dating 30-year-old women. He wasn't a man, he was a force of nature. I would see things happen that were kind of spooky – like women would walk around him then walk toward him. It was as if he was a magnet or something."

After about two years living with Jules, Pat was diagnosed with colon cancer. He decided to return to New Jersey to be with his son, Rick. "He'd been in hospice here – he was in bad shape. But when he got back to New Jersey, his doctor asked, 'What the hell are you taking this medicine for? It's the wrong medicine.' So he changed his medicine and he lived six more months. He lived right on the beach on the boardwalk and was walking a mile or two a day. He was in

16

absolutely no pain. He called me one time and asked, 'Aren't I supposed to be in pain or something?' He was a very funny man, with a
great sense of humor. He was a war hero in WWII, and he figured he
was living on borrowed time so he didn't really care what he did. He
lived a good life."

Pat succumbed to the cancer in 2008.

Although not performing, Jules remains actively involved in
music. In 2010, he became musical director for a production called
"The Blanco Was Blameless or It Was Balcones' Faults," which is a
spoof of the early history of Wimberley, Texas, written by local playwright Russ Marlett. Russ and
his wife, Shirley, have a theater
company in Wimberley, and
asked Jules to write the music
for their first production.

"The thing about Wimber-
ley is there are lots of musicians living here. So when
Russ and I decided to make a
community musical, we invited four other writers to come
in and write songs for it. But
Russ and I wrote most of the
music. I arranged and recorded
it, and we made an album." The
first production of the musical
received such good reviews, in
2011 Jules and Russ proceed-
ed with its second production.

Jules performed a bit after
leaving the Association, but he
had to switch to playing bass
guitar after cutting off part of

Pat Colecchio in 1970. Photo courtesy of
Jules Alexander.

his thumb with a table saw while building a boat. "The Association
is a pretty high mark to go up against," says Jules. "If I'm going to
perform, it's got to be at least as professional, and I just really haven't
found that much around. I haven't been looking for it too much
either."

Jules also is involved in infrared photography as an art form. He
has exhibited his works in galleries in Rockport and San Marcos, Tex-

as. You can view his artwork at his website, Photography by J. Gary Alexander, http://www.pbase.com/lulalake.

Jules looks back on the '60s, it's difficult for him to find nostalgia. "When people look back at the '60s they think, 'Oh, it was just this wonderful time.' I don't think it was. There was more sexism, racism, and I think it was just a horrid, unsettled time. It was a time of wretched excess, and people think it was a time of spiritual awakening. Perhaps it was, who knows? Although I liked being a young adult in those times, I think I would have preferred being a young adult in the '50s or the '40s. Or maybe the '30s would have been cool."

But his experiences in the '60s, '70s, '80s and '90s have helped to shape Jules into the person he's become – a good husband and father. "I'm pretty happy with the way my life is unfolding right now. I know I've put some strokes into it, and it's nice to see some results. But I really like what my life is now, and I feel happier than I have in my entire life, healthier – well, a little heavier – but pretty healthy, and happy."

"Memorial Day 2010." Photo by J. Gary Alexander, www.pbase.com/lulalake.

Epilogue: Ted Bluechel Jr.

Drummer, guitarist and singer

Most people would agree that 20 years at any career, let alone sticking with the same band, is unusual and admirable. And if you've been on the road for any period of time, you'll know that burnout is a common reason for calling it quits. However, it was for the love of family that drummer Ted Bluechel made the painstaking decision to leave the Association in 1984 – the year his wife, Carol, gave birth to son Michael. Born three months premature, Michael experienced some health problems that resulted in autism.

"I wanted to stay on, doing what I could do as time would allow, but we have a motto in the group – you're either in the group or you're out of the group. So I really had no choice but to cut the cord and step back," says Bluechel. When he left the group, Ted Bluechel's resume read "singer and drummer in the Association," which he had done since he was 21 years old.

Ted Bluechel Jr. was born in San Pedro, California, on December 2, 1942, and grew up in Southern California, except for the two years

Ted Bluechel in 1999. Photo by Tracy Coles

during the fourth and fifth grades that he spent in Montana living on a pig ranch. Ted is the youngest of four children. His sister Susie is 13 months older, brother Rodney is four years older, and sister Ann is six years older. Ted's father, the late Dr. Theodore John Bluechel Sr., was a general practitioner, and his mother, Elizabeth, stayed home and raised the children.

"My father said, 'Don't be a musician, son. Get a real job.' And I could go for that for awhile, until I got the fever in my blood. I don't know how to explain it. It's a great big rush when you perform and peoples' energy is concentrated on you. It's just a big surge. My parents were warning me against the evils of it all, but finally when the money was coming in they relaxed because they could tell I'd be comfortable. I was doing all right, and I was able to help the family out for all the help they gave me."

Ted's first interest in music surfaced while listening to drummers march up and down the street while the band was practicing its marching drill at Huntington Beach Elementary School. Soon after, Ted was asked to join the percussion section of the All-Southern California State Band, becoming first chair, until having to make a decision between participating in a track meet or going on the statewide band tour. A league champion pole vaulter, Ted chose the track meet.

"But I really got the hook in me after falling in love with the feeling of the music of the Kingston Trio when I was babysitting for my sister my first year in college," recalls Bluechel. "It just reached my very center, listening to the feeling, the ambience of the music. I was just one of those many people who got hooked into it."

Ted graduated with an A average from North Torrance High School in 1960, and his career goal was to become a zoology teacher. He attended El Camino Junior College for three years, maintaining a B+ average, and in 1965, between his third and fourth years of college, he says, "That's when the hook got set. I got hooked into playing with some friends of mine in a quartet called the Cherry Hill Singers." Ted played guitar with the Cherry Hill Singers, a quartet with a banjo and three guitars, until the group merged with a group of 10 musical arrangers and performers called the Men, for whom Ted played guitar and drums.

"We would all meet at the Troubadour Monday nights, when they had their hoots. We'd all hang out there with Peter, Paul and Mary, and Bob Dylan, the Kingston Trio, and any other entertainers who were in town."

The Men endured a number of changes, eventually splitting into

20

two factions – one interested in pursuing a more contemporary sound, and others who wanted to pursue a pure ethnic folk sound. Ted had no doubt the more contemporary sound was the direction he was heading. "We all came out of folk. Folk is not just 'Michael, Row the Boat Ashore.' There is some hard-driving stuff that was a blend of music that brought about the music of the '60s. Most everybody in the '60s came out of the folk bag. At one time, they all played acoustic guitars and sang at small venues. Then it got developed and it started catching on with the wave of our generation. And all of a sudden, blam! All these groups got electrified, and started singing the same types of tunes, but driving them a little bit harder, getting more effects due to the electronics."

Ted played drums and sang with the Association until 1983. He recalls, "We needed to bolster our vocals, and it's hard to sing and play drums. I can do it, but there is a compromise on each side. So rather than compromise, we brought in drummer Brian Puckett, the brother of Gary Puckett, to strengthen our presentation, while I played guitar and sang." Brian had been playing with Gary Puckett on the Happy Together Tour when the Association met him and asked him to play drums for them.

Ted contributed one song to each of the Association's albums, but only one of his songs, "Bring Yourself Home," became a hit in the Midwest. Two of his other songs, "Standing Still" and "We Love Us," remain popular in Association concerts today.

When Ted left the Association, he looked for jobs that would cause him the least amount of stress, because he'd endured enough for a lifetime being on the road for so many years. "Stress is a big factor that has had its way with me, but as I'm getting older, I really look to enjoy what's left of the span here on Earth. I just go on looking after my own household."

You can take the man out of the music business, but you can't take the music out of the man, at least not Ted Bluechel. Music fever crept back into his life in about 1994, when he began performing with a trio called Sweet and Dandy. "That was a lot of fun for a while, but then one of the guys went his own way, and I needed to replace him. I'd done that so many times during the '70s with the Association. I got tired of repairing the group's sound and putting it back together again every two or three months, so I just went solo. It was a lot less trouble, and I don't have to argue with anybody."

In 1999 Ted began his solo career (billed as Ted Bluechel) in clubs in the Ventura, Camarillo, Thousand Oaks and Santa Barbara areas. He says his favorite Association songs are "Never My Love" and "Windy," which he performs with a mix of other popular '60s tunes, some Jimmy Buffet tunes, a taste of Jamaican and Caribbean West Indies music, and some of his own original material. "I'm choosing to stay in the slow lane. Anything you choose in the fast lane means going on the road, and I've had it with the road. I'm just sort of enjoying doing what I'm doing and sharing my life with Carol and Michael."

Ted had become a Universal Life Church minister in 1968, legally ordained to perform weddings, funerals, baptisms and other functions of the clergy. Since then he has performed wedding ceremonies for about 15 couples, including many friends and members of the Association. "The main reason you become a Universal Life Church minister is to make it easier for your friends to get married without going through a big, expensive church wedding," he says.

In 1981, Ted and his wife, Carol Jamison, were married by a Universal Life Church minister between tours. "I came home and said, 'Well, OK, it's time to get married. Let's go down and get the license, get all that stuff together.' I asked my friend Ray Gann, who lived in the Malibu area, if he'd come over during lunch and marry us. I said 'Come on, Ray, bring your wife over here and a few witnesses and we'll do this thing. We took pictures, had a great time, and we shot off to Mexico for our honeymoon."

Ted and Carol, a financial analyst, moved to Camarillo in 1998 after having to evacuate numerous times due to fires in the Malibu area. In addition, their teenage son, Michael, needed a more socially interactive environment. Their half-acre property in Camarillo has orange and lemon trees, Santa Rosa plum trees, peach trees, and apricot trees. "It's just a neighborhood," says Ted, "but it's very quiet, and it's good for us here. In Malibu we lived in a remote area and there was nobody around for miles and miles. We were like the McCoys. Now we're in a neighborhood where Michael can have some friends and see a little bit bigger piece of the world."

Carol has two grown children (Robert and Tracy) from a previous marriage, and Ted has a daughter, Rhea, from a previous marriage.

Ted and Carol's son, Michael, has a savant gift in art. Ted is involved with Michael's sports, including coaching soccer, volleyball and baseball games. "I enjoy doing all that stuff with the kids. I'm there to help them," he says.

Ted considers his voice one of his greatest assets. "As it has matured, my voice is better now than it's ever been. It has the quality, when I'm singing with other people, to add all kinds of overtones to the sound. That was one of my contributions to the Association. You couldn't hear my voice individually so much, but the voices rang when I'd start to sing. It doesn't get in the way, but it adds a lot of sound when I'm singing with other strong singers. Singing solo, my voice has a very warm texture."

The Kingston Trio had a great musical influence on Ted. In later years, the Association and the Kingston Trio did some concerts together. "It was a thrill for me to meet Bob Shane and hang out with the Trio on the same tour for four or five days. That was great fun."

Ted enjoys being surrounded by nature. Spending a day at the beach with Carol and Michael, walking through the mountains or looking out through the fruit trees in his backyard gives him a shot of serenity he needs to endure the demands of day-to-day life. "I like to take Michael hiking through the hills and get him tuned in to nature. 'See that bug there? This is what he does. See this thing over here?' And we wait and watch for animals coming out of hiding, and I let him understand how things work and how the circle of life works. And it's the same kind of fun I had as a kid."

Michael, Carol and Ted Bluechel in 2010. Photo courtesy of Ted Bluechel.

23

Epilogue: Brian Cole

Bass guitarist and singer

September 9, 1942 – August 2, 1972

"My father was just brilliant and clever," said Brian's son Jordan Cole, who has been performing with the Association since 1998. "If you read a quote from Shakespeare and told my dad what publication it came from, he could name the page it's on."

Vicki Cole, Jordan's mom, agrees. "Brian was extremely intelligent. He had an IQ of over 160. He read everything he could lay his hands on and wrote a lot, but he was not always socially polite. Ask members of the group – he quite frankly pissed people off," she said. "He had a fantastic sense of humor but not everyone got his jokes. He was a little cerebral for many people. Jordan is quite like him in many ways. When Jordan first joined the Association, other musicians who knew Brian remarked about the similarities in their personalities."

Ted Bluechel recalled an incident in which Brian saved the band from an awkward start at the Monterey Pop Festival. "When we were introduced and jumped on stage, I noticed that my drums had been rearranged, so I said, 'Brian, stall us for about 5 minutes!' So he launched into this dialogue of the weirdest collection of facts that diverted the audience's attention long enough for me to set up my drum kit so I could play."

Ted said that Brian could always come up with something to say on stage to fill in the dead space. "When Brian passed, the group lost part of its signature sound – not only his singing but also his talent for dialogue that built great rapport with the audience."

Brian Cole with his sons Jordan (L) and Chandler about 1970. Courtesy of Jordan Cole.

Brian, who was the original bass player for the Association, died of an accidental overdose of uncut China white (a very pure form of heroin) on August 2, 1972, a month before his 30th birthday. His sons Jordan and Chandler were only 10 and 8 years old at the time.

"My dad had a lot of issues with security – his self worth. His insecurities drove him to be remarkably brilliant but also chaotic and unpredictable," said Jordan. "He was kind of scary to me because sometimes he would say, 'Jordan, come here!' and I'd be scared to death that I did something wrong, but he just wanted to give me a hug."

Brian Leslie Cole was born in Tacoma, Washington, on September 9, 1942, to Violet Swan Cole and Perry Anthony Cole. His older brother Michael Perry Cole (born in 1940) became a lawyer, and younger sister Cathy Cole McKay (born in 1953) lives with her husband on a ranch near Grants Pass, Oregon. The family moved from Tacoma to Portland, Oregon, when the kids were young. His father worked for Union Pacific Railroad and his mother mainly stayed home to raise the kids.

Brian graduated from Madison High School in Portland in 1960 and attended Portland State College for a year to pursue his passion for comedy and acting. He performed in class plays throughout his high school years, and "he was hoping to segue from music to an eventual career in acting," said Vicki. He became interested in music while in high school, and his first gig was playing standup bass at a coffee shop on weekends with a small folk group.

Brian and Vicki Cunningham met at a drive-in restaurant after cruising the streets of Portland with friends. "Think of *Happy Days*," said Vicki, "I was in a car with my friends, and he was with a friend. We dated for more than a year before getting married. I was actually two years older than him, but he lied about his age until I was hooked."

The couple married on June 17, 1961, and Jordan was born in Portland on February 17, 1962. "When my mom was in labor for me, she said my dad had to finish watching the *Twilight Zone* before taking her to the hospital," chuckled Jordan. His brother Chandler was born in Portland on October 14, 1963.

In 1964, Brian became a member of a three-person folk group called the Gnu Folk. He and Vicki made an agreement that she and the boys would stay with her parents in Portland to give Brian a year to "make it in LA." Shortly after moving to Los Angeles, the band broke up and Brian joined the Men, meeting Terry Kirkman, Ted Bluechel, Bob Page, Jules Alexander and Russ Giguere, who went on to form the Association in the summer of 1965.

"I moved down to LA with Jordan and Chandler, and we lived in a little fourplex on Western Avenue in Hollywood," said Vicki. "The band's manager paid our rent, and Brian earned just enough salary to buy food for our family."

When the Association started touring and made more money, Brian moved Vicki and the boys to a house in Burbank, where they lived until their divorce in 1968. Jordan recalls, "When we were living in Burbank, I remember one of the neighbors driving by and they stopped and said, 'That's your dad on the radio,' and I said, 'No it's not' because by this time, I was getting conned by other kids. I wanted to be a rock star like my dad, but I assumed that everybody's dad was famous somehow."

All of the touring and fame contributed to Brian's drug use, and the deterioration of their neighborhood in Burbank convinced Vicki that it was time to move the boys back to Portland. Vicki and Brian divorced in 1968, and Vicki and the boys lived with her parents for about a year until Brian put a down payment on a house for them in Portland.

Just prior to his father's death, Jordan was taken out of public school in the third grade and placed in a residential care facility called Edgefield Lodge in Troutdale, Oregon. "No one could reach me. I was cutting myself off from the world. I wouldn't do the work. What I remember is that everyone was out to get me," said Jordan. "The state wanted to medicate me, but my mom wouldn't let them. There were real problem children there – not just juvenile delinquents – children with seizures, severely emotionally handicapped kids. There were also mentally retarded children and children who had been molested. A lot of early '70s hippie-like people were trying to help you just deal with problems and move on. Basically, what they taught me was that no matter whose fault it is, when it's on your lap it's now your problem – deal with it and just move on."

By the seventh grade, Jordan returned to public school, "which didn't go well," he said. He dropped out of school his senior year and took the GED test, which he "aced in the top 99.97 percent." While Jordan experienced difficulty expressing himself verbally, he found that the creative outlet of music enabled him to articulate his thoughts. He discovered a passion in common with his father – a love of music – and has taught himself how to play drums and percussion, guitar (all styles), keyboards, violin, sax and recorder, and can play just about any instrument put in front of him.

After turning 18, the boys received $25,000 from a trust fund from Brian's estate. Jordan used his money to attend an engineering trade school in Phoenix, Arizona. "After about a year and a half at the school, some friends were killed and then I was attacked. Turns out one of my attackers attended the same school. I tried to talk to the administrators and they said, 'His family has more money than you do, so you've just got to learn to live with it,'" said Jordan. "By that time, I was running out of money, so I decided to go back to Portland, where I started my first band at the end of 1982, called Kordrah (hardrok spelled backwards)."

From 1985 until joining the Association in 1989, Jordan performed with several bands, including a traveling top 40 band, working five nights a week, five hours a day. "The first one was called Brothers and Friends, and that was the first band I got to travel with overseas. I went to Japan and played a lot of Army bases and a couple of clubs. They supplied meals and rooms, but it didn't get to be better pay until I started playing in my own bands. I jumped from band to band. I would do the top 40 thing and tour until I had enough money to start an original band and try to get some airplay. I've always had ideas for songs. I can't shut my head off at night when I need to sleep."

Hungering for more information about his dad, in 1998 Jordan called Larry Ramos, who happened to be looking for a bass player for an Association gig and asked if Jordan would send some sample recordings. "My first job with the Association was Christmas and New Year's Eve on a cruise ship in the Caribbean in 1998 to 1999," said Jordan. "A few months went by and Larry called again and said their keyboard player was going to be retiring because his wife was ill and he needed to take care of her." Jordan has been performing with the Association ever since.

While Jordan knew about his half brother Brant Cole, he didn't meet him until 2001. Brant, who was born in Texas to a girlfriend of Brian's, plays drums for a band called the Blackout Trust, based in Los Angeles.

Vicki and Brian Cole have three grandchildren. Jordan, who is happily married and living in Spokane, has two daughters, Savannah Snow Cole (born in April 1991) and Johannah Marie Cole (born in May 1998). Chandler, who is also happily married and works for TriMet in Portland, has one son, Holden Michael Cole (born in April 2010).

Brian was an integral member of the Association throughout the years when they recorded their most memorable songs, and his son Jordan is helping to perpetuate his musical legacy.

Epilogue: Russ Giguere

Guitarist, trombone player and singer

Most Association fans think of Russ Giguere in connection with the exquisite vocal harmonies for which the band is known. But those who know Russ best realize that he's just as likely to issue an outburst of outrageously funny social commentary as he is to sing a tender lyric. For Russ, improvisational comedy has long served as an expressive outlet that stands in sharp contrast with the structured precision of the Association's musical repertoire.

He was born Russell Henry Giguere on October 18, 1943, in Portsmouth, New Hampshire, to Russell Henry Sr. and Marguerite Mary Giguere. Russ never had the chance to meet his father, who was killed during World War II, just before his birth. When he was 5 years old, Russ and his mother moved to San Diego, California, where her sister had been living. His mother remarried and had three more children – Russ's half brother Tyson and two half sisters, Judy and Nancy.

Giguere, pronounced "jig-air," is French and means hunter. "My father was from French Canadian stock. His family was from Flint, Michigan. I have an uncle Pierre Giguere. Can you believe they'd do that to a kid?" he laughs.

Russ's aunt and mother were talented dancers and taught him how to dance at an early age. "They could dance the jitterbug, slow dance, mambo, samba, cha-cha, waltz, you name it. My aunt was an Arthur Murray instructor," says Giguere. "I was into rock and roll dancing in junior high, particularly contests at dances. As soon as I was about 14 or 15, I stopped going to dances, and folk music took over in my life."

As far back as he can remember, Russ always wanted to sing, and began learning the lyrics of songs he heard on the radio when he was 4 or 5 years old. His mother loved music and listened to everything from Johnny Cash to the classics. "The fact that I was interested in music was looked upon as being really neat, so they

Russ Giguere in 2010.
Photo by Henry Diltz.

28

encouraged me to listen to everything. Anything I'd show the slightest bit of interest in, I was just barraged with, so it was great," says Giguere. "The same with books. I couldn't carry all the books from the library that I wanted to check out, so my mom would come help me to check the books out because they wouldn't believe that I was going to read them all."

Russ attended two high schools in San Diego – Hoover High and E.R. Snyder Continuation High School – but left school short of graduating. He taught himself how to play guitar and quickly became enthralled with the folk music scene. "Those were very artistic times. The beatnik era was sort of phasing out but was still there, and very soon they would be called 'hippies.' Although I really quite honestly at the time never related to either name, indeed, I guess I was in the middle of both of the movements."

Russ had his own apartment by the time he was 17 1/2. "High school and me never clicked at all, not at all! Though I must say one of the things I did enjoy when I went to junior high was you got to choose your classes then. You had to take an English class, a math class, a science class, and gym, but then you had three or four others that you chose. Man, I took print shop, drafting, wood shop, general metal. I really learned some stuff in those classes. It was great. It really gave me a well-rounded education as far as just knowing things and how things work. It was wonderful. And I took every art class I could get my hands on."

At the age of 19, Russ moved to Los Angeles and worked sound and lights for the Ice House in Pasadena. It was there that he met most of the guys who would later become members of the Association, including Terry Kirkman and Jules Alexander. He recalls the first time he and Jules performed together in front of an audience in 1962. "One night at the Ice House when I was working lights, the owner says, 'This guy is late, Russ. Can you go out and do a few tunes?' So Jules was there, and I said, 'Jules, you want to play bass?' He said, 'Sure.' So we went out and did three or four songs until the guy got there."

Following his debut performance with Jules, Russ hooked up with a friend of his, Randy Sterling, and formed a short-lived folk duo. "We just called ourselves by our last names, Sterling and Giguere, which could explain why we lasted such a short time. I think we did a couple of graduation parties and a couple of folk clubs and that was it, plus I was still working at my job," says Giguere. "At the same time, I was still learning to play guitar better and gaining some confidence on stage. The hardest thing for me was being on stage. It was so scary. So I just did it 'til I got used to it."

Coincidentally, Sterling was hired by Doug Weston to produce an album for the Men, a highly popular folk-rock group for which Giguere had auditioned to become a member in 1965. "Terry and Jules were playing at the Troubadour with the Men, and Barry McGuire had just left the New Christy Minstrels. The Minstrels took the lead singer of the Men to replace McGuire, so Terry and Jules came to me and asked if I would join the group. I had never seen the group, so I went. They did a few tunes for me, I did a few tunes for them, and I joined the Men. But the reason Randy and I didn't continue our folk duo was that he was producing the Men, which I would later join." Giguere's short-lived career with the Men would pave the way for his lifelong career in entertainment.

Russ contributed a song to each of the Association albums, and two of his songs appear on the live album. He wrote the song "Sometime," which was the flip side of the group's second No. 1 hit, "Windy." After Russ left the Association in 1971, the band continued performing with various new members. "Everything was just too contentious. I think it had gotten real big and everything took on such importance. Everything was a big fat discussion, which is sort of the way the Men broke up."

Following his departure, Giguere put together a couple of his own bands. "I had a band called Hollywood, and another band called the Beechwood Rangers, which was sort of an arty rock and roll group. The bands usually had five to six members, and I always had good singers and good writers in my bands," says Giguere. But none would measure up to the caliber and status of the Association.

In 1972, Russ co-produced an album with John Boylan called *Hexagram 16* on the Warner Bros. label. "It was hybrid music combining a lot of stuff. It's mostly pop-rock oriented but there's a lot of strange art stuff on it. It goes beyond description. I don't think it did anything, but I still sign a lot of copies on the road, so I guess there are collectors out there who have it."

From 1975 to about 1977 Russ was part of a comedy act with a friend, Bill Martin, called Martin and Giguere. The duo performed at the Ice House, the Improv and a couple of smaller clubs around the Pasadena area. Martin had written songs with Harry Nilsson, and he wrote songs for the Monkees and the Dillards. He also wrote a couple of the songs on Giguere's *Hexagram 16* album. "Our comedy was very conceptual. It was rock-um sock-um. We did everything. For instance, friends told us we couldn't do stuff about death, so the first bit we did was called 'Dream Death of a Lifetime.' It was like an ad. We'd say, 'Friends, are you dead or dying? If you die the next 60 minutes you will receive...' and we built this thing up. 'Your yellow Samsonite coffin will be lowered into the world's largest active volcano, Mt. Kilauea!' But it worked, and every time we did it we'd edit it more, and more."

Still the comedian, Giguere offered his facetious observation about one of his favorite singers. "I loved Elvis records. I thought his comeback in the '70s with that TV show was so super. And I was hoping he would really come back. I was so sad when he gained all that weight. Boy, when you get a fat forehead, you're in trouble. You're on your way out. In fact, I now call it – and have since he died – 'Elvis forehead.' And I've seen people that have it, and they die. There was a guy in a band, and I'm saying, 'Man, he's really putting it on. He's even got Elvis forehead.' It was like six months or a year, the guy had a stroke and died. I didn't wish it on him! But if you've got fat on your forehead, you're in trouble. There ain't supposed to be no fat up there."

For Russ, none of his 1970s pursuits could quite measure up to the professionalism and self-fulfillment of being a part of the Association. After the band re-formed for an Association reunion for an HBO special, "Then And Now," in 1978, all of the original members except for Brian Cole, who died in 1972, began touring again. In 1984, the group was invited to be a part of the "Happy Together Tour" with the Turtles, Gary Puckett, and Spanky and Our Gang, and performed 160 shows during that tour. Five years later, they took to the road again as part of Dick Clark's last national tour in 1989. "Our band was the only band that drove cars. All the other bands toured in buses. So we took three cars: two white Cadillacs, and I had a white Chrysler convertible. With six guys in the band, two guys per car, we drove 27,000 miles in three months. We started in New Jersey, and just went everywhere – Radio City Music Hall, all over the place. We played with the Spinners, the Guess Who, and Charlie Thomas and the Drifters."

By 2000, Giguere and Larry Ramos were the only original members carrying on the Association name, with Bruce Pictor, who has been with the group since 1985 and plays drums and sings tenor and baritone; the multi-talented Jordan Cole (son of the late Brian Cole), who plays keyboards, synthesizer guitar and bass; Bob Werner, who plays bass and sings tenor; and Del Ramos, Larry's brother, who has been with the group since 1983 and sings bass. He works the sound board and sings from the board. "We usually put a light on Del when we introduce him. As far as I know, we're the only group who does

31

that. And occasionally, we actually move him up to the stage," Russ told us in February 2000.

To get to the 30-40 concerts the Association plays each year, Giguere must rely on his least favorite form of transportation – commercial airlines. "I still really don't like flying, even though I am rocket man. I've been doing it most of my adult life. I just don't like it much. I'm pretty relaxed about it but, still, how relaxed can you be in a tube shooting through space? When I heard Elton John do 'Rocket Man' I always wondered how he wrote that without knowing me. It sounds like my life. It's always sounded like my life."

By 2011, the Association consisted of Larry Ramos, lead guitar, tenor; Jim Yester, rhythm guitar, first tenor; Russ Giguere, trombone, cow bell, shaker baritone; Del Ramos (Larry's brother), bass guitar and bass vocal; Bruce Pictor (since 1985), drums, tenor-baritone; and Jordan Cole (son of Brian Cole), keyboards, recorder, guitar, and tenor, bass and everything in between vocally.

Association concerts these days include mainly oldies, but, says Giguere, "we always have some surprises in the show. If you don't do the hits, though, they're gonna lynch ya. Some of the people in the audience are named Cherish and Windy. That's just the way it is. And I acknowledge that. I don't resent it in the slightest. Never have, and I don't think I ever will."

Giguere says he doesn't miss much about the 1960s. "Everything transitions from one to the other. I enjoyed the '60s, but I can't say I miss the '60s. In the '60s if you had hair that the longhairs considered short, you were the enemy, and if you had hair that was considered too long by the people who wore it short, you were considered the enemy – both equally off. People still judge you exactly by your looks. They have no idea what's inside. That's something that bothered me in the '60s. I'm just gloriously pleased with the way things are going for me now. If it can go better than this, great, thrill me. But if it can't, I'm thrilled already."

Books, articles and documentaries focusing on entertainers often contain inaccuracies. Oftentimes a rumor or suggestion will show up in print, and writers and editors failing to verify the information will perpetuate the misinformation. But then, again, sometimes stubbornness and stupidity play a role in immortalizing inaccuracies. Giguere recalls being asked to take a look at a book entry about the Association and make corrections to it. "The book said there was a guy in the band named Jimmy Page who was replaced by Jim Yester. When the editor called, I told him, 'There was never a Jimmy Page in the band, but there was a guy named Bob Page.' And he started arguing with me. Now this guy isn't as old as the band is, and he's arguing, 'No, it was Jimmy Page!' And there were a couple of other guys listed as having been band members. I called all the living members of the band, and I said, 'Have you ever heard of these names in any context whatsoever?' No one had ever heard of these people. They had never been part of the Association. And this guy is still arguing with me. So I just said, 'Look. Do me a favor and never, ever call me again as long as you live.' And I hung up the phone."

Giguere still has a passion for reading books. "I've been reading a lot of biographies and autobiographies – everything from Jimmy Durante to Joseph Conrad and Lead Belly. I probably read a thousand books in the three years I was in junior high, but as I started living more, I started reading less. And so in the past couple of years I've been getting into reading again."

He particularly enjoyed a biography of one of his favorite singers, Nat "King" Cole. "I always liked the really stylistic singers, like Nat 'King' Cole and people that really had their own style. I could never pass myself off as a Nat 'King' Cole. But he certainly did some wonderful, wonderful recordings, besides being a great piano player. I really liked Nat a lot."

A collector of band memorabilia and art, Giguere claims to have the largest collection of original Association art among all the members of the band. "I have material from the Monterey Pop Festival, a couple of festivals we've done, some of the early stuff before we had records. I have one painting that a 10-year-old boy did of the band, and nobody wanted it. So I took it and had it framed. I've had it for 40 years, and I still like it as much as I like any of my other pieces."

The complexity of musical arrangements and their intricacy, along with tremendous breadth in repertoire, sets the Association apart from other bands, says Giguere. "One of the things I'm most proud of in the group is the fact we opened so many venues to rock and roll. So many huge venues across the United States that are now common fare weren't in those days – like Ravinia in Chicago, the Greek Theatre here in Los Angeles, Wolf Trap outside of Washington. We are the act that opened these places for rock and roll. The gold records are great and there's nothing wrong with a big fat check, but the pioneering concerts are what I like the most. And I still love doing the shows."

Epilogue: Terry Kirkman

Multi-instrumentalist and singer

A gifted musician, singer, lyricist, poet, journalist and painter, Terry Kirkman is driven by creativity. During the peak of the Association's success, Terry's stage setup consisted of as many as 13 instruments, including variable percussion, reed and brass instruments, as well as an assortment of harmonicas and recorders, and he has played close to 30 instruments for one reason or another during his lifetime.

After a highly successful music career with numerous hits to his credit, and several years as a writer and producer of commercials, ads and movie trailers, Terry has discovered a new sense of fulfillment as a chemical dependency counselor, consultant and teacher. Overcoming his own struggles with chemical dependency in 1984 and helping to run a recovery program in Hollywood Community Hospital opened a new pathway to his personal development and self-contentment.

Born in Salina, Kansas, on December 12, 1939, Terry is the younger of two sons born to Gordon and Lois Kirkman. Music was an integral part of Terry's upbringing. Terry's father played saxophone and was a singer in dance bands in Kansas. His mother played piano

Terry Kirkman in 2001. Photo by Paloma Sendrey.

in theaters during silent movies, was a locally acclaimed church pipe organist and taught piano. His brother, the late Richard Kirkman, who was five and a half years older than Terry, played sousaphone during his college years and also played bass and percussion instruments.

"Both of my parents had come from very educated, very realized parentage. My dad's father built hospitals and Fox theaters in the Midwest. If you ever see the movie *Paper Moon*, notice a scene where Ryan O'Neal and Tatum O'Neal are having a conversation in a coffee shop in Kansas, and across the street you see this little marquee, which was my grandfather's theater. My maternal grandfather built churches and was head pastor of Kansas Wesleyan University."

In 1943, Terry's father, who worked for Montgomery Ward in Kansas, transferred to a store in Pomona, California, later moving his family to nearby Chino, about 35 miles east of L.A. At 14 years of age, Terry began performing music for money. He taught himself to play the saxophone to polkas and waltzes in a Basque hotel and restaurant in Chino. Unfamiliar with any of the band's tunes, Terry would listen to the melody the first time through and then join in by playing harmonies and counter melodies. "I had no idea really how to play saxophone. I just fingered it like I did the little flutes I played when I was a kid."

Terry graduated from Chino High School in 1957 and attended Chaffey College in Alta Loma (now Rancho Cucamonga), near Ontario, where he played tuba as part of a 120-piece orchestra, and began singing as a member of the college choir. It was there that Terry met Frank Zappa, a fellow music major at Chaffey. Kirkman and Zappa performed folk-blues and jazz together in suburban coffee houses from 1959 through 1961. "It wasn't like we were ever a formal act. A lot of the reasons we played together was that I had a car and he never drove. And then we started writing satirical stuff together," says Kirkman. In his original *Mothers of Invention* album, Frank Zappa gives credit to Kirkman for helping to inspire his music.

Terry joined the National Guard his senior year in high school, serving for six years in California and Hawaii, and achieving the rank of sergeant. "When I transferred to Hawaii, they lost my papers and I had to do them all over again. After completing them, a medical officer came to talk to me one day asking about my disclosure of suffering from Osgood-Schlatter's disease. When I confirmed it to be true, he asked if I'd disclosed that on my original paperwork when I first enlisted. I told him I did not because it had never been diagnosed for me at that time. The diagnosis came some years later.

"He smiled, read my performance record and said, 'well, I have some news for you, a little late I'm afraid since it's coming to you in the last year of your enlistment, but we don't take people with Osgood-Schlatter's disease.' The truth is, I really enjoyed most of my service and the guys I got to do the work with – ordnance, communication and jungle engineering in Hawaii."

Following his honorable discharge in 1963, Terry flew to Honolulu with college buddies Bob Bettinger and Miles Lacey. There he met Gary "Jules" Alexander at a party where the two ended up singing folk songs together. "Jules was a key player in the Navy at that time. He was an optical lens grinder for the rangefinders on nuclear submarines. That was during the Cuban missile crisis [October 1962] and they had him locked up in a little lens-grinding vault for about three months."

In the spring of 1963, Terry spent 29 days sailing a 106-foot schooner back to California from Hawaii. Upon returning to the states, he enrolled as a journalism and English major at Orange State College, which was renamed California State College at Fullerton and today is called California State University, Fullerton. He became associate editor of the college's *Titan* newspaper. To help pay his tuition, he began working in a folk club in the town of Upland. "At this time I became very politicized and discovered there was another place for me to be in the world. I was very attracted to folk music and the civil rights movement. And I saw that as a calling. It was a scene, it was a culture, and it was a cause. And I really wanted to be a part of that common and united voice."

By late 1963, Jules had been discharged from the Navy and joined Terry in helping acts including Jackie Miller and Gayle Caldwell (two female singers from the New Christy Minstrels) as well as a trio that included Ted Bluechel. Soon Terry and Jules found themselves part of a spontaneously thrown-together hootenanny folk-jam group that was invited to become a house band, calling themselves the Men, at the Troubadour, a popular and influential folk-pop-rock nightclub in West Hollywood where many musicians launched their acts.

After an impressive eight-year musical sojourn, Terry left the Association in early 1973. "I was totally burned out. Brian [Cole] had just died. Brian was wonderful. He was crazy. He was one of the funniest and brightest people I ever met in my life."

Exhausted from constant touring and recording, Terry realized he needed to spend more time with his 4 1/2-year-old daughter, Sasha, whom he had hardly seen since her birth. He was married to Judy Hyatt Gelbord, Sasha's mother, who had been a waitress at the Troubadour when he met her. They remained married for 22 years. "We were both political activists. So royalties from music gave us income to pursue our activism." Terry was also becoming more involved with an antiwar movement initiated by people in the entertainment industry. "I found a niche with a whole group of people in something that Tom Hayden, who later became married to Jane Fonda, had been working on."They called it the Vietnam Information Project, a program to articulate to the public information about American military involvement in Vietnam."Rather than taking a political point of view, or a polarized point of view, or a propagandist point of view, or a radical point of view, we collected information in an absolutely pure context, backing it up, presenting photographic evidence, and then going off to deliver lectures," says Kirkman.

"Nobody knew what Washington was going to do. We could look back in hindsight and say, well, here's indication that it was winding down. But Washington could have just as easily dropped the bomb. What we knew in the Vietnam Information Project was that Washington had some pretty unthinkable ideas about operations that they were looking to carry out. [Assistant Secretary of Defense for International Security Affairs John] McNaughton wanted to hamburger-bomb North Vietnam, and that's in the Pentagon Papers. The hamburger bombs were two-ton hamburger-shaped explosive devices that he intended to drop on the dike and dam system in North Vietnam and flood the entire country with the intent of killing 6 million people. We knew that."Terry remained involved with the Vietnam Information Project as well as the Entertainment Industry For Peace and Justice until the war ended in 1975.

During those same years, Terry studied acting with Peggy Feury at the Lee Strasberg Theatre and Film Institute for four and a half years, performing in plays while also writing for television game shows *The Crosswits* and **Name That Tune**. In the late 1970s he graduated from game shows to HBO variety shows, writing two musical specials and helping to develop others. One of the specials inspired a reunion performance of the surviving original members of the Association. In 1979 Terry was recruited to become the creative director of Motown Records, which was "a profoundly unpleasant experience that inspired me to re-unite with my former colleagues and get back into the performing business full time."Terry remained with the Association from September 1980 to September 1984, when he finally left the road for good to return to writing television and advertising copy.

Today, Terry's life is almost totally involved in the recovery world. "I am a recovering alcoholic. I was a screaming cocaine addict. And I got sober October 21, 1984, six weeks after leaving the Association, and I've remained so ever since."

Through his own recovery activities, Terry was invited to work in a recovery program at Hollywood Community Hospital. The experience proved to be fulfilling and Terry decided to return to school to pursue a career in chemical dependency counseling. For that, he attended UCLA, met his 4,000-hour intern requirements and then passed his California Certification Board exams in 1994. After working for many public and private facilities, Terry opened a small private practice in Los Angeles, counseling chemically dependent people and their families. In March 2000, he became the clinical director of the Musicians' Assistance Program (MAP) in Hollywood. MAP was a non-profit, independent organization founded in 1995 by a recovering addict, professional jazz sax player Buddy Arnold. Its purpose was to assist people in the music business overcome problems with substance abuse. Terry handled the assessment, referral and funding of treatment for people in the music business throughout the country in need of professional help. MAPS became part of MusicCares, a division of the Grammy Foundation.

"There's no comparison to anything else I've done in my life. It was one of the best jobs I could ever imagine having in the recovery profession," he says. "Someone would call up all helpless and hopeless and broke, and if they met our minimal requirements, I could have them in a treatment facility within minutes. Totally free, if needed. I'd go home with a great feeling of gratitude every night."

In addition, Terry has served as a consultant for sober-living facilities, including a facility that houses members of the homeless population with the purpose of re-entering them into functional, independent living. "By and large, in an urban setting, 60 to 70 percent of anybody who walks into a regular general therapist's office is either chemically dependent or greatly impacted by someone who is chemically dependent. Eighty-five percent of inmates in the California penal system are there because of drug- and alcohol-related crimes. It's just like fighting a war," he said.

Terry met his wife, Heidi Jo Berinstein, a longtime research writer for television and films, in 1987, and they married in 1992. A University of California, Santa Cruz, graduate in American film, Heidi re-entered college in 1999 as a graduate student in clinical psychology, and currently serves as a licensed marriage and family therapist.

Terry's daughter Sasha (whose legal name is Alixandra) graduated with honors from the University of California, Santa Cruz, and went on to complete her master's degree at Columbia University. She's married and taught 10th-grade English in the New York City public school system for years before becoming director of a literacy program in Oakland, California.

Music has always been very much a part of Terry's life. From 1987 to 2002, he was conductor of a choir in Los Angeles made up of other recovering people who sang for different recovery-oriented functions. "We took a lot of pop music and put it in a recovery context. So if you were at a gathering of recovering people and you sang 'Put A Little Love In Your Heart,' the words took on a whole new meaning."

After finishing a session with one of his clients, Terry takes time out to enjoy a little of his own music therapy by either jamming on his soprano recorder, playing his electric keyboard or ukulele, or walking outdoors to sing. In his spare time, Terry enjoys working in the garden, drawing, writing poetry, and painting. "I'm learning how to use color and layer color. I would like to sculpt more. I have done some clay sculpting, not hammer and chisel." He's also a member of a writers group, and he's working on three books – a novel, a recovery book, and a memoir about his music career and activism.

Most individuals could say that a particular person has influenced their lives in some way, either personally or professionally. Terry retorts, "I collect mentors. I'm serious. I meet somebody that knows something that I don't know, and go hook up with them. I want my spiritual connection to be in actions, and not in a beatific, ritual-like conceit. I want to live my spirituality today. Getting on the freeway or when I'm on line or I see somebody that needs assistance, or how I address my wife, how I mend the damage that my alcoholism did with my daughter and other people that I knew. That's really what my life is about. Creating ways to communicate with people without them knowing – that's what I'm doing. How could I say this in a nicer way to you?"

Terry, whose main focus today lies in helping humanity, reflects, "I think the most important commodity that any of us have to exchange with each other is validation. Validate who you and others are. I understand 'postal.' A person who has gone 'postal' feels there's no way to validate themselves. It may be that the spirit of my Methodist theologian circuit-riding grandfather lives in me and in that context I would consider myself an evangelist. I really want to carry that message, without getting into any fundamentalist thought, that there's another way to live. That you can be the person you are and live alongside everybody else and not be in conflict with how hard it is just to be living. And I like to write music about that today. I'm certainly not writing gospel or religious stuff. It may be about having really pissed somebody off and I want to say I'm sorry I did that. It can be done with a lot of humor. It could be about a lot of things. And that's where I would like my art to be today."

39

Epilogue: Larry Ramos

Guitarist, banjo player and singer

The song "Cherish" stands as one of the most stunning examples of vocal harmonizing of the 1960s. One year before "Cherish" became a No. 1 hit for the Association, the song was being sung by a large group that in its time achieved great popularity – the New Christy Minstrels. Larry Ramos was a member of that folk-balladeer troupe during the early to mid-'60s when the Minstrels' "Green, Green" and "Today" were top-20 hits. And Larry was destined to continue singing "Cherish" for more than 30 years as a member of the Association.

"The New Christy Minstrels recorded Terry Kirkman's song 'Cherish' for Columbia Records before the Association recorded it," explains Ramos, "but when the Minstrels asked Kirkman for a license to release it, he refused because he and the Association had agreed to release it. I'm still working today because of 'Cherish.' One way or the other, I was going to be singing 'Cherish.' It was destined, whether with the Association or the Minstrels, because I had been singing 'Cherish' with the Minstrels for months."

Larry's passion for music goes back as far as he can remember. While most kids are more interested in toy trucks and building blocks, at the age of 5 Larry was singing and playing the ukulele for anyone who would listen. His father, Larry Ramos Sr., taught him how to play "My Bonnie Lies Over the Ocean," which consisted of just three major chords. But listening to the radio, Larry taught himself the "Anniversary Waltz," a song in minors. "I had learned the minors by myself. I just put what I heard onto the uke, and it worked out that I learned harmony at a

Larry Ramos in 2000. Photo by Ken Ige, *Honolulu Star-Bulletin.*

very early age," says Ramos. "I sang some Hawaiian things like 'Little Grass Shack' and 'Little Brown Gal' and stuff like that. I call it Tin Pan Alley Hawaiian style, because most of the songs that were popular during that time were actually written in New York, not Hawaii."

Larry was born on Kauai, Hawaii, on April 19, 1942, just four months after the bombing of Pearl Harbor. His father, who owned two billiard parlors in Honolulu, sold them after the war and moved the family back to the rural island of Kauai, where he ran a billiard parlor until the family's move to California.

In 1949, television host and entertainer Arthur Godfrey, who played the ukulele himself and was a fan of Hawaiian music, held a ukulele contest in Hawaii. Larry, who was just 7 years old at the time, entered and won the contest on the night of the semi-finals. The prize was an invitation to appear on Godfrey's television show in New York. Larry recalls, "We went to New York twice. I appeared on his season-opening television show in 1950, which was a big Hawaiian luau. Duke Kahanamoku, Hilo Hattie, some of the more prestigious Hawaiian entertainers had come over too. So it was a real entertaining show. I returned to New York in 1951 again to do another spot on his show."

Following his last appearance on the Arthur Godfrey show, a woman named Ann Baker from Palm Springs, California, discovered Larry performing in Kauai and thought he'd be suited for Hollywood. She paid for his family's trip to Hollywood and carted Larry around to all of the movie studios. "Warner Bros. was very interested in me because they wanted me to become the new Sabu. However, I was so skinny at the time, they wanted me to put on some weight. They gave me six weeks, and I ate everything, but I was one of those kids that you could stuff full of food and I never gained an ounce of weight. So I lost that gig."

Intrigued by the idea of living on the mainland and Larry's potential for success in the entertainment business, his family moved to the south-central Los Angeles town of Cudahy, and Larry managed to land a role in a television show called *Harry Owens and His Royal Hawaiians.* Larry recalls, "Harry Owens was the bandleader of the orchestra that played at the Royal Hawaiian Hotel in Honolulu for a long time, before World War II. I became a semi-regular on his TV show, playing my uke and singing."

In the mid-'50s, Larry toured with the road company of the Broadway musical *The King and I* for almost two years. He played the crown prince and toured with Yul Brynner and Patricia Morison,

41

who played Anna. "I was about 12 or 13 at the time, and played one of the royal children during the performances. I had joined the road company on the leg going back to the East Coast. That was the first touring I actually did. I finally played the Crown Prince at the Royal Alexandria Theatre in Toronto during the month-long run there in 1956."

With music still his passion, and rock and roll filling the airwaves, at the age of 17 Larry and some of his friends from Bell High School formed his first rock and roll band called the Defiants. Larry played the four-stringed tenor guitar and the short-lived group performed at high school assemblies and occasionally local television shows.

After graduating from Bell, Larry attended East Los Angeles Junior College and Cerritos College in Norwalk, California, to pursue a political science major. "Most of my family is either into public service, education or law enforcement. I was supposed to have been either a social studies or history teacher, but I found it extremely boring. I enjoyed political science until I figured out that political science is exactly what it says; it's all about politics."

While attending college, Larry visited a coffeehouse and folk club in South Gate called the Satyr (pronounced Satire). While watching the performers there, he noticed the simplicity of the music that they were playing. Larry recalls, "I went up to the owner of the club after the show and I said, 'Look, I'm a musician and I'd like to work. How many tunes do I need to know to start playing here?' He said, 'Learn a dozen tunes, and come back.' So it took me about a day and a half to learn a dozen tunes. A lot of big people came out of that little club. Hoyt Axton was one, my very good friend Barry McGuire, and the Chambers Brothers. We had some big stars working there, including Brownie McGhee and Sonny Terry, blues icons."

The club hired Larry first as a performer and later made him master of ceremonies for the club's once-a-week hootenanny shows. It was there in 1962 that he was introduced to the New Christy Minstrels, with whom he performed through the group's recording years until 1966. "I was working at the club one night in 1962 and Art Podell saw me and said, 'Hey, are you interested in working for somebody?' And I said, 'Well, what does it entail?' And he said, 'It's a big group, nine people.' And I thought to myself, 'God, it's hard enough for me to make a living as a single act. Nine people. Boy, you're going to have to cut that pie up a lot.' So I said, 'How much money can I make?' And he told me, 'You'll make scale for one thing, because we're going to be working on the Andy Williams television show.'

But it took them six weeks to figure out whether or not I would fit in because I was Oriental. I was the first Pacific Islander-Oriental to break into the major music market with the New Christy Minstrels, and the first in rock and roll with the Association."

Larry met his wife, Helene Luman, in 1963 at a party that the owner of Harold's Club threw for the New Christy Minstrels in Reno, Nevada. "It was at a Chinese restaurant, and it was after the last show, so we didn't get out of the restaurant until about 5 or 6 in the morning. Helene and another lady came in with the owner of the club. And I happened to notice her in the audience at the next show we played at the club. My wife has the most beautiful blue eyes. She's a very, very beautiful woman. After the show, I didn't even go back to my dressing room. I just told one of the guys to take my banjo and I went upstairs, and she was sitting at the bar. I asked if I could buy her a drink and she said, 'No, I get my drinks free.' And I said, 'Oh, that's nice. OK. Do you mind if I sit next to you here?' And she said, 'Free country.' This is great, you know, I'm really getting all these positive signs. So I pursued her for about six months. She was a blackjack dealer at the time. And when we got married in 1964, everybody said, 'You guys won't last more than six months.'"

Larry later adopted Helene's son, Terry, and in 1965, the couple celebrated the birth of twin daughters Stacy Lin and Tracy Lee. "The Minstrels let me off for one day – the day my girls were born because my wife had a scheduled C-section. The next time I saw my daughters, they were 6 months old," said Ramos. "The year my daughters were born, I worked 360 days. They worked us to the bone."

By 1966 Larry was tired of constantly being on the road and decided he wanted to spend more time with his family. So he informed Minstrels owners George Greif and Sid Garris that he wanted to leave the group. "George was kind of ticked off because they had to find another Oriental to take my place, and he said to me, 'You'll never work in show business again if you leave this group.' He gave me the kiss of death speech. And I said, 'Well, I guess I'll have to take that chance.' They offered the position to my brother Del but he refused. A year later, I was in the Association, and the next time I saw Sid Garris was when we were receiving our gold record for 'Windy' at the Coconut Grove in Los Angeles. After the show, Sid Garris comes up to me all smiles and he says, 'It makes us feel good to see one of our kids do well.' And I was about to say, 'You told me I'd never work in show business again,' but I didn't."

43

After leaving the Minstrels, Larry spent the next year working Playboy Clubs up and down the West Coast as a solo artist. One of his opening acts was comedian Pat Morita, who would later appear in the *Happy Days* television series as Arnold, and in the *Karate Kid* movies as Mr. Miagi. "At that time, he was called the 'Hip Nip,' a very politically incorrect name today, but during that time nobody gave a damn. And he was a funny guy. He moved to Hawaii shortly after I met him."

While engaged in session work on an album for former Minstrels member Mike Whelan and songwriter Jimmy Webb, Larry met Pat Colecchio and Terry Kirkman. "Terry said to me, 'Hey, you know we're going to be losing one of our guys, Gary Alexander. He's going to go to India to meet his guru and to seek enlightenment.' He said, 'Do you want to see whether or not you want to be part of this group?' And I said, 'Sure.'"

In 1968, Larry joined the Association, and replaced Jules. "His name has always been Jules Gary Alexander, but he preferred Jules to Gary upon his return." For the next several years, the Association worked a couple of hundred days a year.

In 1970, Helene and Larry celebrated the birth of their son Larry Ramos III. "My wife was just about to turn 30 and she said that she didn't want to have any kids after that. It was during those days when nobody had kids after they were 30. Good God, how far we've come since then. But she said it's now or never, so she flew up to our gig in Duluth, Minnesota. She said, 'If we're going to try to have a son, this is about the best time and by God, she was right!"

Larry recalls performing with the Rolling Stones at Wembley Stadium in 1968. "One of the nicest people I've met was Mick Jagger. Mick was a very cordial person. Very sweet man. You know, you see his persona on stage, some kind of a bad-ass guy. He is really a nice guy. And I met the Beatles when I was with the Minstrels. We were at a Christmas show that the Beatles were having in 1964 in London and we went backstage and met them. And it was quite a thing. And I found them all very nice. I particularly liked speaking with Paul and Ringo, and George. John was a little distant, but I understood that was the way he was, so it didn't bother me at all. You know, you meet all these people and you have these preconceived notions of what they're like, and some of them completely fool you. And some of them don't fool you at all. They're exactly what you think they would be like."

From 1976 to 1979, Larry performed with his cousin Miles Patrick Unite [pronounced you-NEE-tee] and his younger brother Del in a trio called Homegrown. "There's something about a family act that can't be duplicated by anybody else. We played everything from blues to bluegrass. That's probably the most fun I've ever had," says Larry.

During the late '70s, while the Association was on hiatus, a variety of bogus acts were calling themselves the Association and sending out publicity photos that included a cut-in picture of Larry. "They said the guy in the photo was Rudy Ramos, but it was my picture. When I didn't show up for the gig, they said, 'Oh, he's not here because he's sick.' That really bothered me because I've never missed any performance because I was sick. We may have missed performances because of weather or maybe because of bad business, but never because I was sick. I always had enough to get on stage, even if I was running a 103-degree temperature. I always was able to perform. But it bothered me even more that they were using my picture."

In 1981 while the original members of the Association had regrouped to film a Showtime special in Houston, Texas, hosted by Ed McMahon with Phyllis Diller, the Dallas Cheerleaders and Frank Gorshin, they happened to notice a marquee at a Playboy Club that said the Association was featured that night. "After the rehearsal, we went by and caught the bogus group's first show. And here they were on stage saying, 'Yeah, after we recorded this, we recorded this, and we wrote that.' And we couldn't stand it. So we sent a message up to the stage saying that the individual members – Terry Kirkman, Russ Giguere, Jules Alexander, Jim Yester, Larry Ramos – are sitting in the audience and would like to have a word with them after the performance. And the guy who got the message turned white for a second, and then he got his composure back and he said, 'Oh, we're sorry, young lady, but we can't divulge where we're staying' or something like that. But after the show, en masse, we went backstage and the guys were so apologetic. They said, 'We didn't know you guys were back.' They were working for the same guy who had called me weeks before this incident and said to me, 'Hey, would you like to work for the Association?' I said, 'What do you mean, "work for the Association"? How do you have the Association? You don't own the group?' And he said, 'No, but I've leased the name. How about working for the group?' And I said, 'No. You can't pay me enough, for one thing.' So he called Russell, and Russell refused as I did. And they put my picture on the promo photograph because there was no identifiable

45

person. The only identifiable person in the group is me because the rest of guys are all white, and they look like ordinary guys. Except for Jules. Jules looks like Dr. Zorba [a wild-haired character on the old *Ben Casey* television series]. Jules and I were the only two weird-looking guys in the group. The next week they were going to be the Grassroots in another town. And then the next week after that they were the Buckinghams. And it ticks me off because the Buckinghams are good friends of ours.

In 2011, original members Larry, Russ and Jim played about 50 dates with the Association. Although he mostly plays lead guitar, Larry considers himself a musical chameleon. "I could always blend into any kind of music that I had to play. And also I'm a very, very quick study, and that is probably the strongest point of my talent," Larry said. He also plays bass and banjo, and other numerous stringed instruments. "I used to play banjo in the Association every so often. I started with the Minstrels playing a big acoustic upright bass, and I was the littlest guy in the group, playing the biggest instrument. The biggest guy in the group was playing a mandolin, which was the littlest instrument. We decided that looked kind of ridiculous. So Randy Sparks, the leader of the Minstrels, said, 'Hey, can you play banjo?' And I said, 'Sure, I can play banjo.' Of course at that time I couldn't play five-string banjo, but I figured, 'how hard is it to learn?' So it took me less than a week to learn the banjo and play it on stage. And so that's what I mean: I'm a quick study and it takes me very, very little time to learn any new material, or learn any instruments."

Larry and Helene raised their children in San Juan Capistrano, California, but now live on 300 acres in rural north-central Idaho, where Helene grew up. They love animals and have a Mexican hairless dog named Olive Oyl, a dachshund named Lily, three cats named Mitzi, Mrs. Beasley and Wally, five goats (two of which are named after the Righteous Brothers, Billy and Bobby) and three females named Betsy, Lucy and Lola. "I told Bill Medley about the goats while we were performing on a cruise last year, and he cracked up," said Larry.

One of Larry's heroes and a good friend for 40 years is the Kingston Trio's Bob Shane. "I remember hearing Bob and the Trio do 'Tom Dooley.' Little did I know we would become fast friends. Bob and I are both Hawaiians. I like to say the difference between us is that Bob Shane's ancestors put clothes on the Hawaiians," he laughs.

Larry and Jordan Cole (Brian Cole's son, who performs with the Association) are producing a CD of songs Larry has been writing and collecting for years. One of the songs is called "Hawaiian Condominium Fund," which he wrote for Bob Shane. "I saw Bob not more than a month ago. We're like two old farts getting together and having a good time," Larry said in April 2011.

One of the ironies of rock and roll is the toll it exacts upon performers. While love and relationships form the subject matter for many rock and roll ballads, the demands of recording and touring leave a devastating trail of broken marriages and broken hearts. However, Larry and Helene Ramos are rare exceptions. They have weathered the rock and roll road for four decades, and have four children and three grandchildren whom they cherish.

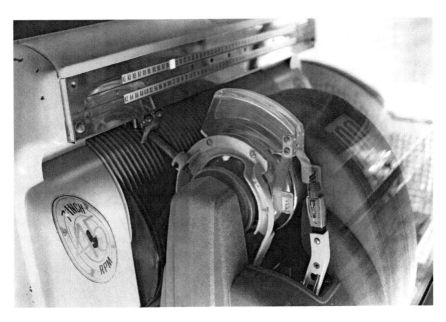

Detail of a 1951 Seeburg Model 100C Select-O-Matic jukebox owned by Terry and Cindy Knight. Photo by Amanda Domingues.

Epilogue: Jim Yester
Guitarist and singer

Jim Yester's musical career had just begun and was gaining momentum in 1964 around the coffeehouses of New York's Greenwich Village. But he set his guitar down in early '65 and picked up a dishrag to help his parents run their restaurant in an isolated desert town. A year later, people throughout the world would hear him singing lead on a song that cleaned up on the music charts: "Along Comes Mary."

Jim's musical roots began in Birmingham, Alabama, where he was born to Larry and Martha Yester on November 24, 1939. His father was a professional musician who played piano, organ and accordion, and his mother sang. "When I was 3 years old, my dad had stars in his eyes and wanted to get involved with the movie industry, so we moved to Southern California. That's where I lived until I went into military service when I was 22." His father managed to land a role as a musician in about a dozen motion pictures, including *Fort Apache* and *April Showers*.

The middle of three boys, Jim attended Catholic school, where he and his younger brother Jerry, who went on to become a member of the Modern Folk Quartet and the Lovin' Spoonful, got their introduction to singing. "You go to parochial school, you sing! So we sang in

Jim Yester in 2000. Photo by Alex Anton, Studio 53.

school, we sang in church, and my mom always sang with us."

At age 16, Jim was drawn to boogie woogie piano music. "I was in a falconry club in Southern California, and there was this guy in his mid-20s from the south side of Chicago who played boogie woogie piano. I used to sit there and watch him play for hours and when he'd take a break, I'd sit down and he'd show me stuff. At that time we didn't have a piano in the house. I was working, so I rented a piano for $10 a month. That just blew my dad's mind. He was so happy."

When his parents decided to move to the California high desert town of Joshua Tree to open a restaurant-bar-café in late 1960, Jim and Jerry had begun performing together and didn't want to go. "I was about 21, and Jerry was 17. Our folks found us a little one-bedroom house in Burbank (right across the street from John Burroughs High School) that was like $50 a month. My brother played the guitar and the two of us sang harmony together, doing Kingston Trio songs. Somebody next door heard us singing, and came over and asked us if we'd sing for a frat party. I decided I didn't want to be up there with my hands in my pockets, so Jerry taught me how to play guitar and sing about 15 songs. That's when I started playing guitar, and it's never stopped."

After graduating from Notre Dame High School, a Catholic college preparatory school in Sherman Oaks, California, Jim began working at a pharmaceutical lab. At 18 years of age he was running the compressing department, which turned powder into tablets and pills. "I had all these older guys working for me, and they wanted to make me assistant production manager, which would have been more money than I ever dreamed of. But they wouldn't do it because I had the draft hanging over my head. I was also going to school from 6 to 9 p.m., and singing with my brother from 10 p.m. to 2 a.m. So first of all, school went, and then I decided, 'well, I'm just going to get the draft out of the way,' so I went and joined the Army."

Jim joined the Army in November of 1961, and after completing basic training at Fort Ord in Monterey, California, he took a battery of tests that determined he had an aptitude for computer programming. But the Army sent him to radar school in Fort Huachuca, southeast of Tucson, Arizona. After radar training, Jim was sent to an artillery outfit in Germany, which was authorized for radar but didn't have it. "I was real gung-ho and I kept putting in for a transfer. Finally my captain, under protest, gave me a transfer to a medium tank battalion, which was also authorized for radar but didn't have it."

Jim was finally assigned to a radio repair unit, and it was there that he met musicians Jim Kirby and Dennis Turechek. Kirby had been involved in a folk group in college that had made an album, and Turechek was a jazz guitarist from Greenwich Village in New York. "The three of us put together a folk-comedy trio called the Yester-years. We sent off a tape to the entertainment director in Nuremberg, who freaked out, sprung us from our outfit, and we toured all over Germany and France entertaining the troops," says Yester.

Jim would later meet up with Jim Kirby again in 1977, when together they started an advertising agency called Media Music. "We had a pretty good run of success, but we were underfunded, and there were so many big advertising companies in L.A., we just couldn't compete. So I wound up going back to the Association, and he wound up opening a very successful advertising company called Bert, Barz & Kirby, in Los Angeles."

Jim was discharged from the Army in October 1964, and moved in with his brother Jerry, who was living in Greenwich Village, New York, and performing with the Modern Folk Quartet. But soon after, their father was seriously injured in an automobile accident, so Jim went to Joshua Tree to help his mother with the restaurant. "I worked at the restaurant for about five months cooking, washing dishes, bar tending and singing behind the piano bar. When my dad was able to work again, I moved back to the Los Angeles area, where I ran into a starting group called the Association. They knew my brother from the MFQ, so I auditioned for them, and Jules pulled me aside and said, 'Come back in about three days.' One guy wasn't working out and they were going to let him go, and I was going to take his place. So I came back in three days, and moved into the house."

In 1965 Jim was married to his first wife, Joellen Shattuck, a member of a group called the Femme Folk Modern – the female version of the Modern Folk Quartet. "They had great vocals, and had recorded 'Baby Can't You Hear Me Call Your Name?' on Capitol Records. Jack Nitzsche did the arranging and produced it with orchestra and everything. Oh, it was gorgeous. She and I were married for four years."

In 1969 Jim met Syleste Wilczynski at the Hollywood Bowl. The couple married, and celebrated the birth of their daughter Corey in 1972. A fashion model, Syleste had been a Playboy bunny for three years, and performed as an actress in about 15 movies.

After seven years with the Association, Jim took a brief leave of absence from the group when his daughter was born, and his brother Jerry replaced him. When Jules left the group in 1974 for family commitments, Jim rejoined the Association, giving him a chance to perform with his brother again. The brothers remained together in the Association lineup for about nine months.

"We had our own recording studio at that time, out in Van Nuys. We had a rehearsal hall in an industrial area, and we wound up turning it into a recording studio, and we were recording a lot of things then. In about 1975, we did get a deal with RCA and recorded a thing called 'One Sunday Morning' and 'Life Is a Carnival.' We had a few single records, but none, unfortunately, that were hits. I mean they went up the chart and then went back down the chart."

Jim left the Association in 1977, the year his father died. "I was raising a family and it had gotten a little crazy, and I was frustrated. I was managing the band at that time, and I think I was just fried making all the travel arrangements and playing." Ted Bluechel, the only original member, kept the band going for awhile, but he gave it up about eight months later.

In late 1979, Terry Kirkman was working on an HBO special, called "Then and Now." After some hesitation, all of the original members of the Association (except for Brian Cole, who had died in 1972) agreed to get together to do the show. "We did the show and the producers were so blown away, they offered to back us to get back together. So I stayed until 1983."

Jim was living in Canoga Park at the time and took a job with Delta Tau Data Systems, making computers, ultimately becoming production manager there. Longing to get back into the music business, after two and a half years, he and Syleste moved with their daughter to Hilo, Hawaii, where his brother Jerry had relocated. The two brothers formed a band called Rainbow Connection with another local musician named Rainbow Page. The group consisted of guitars, flute and conga, and used MIDI technology to synthesize instrumental sounds. It became the hottest band in Hawaii for the next five years. "Then we wound up re-forming Jerry's old band, the Modern Folk Quartet (MFQ), and it became the Modern Folk Quintet with all the members plus myself. We signed with a Japanese record label, and recorded five CDs. About the same time we opened a recording studio in Hawaii."

In 1990, Jerry moved his family to Portland, Oregon, and Jim ran the studio in Hawaii with bassist, songwriter and MFQ member Chip Douglas, who produced recordings for the Turtles, the Monkees and Linda Ronstadt. "One day Jerry called me and said, 'We're putting the Lovin' Spoonful back together. Do you want to take John's [Sebastian] place?' So I said, 'sure.'" After several flights back and forth to Hawaii for performing engagements, Jim decided it would be more economical to live closer to the band. "So I rented a car in Chicago and drove to Arkansas to visit a friend, who had bought 52 acres there. I was there three days and bought a house for $500 down and a handshake, and lived there for a couple of years."

After almost a year performing with the Spoonful, Jim got a call from the band's bassist, Steve Boone, saying a tour had been canceled and there wouldn't be any work for the next six months. "I was really hurting after moving my girlfriend and her two teen boys from Hawaii to Arkansas, but shortly after that, I got a call from David Sommerville asking me to come sing with his group."

Yester spent the next 14 years playing 50 to 60 dates a year with Bruce Belland from the Four Preps – co-founder and co-writer of all the hits – and David Sommerville, founder and lead singer on all the hits for the Diamonds, including "Little Darlin" and "The Stroll." When Yester joined them in late 1993, the group called itself the New Four Preps, because at that time it included Ed Cobb, co-founder and bass singer for the Four Preps. In 1998, Ed Cobb left the band after being diagnosed with leukemia. He died in 1999.

The group performed in tuxedos for corporate events, casinos, and for city concerts in the park as well as performing arts centers. "We did an 18-minute megahit medley at the end of the show of all the three groups' hits. We did some Elton John stuff, some Chicago stuff; we did a medley of 20 years ago: 'MacArthur Park,' we did a capella versions of 'Somewhere Over the Rainbow' and 'Somewhere' from *West Side Story*, and we had a killer version of 'A Whiter Shade of Pale.' In 1998 the group produced a CD titled *Triple Gold by Yester, Belland and Somerville – three golden groups in one.*

"We had a band behind us, plus they monitored a click track off an eight-track digital recorder that had a full orchestra, so it was a big sound. It was a great show. We always got two and sometimes three standing ovations. People just loved it."

In 1994, three years after his divorce from Syleste, Jim performed a concert with the New Four Preps at the Taj Mahal in Atlantic City, New Jersey. There he met Linda Gentille, who was a regular performer at the club. Billed as the "Piano Princess," Linda started playing piano at the age of 9 and had taken acting training at the American Academy of Dramatic Arts. She performed for two years in the late '80s with Liberace on his shows in Las Vegas and at Radio City Music Hall.

Using their combined musical talents, Jim and Linda began a program called Get High On Music, Not Drugs, which intertwined classical and pop music, hip-hop and rap into creative anti-drug messages. They developed age-specific programs for kindergarten through high school-age children and took their show to schools throughout the country. Although Linda had never sung before, she and Jim incorporated a lot of Disney tunes and she started singing along.

"Linda became a very good singer. The last two and a half years she performed at Taj Mahal, I performed with her when I was in town. And we started taking on musicals, in costume, in character, and we'd do duets together – things from *Phantom of the Opera* and *My Fair Lady*."

Linda, who speaks eight languages, toured internationally, and Jim accompanied her on four trips to mainland China, where she had sold-out concerts in 15 cities. Jim and Linda parted ways in 1998, but continue to be friends. They perform together a few times a year with the Jersey Shore Pops (http://jerseyshorepops.org), a 21-piece orchestra Linda established. It stages concerts and music education assemblies in performing arts centers and schools throughout the United States.

In 1999, Terry Kirkman and Jim took part in a songwriters' seminar that was part of a New Jersey Country Music Expo that took place in Paramus, New Jersey. During the expo, they were joined by a country rock band called Circle's End and were billed as Terry Kirkman and Jim Yester, original members of the Association. "We just blew everybody out. We were kinda like the hit of the weekend."

Following that, they performed together as Association Revisited at a big amphitheater in Strausstown, Pennsylvania. "Larry Ramos and Russ Giguere got very upset because they were still out there touring as the Association. So I promised them we wouldn't ever call it that anymore, but the promotion had already gone out."

Until rejoining the Association in 2008, Jim continued performing with Sommerville and Belland until Sommerville took a gig in Branson, Missouri, doing regular shows as a solo act.

"I had already started working with the Association with the understanding that we would juggle the bookings. The guy that I replaced was on a retainer, so if I couldn't make it, they brought him back in because he knew all of the songs." However, after Sommerville was booked in Branson, Jim joined the Association full time.

In his free time, Jim enjoys playing basketball, tennis and golf. "A few years ago, I played in a celebrity tennis tournament out at the Beverly Wilshire Hotel, and gosh, that was fun. I also played on a celebrity golf tournament for one of the conventions that we did, and that was great fun. It was a scramble tournament. And I got the prize for the closest to the pin."

Jim, like each member of the Association, continues to develop and polish his talents and seek new outlets for creativity. As brilliant as they are individually, they each served as a gleaming facet that gave the Association its luster that has remained untarnished over nearly four decades.

Herman's Hermits in 1965. From left, Keith Hopwood, Derek Leckenby, Peter Noone, Karl Green and Barry Whitwam. Photofest photo.

2

Mrs. Brown, You've Got a Lovely Daughter

Herman's Hermits

When the Beatles first soared to the top of the American music charts in early 1964 they opened the gates for dozens of British bands to follow. But missing from that first wave was a band that would rise to become one of the biggest-selling "British invasion" groups – Herman's Hermits – initially left behind because of lack of a recording contract.

Unlike the Beatles, who did their best to disguise their accents while singing, Herman's Hermits took delight in their decidedly working-class dialect that was evident in their first hit, "I'm Into Something Good," a Gerry Goffin and Carole King song that had been a minor hit in the United States for Cookies' vocalist Earl-Jean McCrea. The Hermits' single was released August 7, 1964, and quickly reached No. 1 in the United Kingdom, and No. 13 in the United States.

American audiences couldn't get enough of this new sound from across the sea, and Herman's Hermits were enamored with American pop music. Capitalizing on their British accents, Herman's Hermits traveled to America for the first time in December 1964. They had just released in the United Kingdom their first EP (extended play) 45 RPM disc, *Hermania,* which featured American hits "I Understand," a song first made popular in 1954 by the Four Tunes and later by Freddie and The Dreamers; Frankie Ford's No. 14 hit in 1959, "Sea Cruise"; and Ernie K-Doe's 1961 No. 1 hit "Mother-In-Law."

With seven consecutive hits – "I'm Into Something Good; "Can't You Hear My Heartbeat?"; "Mrs. Brown, You've Got a Lovely Daughter"; "Silhouettes"; "Wonderful World"; "I'm Henry the Eighth, I Am" (a 1911 music hall song); and "Just A Little Bit Better" – Herman's Hermits surpassed the Beatles in a *Cashbox* magazine survey of performance of vocal groups on its charts in the United States during 1965.

While in America, the group was invited to make a cameo appearance in Metro-Goldwyn-Mayer's (MGM) teen movie *When The Boys Meet the Girls*, starring Connie Francis and Harve Presnell. Hermits Peter Noone, Karl Green, Keith Hopwood, Derek "Lek" Leckenby and Barry "Bean" Whitwam joined the likes of Louis Armstrong, Liberace and Sam the Sham and the Pharaohs – who, like the Hermits, had recording contracts with MGM – and introduced their "Listen People," which hit No. 3 on *Billboard's* Hot 100 singles chart in February of 1966. The group also was nominated for two Grammy awards, including Best New Artist in 1966.

Peter Noone was fascinated by the catchy tune "Mrs. Brown, You've Got a Lovely Daughter," written by actor-playwright Trevor Peacock and first recorded and sung by British actor Tom Courtenay. The Hermits featured the song in their stage performances as a novelty number, recording it only reluctantly. The Hermits' producer, Mickie Most, rejected the idea of releasing it as a single, but when advance orders approached 1 million, he relented.

Three days after an American DJ began playing "Mrs. Brown," MGM received 70,000 requests for the single, which was released in early 1965. The song spent three weeks at No. 1 on the *Billboard* Hot 100 chart, topped Australian charts, and sold more than 14 million copies worldwide.

Fueled by the success of "Mrs. Brown," Herman's Hermits selected songs for United States release with a Vaudeville flavor, including "I'm Henry the Eighth (I Am)," distinguishing them from other British invasion acts of the time.

Herman's Hermits began in Manchester, England, as an outgrowth of a group called the Heartbeats, which originally was named the Cyclones and consisted of guitarists Karl Green and Alan Chadwick, bassist Alan Wrigley, and drummer Steve Titterington. When the group's vocalist failed to show up for a gig, 15-year-old Peter Noone filled in and joined in 1963 using the name Peter Novak. The Heartbeats became Pete Novak and the Heartbeats until Peter changed his stage name to Herman after band members said he resembled Sherman in the "Mr. Peabody" segment of the TV cartoon *The Bullwinkle Show*. He misheard the name as Herman and adopted it.

But that version of the band they called Herman and the Hermits didn't last long. Karl Green recalls, "Al Chadwick left, because his girlfriend didn't like him being in a band, so Keith joined. Then we went for a couple of recording tests with different people, and everybody seemed to be saying, 'The band's all right except for the bass player and drummer.' But we didn't have enough balls to say to them, 'You're out of the band. We want someone else.' So the whole lot just split up."

Harvey Lisberg, who had been manager of the dissolved Herman and the Hermits, decided to salvage the group by consolidating it with another band. He sought out a group called the Wailers, which included members Barry Whitwam, Derek Leckenby and a bass player who went by the name of Big Wal. "We said we didn't fancy it, really, because we'd seen the band once before, and we didn't really like them," says Whitwam. "But then Harvey showed us their diary, their date sheet, and they were actually working seven nights a week. So we thought about this – 'well, it's not too bad after all.' So then we auditioned for Harvey Lisberg and his partner, Charlie Silverman, in the basement, and we played a few numbers there."

One of the songs that impressed Lisberg was the Wailers' version of the Jewish celebratory song "Hava Nagila.""We did a great version of it, slowly started it, then we'd speed it up to a frenzy," says Whitwam. "So we played this, and they were over the moon. So we got the job. Thank God for 'Hava Nagila'! But Big Wal's father wouldn't let him become a professional musician."

The group re-formed in the spring of 1964 with Karl Green on bass, rhythm guitarist Keith Hopwood, lead guitarist Derek "Lek" Leckenby, drummer Barry "Bean" Whitwam and lead vocalist Peter Noone. Harvey Lisberg then booked some time for the reconstituted band in a recording studio. He sent a demo of the recording to Mickie Most, producer of hits for the Animals and the Nashville Teens. When Most previously auditioned the early version of the Hermits he was unimpressed, but he was interested in recording the new group. "Mickie liked the new sound," said Whitwam. "It was a lot better musically."

The band members decided they needed to separate themselves from the crowd. "Lek and I suggested we change the name from Herman and the Hermits to Herman's Hermits the day we joined, so the fans would know it was a different band with two new members in it," said Whitwam. "Herman's Hermits was a more modern name, because there were a lot of bands at that particular time – Freddie and the Dreamers, Gerry and the Pacemakers, and so on. And that was the arrangement. I think it was the beginning of April 1964 when we changed the name."

When Keith Hopwood first joined Herman and the Hermits, the group was working four or five gigs a week. He recalls, "Television producer Johnny Hamp of Granada TV in Manchester gave us a TV spot on a little local program. And we did that one, and then he sort of took a shine to us and gave us about four more TV slots. We hadn't had a record at this point. We were still a local band. And not only did he give us the TV slots, but he used to send in an outside broadcast unit to film us. We were playing at the Cavern in Liverpool, and he'd sent the crew down there to film us all day. So we built up a very big following with all this television exposure. The local shows were going fantastically well, although our name didn't mean anything once you got 50 miles from Manchester."

Most, who managed to land a deal with EMI's Columbia label, thought Peter resembled the late President John F. Kennedy and wanted to make him the group's focal point. In July of 1964, Most brought the band into the studio to record "I'm Into Something Good." In September the song spent two weeks at No. 1 on the British charts, and by October of '64, after its release in the States on MGM, "I'm Into Something Good" earned the No. 13 spot in America on the *Billboard* Hot 100 singles chart, which was already crowded with "British invasion" acts.

Herman's Hermits spent most of 1965 in the United States. Karl Green recalls the exhilaration he felt being a young pop star traveling to America for the first time. "The mayhem of arriving at Austin airport, or Fort Worth, or Dallas, and having hundreds and hundreds of people invade the tarmac at the airport, and having to be taken from the airplane straight into cars and taken off to wherever we were going. It was just complete enough mayhem," says Green. "And for a guy 17 to have all these gorgeous girls after him, it was an unbelievable ego boost!"

But all of the traveling and exposure had its price, according to Green. "During the '60s the bands would earn the least money because they were on the road doing all the work while the managers sat in their comfortable offices earning 25 percent with no expenses," he explained. "I mean, when we were on tour, we were paying for all the airplanes that the managers and agents were traveling on, and paying for all the hotel rooms. They had no outlay. We were paying for everything."

While many British groups were striving to sound like Buddy Holly, the Everly Brothers, Muddy Waters, Bo Diddley and other American recording artists, for five years Herman's Hermits turned out hit after hit capitalizing on their heritage and Manchester dialect.

"Herman's Hermits was different from all the other groups," says Peter Noone. "If you want to know about Herman's Hermits, ask the

Beatles, and they'll tell you that it was a great, fun idea that we did the opposite kind of songs of everybody else. Nobody was doing songs with English accents like 'Mrs. Brown, You've Got A Lovely Daughter.' We went to a place where no one else wanted to go. So the perception might be that we were just one of those bands from the '60s. Well, we were, but the reason that we sold 50 million records is because we didn't attempt to compete with the Beatles, or the Stones, or anybody else. We made our own style."

Herman's Hermits' first visit to the United States in the fall of 1964 coincided with the release of "I'm Into Something Good." The group spent a week in New York visiting various radio shows, including an appearance on the influential Murray the K show on WINS. The following spring of 1965, Herman's Hermits joined the Dick Clark Caravan of Stars, a touring ensemble of emerging pop stars on a grueling schedule of one-night appearances.

Keith Hopwood recalls, "It was a bus tour, but not what you'd call a tour bus nowadays. It was like the No. 33 school bus. It was structured so that every other night you got to sleep in a motel, and every other night you had to drive all the way through the night to the next gig. So it was pretty uncomfortable."

Barry "Bean" Whitwam agreed. "If you pulled the short straw and had to sit next to Billy Stewart or Round Robin, there wasn't much room, based on the spillover from that seat to yours," he laughed. "We were so thin in those days, we could actually sleep in the overhead compartments where you put the baggage. We squeezed up in there so we could lay out."

Most Caravan of Stars performers had scored only one or two hits – sufficient to appear on a multi-star bill, but not to draw audiences of their own. But by the time the Caravan reached Philadelphia, Herman's Hermits had four top-five records on the chart – "I'm Into Something Good," "Can't You Hear My Heartbeat," "Silhouettes," and "Mrs. Brown, You've Got A Lovely Daughter." The tour had been booked months prior when the group had only one hit record. Keith Hopwood recalls, "So this promoter, in his wisdom, had obviously booked the Dick Clark thing and then got cold feet about filling this theater. Unbeknownst to anybody, he booked the Rolling Stones as well. But he didn't tell anybody. So we all turned up, and it was quite an entertaining afternoon, because backstage and up the stairs you've got us camped out on one side, and on the other side you've got the Stones, and there was this huge argument about who was going to close the show."

Accompanying Herman's Hermits on the bus tour were Freddie
Cannon, Bobby Vee, Reparata and the Delrons, Billy Stewart, Round
Robin, and Little Anthony and the Imperials. "The bus was quite
full," says Hopwood. "You've got Round Robin, who was 22 stone
[equivalent to 308 pounds]. And Billy Stewart, who was 22 stone. And
Reparata's manager was 25 stone [350 pounds]. But what prompted
us to say that we're not going on the bus anymore was we came out
one morning, and there had been a bit of an altercation in the motel
and a gun appeared at the front of the bus." So we said, 'Excuse me. I
think we're going to travel by car."

Whitwam also recalls the incident. "About halfway through
the tour, Billy Stewart and Round Robin had a disagreement over a
woman, I believe, and pulled guns out at each other. Billy Stewart was
at the front of the bus and Round Robin was at the back. It was like
the wild West. They were pointing guns at each other, and we were
in between this," he said. "So we got off the bus and we rang Dick
Clark and said, 'We don't mind doing your tour, but we're not getting
involved in gunfights.' So he provided us with a station wagon and a
driver. It wasn't much better. There was the six of us and all the bags
in a station wagon."

While Whitwam enjoyed the excitement of being in a different
city every night, at times he found the traveling to be a grind. During a two-week break in the Dick Clark tour, Herman's Hermits performed some shows of their own in Texas. "Just as we were doing
those shows, 'Mrs. Brown' went straight to number 1, and all a sudden
we were playing to thousands and thousands of people, overnight,"
said Whitwam. "We had to go back and finish the Dick Clark tour. And
we still had the overnight traveling in the station wagon. The distanc-
es were quite far apart. So we finished that tour, and then we started
doing tours of our own."

The Hermits continued to churn out hits through 1966 and 1967.
But along with music-hall flavored ditties such as "Leaning on the
Lamppost" in the spring of 1966 and "Dandy" (written by Ray Davies
of the Kinks), that fall they began recording more sophisticated
material. They made memorable recordings of three ballads by British songwriter Graham Gouldman – "Listen People," "East West," and
"No Milk Today," as well as "This Door Swings Both Ways," a mature
portrait about contrasts in life – the jubilance and agony of life and
the choices that must be made. But the band members were perhaps
at their best in 1966, when they recorded the lovely Geoff Stephens-
Les Reed ballad "There's a Kind of Hush All Over the World." The song,

which rose to No. 4 on the American pop charts, earned the Hermits their third and final gold single – a double-sided hit backed with "No Milk Today."

Peter Noone has many fond memories of performing in the '60s. "The whole thing was actually quite a very good time. We were young guys, so everything was a new experience. We played in Hong Kong, Israel, America, the Philippines, France. Every day was a new experience," he says. "We had some of the greatest experiences that any kid could possibly have. So whether we got paid or not, the experience is worth billions of dollars, and I'm grateful for it. If money is the item in the music business, then you'd never make it anyway. If it had been for money, we'd have never been in show business. We would have become doctors."

Peter Noone left the group in 1971 and starred in numerous stage, TV and film productions, during which time he had met David Bowie. Bowie had written Noone's first British solo hit "Oh You Pretty Thing," and played piano on the recording. During the '80s, Noone fronted a new-wave band called the Tremblers, and released a solo album called *One of the Glory Boys.*

Following Peter's departure, Green, Leckenby, Hopwood and Whitwam carried on as Herman's Hermits. Says Green, "And then we were offered to get back with Peter for reunion concerts in the States [without Hopwood, who had left by this time] with Gerry and the Pacemakers and Billy J. Kramer and the Dakotas, the Searchers, and various other bands. And we said, 'yeah.' And it was good fun at the time."

Following Herman's Hermits' 1973 reunion concert at Madison Square Garden, Peter continued for the next 15 years appearing in numerous TV shows, movies and documentaries. In 1986, he was persuaded to start touring again, billed as Herman's Hermits with Peter Noone, performing 40 to 50 shows per year. In 1998, he enjoyed a huge resurgence after touring with Davy Jones and Bobby Sherman in the "Teen Idol" production. He now stages more than 100 concerts per year.

After performing for three decades with the Hermits, Derek Leckenby died on June 4, 1994, of non-Hodgkin's lymphoma, a form of cancer. He left his wife, Leonie, who was at his side when he died, and their two children.

Two versions of the band – Herman's Hermits with Barry Whitwam and Herman's Hermits with Peter Noone – continue to perform concerts worldwide.

The Recording Industry Association of America has certified gold status for four Herman's Hermits albums – *Herman's Hermits on Tour* (August 31, 1965), *Introducing Herman's Hermits* (August 31, 1965), *The Best of Herman's Hermits* (January 11, 1966), *There's a Kind of Hush All Over the World* (June 13, 1969) – and the group has sold more than 60 million records since 1964.

Detail of 1951 Seeburg Model 100C Select-O-Matic jukebox owned by Terry and Cindy Knight. Photo by Amanda Domingues.

HERMAN'S HERMITS U.S. HIT SINGLES ON THE NATIONAL CHARTS

Debut	Peak	Gold	Title	Label
10/64	13		I'm Into Something Good	MGM
1/65	2		Can't You Hear My Heartbeat?	MGM
4/65	5		Silhouettes	MGM
4/65	1	Δ	Mrs. Brown, You've Got a Lovely Daughter	MGM
5/65	4		Wonderful World	MGM
7/65	1	Δ	I'm Henry VIII, I Am	MGM
9/65	7		Just A Little Bit Better	MGM
12/65	8		A Must To Avoid	MGM
2/66	3		Listen People	MGM
4/66	9		Leaning On The Lamp Post	MGM
7/66	12		This Door Swings Both Ways	MGM
10/66	5		Dandy	MGM
12/66	27		East West	MGM
2/67	4	Δ	There's A Kind Of Hush	MGM
2/67	35		No Milk Today	MGM
6/67	18		Don't Go Out Into the Rain	MGM
8/67	39		Museum	MGM
1/68	22		I Can Take Or Leave Your Loving	MGM
5/68	61		Sleepy Joe	MGM

Δ symbol: RIAA certified gold record (Recording Industry Association of America)

Billboard's pop singles chart data is courtesy of Joel Whitburn's Record Research Inc. (www.recordresearch.com), Menomonee Falls, Wisconsin.

Epilogue: Peter Noone

Lead singer

By the time he was 15 years old, Peter Noone had become a household name in his hometown of Manchester, England. But his popularity there wasn't attributed to the music for which he was so well known in America during the '60s. It was more for his acting role as Stanley Fairclough, the son of Len Fairclough, in the popular English soap opera *Cornonation Street.* He also played bit parts in the BBC-TV programs *Knight Errant* and *Family Solicitor.* Combined with local stage appearances, acting seemed the path this young lad would likely follow. But he stopped pursuing his acting career in 1963 because, he says, "Musicians were more fun than actors." At the age of 16, Noone developed a bit of a rebellious streak and no longer wanted to conform to the orders of film directors and producers, and turned his interest toward professional musicianship.

Peter's early interest in music began at home. His grandfather played the organ in the local church, and his grandmother ran the choir. Peter's father was a semi-professional trombone player, and all his uncles were musicians. "My grandfather played classical music,

Peter Noone appeared on *American Idol* in 2007.
Photo courtesy of Peter Noone.

my father played big-band stuff like Woody Herman and Fats Waller, and my grandmother played a lot of Gilbert and Sullivan and light opera," recalls Noone. "I was interested in all of it. In retrospect that's the reason that the Beatles were so good, because our parents listened to this great spectrum of music. They didn't say 'I like the blues and we're gonna listen to the blues or jazz.' It was a spectrum of music. We'd listen to *The Sound Of Music,* and then Little Richard."

Peter Blair Denis Bernard Noone, the second of five children, was born to Denis and Joan Noone on November 5, 1947, in Manchester, England. Named after Peter and Bernard (uncles on his mother's side), his mother's maiden name Blair, and his father, Denis, Noone studied singing and acting at Manchester School of Music and Drama. He began acting in 1960 at the age of 13. Although he didn't have any early childhood ambitions to become a musician, he was always a good singer and played guitar and piano, but considered music a hobby.

"I bought more records than everybody else, and all my friends were into music," says Noone. "We were always interested in the American acts because they were more interesting than the English musicians at the time." Some of the early artists who influenced Peter included Roy Orbison, the Everly Brothers, Buddy Holly, Johnny Cash, Little Richard, Sam Cooke and Elvis Presley.

Noone's parents, who were accountants, moved 35 miles to Liverpool to attend college when Peter was 8 years old, while the children stayed in Manchester. "Part of the history of modern British culture is that our parents were in a world war, and their education was severely disrupted. So my parents went back to school when they were 25 to further their education and their lives," recalls Noone. "So the children of those people were kind of left a little bit to do whatever they want, and I was one of those kids. It was not unusual for kids in my neighborhood to have neither their father or their mother at home at night. Sisters took care of families."

While still in school in 1962, Peter was singer and guitar player for a short-lived band called the Cyclones. In 1963 he jointed the Heartbeats, later to become Herman's Hermits with Karl Green, Derek Leckenby, Keith Hopwood and Barry Whitwam. As lead singer for the Heartbeats, Noone played regularly at youth clubs and dances. Peter recalls at that time the Heartbeats were earning just about enough money to "pay for petrol," and to feed the five members fish and chips on the way home from gigs.

"There were a lot of youth club activities in those days," says Noone, "because the government had set up all of these kinds of activities that kids could do at night to stay out of trouble. We didn't know that's what they were for. We thought they were places where you went to pick up girls, but in fact they were places we could go and play table tennis and nonsense like that, which no one ever did."

Peter attributes Herman's Hermits' biggest break to producer Mickey Most, who took an interest in signing the band after their manager arranged for an audition. "We went for an audition and he tried to sign me on my own without the band, and I refused that," says Noone. "Although I always considered myself the leader of the band, I don't think anybody else in the band did. I think they all thought that they were one team and I was another team, which is kind of strange. I don't know how that happened. But that always does in bands. At the time it was all a little bit confusing, but looking back now at, for example, Aerosmith, in almost every band that you know, there is always some sort of band-versus-singer conflict. You know, the singer gets all the attention. And I got the attention because I was the one who did all of the interviews, and I was best able to manipulate the press, really."

Noone's acting credits, which began in 1961, continue today. As "Herman," Noone performed on hundreds of television programs hosted by Ed Sullivan, Jackie Gleason, Dean Martin, Danny Kaye and other celebrities. Among his many TV and film performances, in 1966 Noone played David, the Duke of Cheshire, in ABC's musical version of *The Canterville Ghost.* In 1968, he played Pinocchio in *Hallmark Hall of Fame's* presentation of "Pinocchio."

Peter left the band in 1971 to continue his acting, while still dabbling in music. "I left because every time I would be off at something that I really wanted to do like a play or a children's theater thing, I had to worry about what my four Hermits would do. And management was not telling me that there were these offers because the offers were for $25,000 a week in plays, and the band was making that in a night. So management wanted to get 10 percent of the huge deal, and it started to get in the way of my life," says Peter.

In the 1980s, Noone starred on Broadway in the New York Shakespeare Festival's production of *The Pirates of Penzance,* winning rave reviews for his portrayal of Frederic. He continued to tour with the United States and international touring company of *Pirates,* performing at the world-famous Drury Lane Theatre in London.

Noone's acting career flourished with guest-starring roles in prime-time television shows such as *Married With Children, My Two Dads, Quantum Leap, Dave's World, Easy Street, Too Close For Comfort* and *Laverne and Shirley.* He also starred in the Los Angeles stage premiere of *Topokana Martyr's Day* and the United States national tour of the smash Broadway hit *Romance, Romance.*

Still a British citizen, Peter has been a United States resident with a green card since 1982. When Herman's Hermits broke up, Peter lived in France and England for awhile. "A lot of people think that the band is your life. It was my life when I was 15, or 16, or 17. But, you know, until I got my own family, my mother and father were the most important people in the world. When you have your own family, your parents take second space," says Noone.

From 1989 to 1993 Noone hosted a VH-1 series called "My Generation," and sang the title track for the 2000 motion picture *Diamonds,* starring Kirk Douglas. In December 2000, PBS ran a special titled "The British Invasion Returns," starring and hosted by Peter Noone. Taped over three evenings in July 2000 at the Fox Theatre, Foxwoods Resort Casino in Mashantucket, Connecticut, the program included numerous musical entertainers – Eric Burdon and the New Animals, Wayne Fontana and the Mindbenders, Billy J. Kramer, Gerry and the Pacemakers, Freddie and the Dreamers, Mike Pender's Searchers, The Troggs, and Clem Curtis and the Foundations. Noone performed "Can't You Hear My Heartbeat?" "I'm Into Something Good," "Wonderful World," "Listen People," "Mrs. Brown, You've Got a Lovely Daughter," "I'm Henry the Eighth, I Am," and "There's a Kind of Hush."

Noone appeared on the televised singing talent show *American Idol* on March 20-21, 2007, as a mentor for male contestants on the show, and he performed "There's a Kind of Hush." In 2010, he appeared in five documentaries featuring '60s entertainers.

Peter and his wife Mireille Strasser (pronounced mir-AY) have been married since 1968. They live in the Southern California coastal city of Santa Barbara, and they have a daughter named Natalie, who was born in 1986.

Sixties music appeals to a wide audience, and especially captures the attention of the younger generation. Says Noone, "While growing up, Natalie's friends and their parents knew who I was because for some strange reason my music was very attractive to teenagers. They all listened to oldies radio stations, and watched all those Monkees TV shows and all that nonsense that they were into during that period."

With about 60 percent of his audience over 40 years of age, and 40 percent teenagers, Noone is pleased with the demographics. "It's what I would have prayed for, really. If somebody had asked me what would I want, I would say, 'to keep having a new audience.' And for some reason, I got them," he says.

Noone says one of the things he still hopes to achieve is a balance between his personal and professional life. "I spend all of my time trying to be creative. Achievements are based on things to do rather than things that are successes or failures. The science of it all is just to keep experimenting with new things. I guess what I hope to achieve is to be able to carry on being creative for a long time."

Noone claims that persistence is one of his greatest assets. "I don't easily get deterred. For some things I'm very impatient and then for other things, I'm very patient. For example, I can wait 10 years to get a record right before releasing it, but I get impatient if a bass player doesn't get a part the first time."

Even though some music critics dismissed Herman's Hermits music as frivolous, the band members were unperturbed and continued recording and performing songs their fans adored. Says Peter, "You know, I've never really cared about how people perceive me. I just hope they like me. But how can you make people like you? Because I dislike people who are too nice. As I grew up, I got more and more nonchalant with being politically correct and stuff like that. I don't care anymore. I care more about what my family thinks about what I'm doing and if they get my jokes. They know when I say something that isn't necessarily what I think."

Noone claims his proudest achievement is that he managed to stay focused while many people in the music business had succumbed to the excesses of the times. "I managed to keep my head while all was going astray," he says. "Many of my friends from those days are dead. You know, I managed to not get involved. And that's based on my education, incredibly enough. I did know the difference between right and wrong and how to take care of myself. I'm just grateful I'm still around, really. You know, I wake up every morning going, 'Wow! Thank you!'"

Peter says one of his greatest pleasures has been to watch his daughter grow up and learn the right way to do things. "You know, there's only one way to do it, and that's the right way. She has a great spirit, and she loves other people, and she would never knowingly hurt anyone's feelings." Natalie has a wonderful voice and, since the age of 8, has been singing with Peter for charity marathons, sponsored by Unity Shoppe (www.unityshoppe.org), a nonprofit organization in Santa Barbara County that helps low-income families. She's currently studying to be a songwriter at Belmont University in Nashville, Tennessee, and has a Facebook page, "Natalie Noone Music."

Peter is personally involved in the creation and maintenance of his own websites where you can find autobiographical information, some great photos and his blog. He says most of what he knows about computers was taught to him by a 12-year-old neighbor.

"Before the Internet," he says, "I think my hobby was probably drinking, and going out, having dinner. And now my hobby is spending lots of time on my own - being creative again. And I'm living the life right now that I lived when I was about 17, where I travel, and I work in my room. In those days I was forced to spend a lot of time on my own, only because of the amazing amount of work and interaction with people. If people start to get on my nerves, I usually retreat to my room. So now I'm a bit of a loner again, which is very enjoyable for me," Noone said.

"I think now is really good musically. And my career is better now than it's ever been. I enjoy what I'm doing very much more now."

For more information on Herman's Hermits Starring Peter Noone, **visit www.peternoone.com** and **www.hermanshermits.com**

Epilogue: Karl Green

Bass player

People have their own definitions for success, but for the most content person success is derived from pride in doing something really well. Many kids, including most future pop stars, envision themselves achieving success on the musical stage. As Karl Green matured, he put that notion behind him. Today he defines his success in terms of the work he has done for his clients. For many years Karl has been a tile setter, known in the United Kingdom as a "tiler." It's laborious but also artistic, and he derives pleasure in creating what his clients can only imagine. He's also an independent sound engineer and continues to perform music, mainly for enjoyment.

Born on July 31, 1947, Karl Anthony Green is the second son of David and Olive Green. Until the age of 10, Karl and his family lived in Salford, near Manchester, England. They then moved to Urmston, the same town in which fellow Hermit Keith Hopwood lived.

In 1956, Karl's only brother David, nine years his senior, was a drummer and washboard player in a skiffle group. "One of the guys in my brother's band was a left-handed guitar player, and I picked up his guitar and said, 'Show me how to play it.'" Captivated by the guitar at the age of 9, Karl asked for one that next Christmas, and received his first guitar with a proviso from his mother and father that he enroll in lessons. He learned how to read music and studied classical guitar from the age of 10 until 13.

"While I was learning to read music, I used to go and see classical guitar players. But my main passion was listening to people like Charlie Gracie, who is a rockabilly guitar player, Gene Vincent, I loved the Everly Brothers, and Carl Perkins, and all those sorts of people – they were the ones who influenced me, and that's the stuff I wanted to play," says Green. "But I under-

Karl Green in 2010. Courtesy of Karl Green.

70

stood I had to have the grounding, and that's why I went for the lessons to find out how to read, which made playing any other type of music quite easy."

Green joined his first band, called the Balmains, at the age of 14. "As soon as I got my guitar, my driving force was just to be in a band and play and become successful," says Green, who was lead guitarist for the Balmains. The band performed at workingmen's clubs and social clubs. "For example, the shipworker's union will have a workingmen's club, and the British Legion, which is like veterans' clubs. I was still in school at the time, so I couldn't go very far, and I couldn't stay out too late. Because my brother was managing us and he was at all the gigs, my mom let me go. Alcohol was served and people were smoking cigarettes, and minors were not really allowed in licensed premises unless they're chaperoned, as it were."

About a year later, Karl was asked to join the Heartbeats with one of the guys from the original Balmains and a bass player and a drummer.

Karl's father, who worked in a bonded warehouse, supervising the loading and unloading of tobacco, wasn't a musical man. "My father was a very practical type of man. He was great with nailing bits of wood together and working around the house, but he had no idea of music. He couldn't even whistle," laughed Karl. "My grandmother was a very good piano player, and all my aunts were quite musical, but my father wasn't at all." Karl's mother, who played piano, served as head of the lunch program for schools in the area. "She prepared the menus and was like a dietitian for the kids, and supervised the cooking of the food," says Green.

Karl left school at the age of 14, and following his 15th birthday that summer, he began an apprenticeship as an engraver of photographic printing plates for a local printer. "I was only there for just over a year. I was what you called a probationer, because I wasn't old enough to sign my indentures for the apprenticeship. So I think I signed my indentures when I was 16. And because my boss realized I was working at night in bands and working during the day doing my engraving, I was getting no sleep, so he said, 'You've got to choose between the band and the job,' and I chose playing in the band. I quit when Keith, Peter and I had got together in the Hermits."

Green, who considers himself a rock and roller, says Herman's Hermits never gained the popularity in England that the band enjoyed in the United States. "I think the English considered us a bit gimmicky and a bit 'twee' [excessively or curiously quaint]. I suppose Americans considered us a bit twee, as well," he laughed. "We were a bit twee, weren't we? We weren't a rock band. I love rock and roll, and I go to see people like AC/DC and Aerosmith. Those sorts of bands are my favorite. But the material we did had to suit Peter's voice. But I'm not moaning about it because it was successful, and I had a wonderful time doing it."

Karl was awe-struck upon arriving in the United States for the first time. He recalls, "My jaw must have hit the ground when we first saw New York and L.A. Just everything was big and unbelievable. I mean, I was 17. I'd never been out of England until we went to the States. We'd had a bit of the screaming audience here [in England], but we'd never known the media hype that America had. Everything was just blown out of proportion over there."

But all of the hoopla was frustrating to Green, who says, "We'd rehearse and try to play well, and then we'd go on stage and no one could hear a damn thing we were playing. So we'd tend to get the attitude, 'Well, who gives a damn?' And the PA systems were rubbish. We didn't have things like monitors in those days, so you couldn't even hear what you were singing. We must have been singing out of tune because we could only hear the screaming and the mayhem out there," says Green. "I've got a PA system here in the house that's 5 kilowatts, and that would have filled Wembley in the 1960s. That would have been big enough for Madison Square Garden in the '60s. So times have changed, definitely."

Karl admits he enjoys playing now more than he did during the height of his musical career with the Hermits. These days he sits in with friends' bands when the bass player has to cancel. "I really enjoy it because I have to think about what I'm doing. And it's a lot more enjoyable, I think, than playing in the band full time. Most of Herman's Hermits' songs were in three-quarter time, and the bass playing wasn't particularly stretching. Only Lek, actually, strove to play better. The rest of us just sort of fell into this attitude, 'Well, this is what we've got, we're stuck with it.'"

Despite the euphoric state of superstardom imposed by thousands of screaming concert-goers aching to make eye contact or to touch the clothing of a musician, Green says, "I've always had my feet very firmly planted on the ground. I've always known that if I wasn't in a band, a woman wouldn't look twice at me walking down the road. But when you're in a band you can interest just about any woman you want, really. And I never thought of kidding myself that they're after me. They were just after what I was. So if you look at life with that attitude, you can really have a good time without kidding yourself."

After Peter left Herman's Hermits in late 1970, Green and the others continued performing in the United Kingdom until Peter came back to perform a United States reunion tour with them in '73. "We hadn't been in the States then since '69, but coming back in '73, we saw that people wanted to see us. And we couldn't believe that people still remembered us," says Green.

Following that tour, Green, Leckenby and Whitwam hired a manager and continued touring from 1973 until 1980. "We had a great time. I was still young enough to enjoy it. I was in my mid-'30s when I left the band, and it was fantastic. We played some really good gigs. We played some shitholes, as well, but the band improved. We actually became very good musicians," says Green. "I fronted the whole thing then, and I really enjoyed it. We played better than we'd ever played, but I couldn't see it going any further. And I wanted to start a family."

Karl's memories of Derek Leckenby, who died of non-Hodgkin's lymphoma in 1994, are sprinkled with conflict and admiration. "When I was in the band, Lek and I used to fight like cat and dog. We were very good opposites. He was very good with the business, and I used to look after the creative side of putting on a show. And it worked very well, but we both were always at loggerheads. And I think it's because we were so alike," recalls Green. "I loved the guy. And I didn't realize until I'd left the band how much he meant to me. Because even after I left, we used to speak on the phone a lot. And it was only just before he died that I actually told him how much I thought of him."

Green had struggled with a drinking problem for several years before joining Alcoholics Anonymous. He hasn't had a drink since April 1990. "I gave up smoking when my first daughter was born, which was '84, and in 1990 I decided that if I wasn't going to stop drinking, I'd never see my daughters grow up. I was really in the bottle quite badly. A friend of my wife's brought a friend with her to our house, and he turned out to be an alcoholic. We were talking and he said, 'Well, come to a meeting.' And I went to AA expecting to see all these dirty people. I was amazed at how smart the people were, good-looking women, very successful businessmen. There were just so many stories of how it nearly wrecked their lives. And I thought, 'Well, that's me! I'm on the brink here.' So I decided to stop. And I went to AA meetings every single night for about four months. The only way for me to do anything is to go cold turkey, stop, bang! I can't cut down, and I can't do anything in moderation. I'm just one of these sort of obsessive people. Like, I play golf; I've got to play every day. And when I want to go shooting, I've got to win every competition. That's just the sort of person I am. I just get totally hooked in what I'm doing at the moment. I get very focused on certain things."

One of the 12 steps of the AA program is for the alcoholic to confront people and explain or admit to having a drinking problem and to apologize for any mistreatment they may have imposed on friends and family members. "I used to treat Lek like shit. So about a year before he died, I had a long evening with him, and just told him how much he meant to me and how sorry I was that I'd put him through all this crap," explained Green. "At that time I think he was aware that he was sick, but he hadn't told anyone. He kept it to himself for a long time. I didn't know until I'd spoken to his wife, Leonie [pronounced LAY-oh-nee], and she said, 'Did you know how bad he is?' And I said, 'No.' And I was thankful that I'd gotten it off my chest. Because it was a big deal for me to actually to open up to the guy."

Leonie told Green that his confession and apology meant a lot to Lek. "I still talk to Lek every day, when I'm at work," says Green. "If things bug me, I just talk to him. I talk to my Dad as well, who's dead. I'm strange like that."

Karl met his wife, Kay Newhouse, in Germany. She was a dancer with an English group called the Young Generation, which had its own TV series in London. A choreographer friend of Kay's invited her to Germany to be part of a four-day filming of a television show called "Lulu's Party," starring British pop singer Lulu. At the same time, Herman's Hermits also appeared. The couple met on the set and they've been married since 1975. "She's been a saint," says Green. "But she knew what I was like when she married me, and a lot of her friends knew me and knew my reputation."

Karl and Kay have three daughters. "It was a house full of women," he laughs. Claire Amy was born in 1984; Lucy was born in 1986; and Daisy was born in 1988. "Lucy was a twin, but we lost her brother. He was two months old and he died of cot death. But we've got three healthy children."

Kay has been an antique jewelry and bead dealer since 1980. After the couple married, she left the dance group and went on the road with Karl for a few years. "We played Bermuda twice a year, and we could bring the whole family out and have a holiday, and work for an hour every night," said Karl. "When Kay decided she couldn't take being on the road all the time, she dabbled in a few things and she started dealing antique beads, and she's been doing that ever since."

Karl and his family live in Sunbury-on-Thames, about 100 yards from the river's edge. "Our road just goes down to the river. So you walk out of the house, down the road, and you can sit in a nice pub that backs onto the Thames. It's lovely. Very nice. And lots of greenery."

Although they've never boasted about their past lives to their children, Karl says from time to time their children will see their mom on TV dancing or Karl in old film clips of Herman's Hermits. "They know that I used to be famous, and they think it's quite funny that their farty old dad used to be a pop star," laughs Karl, who is a sound engineer for the re-formed '70s group Heavy Metal Kids. "The lead singer of the group, Gary Holton, died 25 years ago so the group has re-formed as a tribute to him." The group performed a tribute concert in Croatia for the Harley Davidson Festival in May 2011.

Green and his friends – guitar player Richard Scarfe, former member of Love Affair, a London-based pop, soul R&B group formed in 1966; drummer Greg Terry Short, who played with Peter Green, British blues-rock guitarist and the founder of the band Fleetwood Mac; and keyboard player Kevin Welling, who performed with British singer and actress Elaine Page – make up a group called "Dave's Not Here." The name was derived from the popular '70s comedy duo Cheech and Chong, who had a track titled "Dave's Not Here" on one of their albums. "It just made me laugh, and my father's name was David, so I thought it would be a good name for the band," says Green. "Kevin and I also do an acoustic sort of show, and we call it 'Sons of Dave.'"

The band writes and records songs as demos, and performs in pubs or for an occasional party, but not full time. "I prefer playing in pubs," says Green. "I like the rawness of playing in pubs, and you can blast away at people."

Until his retirement in 2011, Green's main source of income was derived from his career as a tiler. "That was my main business for several years. I would do complete bathroom refurbishments. I'm actually semi-retired. I will do tiling only for very good old customers. I'm not taking any new work, because I'm enjoying my time working with music."

Karl became interested in tiling after having his kitchen tiled and trying in frustration to get the contractor to return and tile his bathroom. "I called this guy and said, 'I need the bathroom done.' And he said, 'Yeah, I'll get around to you.' And I kept calling him and he wouldn't do it. So I decided, 'To hell with it, I'll do it myself.' And I had a go, and I really enjoyed it because it was something completely different than playing in the band, and it was manual, working with my hands. And it was so satisfying. And my wife just jokingly said, 'Well if you ever leave the band, you can go out as a tiler.' And I laughed. I was in the States on one of the tours and I was getting really pissed off. We were working in places like Vegas and Reno and doing like a cabaret where you have to make people laugh, and you have to finish on time. And that's not me. I just like playing rock and roll and having a good time. And I phoned up my wife and said, 'I've had it. I've had enough. I'm leaving the band.' And she said, 'What are you going to do?' And I said, 'I've no idea.' And she said, 'I'll put an advert in the paper, "Tiler".' So I just started. It was a growing business when I started, and I was very lucky. It's been very good for me."

A perfectionist in his trade, Green says, "I've always thought if you're going to be a dustman [trash or garbage collector in Britain], you want to be the best. And that's the way I treat my tiling. I'm the best. I'm not the cheapest, but I'm the best." Green employed laborers until the early the '90s when England experienced a downturn in business. "I didn't lay anyone off," says Green. "I just said to them, 'You can earn by the yard if you want.' And they said, 'Yeah, we'd rather.' So after that, I would subcontract people when I had big jobs, and I didn't have to worry about making salaries."

Green also performs work as an independent sound engineer for various promoters in London. He worked on a large venue called the Festival Hall in South Bank in London, and has done as a lot of work at the Royal Festival Hall and the Queen Elizabeth Hall in London for specific promoters who bring in French musical artists and flamenco dancers. "Recently, I worked for Dave Brubeck's sons, who call themselves the Brubeck Brothers. They're fabulous fellows, really nice blokes! I was a little bit in awe, because I had bought a lot of their father's stuff in the '60s."

Karl and Kay's daughters have done well in their own right. His oldest is a teaching assistant for a headmaster at a private school and has her own business featuring retro fashions from the '60s and '70s.

In his spare time, Karl enjoys fishing and shooting (clay pigeons with a shotgun). "I've been shooting for years, and I've been fishing since I was a kid." He enjoys fishing the Thames and around the Isle of Wight in the English Channel. For years his family would travel to Saint-Tropez, France. "We'd stay at a house right on the Mediterranean, and we fished off the dock at the back of the house there. Or if we took the boats out, the girls would do a bit of fishing. But it's only a sort of holiday thing for them," he says. "I used to go out in all weather to fish matches competitively. Just like I used to shoot competitively."

Green enjoys listening to bands such as Steely Dan, Aerosmith, Whitesnake and Eric Clapton. "I've always liked Steely Dan, Donald Fagen and Walter Becker doing their own personal projects," says Green. "I went to see the Eagles when they were over here in 1998. They played Wembley Stadium as part of their 'Hell Freezes Over' tour, and it was absolutely superb. The sound was magnificent. And I sat right in front of Joe Walsh, and he blew me away. It was great. Fantastic."

People who have influenced Green include his father, who died in the fall of 1996. Green describes his father as a very gentle man. "When he died, I didn't realize how many friends he had. You can measure your success in life by how many people stand up and say 'I knew him, and he was a good friend'."

Other influences in Green's life include skiffle player Lonnie Donegan, whose guitar playing persuaded him to learn how to play the guitar. Derek Leckenby made an impression on him as well. "Lek taught me how to calm down, eventually," says Green. "Early on, I just drifted through life, and I learned a lot by my mistakes. So I think everyone's got to do that, haven't they? You've got to try and experience as many things as you can in life, and try and learn from them."

Green says his proudest achievement is keeping his family solvent since he left the band. "Before I left the band, the business was out of my hands. When I left the band, I started again. So I'm quite proud of the fact that I built up this business into a going concern. And I suppose I'm proud of being successful. I enjoyed that success, and the mid- to late- '60s was great. And the rest of it was just sort of a treadmill. I'm proud of the way the band played from '73 until '80, when I left, because we really tried to get it together and play well rather than just rely on hits. We had to go out and do a show and try and be entertaining."

Epilogue: Keith Hopwood

Rhythm guitar

Since 1977, Keith Hopwood has been known not so much for his role in Herman's Hermits, but rather for his commercial soundtracks, scores and theme songs for full-length TV and movie features, as well as music for children's animated features. His company, Pluto Music, has earned accolades for turning out winning tunes.

Keith recalls his introduction to music as a child growing up in England during the 1950s and '60s. "Unless someone in the house collected records, you didn't hear much on the radio, apart from Radio Luxembourg, which played a lot of the pop stuff from the early '60s. But it was very bad reception, because it was broadcasting from Europe," recalls Keith. "I suppose I was about 10 or 11 when I started becoming aware of the radio kind of pop music. That's really what drew me into music. Once I got interested enough to get a guitar, I used to go out to a couple of clubs in Manchester that brought a lot of blues singers over from America. And I became a big fan of that kind of music – Sonny Terry and Brownie McGhee, and all these different people."

Born on October 26, 1946, in Manchester, England, Keith grew up in the rural town of Urmston, about eight miles outside of Manches-

Keith Hopwood in his studio in 2011. Photo by Dan Hopwood.

ter. The only child of Lyllian and Jack Hopwood, Keith completed the required general education in England, and then decided he'd rather perform music than to go on to technical school.

"I finished the first part. You do it to one level, then you study for the further two years and get what we call 'A' level – advanced level examinations – on just three subjects. But I didn't do that; I left before that happened. Probably most people at the grammar school would stay on and do the extra two years, but the music really did take a bit of a hold, and when it came to the point of leaving school, I remember being handed all these books full of careers, and they were just all very uninteresting. All I wanted to do was just do music all the time, although it must have seemed very impractical."

At about 10 years of age Keith had begun singing in the school choir, which occasionally performed concerts in large auditoriums in Manchester. His mother played the piano and gave piano lessons, but Keith, who plays by ear, refused to take formal lessons. Instead Keith took classical guitar lessons for awhile. He recalls, "It was the proper tuition and the whole thing, but unfortunately at that time I was about 14, and playing classical music wasn't really where I wanted to be going. I wanted to play rock and roll, so I left and found a sort of informal tutor – the guy down the road who knew three chords. So we took it from there," says Hopwood. "And then eventually, after the Hermits had been going for three or four years, I thought, 'This is silly, I should really be able to play the piano.' So I worked it all out backwards from the guitar onto the piano, and just figured out where everything was and started playing it. That's what I work on now most of the time, is piano and keyboards."

Keith's father, who died in 1974, was a chemical engineer. "My father was a very clever man. He could understand televisions, and when tape recorders first came out, I must have been about 6, I guess, when he made one at home, with all the foil tape that you used to use. This thing took up the whole table, but it worked. He was very clever like that. He invented a couple of things. He had the sort of brain that could figure these things out. I remember that a friend of his had formed a company that had something to do with industrial lighting. They had the right idea, but they couldn't work out how to do it, so my father sat down and worked out what they should do."

Initially Keith's parents weren't too happy about his choice of careers, but his success in the music business made them proud. "It frightened them to death when I said I wanted to play music as a job. You can imagine. They were from a sort of very traditional background. What parents always say is, 'Oh, go and learn a trade somewhere and do it afterwards.' Well, you can't, because it's too late then. In the end, the Hermits were working so much my parents were so worried about me coming in at 4 o'clock and getting up at 6 o'clock to go to work as a trainee telephone engineer that they said, 'OK. Well, do it!' And we were very fortunate. We cracked it in a very big way, so they were over the moon. I don't think they could understand the style; it's a lot to take in. But they were very pleased and very proud," says Hopwood. "But I suppose having done it, I would say that if I had a child that was desperately passionate about something, I'd find it hard to say, 'No, you can't do it. Go and get a degree in something or other.'"

Prior to his involvement with Herman's Hermits, Keith had a band with a friend named Malcolm Rowe. "We started a band. He was the drummer, and I was the guitarist. We were very enthusiastic. We used to thrash away for hours. We were doing a couple of gigs a week. The band was quite good, but the problem was the other three guys were a bit apathetic. They weren't too bothered about it, and we were very keen," says Hopwood. "What happened was the other lot, the Hermits – who I'd never seen, but they were buzzing around – were about to lose their guitarist. And they came to see me and said, 'Do you want to join our band?' So I went to see them do one of their shows, which wasn't very impressive. I wasn't too bowled over. But the point was they had lots of gigs, and they were all dead enthusiastic. So I thought, it's probably better in that band than the other one. So I joined them in 1963."

With no MTV and very little media exposure on radio or in newspapers for new talent, Herman's Hermits spent virtually 350 days a year on the road. According to Hopwood, the band would finish a three-month tour in America and fly to England for a booking in Yorkshire the next day, without a day off.

Although exhilarating, performing live concerts in America could be frustrating for British groups during the 1960s. Bands didn't have to worry about singing or playing their instruments on key, because the audience couldn't hear them anyway. "The screaming was a bit bizarre in America," says Hopwood. "I suppose it had been a bit screamy over here in England, but nothing like when we were in America through 1965. I suppose it's just something you get used to. You can't hear a damn thing. I think it was probably quite upsetting for the English acts we brought over to support us. The deal with the promoter was that we would supply the support act from England. So we would say to an English band, 'Do you want to come on this tour,' and it would just be the two bands. So we took the Hollies one time, and then the Animals, and then the Who. And I think sometimes for them, if they were good bands and they were quite proud of what they did, they'd go on and all anyone had come to see was us. That was very frustrating for them. I remember Graham Nash being particularly brassed off about it, because they were playing to deaf ears, as it were."

Hopwood recalls performing for a crowd of 60,000 at the Pasadena Rose Bowl the summer of 1965. The concert appearance was sponsored by KFWB and the tickets were 98 cents apiece as a tie-in to the Los Angeles radio station's dial position (980 AM). "I do remember that one very clearly because it was so damn big," says Hopwood. Herman's Hermits headlined at that show, which included the Lovin' Spoonful, The Midnighters, the Bobby Fuller Four and the Turtles. "I also remember doing Birmingham, Alabama. For some reason, we were very big in Birmingham. I remember the theatre there only because we used to go there a lot – six times a year."

As glamorous as it sounds to be a famous rock star, life on the road for more than 300 days a year in a foreign country can be grueling. "The thing that was difficult in those days was we were not sort of just holed up in L.A. or New York with people running around after us, or doing three months here and six months there. We were just on the road, which is fairly boring, just workaday stuff. And it's more the boredom that gets to you," says Hopwood. "It's difficult to cope with because you've got all the booze that you can drink and all the rest of it. I suppose the saving grace for most of us, we were young enough to actually get through it and write it off. So it's not the easiest thing to get thrown on you if you're 18, but for whatever reason, I don't know, we seem to have come out the other side in reasonable shape."

Hopwood recalls the breakup of Herman's Hermits. "As I remember it, our record company, for whatever reason, had sort of lost the plot a bit and was putting out the wrong singles. They even at one point put a single out, whichever one it was, and put a full-page ad in *Billboard* for the single, but the ad was for the wrong track. And this sort of stuff got us very frustrated, because the songs we were giving them had been hits around the rest of the world, so we knew they were hits. I think it was a bit of a problem with the record company, coupled with the fact that you'd obviously got the Monkees coming along, which was aimed very much at our marketplace. So I think that by '68 they'd started to make a big inroad into it all. And America just sort of wrapped itself up, which left us to the rest of the world and England."

Hopwood remains in contact with the rest of the band through the holding company, which he administers, that handles the financial affairs of the group. "Before the breakup I'd started Pluto Music with Lek – Derek Leckenby from the band – because we thought we'd start with a little outfit. And it was a little studio. While we were on the road, we had another guy running it for us who had been in radio as a deejay. And he started to get into TV and radio commercials and that sort of thing. Lek wasn't too interested in that so he left, and I took it all over."

Following Noone's departure, Hopwood, Whitwam, Leckenby and Green recorded an album with new band member singer-guitarist Pete Cowap, who had written songs for Herman's Hermits in 1967. "But the album never got released because the record company shelved it," says Hopwood. "At that point, the other guys decided to carry on, and I didn't want to do that, so I left and started to build up the production company."

Through the years Hopwood's company has produced a number of soundtracks for big television commercials, as well as producing music for animation films and documentaries. "So that's more or less what I've been doing ever since. I've moved the studios about three times, but that's really what I still do."

In addition, Hopwood owns a publishing company, working with other writers to develop their work, and he assists them in getting record deals. "I don't do it too often because there's only me, and it's a bit time-consuming. I've done that two or three times. I get sent stuff all the time, so if I find something that's really *really* good, then I'll usually try to get involved and do something with it."

But Keith no longer performs concerts. "I helped the Hermits out a few years ago when Lek died, because it was all rather sudden, and they'd got some work in Europe. So I did a few shows with them to help out. And then also when Peter was over here in about 1998, I got us all back together just to sort of chat things through, and it was just before he was finishing the tour. Peter was finishing at the London Palladium, and he said, 'Why don't you come down?' In the end the three of us went down and did half of his show with him, which was fun because it was real spur-of-the-moment. We just did about eight of the songs."

Hopwood fondly recalls his last days with Derek Leckenby, who died in 1994 of non-Hodgkin's lymphoma, a form of cancer. "He'd been poorly with it for three or four years, most of which he'd worked through. He had a lot of treatment, and he appeared to have beaten it. In fact, he came out here to see me, just before he went on a trip to America. And he seemed in fine faculty. He went to America – it was only a short trip – once he got over there he started getting very anemic, and he was obviously in a bit of a bad way. And he wouldn't come back. He was determined to see this two-week thing out. Fortunately his wife, Leonie, was with him. So he persevered to the end, and then he came back, and I think it was within about two or three days, it had him beaten."

After Hopwood left the band, he says Lek was very much the driving force behind Herman's Hermits and fought for legal rights for the remaining group to own the name. "Lek was quite happy," says Hopwood. "I think a couple of times he thought, 'Oh, perhaps I should just go and do something else.' And then he'd gone through and thought, 'No, I really don't want to do anything else.' He carried on, and he loved it. And he was a very musical guy."

During the 1970s Keith's studio was a large commercial operation located in Manchester and he recorded bands. "At that time there would be lots of different people and bands recording. And we had quite a lot of interesting people in the '70s and '80s, when we were in Manchester – you know, the Smiths and people like that. But they really weren't of an age when they could do much then."

After traveling extensively in his younger years, Keith says he actually misses it now. "I really miss traveling. I'd like to travel for pleasure, and not particularly to work. I traveled to so many places when I was young, but I never got to see them then. But I think now, that's what I want to do. That's my ambition, to travel."

Keith lives near Chester, on the Welsh border south of Liverpool, and his studio is in a village called Tarporley. In 1989 Keith married Maria Verdellis, who now has her own online retail company called Deckchairstripes Ltd. (http://www.deckchairstripes.com). Keith and Maria have a son named Daniel, born in 1991. Keith has three children from his first marriage to Penny Pagni, which lasted 17 years. His sons Dax and Joel were born in 1968 and 1976, respectively. Daughter Zhian [pronounced ZHEE-an, like Zhivago] was born in 1978.

"My children are all interested in music, though not in a performance sense. My two older boys both play the guitar, Daniel is now studying sound engineering and production. He is the keen one!"

Dax lives in Manchester and runs a consulting service. Joel lives in London and has his own marketing company, and Zhian works for a large fashion house.

Hopwood has won numerous awards for his work, including a 1994 RTS award for "best network documentary and best factual" for *Countrywomen*, a documentary consisting of six 30-minute segments for BBC2. He won a gold medal at the 1989 New York Festival for the score and songs of *The B.F.G.*, a full-length, animated feature. The CDs of the music he wrote with Malcolm Rowe for *The Wind in the Willows* feature and TV series are still in demand, 25 years after the event.

Keith recalls the '60s as the beginning of a more prosperous time in England. "Particularly in England, the '50s were still very austere," he says. "We had rationing for half the '50s, and it was a very black-and-gray decade, even though the war was well and truly over. But there wasn't that much money around. Things were very tough. I wasn't aware of all that at the time, but looking back on it I can remember it being like that. And then suddenly in the '60s, we turned a corner, and there was lots of work around. You could almost say, 'I'm fed up with this job. I'll resign tonight and go find another one tomorrow.' And just the general freedom and opportunity that was in the air was very memorable. It was just a wonderful age of coming out of all that darkness of the war period. The opportunities were there even more then. You could say, 'Well, I'm going to do this,' and just get off and do it."

Keith says he listens to a wide variety of music. "At the moment, I'm listening to Van Morrison, Macy Gray, Dinah Washington, Malcolm McLaren, Oscar Peterson – just a big mixed bag. With technology today, you're never really quite sure what you're listening to. Because you can virtually do anything, and I think there are some great bands around and quite a lot of good music around now. Obviously there's a lot of the formulated stuff – the boy bands and the girl bands and the rest of it. But I seem to hear quite a lot of stuff that I like now, more than I heard a couple of years ago.

"The Internet has changed the music business forever. Although very difficult to get signed by a major, the tools are now there for talented people to create and market their music without the majors. Utilizing music download sites such as iTunes and social networking sites like MySpace and Facebook, this can either mean that an artist can make a satisfactory living from their music without major exposure, or it can lead in the end to being signed by one of the majors if their profile gets big enough."

Keith enlists in the philosophy that putting your heart and soul into whatever you've chosen to do brings pleasure, whether or not

you become a big success at it. Unlike his parents, who initially wanted him to pursue education and a career outside of music, he says to
his children, "Being passionate about something counts for a lot more
than just a piece of paper, and you can't count the cost of the energy
that you put into doing something that you're passionate about. So
I think I'd have to say, 'OK, give it a go. Go and do what you want to
do.' Because at the end of the day, really, the most important thing is
being happy in this rotten old life. It doesn't really matter whether
you make a big success of it or whether you just make a medium success or get by. What's more important is that your heart is in it."

For more information on Keith's production company,
visit **http://www.plutomusic.com**

Epilogue: Barry Whitwam

Drums

Barry "Bean" Whitwam is proud to say that one of his finest achievements has been "staying power" – the ability to remain with one band through all of its trials and tribulations for well over three decades. And one of the bonuses he recognizes is the realization that audiences today are as excited about seeing Herman's Hermits as they were during the 1960s. With all those years of experience under his belt comes excellence in his craft. His precision drumming reflects the refinement of all those years of practice.

Barry picked up his nickname "Bean" in 1950. "I was always inventing and building silly things, so a close friend of my father's, Frank Evans, christened me Billy Bean after a cartoon called 'Billy Bean and

Herman's Hermits starring Barry Whitwam in 2010. From left, Mike Harling, Kevan Lingard, Barry Whitwam and Geoff Foot. Photo courtesy of Barry Whitwam.

His Funny Machine.'A few years later, it was shortened to 'Bean.'"

Barry recalls becoming interested in music at about the age of 10, after hearing Buddy Holly records."A friend of mine had the records, and he played a guitar and he sang," recalls Whitwam."At about 12, I had the opportunity to join a group of local boys playing in a band. But they wanted a drummer with a drum kit, and I couldn't play the drums and they didn't have a drum kit.And so I persuaded my mother to buy me a secondhand drum kit, which came to about $60 in those days, which was quite expensive.And I joined the band, but I couldn't play the drums. Eventually after about six months I got some kind of rhythm together.After struggling for about two years I took some lessons for 18 months when I was about 14."

Eager to learn popular music, Barry would listen to a record and copy the drumming in it the best he could."It worked out pretty well in the end," he says."It's like riding a bike, really. Once you've got your balance and you can separate your feet from your hands, it becomes a lot easier. It's just getting over that first barrier, separating your limbs."

His drum lessons proved to be a very valuable experience, especially in discipline."Most of the time I played just on a rubber pad. I wasn't on the drum kit. I was studying the Buddy Rich snare drum rudiments.And that was very good, indeed. I still use that book. I've still got the original I had. It's real beat up, but I've still got it, and I go back to it every now and again, just for fun, because it is enjoyable playing these patterns on a rubber pad."

Barry's first band was a five-member group called the Demons. "We first started playing instrumentals – songs by the Ventures and the Shadows and things like that, and old classical instrumentals revamped.Then we got a singer, and we were called Danny and the Demons, and we were doing copies of American singers – Elvis, Buddy Holly, and Dion.

Fifteen-year-old Whitwam was performing two to three days a week with the Demons for youth clubs and workingmen's clubs. "Nobody ever asked us how old we were," he laughs.The band, which retained the same members, changed its name from the Demons to the Hellions, and then to the Wailers.

Born Jan Barry Whitwam on July 21, 1946, in Prestbury, Cheshire, Barry says, "Prestbury is in the country. It was sort of a place people settled in during the war. No babies were born in Manchester in case they were bombed. It's a very nice house. It's still there." He grew up in Didsbury, a suburb of Manchester, and graduated from Ladybarn Secondary Modern in Manchester. He then entered into a college for women's hairdressing in the center of town.

"I didn't want to go into a factory or be like everybody else. I wanted to try to get into a career where there was hardly any competition. My mother fancied me going into it as well because she could get free haircuts," he laughed.

Barry took a six-month course in hair styling. The owner of the college, who had several shops in Manchester, thought having a male hair stylist would help to increase his business since there weren't many men in that profession at the time. "He took me aside, and I was supposed to be the whiz kid in the shops. So he gave me an extra three months' training at no cost.

But Whitwam's hair styling career proved to be short-lived. He worked as a stylist at a shop in Manchester for almost two years, before deciding it wasn't a career he wanted to continue. "It was hectic, really," he says. "It's like cooking seven different meals at the same time – one woman's got the color on, another one's got the perming lotion on, another with bleach. If you get the timing wrong, you can lose somebody's hair."

Whitwam decided he'd much rather pursue a career in music and asked his father if he could spend some time concentrating on becoming a professional drummer. "My father said he'd think about it, and I didn't know this 'til 20 years later, but he'd had a word with my boss. He asked him if I could take some time off to get this drumming out of my system. And if it didn't work, could I have the job back? So the two of them made an arrangement," says Whitwam. "There was one condition: When my father went out to work at about 8 o'clock in the morning, I took practice for four hours, had a good lunch, and practiced for another four hours. So I wasn't just sitting at home. I was actually practicing the drums for eight hours a day. The next-door neighbor didn't like that, really."

Barry's father George Vincent Whitwam, who died in 1985, had made a living as a refrigeration engineer. His mother Elsie, who had worked as a seamstress, died in 1992. Both parents were very proud of Barry's musical success. His only brother, two years his senior, died of electrocution at the age of 14. He had been playing a record while taking a bath.

In coping with the Hermits' stardom, Barry recalls, "We were sort of brought down to earth very quickly with our second record. It only got to No. 20 in the charts in England, and the press really went to town on us. You know, 'we're a flash in the pan,' 'one-hit wonders,' 'you will never see Herman's Hermits again.'"

But the band carried on, and not long after the negative publicity the Hermits returned to the studio and recorded "Silhouettes," which quickly reached No. 2 in England and No. 5 in the United States. The next four years would be spent touring the world.

"Stardom really doesn't affect you individually," says Whitwam. "It affects your friends more than anything. You go back into the local bar and have a drink and your friends all seem to be saying 'you've changed' because you can afford to buy a drink and they expect you to buy them one. Your friends sort of disappeared slowly. And you really didn't make any, because you were always on the road. You'd make friends with other bands, then, who were in the same situation."

Some of Barry's fondest memories of performing with Herman's Hermits during the 1960s include a Royal Command Performance show in London in front of the Queen Mother and royal family, and meeting and talking with Elvis Presley while in Hawaii. "We had just finished one of our U.S. tours in Hawaii, in 1966. Elvis was making a film, *Paradise, Hawaiian Style.* We were due to fly out, and the night before Elvis' manager, Colonel Tom Parker, phoned us and said Elvis was filming, did we want to meet him. And we said, 'dead right, yeah!' But three of the boys went home, and just Peter and I stayed behind. And that was something the rest of the boys truly regretted," he says. "We talked with Elvis about nostalgia music, the different way our hair was, and how we liked his songs and films. He was real cool. I have a picture of myself and Elvis on my wall of fame, as it were, at home."

Today, Whitwam tours with his Herman's Hermits band for about 12 weeks a year in America and around the world, including Japan and the Middle East. The rest of their time is spent touring Europe and Scandinavia. In 2011, Whitwam's Hermits included Kevan Lingard, lead vocal and keyboards; Mike Harling, lead guitar; and Geoff Foot, who wrote the first single for the band after Peter Noone left in 1971.

"Geoff Foot joined the band in the '80s after the Hermits recorded one of his songs, 'She's a Lady.' Geoff toured with the Hermits in the U.S., Germany and Scandinavia before leaving to raise his family. He rejoined the band in 1996," says Whitwam. Foot had been a member of Wayne Fontana and the Mindbenders, and Mike Sweeney and the Thunderbirds.

A friend of the band for more than 30 years, Graham Lee played lead guitar with Herman's Hermits on a five-week tour of Sweden in 1992 while Derek Leckenby was undergoing chemotherapy. Lee had been a member of the Scorpions in 1965 and moved to Holland where the band had a No. 1 hit with "Hello Josephine," and went on to make four albums and seven chart hits.

Whitwam's Hermits regularly tour the United Kingdom, Germany, Belgium, Holland and Scandinavian countries, the United States, Canada, Australia and New Zealand. Although a large part of their show is made up of the ever-popular "oldies" tunes, they throw in a few of their more recent creations.

Barry has made Herman's Hermits his sole career since 1964; however, he says, "Business slowed down in America after about 1969, when MGM was putting out the records, and we got into a litigation with them. During that 18 months of litigation the Monkees replaced us. Our fans were young teenagers. They got straight stuck into the Monkees. They liked them. I liked them too. But we carried on doing songs and tours in Europe, up until Peter Noone left. Then we continued onwards without him, and we've never stopped."

Whitwam believes that Herman's Hermits fared financially better than most '60s bands, whose profits were mishandled or scooped up by greedy managers. "Our money wasn't handled by management. It came in when we did a tour and it was just split up into individual bank accounts. They had managed projects or investments. Management helped organize insurance and endowment policies and introduced us to people in very reputable companies, and we invested our money with them," he said. "Once we made a bit of money, we all bought our parents houses."

Whitwam lived with his parents for about three years while the band was touring. "But I was hardly ever there. I was always on the road, traveling," he said. "We upgraded the house. We used to live in a semi, which is sort of a house you add on to another one. We bought a big detached house, about a six- or seven-bedroom house. And then I got stuck into cars. I used to love cars. I'd buy a car for three months and change it. I think up to now I've had about 60 cars, but between 1964 and '70 I must have had about 30 cars. We used to say, when the ashtrays were full, you'd change it and get a new one. I used to have Jaguars, Aston-Martins, Daimlers, sports cars. I used to love them."

Barry was married to his first wife in 1967. His daughter, Emma, was born in 1969, and son, Richard, was born in 1974. Both of his children are married and have children of their own. Emma has three sons – James was born on Christmas 1998, Harry was born January

2001 and Freddie was born in January 2011. Richard has a daughter, Meghan, who was born during the summer of 1996, and a son, Sam, who was born in 2000.

When Emma was born, Barry was on the road a lot. "I remember coming home and my daughter was sort of hiding behind my wife's legs – you know, like, 'Who's this man?' 'It's your father.' After you've been away three months, it was a strange feeling. I had to sort of break the ice again."

Barry met his current wife, Patricia Prendergast, when their children were going to the same school. The couple has been married since 1987. "I had a golden retriever and she had a big German shepherd. And we'd take the kids to school. On my way back there's a big park, and I'd take the dog for a run, and the two dogs met first fighting. So we separated them, and got to know each other. Then eventually I got divorced from my first wife and married Patricia."

Patricia, who has a son named Jonathan, born in 1974, owns her own air cargo business, arranging for air shipment of animals worldwide. When he's not on the road, Barry enjoys playing golf. "I've just joined a club for the first time," he says. "I've been playing for many years, but I've never been around long enough to join a club."

Patricia accompanies Barry when the band plays resort areas or when he expects to be away for a week or more. "Patricia came to San Diego when we were playing there for two weeks. In 2001, she actually won the air travel on a TV show phone-in. She was asked to pick a number between 1 and 5, and that represented how many you think the panel will score, and I think she picked none. The panel was hopeless," laughs Whitwam. "We also went to Death Valley, and that was fabulous!"

The group members collaborate on songs while they're on the road. "It works well," he says. "We've written some great songs together. It's difficult getting a record company to back Herman's Hermits, but we're hopeful."

Herman's Hermits made two films during their career. The 1966 movie *Hold On!* was filmed in America. Barry explains, "The space program, NASA, decided to let the children of America name the next rocket to go up, and the kids chose the name Herman's Hermits. So then the FBI and special agents had to follow the group around to make sure we were worthy of our name going on a rocket." The group also made a movie in England in 1968 called *Mrs. Brown, You've Got a Lovely Daughter.*

"Basically, we had to act like ourselves. The director said, 'here's your lines. Just do them the best you can,' and we had a good laugh with it." said Whitwam. "*Mrs. Brown* was probably better than *Hold On!* It was about a greyhound dog. The dog was called Mrs. Brown. And the puppy was Mrs. Brown's daughter. I get the movies out for a laugh every now and again. Basically MGM wanted to make the films. It was in the contract so they'd sell more records, soundtracks."

Barry says he feels his greatest enduring talent is playing the drums. "It's probably the best thing I do. I think my best ability is to look at the world and take it with a pinch of salt. Don't take it too seriously, or you'll worry yourself to death in this business."

Any misperceptions? "No. Everybody knows that Peter Noone is not in the band. People who come see us expect not to see him, because Peter's done a good job saying he left the band by 1971, especially when he did his VH-1 TV show. So everybody knows that Peter's not in the band and everyone has a great time enjoying the music."

Barry says the individual who made the biggest influence on his musical career was Elvis Presley. "When I saw *Jailhouse Rock,* the video clip of that was incredible. That changed my whole way of looking at music. It was incredible. It was like three rows of cells, and they were dancing along it. That was brilliant."

Whitwam observed there are three generations of Herman's Hermits fans. "When we do a state fair, where there's no alcohol served and kids can go in, we get a lot of young kids, from 5 years old, upwards." With them are their parents, who are typically the children of baby boomers. "And then we obviously get the old fans who want to see us again. But it's really good to see like 5-year-olds that know the words to 'I'm Henry VIII, I Am.'"

Barry is "a typical Cancerian," in his estimation. "I was born on the 21st of July, so I'm nearly a Leo. So I'm a bit of an extrovert. I think I approach excess with caution, shy sometimes. My wife would say I'm a safe old dog. Always by the side," he added. "I don't cause any trouble. I have a wonderful sense of fun."

For more information on Herman's Hermits starring Barry Whitwam, visit **www.hermanshermits.co.uk/**

1951 Shure SH55 Series II microphone, commonly used in the 1950s and '60s. From the collection of Terry and Cindy Knight. Photo by Amanda Domingues.

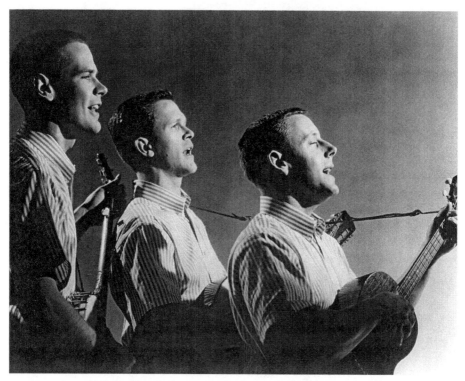

The Kingston Trio in 1959. From left, Dave Guard, Bob Shane and
Nick Reynolds. Courtesy of Frank Werber.

3

Where Have All the Flowers Gone?

THE KINGSTON TRIO

Rock and roll had been a vibrant part of American culture for three years by 1958, but it still had not won acceptance as a legitimate musical genre. Parents denigrated it, religious leaders vilified it, and national advertisers shunned the "Top 40" radio stations that played it. Pop music had become a wedge that was widening the generation gap. In those chaste days, respectable adults who favored the tame musical stylings of Doris Day, Pat Boone and Nat "King" Cole criticized the raucous beat of rock and rhythm 'n' blues, and denounced the uninhibited gyrations of Elvis Presley, Little Richard, Jerry Lee Lewis and other performers.

It took a trio of West Coast college kids to develop a pop music style that engendered widespread appeal among the youth genera-tion as well as parents. Fusing the exotic rhythms of Caribbean calypso and Polynesian music with the playful whimsy of country songs and sea chanteys and the thoughtful messages of folk music, the Kingston Trio - consisting of banjo player Dave Guard and guitar-ists Bob Shane and Nick Reynolds - brought a measure of intellectual sophistication to pop music. With their robust vocals, humorous satirical monologues, and their clean-cut appearance, they quickly became the most popular vocal group in the nation.

The Trio, as they were known simply to their fans, ushered in numerous trends and fads. They launched the folk music craze of the late '50s and early '60s, even though they did not consider them-selves to be folk musicians. They catapulted pop music from the confines of the 45 RPM single record with enormously popular top-selling albums, documented in a *Life* magazine cover story on August 3, 1959. They established the college circuit - previously the exclu-sive realm of lecturers - as a viable concert touring platform. They set a fashion trend with their wide-striped shirts - a style the Beach Boys later adopted. And they influenced numerous iconic performers who followed them. Pulled over in Minnesota by a police officer, young Robert Zimmerman driving with a guitar in his car's back seat explained, "I'm a folk singer – you know, like the Kingston Trio." The world would soon know Zimmerman as Bob Dylan. In February 2011, nearly 57 years after Dave, Bob and Nick began performing together, the Recording Academy honored the Kingston Trio with a Lifetime Achievement Award during Grammy presentations.

The Kingston Trio inspired the musical careers of members of groups as widely divergent as Fleetwood Mac, the Eagles, Peter, Paul and Mary, the Smothers Brothers, and the Allman Brothers. "Many rock and roll performers have said if it hadn't been for the Kingston Trio, they never would have picked up a guitar," Shane said. Those are mighty impressive credentials for a group that began as the impromptu, undisciplined product of after-hours gatherings in Redwood City, California, at a place called the Cracked Pot, a watering hole no larger than a garage frequented by students from Stanford University and Menlo College on the peninsula south of San Francisco.

Their rise to fame became a matter of legend – how nightclub entertainment publicist Frank Werber discovered the Trio at the Cracked Pot, became their manager and signed them to a lengthy engagement at San Francisco's Purple Onion nightclub, leading to their contract with Capitol Records. The truth is more complicated than that romanticized legend. The group that Werber originally saw was spontaneous, unorganized and undisciplined – simply a collaboration of Dave Guard and a rotating cast of his friends who performed with him when they happened to head over to the Cracked Pot for a little fun.

Guard, Shane, Reynolds and Werber converged in the San Francisco Bay Area by happenstance after traveling circuitous paths. Dave and Bob had met in 1947 as junior high students at Punahou School, a college preparatory school in Honolulu. Participating with other students in a group singalong of Huddie "Lead Belly" Ledbetter's "Goodnight Irene," Dave and Bob discovered their mutual interest in the Weavers and other folk singers. Shane taught Guard how to play guitar, and they began performing at school events. In the fall of 1951, Dave enrolled for his senior year of high school at Menlo School, a private high school and college in Atherton, California. The school's well-regarded college preparatory curriculum gained Dave entry as an undergraduate majoring in economics at prestigious Stanford University, only two miles away, in the autumn of 1952 while Bob enrolled as a freshman at adjoining Menlo College. For enjoyment, they performed at local clubs, often with other friends of theirs. In lieu of payment, they played for beers. In the spring of 1954, Bob met Nick Reynolds, who had enrolled at Menlo College after transferring from the University of Arizona. They quickly became inseparable pals. "Nick had a car and I had a guitar," Shane grinned. Reynolds, who played congas and ukulele, began performing with Guard and Shane at fraternity parties. "We didn't think of what we were playing as folk music. We did what we could do with what we had – guitars, bongos and a banjo," said Shane. The music they played was influenced by Hawaiian, Tahitian and calypso rhythms as well as folk songs with lyrical importance. Even so, the guys didn't take performing too seriously. "We played a lot of risqué stuff at parties," Shane chuckled.

By the summer of 1956, following graduation from Menlo College, Shane returned to Honolulu and started a solo nightclub act as "Hawaii's Elvis Presley" – the world's first Elvis impersonation performer. Guard, accepted into the MBA program at Stanford's School of Business, and Reynolds, with a year remaining at Menlo, replaced Shane with a musician named Willie Gage. When Gage went his own way, the trio became a quartet with the addition of singer Barbara Bogue and bass player Joe Gannon. Sometimes calling themselves Dave Guard and the Calypsonians, or at other times appearing as the Dave Guard Quartet, they regularly played at the Cracked Pot and at other beer gardens and private parties on the peninsula.

Nick had planned to return to San Diego to enter the restaurant and hotel business, but found entertaining too alluring to resist. "After having some acceptance on the peninsula at these clubs, we sort of got it in our blood," Nick told us in 1999. "When people applaud and like what you're doing, even though you're just having fun, it's kind of like a narcotic." Just about the time they came to that realization, Frank Werber came calling.

Werber, born in Cologne, Germany, in 1929, spent his youth on the move, initially as a refugee from Nazi persecution. Werber's father, who was Jewish and worked in banking, was an amateur photographer and a politically active critic of the Nazi regime. The family left nearly all their possessions behind when they hurriedly relocated to Holland, where they moved in with friends. Shortly afterward, when Frank was 5 years old, his mother died. He and his father moved on to Belgium, where Frank attended school speaking French. "We were refugees, and we were scrambling," Frank told us in 2000. As the

Nazis closed in, father and son journeyed to Africa, then to the United States in 1940, ultimately settling in Denver because Werber's father had read that the schools were good there. As a young man in Florida, Texas and Colorado, he endured anti-Semitic prejudice, from which he found relief by traveling to San Francisco in 1950. "I found North Beach, and I thought I'd died and gone to Heaven," said Werber, who took comfort in the area's "European ambience." Sleeping in a bus station upon his arrival, the nearly broke Werber landed a job with United Press International as a photographer, based upon skills he had learned during his stint with the U.S. Navy in the late '40s.

Werber rented a one-room flat with orange-crate furniture, and discovered he could supplement his income at nightclubs. "I had a Speed Graphic [camera], courtesy of UPI. I traded my photos for good will, a glass of wine, pizzas – whatever I could get," Werber chuckled. He had no idea where that might lead him. "Truly, I had never had the ability or the desire to figure out this was the first step to…. I'm confessing to ignorance," Werber said. One of those clubs was the hungry i (which was spelled in all lowercase letters). The dark, moody club at 599 Jackson Street was owned by Enrico Banducci, who had big ideas but a tight budget. "He was always great at picking up young people who were just totally enamored with the ambience of the place, and letting them work their asses off for no money," said Werber, who saw his newfound friendship with Banducci as an opportunity to learn about the nightclub business.

Werber was burning the candle at both ends, however, and because of his late nights at clubs he wasn't his sharpest when he began his workdays at UPI at 4 a.m. When the wire service fired Werber, he went to work full time at the hungry i, handling all the chores that Banducci shoved his way, including painting, carpentry, installing wiring for lights and sound, and removal of old plaster from the walls to reveal the ancient bricks that became a well-recognized backdrop for the club's stage. By night, Werber watched the performers and became a student of staging. He absorbed all he could about lighting, comedy, music presentation and audience rapport techniques used by folk singers Josh White, Theodore Bikel and the Gateway Singers. He also studied the techniques of Shelly Berman, Mort Sahl, Bob Newhart, Bill Dana, Mike Nichols and Elaine May, Jonathan Winters and other comics and social commentators who appeared there.

Werber spent much of the winter of 1956–'57 working for the family that owned the Soda Springs ski resort, 170 miles northeast of San Francisco in the Sierra Nevada. He took publicity photos of celebrities who visited the resort, worked as a member of the ski patrol and operated chair lifts for the resort. "I don't think it's ever snowed there as much as it did that winter. The plows would go through and the snow banks would be 30 feet high. It was an incredible winter. We had to shovel out a channel so the chairs could get up the hill. The snow got *that* high," Werber said. There, amid the white-blanketed splendor and solitude, he determined a career path to follow. "It was a very good moment in my life," Werber told us.

With the knowledge he had gained at the resort and at the hungry i, Frank decided to return to San Francisco to become a freelance press agent specializing in publicity for nightclubs. He set up shop in a low-ceiling loft he rented for 30 bucks a month above a barber shop that was next door to the Purple Onion which, at 140 Columbus Avenue, was around the corner from the hungry i. A back door from the loft led to an accordion factory owned by Italian immigrants. Werber, a two-finger typist, bought a used typewriter and hit the pavement, building a clientele of nightclubs that came to include not only the hungry i, but also the Purple Onion (of which Enrico Banducci was part owner), elegant Romanoff's, Al Williams' trendy Papagayo Room in the Fairmont Hotel, and Ann's 440 Club, where Johnny Mathis and Lenny Bruce entertained. "The Papagayo was the place to be seen after the clubs closed. Past 2 a.m., you could get your booze in a teacup there," Werber winked.

Although Werber had no intention of managing entertainers, he credited Chuck Marcoux, a waiter at the Purple Onion, for urging him to catch an act at the Cracked Pot. Werber watched Dave Guard and the Calypsonians perform there one night in the spring of 1957 and again a few weeks later at a San Francisco club called the Facks II. Werber was impressed by the quartet's energetic, almost boisterous approach, and their ability to energize an audience, but said he would be interested in working with them only if they trimmed the group to a trio. "With my limited understanding, I was concerned that local clubs that were willing to pay scale for three performers might not do so for a quartet," Werber explained. He suggested elimination of bass player Joe Gannon. Since singer Barbara Bogue was romantically involved with Gannon, she quit as well. In search of a third member, Dave and Nick persuaded Bob Shane to leave his family's business, drop the Elvis act at the Pearl City Tavern in Hawaii and join them. The group solidified in early May 1957 with Dave on banjo, Bob on rhythm guitar and Nick on four-string tenor guitar, and they and Frank agreed to give the effort a one-year trial. They settled on the name Kingston Trio, inspired by Kingston, Jamaica, where calypso music originated, and Kingston, Rhode Island, evocative of the Ivy League.

But from the beginning, the group was really a quartet, and was organized as a business enterprise with a specific plan to avoid the financial squabbles that often infested other performing groups. "Knowing that other groups were being screwed by their manager who was the first to take money off the top, we decided that expenses would be paid first, and then we would share in the profits, like partners in any business," said Werber, who came to be recognized for his neatly trimmed goatee. "We worked out a partnership. Four of us were involved, four of us did the work. I did everything but get up on stage and sing. And that's how we started," Werber told us. "Through an insurance man I knew, I found a lawyer who drew us up an agreement and incorporated us."

Werber bought a Wollensak tape recorder so the Trio members could hear themselves and improve their harmonies. Under Frank's direction, the group rehearsed assiduously, created comedy monologues and routines, and were fitted with Ivy League-style shirts and slacks. Werber also enrolled them in singing lessons with vocal coach Judy Davis, who helped shape their harmonies. "She was a great vocal coach. We had to do exercises that sounded like eeeeee-ooooo-eehhhhhh. She taught us how to use and strengthen our voices to withstand the rigors of the road," Shane said.

When Werber learned that comic Phyllis Diller had cancelled a two-week engagement in late June at the Purple Onion, he managed to book the Kingston Trio in that slot for a little less than $300 per week. Calling upon their college buddies down the peninsula, the Trio packed the little basement nightclub, and as word about the group spread they attracted patrons from throughout the area. "The socialites of San Francisco started hearing about us and coming down to see this new phenomenon, three young brats having way too much fun," Nick said. "Our rapport with the audience became infectious. We've always played with the audience, involving them in our conversation, because we certainly weren't great musicians or great singers." They knew about 15 songs at the time, but their presentation electrified packed-house audiences four shows each night, and the club extended their engagement to seven months.

Werber sat in the audience and studied each performance of the Trio, observing crowd reactions and continually making notations on his clipboard. "I'm a big believer in paying attention," Werber explained. At rehearsal the day after each performance, he gave them directions: "I would tell them, 'No, don't move over here for this part, move over there. Dave, try this.' The shows became very tightly choreographed, but we worked hard to make it look like it wasn't. And nobody figured it was."

Werber's direction developed a well-rounded stage act that harnessed yet refined the Trio's boisterous enthusiasm. They selected their songs with conscience: "We wouldn't feel right singing, for example, chain gang songs or Muddy Waters songs because here we were, three middle-class white guys," Reynolds said. They sandwiched their songs between good-natured comedy routines and involved their audiences in their dialogues. Their repertoire of crisp, resonant vocals drew from Harry Belafonte-inspired calypso numbers, as well as Appalachian folk songs, Hawaiian and Tahitian melodies, and a smattering of country music. They had no designated lead singer, but traded vocal parts within songs to best suit each member's range.

Werber concentrated on the group's stage persona, but had given little regard to the possibility of developing the Trio as a recording act. Nevertheless, the publicity that Werber and the Trio generated soon attracted a man named Jimmy Saphier, who was Bob Hope's television agent. It was Saphier who persuaded Capitol Records executives to catch the Trio's act at the Purple Onion, after which they signed the group to a recording contract. Working with staff producer Voyle Gilmore in Capitol's monaural studio at 1750 N. Vine Street in Hollywood, the group recorded *The Kingston Trio* album with the Purple Onion's upright bass player, Elmer Lynn "Buzz" Wheeler, in just three days beginning February 5, 1958. Singing into one shared microphone as they played their instruments, the boys efficiently laid down the songs they regularly performed in their Purple Onion stage act. Their repertoire included folksinger Terry Gilkyson's "Fast Freight," the bluesy "Scotch and Soda," the traditional ballad "Sloop John B" (popularized once again by the Beach Boys in 1966), and the song that seven months later would soar to the top of the charts – "Tom Dooley," a rural folk ballad about a man who was convicted of murder and sentenced to death by hanging. The recording session cost Capitol just $900 in studio time, and the label had only modest expectations for it, according to Werber. "They weren't planning to release any singles, and they pressed only 1,000 copies of the album," Werber said.

After the extended Purple Onion run ended, Werber booked the Trio for a succession of engagements on the road in the spring of 1958, first the lounge of the Holiday Hotel in Reno. "That was a disaster that taught the Trio humility. It was a small club with a little raised platform in the slot machine room, and we were told to keep the sound down to background level," Werber recalled. Subsequent bookings that provided a better showcase for the Trio's talents included the prestigious Mr. Kelly's in Chicago and the Village Vanguard and the Blue Angel in New York. Coinciding with the release of *The Kingston Trio* album in June, the Trio returned to San Francisco to open for comic Professor Irwin Corey at the hungry i. The billing drew sellout crowds over a four-month period. Capitol Records used that opportunity to record a live album, ... *from the hungry i,* which captured the energy of the group's stage performances. The album encompassed a broad repertoire, ranging from traditional folk ballads to Broadway show tunes, including a stirring version of Frederick Loewe and Alan Jay Lerner's "They Call the Wind Mariah," from the musical *Paint Your Wagon.* Guard, Shane and Reynolds were backed in that gig by upright jazz bassist David "Buck" Wheat, a "beat generation" musician who had played with the Chet Baker Trio and other jazz ensembles. Buckwheat, as he was known, would perform on the remainder of the Trio's recording sessions during the next three years. The group got a publicity boost when Werber persuaded a *Look* magazine photographer to include photos of the group in a feature article on San Francisco. The Trio members gained their first TV exposure when they were cast as airline pilots and performed "When the Saints Go Marching In" and "Scarlet Ribbons (For Her Hair)" in a *Playhouse 90* drama presentation titled "Rumors of Evening," which aired on CBS May 1, 1958. Four days later, Capitol released "Scarlet Ribbons" as the first Kingston Trio single, but it failed to reach the charts.

While the Trio entertained at the hungry i, the live album was released. Radio station KLUB in Salt Lake City, meanwhile, had begun playing the "Tom Dooley" cut from the Trio's first album. The track began with Nick's somberly recited prologue – "Throughout history, there have been many songs written about the eternal triangle" – before the group broke into rousing song backing Bob Shane's impassioned lead vocal. The listeners loved it, and lit up the station's phone lines with requests for it. Stations in Miami and Boston got the same reaction when they played it. Since the song was not available as a single due to Capitol's lack of confidence, people began buying the album. Capitol then reluctantly pressed more copies to meet the demand and, upon urging by radio programmers, released "Tom Dooley" as the Trio's second single. It hit the charts on September 29, rose steadily and the week of November 17 it hit No. 1. Television called, and the Kingston Trio made appearances on the top variety programs hosted by Perry Como, Dinah Shore, Milton Berle, Garry Moore and others.

The December 15, 1958, edition of *Time* magazine devoted a full-page article to the hit tune, noting that "The real-life reprobate all the singing is about was a Blue Ridge Mountain folk hero named Tom Dula, who was hanged for the 1868 murder of a young woman." The article described Dula, who had been a Confederate soldier in the Civil War from Wilkes County, North Carolina, as "a handsome young country fiddler, devoted to the jug, averse to the plow, and a constant delight to the ladies." The ladies' delight understandably diminished after learning that they had contracted syphilis from Dula, who was infected with the potentially lethal infectious disease. The song's mention of "Mr. Grayson" refers to Lt. Col. James W. M. Grayson, who led the posse that captured Dula. The day after his conviction, Dula reportedly rode to the gallows on his own coffin and "rambled on blasphemously for an hour when asked if he had any last words to say." Dula also reportedly declared, "I want everybody to know that I did not harm a single hair on that fair lady's head." The deathbed confession years later by a married woman with whom Tom had recurrent sexual relations suggested that Dula was innocent of the murder for which he had been convicted. The Kingston Trio's hit song spurred a movement of sympathy for Dula, and resulting financial contributions were sufficient to commission a tombstone for the man who had died and was buried in Ferguson, North Carolina, 90 years earlier.

The new year brought a new distinction: the Recording Industry Association of America (RIAA) certified gold record status for "Tom Dooley" in January 1959. In the first Grammy Awards ceremony, held that May, "Tom Dooley" earned the Kingston Trio honors for 1958's "best country and western performance" – for reasons that Bob Shane explained: "In 1958, the first year of the Grammys, there was no folk singing category. And since country music was dead in sales in 1957 and '58, they figured they'd use the Kingston Trio." The Trio was in good company; other award-winners that year included Henry Mancini, whose *Music From Peter Gunn* was named best arrangement; Meredith Willson, whose *Music Man* was named best original cast album; Keely Smith & Louis Prima, whose jazzy "That Old Black Magic" was named best performance by a vocal group; and Domeni-

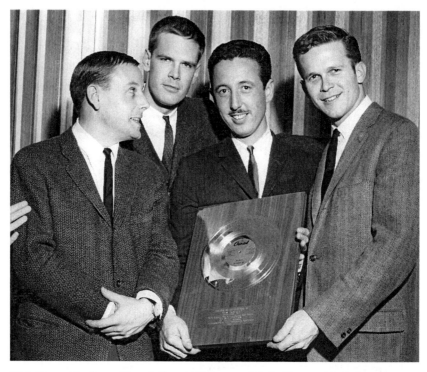

Nick Reynolds, Dave Guard, Frank Werber and Bob Shane with their gold record for "Tom Dooley" in January 1959. Photo courtesy of Frank Werber.

co Modugno, whose haunting romantic ballad "Nel Blu Dipinto Di Blu (Volare)" was record of the year. The Trio was red-hot, making the first of about 500 campus appearances during a three-year period, playing auditoriums, gymnasiums and field houses to wildly cheering fans. Between concert performances, they squeezed in visits with disc jockeys at radio stations, granted interviews with newspaper and magazine reporters, and autographed their records at stores.

The group's third single, "Raspberries, Strawberries," released in the closing days of 1958, reached only the No. 70 position on the chart. Their fourth single, however, the whimsical "The Tijuana Jail," sent the Trio soaring back up the singles chart, to No. 12 in the spring of 1959. A concert at Liberty Hall in El Paso, Texas, provided the content for the Trio's third album and their first in stereo, called *Stereo Concert*. Their popularity was cemented with the June release of their fourth album, *At Large,* which hit the No. 1 spot on the album charts and remained there for nearly four months. In 1959 the

Trio won the first Grammy for best folk performance on the strength of *At Large*, from which Capitol culled the group's next hit single, "M.T.A.," a rollicking banjo-flecked ballad that began with a Dave Guard monologue about a man doomed to forever ride the Boston subway system because he lacked the fare to exit the train. That single, which reached No. 15 on the charts, took the group through the summer of 1959. They inaugurated the fall with a follow-up top-20 hit, "A Worried Man," an ideal showcase for their hallmark robust harmonies. The Trio maintained an exhausting pace, cramming themselves into their small twin-engine Beechcraft airplane that shuttled them from city to city 300 days a year, all the while fulfilling their obligation to record three albums each year.

Amid that frenetic activity, the Kingston Trio was signed in September 1959 to appear in a series of 7-Up radio and television commercials that Buster Keaton directed. The commercials cast the Trio members in some improbable situations as they sang variations on their songs. In one spot, the Trio appeared to be balancing on an I-beam high above the New York streets on a skyscraper construction project. As they toyed with "Worried Man" and sang "I'm thirsty now, but I won't be thirsty long," Nick toppled – but landed safely on a store awning far below. In another spot, the Trio members were performing aboard a rolling subway train to the tune of "M.T.A." as Nick sang, "I need a real thirst-quencher from the 7-Up vendor, but I gotta get outta here first."

Riding the crest of their wave of popularity, the Kingston Trio ended 1959 triumphantly when *Here We Go Again* burst into the nation's top 10 album list, giving the group the unprecedented distinction of having four LP records in the top 10 simultaneously. During 1960, the last full year of Dwight Eisenhower's presidency, Capitol Records released three more Kingston Trio albums: *Sold Out, String Along* and *The Last Month of the Year,* a Christmas music collection.

The Trio made a conscious decision to avoid turning their stage into a podium for political commentary, which would have caused difficulties because the group members held differing political views. "We believed in entertaining people, not preaching to them," Shane explained. "The Kingston Trio always was primarily an entertainment group, and the records were always secondary. We used the record sales to promote our shows. The act itself was the most important thing to us. Even in our biggest years, we still made more money from personal appearances than from records."

In January 1961, the Kingston Trio embarked on its first international tour. Stops included television and concert appearances in Japan, the Philippines, New Zealand and Australia – with which Dave Guard became enchanted. Back in the States, the Trio's fan following remained loyal and their albums continued to sell well, but their performance on the singles charts began to lag. Philosophical differences about the musical direction of the group had surfaced by then. Guard wanted to steer toward traditional folk music. Reynolds, Shane and Werber firmly believed that the group should retain the whimsical, eclectic, singalong repertoire that formed the group's foundation. Dave thought the group's song arranging had been too casually done and advocated a more structured approach. The building pressure caused a fracture. *Make Way,* released in January 1961, and *Goin' Places,* the Trio's 10th album, released in June 1961, were the last two Kingston Trio albums on which Dave Guard would perform.

"Dave was a very mathematical musician-performer, and as he started learning to read music he wanted to exert more control over the harmonizing that Bobby and I did," Nick had said in August 1999. "Dave wanted to write out parts for us to sing. More mathematical, no spontaneity. Bob and I thought that didn't sound like much fun, and we wanted to stick with what we had been doing."

Gretchen Guard, who was married to Dave for 21 years, said that he wanted the group to advance and grow as any enterprise must if it expects to thrive in the long run. "A perfect example of this is the Beatles, who never did the same thing twice, who never even recorded two songs side by side in the same key. They were constantly reinventing themselves and never became complacent about their audience. This is what Dave wanted for the Kingston Trio," Gretchen said.

Nick recalled, "Dave finally told us either we would do it his way or he would just leave. And we said, 'See ya later!' We were on the absolute top of the charts, and we didn't know if we'd be able to continue after that. It was a very scary period."

Dave began forming a new traditional folk music group, the Whiskeyhill Singers, which Kingston Trio bass player David "Buck" Wheat subsequently joined; the following year, the Guard family moved to Australia. The Trio auditioned numerous musicians to replace Dave. Chip Douglas, who would later become a member of the Modern Folk Quartet and the Turtles, was still in the running when the list was shortened to two names. Chip knew all of the Trio's songs, but at 19 years of age, he was eight years younger than Bob and nine years younger than Nick. The Kingston Trio ultimately turned to a group

106

called the Cumberland Three, which Werber also managed. Cumberland Three banjo player-guitarist John Stewart, then 21, had a voice that blended well with the harmonies of Nick and Bob, and was an accomplished songwriter to boot. "John Stewart was a Dave Guard clone. There was really no contest, because he had been prepped. I was hoping for a smooth segué, to make the least noticeable change, and with John, it worked," Werber told us in March 2000. "John was a natural," added Bob Shane. "He'd written songs for us and he knew the style that we were into. We put it together and rehearsed and went right back out six weeks after Dave left. We were still getting sold-out crowds and standing ovations, so we knew we had done something right."

After Stewart joined the Trio in August 1961, the group headed into the studio to record new material. In October, Capitol released *Close Up,* the first Trio album with John Stewart. Among the tracks the group laid down that fall was a poignant rendition of Pete Seeger's "Where Have All the Flowers Gone?" The somber song, lamenting the human toll of war, was decidedly different from much of the carefree fare for which the Trio had become known. Released as a single in January 1962, the song reached the No. 21 position on the national charts. The *College Concert* album, compiled from two performances at UCLA, followed in February 1962. That spring, Capitol Records issued *The Best of the Kingston Trio,* which became the group's seventh gold album and remained on the charts for more than two years.

By the time Capitol released the Trio's *Something Special* album in June 1962, upright bass player Dean Reilly had replaced Wheat. Reilly performed on the remainder of the Trio's albums until 1967. The *New Frontier* album, which Capitol released in November 1962, contained the Trio's version of Hoyt Axton's self-assertive ballad "Greenback Dollar." The Trio's interpretation of the song was decidedly different from Axton's rendition. "When Hoyt did it, it was a very dark, angry song, but with the Trio's let's-have-fun attitude it was a 'who cares' song – you know, don't have a dollar, but who gives a damn? So the real difference was in the attitude, but not the arrangement, which was Hoyt's all the way," Stewart told us in January 2000. With Bob Shane singing lead, that tune reasserted that the group was still at its boisterous best. Because of the far more conservative regulatory environment in those days, Capitol edited the single version of the song, replacing the word "damn" with a loud guitar strum so that radio stations could air it without fear. (So volatile were the '60s that only five years later, social changes enabled Spanky and Our Gang to have a successful hit single called "Give a Damn," derived from a public service spot that had aired on radio stations in New York.)

The Trio achieved their big sound in studio recordings and during their live performances without using electrical pickups on their acoustic instruments. John Stewart explained how. "Bobby Shane, I've got to say, is simply one of the best rhythm guitar players. He plays with a big, heavy pick and heavy-gauge strings, and would break them several times during a show. He's a very strong man and he would really lay that guitar down. It was like a drum section," Stewart said admiringly. "While Peter Paul and Mary were terrific pickers and they strummed, Bobby attacked. When you put that together with Nick's tenor guitar, which was like a mariachi band, it would really

The Kingston Trio in 1962. From left, Bob Shane, Nick Reynolds and John Stewart (seated). Courtesy of Frank Werber.

add to the drive. Nick would play these terrific triplets and double-time riffs like on 'M.T.A.,' and no other group had that."

The Trio closed '62 by headlining at the Dunes Hotel and Casino in Las Vegas. "Greenback Dollar," which hit No. 21 on the charts in the early spring of 1963, gave the Trio new momentum. They turned to their #16 album for their next hit, "Reverend Mr. Black," in which John Stewart's gritty lead vocal taught a lesson about physical fortitude embedded in spiritual strength. After that song peaked at No. 8, the Trio followed up with "Desert Pete," containing a moral message about the need to prime the pump before reaping rewards. That turned out to be the group's last record to make the top 40.

Through the years, the Kingston Trio had developed a reputation for bringing success to performers who became associated with them as opening acts. But the radiant success they brought to others ultimately undermined their own popularity through a twist of fate. "It was a gas because everyone who opened for us at our peak – Barbra Streisand, Henry Mancini, Woody Allen, Roger Miller, Bill Cosby, Bob Newhart – became gigantic in show business," said Shane.

The Trio's final Capitol single to reach the national charts, "Ally Ally Oxen Free," made its debut during the week in which President John Kennedy was assassinated, just as parent company EMI forced Capitol to release the *Meet the Beatles* album. As it did, it allowed the Kingston Trio's contract to expire. At the height of Beatlemania in March 1964, the label released its final Kingston Trio single, "Seasons in the Sun," which failed to hit the charts. Ten years later, however, that song became a No. 1 hit for Terry Jacks. In June, Capitol released its final Kingston Trio album, *Back in Town,* recorded live in March at the hungry i. It was Capitol's 18th Kingston Trio album, not counting four "best of" compilations issued between 1961 and '66.

After the expiration of their Capitol contract, the Kingston Trio signed with Decca Records in 1964. But Werber knew the group's season in the sun was just about done. "While we were at Decca's offices negotiating the contract, I looked outside and saw police officers holding screaming teenagers behind barricades outside the theater where the Beatles were appearing on the *Ed Sullivan Show.* In my heart, I knew it was over," Werber told us.

Even so, the group was doing fine financially, thanks to savvy investments over the years. The Trio's deal with Decca encompassed a contract to record and produce other recording artists through their newly established Trident Productions. Kingston Trio Inc. had purchased the Sentinel Building at the intersection of Columbus Avenue and Kearny Street in San Francisco, and renamed it Columbus Tower. The flatiron-shaped building had been the original location of the hungry i before Enrico Banducci moved the club around the corner to 599 Jackson Street in 1954. On the adjacent block the Trio had bought, refurbished and expanded the old Midway Theater at 535 Pacific Avenue and reopened it as a performing arts venue under the name Little Fox Theatre. It became best known as the locale of the Trident-sponsored musical *You're A Good Man, Charlie Brown,* which ran through 1968. In addition, the Trio owned SFO Music, Treaty Music and other music publishing enterprises.

Werber also had opened and was operating the famously hip

From left: Dave Guard, Bob Shane, C.F. Martin III (president of musical instrument manufacturer C.F. Martin & Co.), bass player David "Buck" Wheat and Nick Reynolds in Dillon Gym at Princeton University (C.F.'s alma mater), November 5, 1960. Courtesy of C.F. Martin Archives.

Trident Restaurant, a favorite hangout of many elite Hollywood and musical stars at 558 Bridgeway on the Sausalito waterfront, just across the Golden Gate Bridge from San Francisco. Established as a jazz lounge, it became the Bay Area's most fabled after-performance hangout for high-echelon rock stars. In early 1965 in the Columbus Tower basement digs of the original hungry i, Werber built a top-notch studio, Columbus Recorders. Under the Trident umbrella, Werber hoped to manage and produce newer musical groups. One of those was the Michael Stewart Quintet, which John Stewart's brother had formed; in the spring of 1965 Werber began recording the band, which he renamed "We Five," and leased master tapes to A&M Records, on which the band scored a top-10 hit that summer with the song "You Were On My Mind." Trident Productions also worked with the Sons of Champlin, Blackburn & Snow, and Mystery Trend. In 1968 Werber sold his publishing catalogue to Irving Music-A&M Records.

The group's first Decca album, *The Kingston Trio (Nick Bob*

John), was released in December 1964. *Somethin' Else,* the third of the Trio's Decca albums, released in November 1965 with the accompaniment of an electrified backup band, had the distinction of being the group's first album recorded entirely at Columbus Recorders (where the Beau Brummels, the Mojo Men, Quicksilver, the Tikis and Steve Miller also did some sessions). *Somethin' Else* also, unfortunately became the first Kingston Trio album to fail to reach the charts. Decca released only one more Kingston Trio album, *Children of the Morning,* in May 1966.

The group pressed on, playing concert and club dates until 1967, when John Stewart's decision to go solo precipitated the breakup of the Kingston Trio. "We were running out of steam and I knew if I was going to go out and be a singer-songwriter, I had to leave before I turned 30," Stewart explained. He remembers that the group members were on an airplane flight to a show in the summer of 1966 when he told the others of his intentions. After eight years on the treadmill, Nick realized that he wanted to exit the group as well. "So we decided to play every farewell gig we could during the next year," John said.

For their final performance, the Kingston Trio returned to their old stomping ground – a 12-night engagement at the hungry i in San Francisco. Robin Callot and Paul Surratt, who wrote the liner notes for the 1990 Capitol compilation CD *The Kingston Trio Collectors Series,* noted that the last two songs of the Trio's last set were particularly fitting. They closed their appearance that night with "Where Have All The Flowers Gone?" and "Scotch And Soda," two of their signature songs. The engagement ended on Saturday, June 17, 1967 – the same weekend on which throngs of fans had assembled 75 miles south for the Monterey Pop Festival, which inaugurated a new era in rock music style and staging.

Bob Shane – who resisted disbanding the Trio – and John Stewart both began carving out careers as soloists, while Nick relished the opportunity to find solace away from the spotlight. In March 2011, Dave's son Tom Guard reflected on the 1961 clash among the Kingston Trio members. "If there's anything my mother, Bob Shane and I seem to concur on most, it's this: Dad was pretty stressed when he presented ultimatums to the others while a big money shakeup went down," Tom told us. "Like a lot of overworked people, he left a pretty good 'guarantee' behind and sacrificed a brain surgeon's salary but felt he would 'go crazy about all the rip-offs' if he didn't get out. He had few friends better than Bob and Nick, so the break was hard in more ways than one. By 1969 he caught the performing bug and was ready to reunite with the originals, but Nick had just begun a long rest and Bob had done what he could to keep the band going and that involved securing loyalties to anyone willing to go out on the road with him."

Eventually, the Trio business enterprise sold the Columbus Tower building to Francis Ford Coppola. When Frank Werber became a father at age 43 in 1973, he moved with his family to a ranch in the Gila Wilderness near Silver City, New Mexico, where he established a health-food store and for a period published the *Silver City Enterprise* newspaper. There he remained for three decades, enjoying solitude. His health declined following a stroke in 2004, however, and he died of heart failure at the age of 78 on May 19, 2007.

Ace Records, which had reissued many of Werber's mid-'60s productions during past decades, subsequently bought Werber's entertainment-related holdings, which included the Trident Productions catalog, master tapes and historical artifacts. "I was very good friends with Frank Werber. He was a truly charismatic fellow. Frank had spent a large part of the later '70s and '80s living in Santa Barbara and Hawaii, but Silver City was his spiritual home," Ace Records music archivist and reissue consultant Alec Palao told us. "My personal opinion is that Frank was a far more visionary and path finding manager-entrepreneur than has been documented. Most any kind of artist representation before Frank was exploitative. Frank established the college circuit as a lucrative venue for folk and rock music, and also via his experiences with the Trio, designed the 'rider' for equipment and backstage facilities that became a basic constituent of any professionally-run engagement or live performance," Palao added.

Bob Shane alone persisted in his commitment to the Kingston Trio musical tradition. After a brief stint singing with Travis Edmonson of Bud and Travis, Bob recruited guitarist and vocal tenor George Patrick Horine (known as Pat Horine) and banjo player Jim Connor in late 1968 and started the New Kingston Trio, leasing the name from the other Trio members. While in Tokyo, the New Kingston Trio recorded an album in 1970 titled *Try to Remember* for the Birdree Record label, which was available only in Japan. Ken Bradshaw, a researcher of Dave Guard's Australian work, said "This is a very rare record, a copy of which sold at eBay auction for over $420" in U.S. currency. Bradshaw noted that the New Trio recorded several tracks for Capitol in the United States, but the label released only one single, "Tell the Riverboat Captain" backed with "Windy Wakefield," in

112

1971. Connor, who hailed from northern Alabama, gave the New Trio somewhat of a country flavor, exemplified by the sentimental ballad "Grandma's Feather Bed," which he had written in 1964. That song was included on *The World Needs a Melody,* the first U.S. album by the New Kingston Trio, which Longines Symphonette released in the spring of 1973. Jim left the Trio that year, later performed with John Denver, and eventually joined the ministry.

The KT - as hardcore fans sometimes refer to the Kingston Trio - has since undergone numerous personnel changes. From 1973 to 1976, the group consisted of Bob, former New Christy Minstrels singer, guitarist and banjo player Bill Zorn, and guitarist Roger Gambill, who was born in Wilkesboro, North Carolina, about 12 miles from Tom Dula's grave. When Zorn left the Trio in 1976 to join his brother Pete as a singing duo and to try his hand at acting and comedy, banjo player George Grove stepped in. Grove, who grew up in Hickory, North Carolina - about 35 miles from Tom Dula's grave site - has remained a KT member since then. In 1976, Bob bought the name Kingston Trio from Nick and Frank. On November 7, 1981, Shane, Gambill and Grove were joined by Dave Guard, Nick Reynolds and John Stewart for a remarkable one-event reunion concert at Six Flags Magic Mountain in Valencia, California, at the northern outskirts of Los Angeles. It was the first time Dave had performed with Bob and Nick since 1961. Mary Travers of Peter, Paul and Mary made a guest appearance to sing "Where Have All the Flowers Gone?" The bass player for the concert was Lindsey Buckingham of Fleetwood Mac, whose early musical development was inspired in part by the Kingston Trio. With Tom Smothers as host, the concert was broadcast as "The Kingston Trio and Friends Reunion" February 21, 1982, on PBS television.

After the death of Gambill on March 20, 1985, resulting from a heart attack and stroke, former Brothers Four singer, banjo player and guitarist Bobby Haworth joined the Trio. Haworth remained in the Trio only until 1988, when Nick Reynolds decided to return to the group. Discussions soon began with Dave Guard about the possibility of his return to the Trio but no reunion occurred; Dave died of cancer in March 1991. Nick, Bob and George Grove continued touring until the close of 1999, when Nick decided to take life easy and retire. After an 11-year absence, Bobby Haworth rejoined George Grove and Bob Shane, and the KT continued performing into the 21st century.

When a heart attack sidelined Bob Shane in March 2004, he hired an able replacement: former 1970s Trio member Bill Zorn, who had joined the Limeliters in 1996 following the death of Lou Gottlieb. In August 2004, former Kingston Trio guitarist Pat Horine died at age 59 of smoke inhalation when fire broke out in his apartment in Lexington, Kentucky. Rick Dougherty - another former Limeliters member - joined the Trio in place of Bobby Haworth, who once again left the group in August 2005. The year 2008 was a sad one for the Kingston Trio family. That January, John Stewart died as the result of a ruptured aneurysm in his brain, and in October, Nick Reynolds died of causes related to acute respiratory disease syndrome.

Bill Zorn, George Grove and Rick Dougherty compose today's Kingston Trio. "They are a knock-out. They sell out every venue and blow me away by how good they are," said Bob, who from his Arizona home oversees the group's tours and online CD and souvenir sales (www.kingstontrio.com). Folk Era Records (www.folkera.com) of Naperville, Illinois, also offers a selection of Kingston Trio and John Stewart CDs.

Between 1958 and 1969, the Kingston Trio recorded a voluminous library of musical treasures encompassing 23 U.S. albums of new material (not counting four "best of" compilations). In 1985-86 Folk Era Records released two new KT vinyl albums and one CD.

"The two LPs were of previously unreleased songs, or tracks that until then had been only on 45 RPM records, and are legitimately added to bring the total number of albums to 25," said Allan Shaw, president of Folk Era. "The CD consisted of what we then thought of as the *Stereo Concert* album with previously unreleased additional tracks derived from what we thought were the original tapes from

Sign at the hungry i announcing the final appearance of the Kingston Trio, June 1967. Photo by Pete Bentley.

which that album was made. We later learned that they were from a different concert recorded at about the same time. Of the 18 songs on the CD, nine were previously unreleased, so I would include it to bring the total to 26." Six more live performance albums (one by the Guard Trio, the others by the Stewart Trio) and two studio albums of previously undistributed material were released between 1987 and 2009, bringing the total to 34, according to Shaw. Latter-day configurations of the Trio have recorded a combined total of 14 additional vinyl albums and CDs, and nearly 20 more compilations have been released since the early '70s. The Recording Industry Association of America certified seven Kingston Trio albums as gold records between 1960 and '64.

But the cultural imprint of the Kingston Trio vastly transcended their own record sales. "Prior to the Kingston Trio, folk music was the 'Cinderella' of popular music, too crude and unsophisticated to be appreciated in the same way as were classical music, big-band music, and other musical genres," Shaw observed. "This disdain was frequently enhanced by folk music's affiliations with socially unacceptable political movements such as Communism and labor activism, as well as ethnic connections. By eschewing socio-political causes, the clean-cut Kingston Trio made folk music acceptable to and by the educated, intellectual and upper middle-class segment of the population." Shaw attributes his love of folk music to his interest in history. "Folk music tells tales, often with historic origins, of people and life, and frequently brings history to life."

The legions of ardent Kingston Trio fans include preeminent rock musician photographer Henry Diltz, who as a member of the Modern Folk Quartet performed with Dave Guard. "When I was a college student studying psychology at the University of Hawaii, I eagerly awaited each new Kingston Trio album, and each time a new one was released, I ran to the store to buy it, and played it over and over," Diltz recalled. "The Kingston Trio were like the Beatles to my generation. The Trio excelled in finding just the right songs, and with their superb three-part harmonies they infused such joy and life into their music. For me, that was the pinnacle of entertainment. And I can tell you that Stephen Stills and David Crosby, among many other musicians, bought guitars because of the Kingston Trio," said Diltz, whose insightful, evocative photography has graced record albums for Crosby, Stills and Nash, the Eagles, the Doors, Jackson Browne, and scores of other musical artists since the late 1960s.

Many KT albums introduced songs that would later become hits for other performers. The Trio's 1961 album *Goin' Places* included "It Was A Very Good Year," which became a top-30 hit for Frank Sinatra four years later, and "Lemon Tree," with which Peter, Paul and Mary made their first appearance on the charts in May 1962; the Trio's 1962 album *New Frontier* included a song called "The First Time," which became better known as "The First Time Ever I Saw Your Face" when Roberta Flack turned it into a hit in the spring of 1972; and the Trio's 1963 album *Sunny Side!* included "Jackson," which became hits for Johnny Cash and June Carter Cash, and for Nancy Sinatra and Lee Hazlewood in 1967. Alec Palao added, "The Trio were the first to commercially release the future anthem 'Let's Get Together' on their 1964 live album *Back In Town*. Frank [Werber] had purchased the song from the composer, Dino Valenti. The tune also constituted We Five's follow-up single to 'You Were On My Mind,' and the We Five version, which Frank produced, was the song's highest-charting recording until the Youngbloods' 'Get Together' hit the top five in 1969."

But the greatest legacy of the Kingston Trio has been the entertainment value of their concerts, and those lucky enough to have seen them perform will never forget them.

The Kingston Trio performing at Kingston Trio Fantasy Camp, August 8, 2009. From left, George Grove, Paul Gabrielson (bass), Bill Zorn and Rick Dougherty. Photo by Howard Bruensteiner.

KINGSTON TRIO U.S. HIT SINGLES ON
THE NATIONAL CHARTS

Debut	Peak	Gold	Title	Label
9/58	1	Δ	Tom Dooley	Capitol
1/59	70		Raspberries, Strawberries	Capitol
3/59	12		The Tijuana Jail	Capitol
6/59	15		M.T.A.	Capitol
9/59	20		A Worried Man	Capitol
12/59	98		Coo Coo-U	Capitol
2/60	32		El Matador	Capitol
6/60	37		Bad Man's Blunder	Capitol
10/60	60		Everglades	Capitol
1/62	21		Where Have All The Flowers Gone	Capitol
4/62	81		Scotch and Soda /Jane, Jane, Jane	Capitol
10/62	97		One More Town	Capitol
1/63	21		Greenback Dollar	Capitol
4/63	8		Reverend Mr. Black	Capitol
8/63	33		Desert Pete	Capitol
11/63	61		Ally Ally Oxen Free	Capitol

Δ symbol: RIAA certified gold record (Recording Industry Association of America)

Billboard's pop singles chart data is courtesy of Joel Whitburn's Record Research Inc. (www.recordresearch.com), Menomonee Falls, Wisconsin.

Epilogue: Bob Shane
Guitarist, banjo player and singer

For more than 50 years beginning in 1957, through the numerous personnel changes that have taken place within the Kingston Trio, Bob Shane has maintained a constant presence. The Kingston Trio might never have existed at all if not for Bob, for it was he as a high school student who persuaded Marjorie Guard to buy a guitar for her son, Dave. Yet Shane himself nearly missed being a part of the group.

He was born Robert Castle Schoën on February 1, 1934, in Hilo, Hawaii. Bob's father and his maternal grandmother were also born in Hilo. Bob's great grandfather, born on Molokai, grew up in a fam-

ily of missionaries from the Boston area who had settled in Hawaii. Bob, who is of German lineage, adopted the phonetic "Shane" spelling. He quipped, "I 'became' Irish just because I got tired of people mispronouncing my name as *Shone.*"

Bob's parents, Art and Margaret Schoën, operated Athletic Supply of Hawaii, a wholesale toy and sporting goods company in Honolulu. But he became enchanted by the musical exploits of a fellow named Harold Harvey, a close friend of Art's and Margaret's. Harold, who had been in the cast of a famous musical comedy stage revue called *George White's Scandals* during the 1920s, was a guitarist and singer with

Bob Shane performing at Fantasy Camp 6 on August 14, 2005. Photo by Paul RyBolt.

118

an expansive repertoire of comic and novelty tunes. "Harold Harvey used to come to our house during the war years when I was growing up, and he always came to our parties. He would play and sing some interesting songs, not just the run-of-the-mill stuff," Bob recalled fondly. "He had one called 'So the Bluebirds and Blackbirds Got Together.' It was priceless. The attention he got and the pleasure that he brought made me want to be in show business. Right after that I picked up the ukulele and the tenor guitar."

Bob acquired an inexpensive four-string tenor guitar when he was in ninth grade. He likes to say that he learned to play and sing as a matter of self-defense. Because music was such an essential part of Island upbringing, anyone who wasn't musical was considered somewhat of an outcast. Bob enrolled in glee club, and began to seek roles in school plays and musicals. That's where he gained his first exposure to the stage, and he and his friend Dave Guard found they really enjoyed appearing before an audience.

Bitten by the entertainment bug, Bob and Dave began performing together for friends. They were influenced by an eclectic mix of musical styles and performers, including Harry Belafonte, Hank Williams Sr., and Elvis Presley, as well as Hawaiian musicians they knew.

Bob enrolled in Menlo College in Atherton, California, in 1952 with the intention of transferring to Stanford University, which both of his parents had attended. While attending Stanford in 1954, Dave began dating a girl named Katie Seaver – whose younger brother Tom would become a star New York Mets pitcher, and later would be inducted into the National Baseball Hall of Fame. While driving to Los Angeles in 1954, Bob and Dave stopped at the Seavers' home in Fresno for dinner. "Katie and Tom's parents told us they knew of a song we might like. They had heard it at a place in Phoenix in 1932, performed by a backroom piano player who had written it. When they said they liked the song, the piano player wrote out the sheet music for them, and Katie's parents gave it to us," Bob said. The pianist didn't sign the music notations, and his name remains unknown, but Shane would in 1958 immortalize the song – "Scotch and Soda" – after recording it for the Kingston Trio's first album.

After receiving his bachelor's degree from Menlo College with a business major in 1956, Bob decided to take a break from school and returned to Honolulu, where he joined his family's business in preparation for ultimately running it. The Elvis impersonation act he developed was then just for personal enjoyment. But he soon realized that he found the allure of the stage and popularity magnetizing and began to grow disenchanted with the toys and sporting goods wholesaling business. While in Honolulu, Bob went on a date with a young woman named Louise Brandon, arranged by his father. "My aunt was returning from the mainland to Hawaii aboard the S.S. Lurline, and Matson Lines, which owned the ship, had a rule that all unaccompanied women must be paired with someone else," Bob explained. "My aunt was paired with Louise, who impressed my Dad when he met her. So he fixed us up on a blind date." The couple enjoyed each other's company, continued dating, and became romantically involved.

Bob married Louise, who hailed from Georgia, on March 15, 1959. "Yes, I got married on the Ides of March, and I'll not do that again," Bob laughed. Bob and his mother, who had a beautiful voice, sang as a duo at the wedding, which took place in Washington, D.C. The couple settled initially in the San Francisco Bay Area community of Tiburon – where the first of their five children, daughter Joan Glancy (known as Jody), was born May 4, 1961. Bob calculated that he was on the road with the Kingston Trio 285 days during his first year of marriage. Shortly after the birth of their second child, Susan Hull, on November 6, 1963, the couple relocated to Alpharetta, Georgia, just north of Atlanta. There they bought property, which they named Kingston Farm, and began raising horses – and a larger family. Their son Brandon was born June 4, 1967.

After the breakup of the Kingston Trio that month, Bob went solo for a brief time. Decca Records, for which the Trio recorded beginning in 1964, signed Bob to a contract. He recorded four singles for Decca, including "Honey," written by Bobby Russell. Bob was given a two-week exclusive on the song, but Decca lagged in promoting the record. Bobby Goldsboro's version of the song quickly surpassed it and went on to become one of the top-selling songs of 1968. Shane, irritated at Decca as a result, declined the label's request for him to record another Bobby Russell song, "Little Green Apples." That turned into a substantial hit for both O.C. Smith and Roger Miller.

After Bob's short-lived outing as a soloist, he resurrected the group he loved by leasing the name New Kingston Trio from Nick Reynolds and Frank Werber in late 1968. He performed initially with Jim Connor and Pat Horine. Connor speaks fondly of the five-year period during which he and Pat performed with the New Kingston Trio. "We worshipped Bob Shane. He was such a star," Jim said. "The girls and the young ladies clustered around him. They would sort of ignore us, because we were just new in the group. Shane's a phenomenon. If he'd had a different break or two in his life, there's no doubt he would have been as big a soloist as Sinatra, because he sings so fabulously."

The Shanes' daughter Robin was born May 23, 1969; then came son Jason, born June 3, 1971. Through personnel changes, Bob kept the KT on the road and in the spotlight, and he purchased the name Kingston Trio from Reynolds and Werber in 1976. During much of the childhood of his five kids, Bob was on the road. "I have no idea what it was like for them to grow up knowing they had a well-known father, because I was never there," Shane told us. Life on the road took its toll on Bob and ultimately destroyed his nearly 23-year-long marriage to Louise. "I had some strange years going through various drugs and booze, marriage and divorce. It was the result of the pressure of being on the road. We used to say we got into the business for women. We had quantity, if not quality," he laughed heartily.

After Bob and Louise divorced in 1981, the couple lived together for another 11 years, until Bob and longtime friend Bobbie Childress began seeing each other. Bob had met Bobbie years earlier when the Trio was booked at the Four Queens Hotel and Casino in Las Vegas, where she was the maître d'hôtel. With each other's help, they made an important decision. "Together, we quit drinking. I was very lucky that I was raised in a family that taught moderation, so I didn't have to go into rehab," Bob said. "Whenever I was told I was doing the wrong thing, I would just quit. So when I went to a doctor in 1992 and acknowledged that I was a pretty heavy drinker, he told me, 'If you don't quit drinking, you're not going to be able to sing anymore.' So I quit that day." The couple settled in Phoenix, where Bobbie was living. "It's a good place to live. She and I both like the heat," Bob explained. After eight years together, the couple married in November 2000.

Bob continued entertaining audiences until March 21, 2004. He had fallen deeply asleep aboard an airline flight following a gig. When the plane landed in Phoenix and the cabin depressurized, he awakened, stood up and although he felt strangely lightheaded, he filed down the aisle in line with other passengers. As he reached the doorway, he felt woozy. "I started to faint, and a redcap caught me as I fell, and put me in a wheelchair that he had been holding for another passenger," Bob said. After he rested briefly, the lightheaded sensation diminished. He carried his guitar and luggage to the passenger pickup area, where he waited for his wife to pick him up. "By then I was feeling OK." But when they arrived home, Bobbie noticed that

Bob still appeared dazed, and she took him to see his doctor. "The doctor hooked me up and took an EKG, and told me I had a heart attack, and then I was taken to the Mayo Clinic and hospitalized for a few days." Although he had no artery blockage, he was diagnosed with chronic obstructive pulmonary disease (COPD), a lung condition that impedes breathing. Bob was prescribed medication and has since used liquid oxygen around the clock to enrich air intake in his damaged lungs. His doctors advised him to retire from performing. Bob called upon Limeliters alumnus and former 1970s Trio member Bill Zorn to replace him and perform with Bob Haworth and George Grove. That marked the first time that the Kingston Trio had appeared on stage with no original members.

Although Bob was unable to resume touring, he continues to oversee the online store operations and schedule for the group, which now consists of George Grove, Bill Zorn and Rick Dougherty. The Trio is typically booked a year in advance for engagements at clubs, casinos and concerts. As much as Bob likes Phoenix, he still feels a deep connection with the coast. "I'm a West Coast person. I keep a place in Hawaii so I can go back and chill out. I need to be near the ocean at times," said Bob. His once-short, dark, wavy hair is

Bob Shane performing at Kingston Trio Fantasy Camp, August 8, 2009.
Photo by Howard Bruensteiner.

now long and white, often pulled back in a ponytail.

Bob enjoys being a homebody. Unlike many other entertainers, he isn't a sportsman during his off-hours. "At my age, I'm just glad to get around," he laughed. "We've got a nice house with a pool. We listen to good music, eat good food, we have lots of friends, and we occasionally take sightseeing trips to national parks. In show business you don't go out for active sports because if you get hurt you're out of a job and you put other people out of work, too." Asked if he reads for pleasure, Shane responded, "I've read only three books in my life: *War and Peace,* and the Harry Lorayne Memory Course, and I forgot what the other one was." After a well-timed pause, as if waiting for a rimshot, he broke into buoyant laughter.

Bob said his proudest professional achievement is his lifetime performance record: on stage, he entertained more than 10 million people. "That's what I really enjoyed doing most," he said. In 2006, Menlo College presented Bob and his fellow alumnus Nick with its inaugural Alumni Lifetime Achievement Award. Through the years, Bob remained true to his ideals. Another source of pride was learning that Frank Sinatra rejected suggestions to record "Scotch and Soda," declaring that Bob Shane already had sung it to perfection.

"Frank Sinatra was my favorite pop singer, and that gesture of his was the nicest compliment I've ever had from someone who I admired," Bob told us. Even though Shane's rendition was recorded in a sterile, cavernous recording studio, it oozes the intimacy of a dimly lit hideaway. During the recording session, Bob had little difficulty transcending his surroundings to attain the moody feel of the song. "It was easy. I was after women," he laughed.

"I am not a folksinger and never will be," Bob wrote in an autobiographical statement that appeared in the Trio's 1967 farewell tour concert program. "I am a singer of folk songs, among other things like show tunes and songs written today. My pet peeve is the so-called ethnics who put me down because I'm putting a lot of work into making it a good living. These people should remember that show business is a business intended to entertain, not exclusively a medium for airing personal and world problems. When asked if it's fun, I reply, 'If it weren't enjoyable, I shouldn't and wouldn't be doing it.' This means all of it, including all of the shows, promotion, advertising, rehearsing, public relations and charity. I enjoy it all." He added, "One of the things that can kill you the quickest in show business is your own ego. Sometimes you get so puffed up with yourself without realizing it that when someone asks why you think so much of yourself, the air goes completely out of you and you feel like quitting. You have to constantly remind yourself that you're a human like everyone else – no better, no worse – and treat all others with the same respect that you require for your own peace of mind."

Bob now presides over the four-day Kingston Trio Fantasy Camp in Scottsdale, Arizona, an annual event that Nick Reynolds and John Stewart created and operated beginning in 2000. The program for KT fans and musicians includes performances by the new Kingston Trio and impromptu jam sessions, and enables "campers" to fulfill a fantasy by wearing striped shirts, slinging an instrument over their shoulder and becoming a member of the Kingston Trio, if only for a day. Bob appears on stage each evening of the festival to sing two or three songs. He takes great pleasure in the Kingston Trio's durability as a popular entertainment attraction. "I visited Dave Guard two weeks before he died, and we talked, among other things, about the legacy of the Kingston Trio. He said to me that quitting the Kingston Trio was the most foolish thing he'd ever done in his life."

Today Bob greatly enjoys his relationship with his adult children. His daughter Jody, who married a country music singer, lives in Nashville. Bob's other daughters and sons live in Atlanta. Susan and her husband are raising their three daughters. Bob's sons Brandon and Jason – who now has two sons of his own – have shown an interest in music recording and have begun engineering sessions for local rock groups.

Now that he has time to relax, Bob has had a chance to assess his life and think about its meaning. Still kidding, he feigns bewilderment. "When I die I'll be like Marlon Brando and on my deathbed I'll say, 'What was *that* all about?' I think life is meant to be lived as straight as you can. You do the best you can and try and make a mark for yourself without stepping on people. Unfortunately, most people who get ahead seem to step on somebody," Bob told us. But he isn't ready to annotate his life story in greater detail just yet.

"People have asked me for years why I haven't written a book, and I say the same thing Audrey Hepburn said: 'First of all, my life is not over, and second of all, you don't cop out on your friends.' Most of the people who would make my book interesting are still alive," he said. "I've had a great life."

For more information, visit **www.kingstontrio.com**

Epilogue: Dave Guard

Banjo player, guitarist and singer

October 19, 1934 – March 22, 1991

Peering from behind black-framed glasses, Dave Guard
had a penetrating gaze that appeared capable of piercing
anyone's veil of pretension, dishonesty or hypocrisy. His face
epitomized the look of the collegiate male of the late 1950s and early
'60s. Clean shaven, with a closely cropped, forward-brushed hairstyle,
square-jawed and confident, Guard was the embodiment of youthful
American optimism in a post-Sputnik world.

Bound for a career in business, Guard often was regarded as the
serious, intellectual, studious member of the Kingston Trio. He also
had a spirited, humorous side that helped infuse the lively presence
of the Trio. Guard initially pursued music purely as a diversion, along
with numerous other interests in the arts and athletics. As a student
in the San Francisco Bay Area, he enjoyed running, body surfing,
playing baseball and basketball, and earned letters in football and
track. In the autumn of 1952, however, just a few weeks after enter-
ing Stanford University as a freshman economics major, he suffered
frightful injuries that could have
pre-empted his career – or ended
his life.

Dave Guard before performing at a folk
festival in Västervik, Sweden,
July 1990. Photo by musician
Totte Bergstöm.

His parents had sent him a
generous check for his 18th birthday on October 19. He invited his
schoolmates in Encina Hall to celebrate with him, but unfortunately he consumed too much beer.
He got up during the night in
his second-floor room of Encina
Hall and groggily walked to his
window. Apparently sleepwalk-
ing, Dave opened the window,
stepped onto the sill, stumbled
and fell 20 feet to the ground,
seriously injuring his back. After
being placed in a body cast
he was carried onto a military
transport aircraft and flown to

Honolulu, where he underwent further treatment. His recuperation consumed the remainder of the school year.

The following fall he returned to Stanford, and in the ensuing three years completed his four-year undergraduate curriculum. He had begun his senior year in 1955 when he was introduced to his future wife, Gretchen Ballard, through a mutual friend. "I first met him when I was a freshman, and he was a senior. We started going around together the following year," Gretchen recalled. "He was unconventional, to say the least, yet he had terrific grades, so I knew he had to be really bright. I was young and impressionable, and he was fascinating."

Immediately after earning his bachelor's degree in economics, Guard entered the Stanford Business School. He found the curriculum dreary, however. His growing pleasure in music corresponded with declining interest in his studies. "He became a bit bored with the business school. Playing music was much more fun for him," Gretchen explained. "We used to spend a lot of time at the Cracked Pot. I was really amazed when Frank Werber came and listened and showed some interest in Dave, Bob and Nick. The three of them knew maybe a combined total of 100 songs, but they knew how to perform about 15 songs together, and that was enough for a full set."

Dave and Gretchen became increasingly serious about each other. Gretchen said she wasn't worried about Dave's ability to support her and a family on a musician's salary. "I was 19 and I was happy to be involved with an artistic person," she explained. "At the time I thought David was a lot smarter that I was. He was three years older, worldlier, and funnier. He was so bright, so quick, your jaw would drop." He reveled in being inscrutable. "When we were in college, friends of his walking on campus might see Dave and say, 'Hi, how are you doing?' And Dave would answer, 'Abstract.' And they would wonder

Dave and Gretchen Guard at Sea Ranch, Sonoma County, California, in 1973. Photo by Tom Guard.

126

'What? What does he mean by *that?*' He used his intellect and his humor to entertain people and to keep them off balance, too."

Gretchen dropped out of school after completing her sophomore year, and the couple married in the fall of 1957. "The Kingston Trio were playing at the Purple Onion by then, and David was still enrolled in business school until the end of that year. I don't think he was attending classes, but he was enrolled, she said."

Although the success of the Kingston Trio permitted Dave to abandon his MBA studies at Stanford University, he remained a lifelong student, developing expertise in musicology, photography and, eventually, teaching. Dave Guard's sense of discipline likely was influenced by his father, who had been a civil engineer and a colonel in the U.S. Army Reserve.

Donald David Guard was born an only child October 19, 1934, in Honolulu, Hawaii. His maternal grandmother, Jeanne Thielle Kent, was Belgian, a pianist and a music teacher. Her husband was an officer in the Navy and, as a result, David's mother, Marjorie, grew up in Honolulu on Ford Island. After graduating from high school, she began working as a secretary for the Air Force at Hickam Field. Dave's father, Carl Jackson Guard, (who was always called Jack) was from Florida but moved to Honolulu after completing his university education. He served in the Army as a civil engineer during World War II and the Korean and Vietnam wars. Between wars he returned to civilian life so that he could remain in Hawaii.

When Dave turned 7 years of age in 1941, he and his family were living in an apartment complex at Hickam Field, adjacent to Pearl Harbor. On Sunday morning, December 7, young Dave was awakened by the sound of explosions and artillery fire. "He got up, went outside to get the Sunday funnies, and he saw Pearl Harbor going up in smoke," Gretchen said. "When he tried to wake up his parents they said, 'No, go back to bed, it's only a drill.' So he got out some paper and colored pencils and drew pictures of the whole thing, from a 7-year-old's point of view."

Dave later wrote about his childhood Pearl Harbor experiences in a diary that he compiled in 1978. His son, Tom, transcribed an excerpt for us:

November 1941:
Big night drills over Pearl Harbor with searchlights and sirens. Listen to Green Hornet *and* Bulldog Drummond *on radio.*

December 1941:
Japanese bomb Pearl Harbor. I can see the faces of their pilots, see

bombs and burning planes falling. Chaos and panic. Mama and I return to old landlord on Makiki Street with Smiths. We sleep under the street in the drainage tunnel, among the sandbags. Dog bites me and I'm taken to the doctor at Pearl Harbor, which still burns. We go back out to Hickam but it just doesn't look safe. Dad comes out of underground command post for first time. No Santa Claus, no Christmas presents.

January–February 1942:
We move back to Punahou Court in a different cottage. Put tar-paper over all the windows and just sweat the war news. No one can go out after dark at all. We listen to Ozzie and Harriet, I Love a Mystery, Bob Hope. *Parents won't let me go to Lincoln School because they fear bomb attack on town. So they have me stay with the maid, but the maid lets me go to movies every morning all day long. The movies (Palace Theater, 9 cents) I saw the most were* Suez *and* The Mummy's Curse. *I would sit in the front row all day long and let World War II take care of itself. Parents gain lots of weight. All the talk is about leaving for the mainland. A ticket is status.*

Dave left with his mother aboard an airline flight to Washington, D.C., to stay for a while with his grandmother. After U.S. forces inflicted a crippling blow to the Japanese Navy in the battle of Midway in June 1942, Dave and his mother returned to Honolulu and the Guard family rented an apartment in Waikiki. Dave entered nearby Punahou School – where he would meet fellow student Bob Shane. On one of several visits with his mother at the Honolulu Academy of Art, Dave saw a group of itinerant folksingers, and he was transfixed. "That was an important early influence on him," Gretchen said. Despite his early interest in music, he agreed to follow his father's recommendation to study business. His enrollment at Menlo School and subsequently at Stanford University enabled his introduction to Gretchen.

When the Kingston Trio took to the road in the spring of '58, Gretchen went along so the newlyweds could spend as much time together as possible. "The dynamic of that group was something that could never be duplicated. Each one of them had his own kind of energy that contributed to the success of this group, and to the spirit and the fun of it. And I think that's what people loved so much about it. Before we had children, I spent a lot of time sitting in dark places and applauding," Gretchen told us in December 2001. The couple's first child, daughter Catherine, was born June 1, 1958. "When Catherine was 3 months old we began to tour with David and the group, to Hawaii, to Juarez, Mexico – which was fun and safe then – and to

New York for a few months. By then Catherine was becoming very active, so she and I moved back to the Bay Area, and David came home as often as touring would allow, usually every other weekend."

Gretchen said that in those days, Dave had no pretensions about becoming famous. "He never thought he was going to be a superstar. When he started, he was only 22. For someone that young, he handled it pretty well. It's difficult to have a great success at the beginning of your life, and then to try to live up to that afterward. But I think he did pretty well," Gretchen said. Despite Dave's fame, the couple lived modestly and engaged in typical family activities.

While fans perceived Guard as the intellectual conscience of the group, he didn't think of himself that way. "Dave wasn't as entirely serious as some people thought. He also was a very funny guy with a keen sense of humor," Gretchen said. "Living with Dave was fun, especially when the children were little. Home was much livelier when he was there, and we would bundle up the kids and take them all over the place. We went to Big Sur a lot, we visited his parents in Honolulu and my parents in Pasadena – we did a lot of running around like young families do," Gretchen said. "We always lived in modest places. I think because he didn't trust the Trio's popularity to last, he didn't want to get overextended. Our first nest was a rented apartment in San Francisco for $75 a month. Then after a few months of traveling with the group, we rented an apartment in Palo Alto, before renting a house there later."

The couple's only son, Tom, was born April 20, 1960. By the time their second daughter, Sally, was born nearly three years later, Dave had left the Kingston Trio. "He was tired – tired of touring, tired of being away from home, tired of producing three albums every year" Gretchen said. "I remember one time he said, 'If I have to walk on stage for the three thousandth time and sing "Tom Dooley" again, I think I'm going to throw up.' I sympathized with him, but I didn't know he was going to issue an ultimatum to Nick and Bob. I think if he had talked to me about it first, and if he had provided some wiggle room when he approached the others, things might have turned out much differently."

As the Kingston Trio members were en route for a tour of the Far East and South Pacific in January 1961, Dave returned briefly to Hawaii and sought out slack-key guitar virtuoso Gabby Pahinui. As a youth, Dave had been enthralled with the delicately crisp voice and hypnotic playing style of Pahinui, who was 13 years Dave's senior. The first record Dave had bought as a kid was "Hi'ilawe" by Gabby

Pahinui. Dave said that Gabby "plays the sweetest, cleanest most soulful, most Hawaiian guitar music ever heard." Through the years, Dave had continued to collect Pahinui recordings but was disappointed that orchestral accompaniment on most of them drowned out Pahinui's shimmering falsetto singing and masterful playing. "For the slack-key method, the guitar is loosely tuned, not like traditional Spanish tuning, so you can hear the strings vibrating. The melody is sung, and the chords are strummed and plucked, providing a rich, luscious background, always in a major key," Gretchen explained.

Dave wanted to produce a recording that emphasized Pahinui's musicianship, with subtle ukulele and bass guitar accompaniment. He hired recording engineer Bob Lang, who had worked with Gabby previously, along with bass player Sonny Nicholas and ukulele player Danny Stewart. The two recording sessions for the double album took place in the meeting hall of Central Union Church in Honolulu. They had to pause recording every 15 minutes, during the chiming of the church bells. Dave contacted numerous record labels, but at the time he was unable to interest anyone in releasing the Gabby Pahinui album.

Yearning to explore new musical directions, Dave set about creating a new group and enlisted an old friend from Hawaii, singer-guitarist Cyrus Faryar. Bass player David "Buck" Wheat, who had accompanied the Kingston Trio in their recording sessions, also joined the group, dubbed the Whiskeyhill Singers. "David knew Buckwheat well and appreciated his musicology and his wisdom," Faryar told us in March 2011. "Bucky was from a generation earlier than us, and turned out to be a resource far beyond just being a bass player for the Kingston Trio. He never got to sing much with the Trio, but with the Whiskeys he became the fourth voice."

When Dave said that he would like to include a female singer to add vocal texture, Cyrus recommended folk and blues singer Judy Henske, an imposingly tall woman who belted out songs with a commanding presence. "I had been the opening act at a club in San Diego on a bill that included Judy Henske with [guitarist] Eric Hord as her musical accompanist," Faryar said. "She could croon a sweet ballad with great tenderness, but she also was a powerful blues shouter. Some clubs that booked Judy had to reinforce the floor because when she kept time singing, she didn't just tap her foot; she pounded her heels. The floor was at risk when Judy sang. Dave and Buckwheat went to see Judy perform, and they were as knocked out as I was by her singing."

Judy agreed to join the Whiskeyhill Singers, which began developing an eclectic repertoire encompassing folk compositions, traditional melodies from Hawaii and Fiji, and indigenous music from Africa. "David had a very exploratory mind musically, and was keen about global music, and really felt a powerful calling to not just sing 'Tom Dooley,' but to sing African and Brazilian and any kind of music. An academic musicologist named Erich Schwandt, who was a buddy of David's, was a large mainstay in the discussion. At David's house, with Erich there, we would listen to a great number of songs from around the planet, to see what would fit in what became an extremely eclectic package of tunes," Faryar said. The group began rehearsing and laying down tracks at Henry "Sandy" Jacobs' recording studio in Sausalito, not far from Faryar's apartment above the Tides bookstore.

The Whiskeyhill Singers soon recorded four songs for the motion picture *How The West Was Won*, which captured an Academy Award for "best motion picture soundtrack" of 1962. Capitol Records signed the group and in the spring of 1962 released a multifarious album, *Dave Guard & the Whiskeyhill Singers*, but the musically adventurous recording failed to generate sufficient attention.

That June, Dave and Gretchen took a vacation trip. "David and I went to Australia because he wanted me to see it, especially the beaches north of Sydney. He had first seen this area during the KT tour of the Pacific and was impressed with its beautiful sunny beaches and friendly people," Gretchen said. "We left Catherine and Tom with their grandparents and were away for only a week or so before returning to California." As preparations were under way to record a second Whiskeyhill Singers album, Judy Henske left the group to pursue a solo career. Guard replaced her in July 1962 with singer Liz Seneff.

The Guards began making plans to return to Australia – with the intention of remaining for an extended stay. "For a long time, David and I had been looking for a place to live along the beach in California. There wasn't much left in Southern California, where it's warm, and up north where land was plentiful, the water was too cold most of the time for swimming," Gretchen said.

Ken Bradshaw, a researcher of Dave Guard's Australian work, tells what happened next. "Cyrus Faryar recalls Dave saying later that he planned to give the Whiskeys a rest for a while and go to Australia, returning to the U.S. from time to time for Whiskeyhill Singers tours," Bradshaw told us in March 2011. "This, of course, did not happen." Tom Guard said that when his father informed Capitol of his plans to move with his family to Australia, the label cancelled release of a second Whiskeyhill Singers album because the band wouldn't be able to promote it by touring.

"Because David was so burned out at that point, we thought it would be a good idea to take a year off," Gretchen explained. "We were expecting our third baby then. While touring, he had missed the birth of our first two children, and he didn't want to miss this one." The Guards bought a contemporary-style house – the first they had ever owned – and moved into it in October, which is springtime in Australia. The house was about two-thirds the way up a bluff, overlooking the crystal-blue Pacific Ocean on Morella Road at Whale Beach, on a peninsula about 30 miles north of Sydney. "Our daughter Sally was born there on a national holiday – Australia day – January 26, 1963, and Dave was there," Gretchen said.

Dave severed his final ties with the Kingston Trio by cashing out his share of ownership in the group collective. That enabled him to concentrate on development of *Colour Guitar,* a music instruction package he had conceived. It was based on jazz composer George Russell's theory called *The Lydian Chromatic Concept of Tonal Organization.* Guard had sought a way to teach music theory to guitarists without requiring them to study piano. Using visual color as an analogy to the musical spectrum, he assigned colors to each of 12 musical notes; in the *Colour Guitar* method, which he developed over a period of five years, he used warmer colors to represent whole notes, and cooler colors to designate sharps and flats. Patterns of colors represented chords. Dave designed a package consisting of a series of lesson folders with die-cut holes correlating the guitar

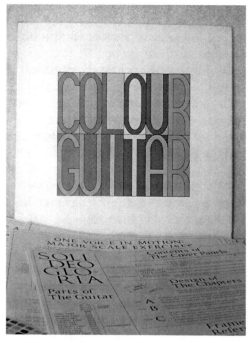

The Colour Guitar instruction package, designed by Dave Guard.

132

fingerboard to a coded color grid. *Colour Guitar* explained scales, chords, tonal relationships and how to interpret sheet music. The 16-inch-square package contained color chips to attach to the guitar neck between the frets. Gretchen helped design the cover of the package.

During the time Dave designed and refined *Colour Guitar,* he did recording session instrumental and background vocal work for Australian folk artists, performed occasionally as a soloist on stage, and recorded music for television commercials. Doing advertising work was not at all distasteful to Dave. "David had vocational testing early on, before he got into business school. All the profiles said that he would be good at advertising," Gretchen said. "He was always devising funny sayings, all through his life. When he would sign off a phone conversation or a letter, he often said, 'Strangle the falcons.'" When writing letters to friends, he sometimes used fictitious names, including Mutt Blankenship and "Dynamite" Finkelstein, in the return address. "He would say off-the-wall things, and nobody had any idea what he was talking about. They didn't mean anything. His idea was to baffle people, and set himself apart by saying something screwy or funny or witty, so people would say, 'Huh?' He loved getting that reaction," Gretchen explained. "When a visitor was leaving our house at night, he would say, 'Drive wreckless. Or without wreck.'" Another favorite saying of Dave's was "Bombs away, dream babies." That phrase tickled Henry Diltz, who wrote that phrase when he was autographing John Stewart's copy of the book *California Rock, California Sound: The Music of Los Angeles and Southern California,* which contained numerous photos by Diltz. John found the "bombs away, dream babies" phrase so amusing he later used it as the title of one of his solo albums.

In 1964, Dave became a folk music consultant for an Australian Broadcasting Corporation (ABC) program called *Jazz Meets Folk.* That prompted ABC to sign him to host a musical-variety television program called *Dave's Place* beginning October 3, 1965. The set, adorned with bamboo, an imposing large mask, tropical birds on perches and other vestments of the South Seas, was designed to look like a tea room, in which Guard welcomed his guests. He sang solo and performed with the program's in-house ensemble, the "Dave's Place Group," consisting of bassist Chris Bonett and female singers Kerrilee Male, Frances Stone and Norma Shirlee Stoneman. Guest performers who appeared on the program included Sonny Terry and Brownie McGhee, the New Lost City Ramblers, Nina and Frederik,

133

and Judy Henske. Gospel music was among the repertoire of the Dave's Place Group, and many of the show's guests performed gospel songs as well.

"Dave had an idea that gospel songs with an electric touch would be the next thing to take off," Ken Bradshaw explained. "Just as the Weavers inspired the Kingston Trio, Dave was inspired by the Staple Singers. Gospel songs took up about half of the songs that Dave and his group performed on the *Dave's Place* TV show, and many of them were obscure." Broadcast on Sunday evenings, *Dave's Place* also aired in Canada. But ABC recorded only 13 programs, and did not renew it after its last broadcast in late December '65.

Guard continued conducting music theory research and refining *Colour Guitar* until he self-published it in 1967. Early that summer, he traveled to California to begin promoting *Colour Guitar*. In Los Angeles, he stayed at the Laurel Canyon home of Judy Henske and her husband, Jerry Yester. By that time Yester was a member of the Modern Folk Quartet, along with Cyrus Faryar, Chip Douglas and Henry Diltz. "Dave slept on our couch. I remember him in the kitchen listening to his portable radio as it played 'A Day in the Life' by the Beatles, which had just been released then. He came to sell his *Colour Guitar* method, but instead he got bitten by the music bug here," Yester told us in March 2011. Tom Guard told us an entry in his father's journal indicated that he had difficulty sleeping "because Phil Ochs would sit up all night talking in the kitchen." Before returning to Australia, Dave sat in as a session musician during recording of Tim Buckley's album *Goodbye and Hello*, which Yester co-produced.

Meanwhile, in Australia, Gretchen planned to return permanently to the United States. "David had spent a lot of time on his *Colour Guitar* theory. It was a deeply intellectual exercise, and he was married to it for years. I think it took way too much of his time, and we stayed in Australia too long. While we were there, Phil Spector came into the music scene with his 'wall of sound,' the Beatles came along with their genius arrangements and multiple-track recording, and everything went from acoustic to amplified. The whole industry was turned on its head, but David wasn't there to take part in it," Gretchen told us. "Whale Beach was a wonderful place to live, with good people and fine weather, and it was a safe place to raise children, but we stayed too long. I had always promised myself I would return to Stanford and finish my degree as soon as Sally started kindergarten, and that's what we did."

In early 1968, the Guard family returned to the San Francisco

Bay Area and settled in Portola Valley, west of Palo Alto. Gretchen resumed her studies at Stanford University, and Dave began teaching individual students using his *Colour Guitar* approach. He also intermittently began performing with impromptu and established singing groups at a club called Chuck's Cellar on El Camino Real in Los Altos, about 10 miles from the location of the Cracked Pot, where the Kingston Trio had formed. "Dave and other musicians and singers, whoever wanted to play, would get together, and perform at Chuck's Cellar. I remember [folksinger] Holly Near performed with him at least once there, and our daughter Catherine sat in and sang with him on several evenings there," said Gretchen, who obtained her bachelor's degree in art from Stanford in 1970. She became a watercolor painter and in her home studio began a freelance graphic design practice.

In 1972, Dave and Gretchen began conducting research for a book about a 2,000-year-old Celtic tale that had first stirred his interest when he was a high school senior. He had read the story, about the Irish heroine Deirdre, at Menlo School after seeing it in an optional reading list. Although Gretchen was unfamiliar with the story, she became intrigued because she had been searching for something to illustrate. After reading the story, they conducted a substantial amount of research, which included visiting several museums in England, Ireland and Scotland, speaking to the curators, and traveling around the parts of Ireland and Scotland where Deirdre had lived. The Guards rewrote the old tale in contemporary English under the title *Deirdre: A Celtic Legend,* and Celestial Arts of Millbrae, California, published it. Ten Speed Press and Tricycle Press later published it, and it remained in print for more than 20 years. Dave subsequently resurrected an ancient Hawaiian story upon which he based another book, titled *Hale Mano: A Legend of Hawaii.*

Through the mid-'70s, Dave performed at clubs throughout the San Francisco Bay Area and Southern California. Then he joined in forming a folk music group with Limeliters founder Alex Hassilev and singer-songwriter Mike Settle, who had been a member of the New Christy Minstrels and Kenny Rogers and the First Edition, and had toured with Mason Williams and with John Stewart's Cumberland Three. The group, known as Hassilev, Settle and Guard, performed in the "Great Folk Revival" concert February 2, 1974, at Nassau Coliseum on Long Island. Other performers on the bill were Dave Van Ronk, Odetta, the Brandywine Singers, Carolyn Hester, the Highwaymen, the Tarriers, Bob Shane and the New Kingston Trio, and comedian David

Steinberg. ABC television broadcast the concert on its *Wide World of Entertainment* program four nights later. Hassilev, Settle and Guard performed together on stage for a few months, but the collaboration ended when the Limeliters' touring schedule resumed.

In 1977 Yester produced some demo recordings for Dave in Cyrus Faryar's studio, which was installed in the five-bedroom ranch house called "the Farm" that Faryar was renting for $150 per month on a 43-acre plot off Barham Boulevard between Hollywood and Burbank. "John Hartford came and played fiddle on the session, with Peter Klimes on guitar, and the result was great," Yester said. (The song on which Hartford and Klimes played was called "Above and Beyond"; Tom Guard liked it so much that he included it on his 2008 CD *Shy River*.) "That recording at Cyrus' studio was a precursor for Dave's eventual solo album that he completed 11 years later," Jerry added. "I went into show business because of the influence of the Kingston Trio. But I became a banjo player because I was mainly drawn to Dave, who was like an icon for all of us in the MFQ."

The Ice House in Pasadena booked Dave for an engagement in June 1977 with the Modern Folk Quartet, which had been headlining there. The MFQ initially appeared as the opening act for Guard's solo show, but soon functioned as Dave's backing band. They were whimsically billed as "Dave Guard and the Handful o' Nuts" for some appearances. MFQ member Henry Diltz relished the opportunity to perform with Guard. "Dave was a wiggy genius. He thought about and approached things way differently from most people," Diltz told us in May 2011. The gig was a reunion as well for MFQ member Chip Douglas, who as a young teenager two decades earlier had performed a couple of tunes backstage after a Kingston Trio performance at the Royal Hawaiian Hotel. Chip was seated in the audience with his own group, the Wilcox Trio, which emulated the Kingston Trio. Nick Reynolds noticed the young musicians dressed in Trio-inspired striped jackets, and invited them to visit backstage after the show. "When we went backstage to meet the Trio, Dave Guard said, 'OK, babies, let's hear it.'" The Wilcox Trio obliged by singing "Molly Dee" and "Corey, Corey." For the Ice House gig in 1977, Dave and the MFQ rehearsed at Cyrus Faryar's place. Dave's set list was a musical mosaic. "It was very eclectic. We'd play a Steeleye Span song. Then a song by Bryan Ferry of Roxy Music," Diltz said. They also rehearsed and performed "Saucy Sailor Boy" and the Kingston Trio favorite "Zombie Jamboree," Chip Douglas recalled. "Dave would drill us on musical parts, because he wanted arrangements a certain way. Performing with him at the Ice House was fun, though," said Douglas, a bass player who also had been a member of the Turtles and producer of recordings for the Monkees. The MFQ-Dave Guard collaborations ended when the Modern Folk Quartet temporarily disbanded in 1978. By then, Dave found contentment increasingly elusive.

"David was a very bright human being. But he had a funny habit of trying to keep people at arm's length. It was hard for him to get really close to people, and he would use his intelligence and his quickness to set up little barriers," Gretchen explained. "There were so many people who loved him, and for all the right reasons. I think this is true for a lot of entertainers: they really want to be loved, but maybe at a distance. Dave had trouble dealing with the banality of day-to-day life. I mean, just doing the ordinary things that we have to do every day in order to be good citizens, good parents, good partners. He was very engaging, when he wanted to be, and he could be pretty remote, too."

By the mid-'70s, the Guards' marriage was coming undone. "I've always been an optimist, but I knew that David and I would not be able to share our future. We separated in 1977 and divorced in 1978. It was difficult as divorces are when children are involved," Gretchen said. "Catherine was in college, Tom was college-bound, and Sally was 15, a junior in high school and living at home with me," said Gretchen, who became an art director for *Sunset* magazine in 1977.

As their divorce proceedings were under way, Dave resuscitated a long-dormant project – the recordings of Hawaiian slack-key guitarist Gabby Pahinui that he had produced in 1961. He had kept the master tapes all those years, and finally persuaded Hula Records of Honolulu to release the double album, titled *Pure Gabby*.

"I think this was one of David's finest efforts," Gretchen told us in March 2011. "He was prescient in recording it in the early '60s, then producing and distributing it many years later. In the meantime, Hawaiians and many other indigenous people had come to value their own cultures. Although Gabby is no longer living, he is an icon of Hawaii's native music. I like to think part of that is because of David."

Dave's long-held fascination with Eastern philosophy and religion, and Chinese medicine, intensified after he met Sarah Scott O'Brien. She was involved with a Hindu ashram – a communal center for meditation and spiritual study – in Oakland. Dave became a follower of Swami Muktananda, adopted a vegetarian diet, became an adherent of Siddha Yoga, and in October 1983 married Sarah. The couple lived modestly in Los Altos, south of San Francisco, before moving in 1984 to South Fallsburg, in the Catskill Mountains of New York, where Dave and Sarah agreed to serve as editors for a Siddha Yoga meditation magazine. As Dave prepared to begin work at the publication, he told a radio interviewer that he was playing mostly Indian music at the time – "thousand-year-old hits," he joked. Dave's interest in contemporary music was revived, however, when his old friend Jerry Yester sent a few tracks from his solo album *Just Like The Big Time... Only Smaller,* which he had begun recording. "Dave came up with the idea of forming a new trio with me and his daughter, Catherine. But I declined because I really wanted to concentrate on finishing my solo album," Yester told us.

"In January of 1986, I moved to New Hampshire with the ambition of making a living once again as an entertainer," Dave wrote in an article he prepared for Allan Shaw's *Popular Folk Music Today* newsletter. "I had spent the previous two years editing a magazine, which had been most satisfying – had even taken me to India – but my ego was nagged by the opinion that there were several lifetime goals remaining unfulfilled: some books, some video projects and some musical offerings. I had done a lot of homework along these lines and was eager to get started – at the same time feeling I'd have to approach matters on contemporary terms rather than trying to get by as a famous, rotting has-been. Nothing against the dear old records, the dear old friends or the dear old days; I just can't get my clock to stop."

Gretchen, meanwhile, had remained in her position at *Sunset* magazine until 1982, when she moved to Idaho to accept a position as editor of *Sun Valley Magazine.* She followed that position with several "mini-careers," including a catering business, teaching art at the Community School in Sun Valley, and devoting six years to establishing public radio in the Wood River Valley of Idaho. She began painting full time in 1990, and two years later moved to Santa Fe, New Mexico, where, as Gretchen Ballard Guard, she has become a prolific oil painter. Her work, which she describes as "representational rather than realistic, with fairly loose brushwork," has been shown in various galleries in Santa Fe and San Francisco. During the past few years she has been concentrating on large-scale commissions.

After Dave had moved to Nashua, New Hampshire, he began appearing on stage with Rick and Ron Shaw, a folk duo who perform as the Shaw Brothers. Identical twins Rick and Ron had been members of the Brandywine Singers before joining the Hillside Singers, who had recorded the 1971 hit "I'd Like To Teach The World To Sing (In Perfect Harmony)." The Shaws had first met Dave in Ipswich, Massachusetts, when he was performing with the Kingston Trio. They strengthened their acquaintance when the Brandywine Singers appeared along with Hassilev, Settle and Guard in the "Great Folk Revival" concert in 1974. "It was quite a lineup, and was a huge success. The Coliseum was packed. Oscar Brand was the MC, and it was a thrill – one of the highlights of our career," Rick Shaw said.

When Rick learned that Dave and Sarah were living in Nashua, he met them for lunch there. Not long after that, Dave and Sarah separated and divorced because Sarah wanted to return to life on the ashram, and Dave was intent on resuming his music career. As

Gathering of performers for Folk Era Records' 1987 "All Along the Merrimac" tour. From left, bass player Bob Smiley is standing alongside White Mountain Singers members Scott Fisher (guitar) and Steve Fiott (banjo). Seated are, from left, Dave Guard, Ron Shaw (wearing vest) and Rick Shaw (in striped shirt holding a guitar). Courtesy of Allan Shaw, Folk Era Records.

MIDI (musical instrument digital interface) technology emerged, Dave studied techniques with a teacher named Kevin Garant and set to work composing and digitizing material for a solo album. Mastering MIDI technology to Dave's satisfaction turned into an 18-month endeavor. When Dave's apartment lease ended, he accepted the invitation of Rick Shaw and his wife at the time, Ingrid, to move into an apartment above a barn at their Melody Pond Farm in Rollinsford, New Hampshire, where Ingrid trained thoroughbred horses. Guard became captivated by the horses, and developed a close relationship with the Shaws.

Preparatory for his re-entry into music, Dave journeyed to Sweden to spend the better part of a year studying with a guitar maestro he admired. When he returned to Rollinsford he began feeling fatigued, then increasingly ill over a period of months. Unsure of what was wrong, he tried for nearly a year and a half to treat himself with Chinese herbal teas. Observing that his condition was worsening, his children, Sally, Catherine and Tom, grew concerned and urged him to consult a doctor. In 1988 he relented and visited a physician, who prescribed tests that confirmed that Dave had developed non-Hodgkin's lymphoma – cancer of the lymphatic system. Dave began treatment, and responded well; the cancer went into remission.

Elated, Dave resumed concentration on his music. "In the early stage of his illness he spent a lot of time in the apartment rehearsing the banjo. He had such a great style," Rick Shaw told us in April 2011. Dave completed work on his new album, titled *Up and In* – a counterpoint to "down and out" that reflected his lifelong love of word-play. He created his own label, Ball Bearing Records, and – with Folk Era Records serving as distributor – he released the album in August 1988. And he began dabbling in video production. Working with Rick Shaw's wife, Ingrid Gsottschneider Shaw, an equestrian physical trainer, Dave produced a videotape called *The Workout for Equestrians* to help riders improve their balance, flexibility and stamina.

Allan Shaw, Folk Era's president, had known Dave since meeting him at the "Kingston Trio and Friends Reunion" in 1981. "I came to know him personally during the next decade as he attempted to re-enter the world he'd largely put behind him for the better part of the past two decades. Intentionally or otherwise, he kept me off-guard, as he did so many others, with his obfuscating remarks that frequently left me confused both as to what he said as well as what he meant. I can understand this bothering some folks; I loved it since it was so *Dave*," Allan said. "He was also stubborn and non-compromising, as he had been when he left the Trio. I questioned his intent to take his MIDI-guitar on the second reunion tour – which was not to be – and urged him to do what Trio fans wanted to hear. He responded, 'That's no longer me, and it's not what I do anymore. And I'm not sure that I could, even if I wanted to.'"

The return of Nick Reynolds to the Kingston Trio in 1988 after a 21-year absence prompted the possibility of a reunion of the original Trio. In 1990 Nick and Bob began earnestly discussing a reunion tour with Dave. They set their sights on the summer of 1991, but it was cast in doubt when Dave suffered a medical setback in October 1990. A CAT scan revealed that his cancer had returned. He began a course of oral chemotherapy, but his condition worsened. Dave was hospitalized and given a more potent mixture of chemotherapy drugs. Numerous concerned friends, including Lou Gottlieb, Alex Hassilev, Bob Shane and John Stewart, visited him. "Dad had a strong heart, but said the oral chemo left him feeling like he'd been beaten up. He was just a saint about not complaining, and he managed to maintain a very strong, positive attitude," said Tom, who saw his father for the last time in early January 1991. "My wife and I visited him in the hospital, and we knew that probably was it, because after being in remission he wasn't doing well. He was a great father in that he was always teaching and showing us new things. He disliked stagnant, predictable patterns. He invented games for us to play, read to us, and encouraged us to think about 'advancing the plot,' as he would say in reference to discovering things in life."

Rick and Ingrid Shaw took care of Dave as the disease continued to spread. "He had been so vibrant, witty, intellectual and genuinely humorous. I must say he was a very brave person. He never complained," Rick said. Dave slipped into a coma, and his daughter Sally and Ingrid Shaw were with him in the apartment over the barn when he died the evening of March 22, 1991, at the age of 56. "His body was cremated, and Sally brought his ashes in her backpack from New Hampshire to Honolulu, where a memorial service was held at Punahou Chapel," Gretchen said. "After the ceremony we left his ashes and our leis at Makapu'u Point, his favorite body-surfing beach. All of his family were there, along with a few old friends, including Cyrus Faryar and Joan Brownlee, who had been a neighbor in Waikiki when Dave was a teenager." Ten years later, in July 2001, Sally also died of non-Hodgkin's lymphoma; she was 38 years of age.

"The last time I spoke to Dave was probably a month before he died," Jerry Yester recalled. "I believe if he had lived, we would have worked together again."

In 2007, Silverwolf Records (www.silverwolfmusic.com) of West-minster, Vermont, released *Up and In,* which is available as a single CD or in a package paired with the 2004 Kingston Trio release *Live at the Crazy Horse.*

Tom Guard, who plays guitar and is a music instructor in Attleboro Falls, Massachusetts, has begun work on a Flash version of *Colour Guitar* (www.tomguard.com/colour-guit.html). "This computer version of what was initially an interactive tool will offer the advantage of self-contained templates. I think Dad would love to see his revolutionary idea manifested in this capacity. By passing away in the early '90s he just missed some profound advances in technology, but I feel it was minds like his that inspired them," Tom told us in March 2011.

"I miss him immensely. He'll always be a brother to me," Nick Reynolds wrote about Dave in a tribute message published in the spring 1991 issue of *Popular Folk Music Today.* "He had one of the sharpest minds I met in my life, but sometimes it seemed that he had the curse of being smarter than was necessary. I mean that as a positive statement about him – when you talked to Dave, his mind worked so fast that his thoughts were way ahead of his words so you wouldn't understand him unless you knew him real well, which I did."

Epilogue: Nick Reynolds

Guitarist, percussionist (conga and bongos) and singer

July 27, 1933 – October 1, 2008

Nick Reynolds thought he always would be a member of the Kingston Trio, and he never considered any other pursuit until John Stewart announced his intention to leave the group. That's when Nick began thinking about life after the Kingston Trio. "We had satisfied Capitol Records by going out and singing and shaking our asses on stage, but I was getting pretty burned out at that time by all of the traveling. I had a wife and a 6-year-old son, Josh, and I hardly ever saw them. We talked to our accountants and they told us that we could financially afford to quit singing," Nick told us in August 1999. "So we worked real hard for one more year, playing everything we could get, to build up a little capital stock."

Nick had met his first wife, Joan Harris (pronounced ha-reece), in San Francisco when she was working as a comedian at a club near the hungry i. She later became Frank Werber's assistant. After mar-

Nick Reynolods embraces his wife, Leslie, at his last Kingston Trio concert appearance, December 2, 1999, in Scottsdale, Arizona. Photo by Nick's cousin Tom Keck.

rying in September 1958, Nick and Joan moved into a houseboat anchored at the San Francisco Bay waterfront town of Sausalito. Nick took up water skiing, became a sports car racing enthusiast, a skilled photographer and developed expertise in skeet shooting, in which he won numerous awards. The couple, who later moved into a conventional home in Sausalito after their houseboat sank, celebrated the birth of their son, Joshua, on March 31, 1960.

After the Kingston Trio played its last performance in June 1967, Nick and Joan decided to take a month-long vacation with Josh. To give themselves time and space to figure out what they'd do next, they drove 430 miles north from San Francisco to the southern Oregon coastal village of Port Orford, an isolated, rural area populated primarily by loggers, farmers and fishermen. Nick had developed a strong interest in restoring classic cars and building racing cars, and had intended to immerse himself in that field upon their return from vacation. The Reynolds family found a rustic cabin in a canyon on Elk River Road, at the fringes of the Siskiyou National Forest. The cabin had only the bare essentials, but they fell in love with the land and decided to stay. For the next 10 years, the family lived in the cabin, which they leased for $100 per month. "We had no TV, no phone and no radio for 10 years because we couldn't get those services in the canyon," Nick said.

The family paid their meager expenses from savings and the salary that Nick continued to draw from Kingston Trio Inc., as he busied himself with homesteading chores. "I cleaned up the place. I learned how to chop wood, I learned how to fish. The Elk River was full of salmon and steelhead. And no fishermen were around other than a couple of neighbors of mine who I became good friends with," he said. The rural isolation appealed much more to Nick than it did to Joan, however, and the couple divorced.

In 1977 Nick purchased the neighboring ranch, and he became a cattle rancher. "It was a beautiful ranch with the river running right through it, and it was an ideal place to bring up a kid. Josh went to school there and played in Little League. I was umpiring Little League and coaching the All Star team. I'd travel to San Francisco for business meetings every now and then, but I pretty much put it all behind me. I did all of the ranch work myself. I had help only during the haying season. I'd cut and bale all the hay, and I'd hire some high school kids to help me put it in the barn," Nick said. He also operated the Star, the only movie theater in Port Orford.

After building a nice house on the ranch property, Nick met a woman named Linda Peacock. They fell in love and married. Nick adopted Linda's daughter Jenni (who was born in September 1973). Together, Linda and Nick had a daughter of their own, Annie, who with the aid of a midwife was born on the ranch in 1978. Three years later, they had a son, Johnny Pike Reynolds.

After nearly 17 years away from the music business, Nick – whom his Kingston Trio pals affectionately called "Budgie" because he was the shortest among them – dusted off his tenor guitar in 1983 upon the urging of John Stewart. Together, Nick, John and Lindsey Buckingham of Fleetwood Mac recorded an album called *Revenge of the Budgie,* which unfortunately did not succeed commercially. But that alerted Bob Shane and George Grove, then doing Kingston Trio dates with Roger Gambill, that Nick's interest in music had been aroused once more. They drove to the ranch to visit Nick, but nothing immediately developed.

In 1987, Nick and Linda sold the ranch and moved to Coronado, near San Diego. They relocated for the sake of the children. "The schools up in Oregon were good, but our kids were getting old enough that they needed to have a little more input. For example," Nick explained, "my daughters had never seen a person of color, other than on TV. We did have TV in the new house, although we didn't have cable. We got just a couple of channels in grainy black and white. Bill Cosby and his TV family were the only black people our daughters had seen in their lives. We wanted them to have far more exposure than they were getting."

The move to Coronado took Nick back home. Nicholas Wells Reynolds was born in Mercy Hospital in San Diego on July 27, 1933, and grew up in Coronado, which is situated on a peninsula directly across San Diego Bay from the city of San Diego. Nick was the son of Jane Keck and Stewart Reynolds. Nick's father was a Navy captain who had served on a mine tender during World War I and was assigned duty aboard an oil tanker in the North Atlantic during World War II. He was then placed in charge of a big troop transport vessel that took part in the invasions of North Africa and Normandy, France, and participated in operations at Okinawa. Stewart Reynolds, who also was an accomplished guitarist, taught Nick and his older sisters Jane and Barbara to play ukulele. When Nick was 6 years old, his father bought him his first instrument, a little wooden Martin ukulele. "We would sit around and sing almost every night that he was home. We learned our harmony from our daddy, who had perfect pitch. My sisters and I would harmonize and my dad would sing bass. My

145

sisters have perfect pitch. I wish I could say the same for myself," Nick laughed. "We would sing barbershop and calypso and Hawaiian songs and Burl Ives tunes when I was growing up. My sisters and I still have the ukuleles that our father bought for us and, when we get together, we still sing old Andrews Sisters songs and Trio songs and other things."

Nick never took any formal ukulele or guitar lessons, nor did he ever learn to read music. Despite that fact, athletic Nick – whose pursuits included skin-diving, tennis and basketball – played tuba in the Coronado High School marching band. "I was the smallest guy in the band, but I was strong at the time. I just liked the thing," Nick shrugged.

After graduation from Coronado High School in 1951, Nick enrolled at the University of Arizona in Tucson. There he found a job at a hardware store, became a Phi Delta Theta, and ran the fraternity's glee club. His friends there included Travis Edmonson (who later joined the Gateway Singers and then formed the Bud and Travis duo with Bud Dashiell). But Nick never really adjusted to what he regarded as the elitism of fraternity life, and after completing two years of course work he returned to the San Diego area. There he remained for about six months, working as a soda jerk at a Coronado drive-in restaurant. "That was a cool job," Nick reminisced. "My best friend, who married my sister, was the cook, and another friend was the waiter at night. We had a great time." Nick kept his scholastic skills in tune with a couple of summer school classes at San Diego State College. Then he made a decision that would help lead to the formation of the Kingston Trio: in early 1954 he enrolled at Menlo Business College in Menlo Park, which then accepted only male students (but subsequently became a coeducational institution). Menlo was about two miles from Stanford University on the peninsula south of San Francisco.

At the time, Nick was planning to go into the restaurant and hotel business with a friend whose family owned a hotel in Coronado. On his first day at Menlo, Nick met Bob Shane. "I walked into my accounting lab and there was this kid in the back of the room sound asleep with his head on his books, and I said to myself, 'I gotta meet this guy.' After class we talked, he got his guitar and I got my bongo drums, and then we went to the local beer joint and began playing," Nick recalled. "I knew a lot of Hawaiian songs through my dad, and Bobby taught me a lot more. Bob used to get together with Dave, who was going to school at Stanford, so the three of us got together and I became their rhythm, playing bongos and singing with them." By the time Nick graduated in 1957 with a bachelor's degree in business administration, the popularity of Dave Guard and the Calypsonians was growing, and the course was set for the establishment of the Kingston Trio.

Throughout the height of their renown, the Trio members were labeled trend-setters, but Nick dismissed any notion that they tried to influence fashion in any particular way. "During those years when our schedule was so hectic between performances, rehearsals and recording sessions, we had no time to think about being trendsetters," he said.

After Nick and his wife Linda relocated from their ranch in Oregon to Coronado in 1987, they separated and eventually divorced. Fulfilling his original youthful intention of going into the restaurant business, Nick was at Bula's Pub & Eatery on Orange Avenue in Coronado in 1988, tending bar and managing the small restaurant for the fun of it, when Bob Shane and George Grove walked in and asked Reynolds to join them. "I got my guitar and we sat around and sang for three hours. I was back on the road with the Kingston Trio in two weeks," Nick grinned. "It worked out well for me because Bobby then owned the Kingston Trio name, but Frank and I still own the corporation. We've sold most of the real estate properties now, but we get all of the recording royalties," Nick told us. "Bobby became the group's leader and I was paid a percentage. I knew exactly what I was going to get. I had no responsibility; I just brought my guitar and got on the plane, sang the songs, and had a great time. The reaction from the audiences when I came back in the group was very rewarding. The basic sound of the Kingston Trio is really Bobby and me." In contrast to the college gymnasiums and large auditoriums the KT played during their peak popularity, Nick favored the smaller rooms in which they performed after he rejoined them. "We played a lot of performing arts cen-

Nick Reynolds in Sacramento before a performance on August 28, 1999. Photo by Amanda Domingues.

147

ters, which are really nice and have great sound, and we did quite a few pop concerts with symphony orchestras. We were making good money in the early days because we worked all of the time, but during the 1990s we were able to make twice the amount of money," he told us.

In 1994 Nick married Leslie Yerger, who, like himself, had a father in the Navy. Their families were close friends, and Nick and Leslie had known each other most of their lives. "After my wife and I were separated, Leslie and I got together and fell madly in love. Finally I met someone who could put up with me," Nick said, breaking into laughter. When Nick and Leslie became reacquainted, she was a vice president at San Diego State University in charge of fund raising. "It was very stressful for her, and I talked her into retiring."

Nick had undergone three hip replacement and back surgeries due to arthritis beginning in 1984. Touring and air travel became too arduous for him, and he reluctantly stepped down from the stage again at the end of 1999. "I'm at a point where I'd like to enjoy life without having to run around the country and chase a buck. I've done fairly well, and I don't have to worry about it too much," Nick told us.

Nick became active in community activities, including performing volunteer work for the Chula Vista Nature Center and serving on the board of directors for the Friends of San Diego Wildlife Refuge. He was sidelined in 2002 by a stroke that affected his speech, but he managed to recover. Additional health problems began to take their toll on Nick, who contracted acute respiratory disease syndrome, a complication of a ruptured diverticulum, that proved far more damaging than the stroke. He died in his beloved San Diego at age 75 of causes related to the disease after being removed from life support on October 1, 2008.

Leslie still struggles with the emotional pain of her loss of Nick. "There is so very much to be said, and known, about this beautiful person that I could spend the rest of my days trying and still not capture his essence," Leslie told us in April 2011. "Having said that, I am so grateful to you for honoring the Kingston Trio."

In 1999, we had asked Nick what he regarded as a defining characteristic about himself. "I'm a pretty compassionate guy. Maybe too much so," he reflected after a pause. He didn't hesitate in identifying what he had learned from life: "Too much fun is not enough!" he answered, then broke into hearty laughter.

Epilogue: John Stewart

Guitarist, banjoist and singer

September 5, 1939 – January 19, 2008

Among the members of the Kingston Trio, John Stewart
always stood apart. Scrutinizing the world through dark,
deeply set eyes, the tousle-haired musician was a soloist among a
group. A loner among his gregarious fellow performers. A champion
of America when some people viewed patriotism as unfashionable.
A songwriter who avoided the "hindrance" of learning to read music.
A self-described "oddball" who considered himself more of a reporter
than a songwriter and acknowledged that he bewildered even himself.
But Stewart also was an accomplished songwriter whose composition
skills first brought him to the attention of the Kingston Trio, and
whose songs include one that became a No. 1 gold-certified record
for the Monkees. He had been in the company of presidents and
astronauts, and his works have been likened to musical interpretations
of the spirit of John Steinbeck. And he and his wife Buffy Ford became
for a time one of the highest profile duos in folk music.

Despite the grueling nature of concert touring, John Coburn Stewart held a deep fondness for the road. That affection, which colored

John Stewart in Coronado, California, on January 17, 2008, two days before his
death. Photo by Buffy Ford Stewart.

149

his songs and cast him in the role of documentary troubadour, has its origins in his childhood, when he spent many days on the road traveling with his father, John Smith Stewart. The senior Stewart was a horse trainer who worked the Southern California racetrack circuit. John was born in San Diego on September 5, 1939, but his family moved frequently during his childhood years as his father pursued work. "My dad was on the road on the day I was born," John told us in January 2000.

John spent much of his childhood years in Pasadena and in Pomona, among the eastern portions of the sprawling Los Angeles metropolitan area. While his mother, Alice, stayed at home to look after his brother and two sisters, young John tagged along with his father from one racetrack to the next – Santa Anita Park, Hollywood Park, Bay Meadows, Del Mar Thoroughbred Club – training trotters and show horses. "As far back as I can remember, I was on the road and working on the track," John recalled. Even though his father showed him the ropes, John wasn't interested in that line of work – "especially," he said, "because the chores that I was assigned were deep in the bowels of the no-fun category."

John got an early taste of entertaining when he and his best friend in school, George Yanok, created a comedy act, for which they won a prize in a local talent show. John didn't give music much thought until he was about 16, when he first heard Elvis Presley. After teaching himself to play guitar and banjo, he formed his own group: Johnny Stewart and the Furies. For a while, John's interest turned to cartooning, and his heroes were "Dennis the Menace" cartoonist Hank Ketcham, "Woody Woodpecker" creator Walter Lantz, "Dick Tracy" artist Chester Gould and the wacky cartoonists at *Mad* magazine. But during his senior year at Pomona Catholic High School, something new and fresh riveted him to music for good. "I heard the Kingston Trio, and that just spun me around," he said.

After graduation from high school, he enrolled at Mt. San Antonio Junior College in Pomona, and his interest in American history and the Civil War – then approaching its centennial – compelled him to write songs about that period. When the Kingston Trio appeared at the Coconut Grove in Los Angeles, John boldly knocked on their stage door and persuaded the Trio to listen to his compositions. After encouraging him to hone his craft by writing more music, the Trio eventually did record two of John's songs: "Molly Dee," the opening track on the *Here We Go Again* album, released in October 1959; and "Green Grasses," the flip side of "Coo Coo-U," which charted as a single that December.

When his first royalty checks arrived in the mail after he had completed a year and a half of college, John quit school and moved north to San Jose, where he roomed with a high school friend and nine other guys in a house near Santa Clara University. John slept on a mattress on the floor and began playing songs with John Montgomery, a friend from Mt. San Antonio College. They landed a gig at the Kerosene Club in San Jose, opening for the Smothers Brothers. Then Montgomery and Stewart were hired for a few Tuesday night sets at the hungry i, the San Francisco nightclub that was known for exposing talented young performers. All the while, Stewart maintained contact with the Trio and kept sending them songs. Before long, the Trio's manager, Frank Werber, called Stewart to tell him that Roulette Records in New York was looking for a folk group, and asked Stewart if he could assemble one. John called upon his high school choir teacher, Gil Robbins, who often drove to San Francisco to play bass in clubs. Gil was the father of actor-director Tim Robbins, for whom John Stewart used to babysit. (Gil later became a member of the Highwaymen folk music group.) With only three days' notice to fly to New York, Robbins agreed to join Stewart and Montgomery. They decided to call themselves the Cumberland Three, and rehearsed on the airline flight. They auditioned and signed with Roulette Records, which promptly sent them into the studio to record a couple of albums and then sent them out on the road with comedian Shelly Berman for a year. On June 8, 1960, shortly before he headed out on the road, John married his high school sweetheart, Julia Koehler.

The Cumberland Three performed traditional folk songs along with contemporary compositions by John Stewart and Bob Gibson and whimsical material by Shel Silverstein. Other performers, including the Limeliters folk group and pop singer Jimmie Rodgers, began recording Stewart's songs. The Cumberland Three recorded a third album, but times were lean. "We spent a year starving in New York, collecting bottles to make phone calls and living on pancakes," John said. The band broke up, but within a few days he learned about the departure of Dave Guard from the Kingston Trio. "I remember calling Nick Reynolds and saying, 'Here I am, I'm your man.' Finally they flew me out to Sausalito to audition for the group, and my wife was pregnant at the time," recalled John. The audition took place in Bob Shane's den, and John said the experience was excruciating because so much was riding on it for him. "After a couple of days had gone by the Trio called and said, 'You've got the gig.'"

151

After having pursued the Kingston Trio for three years, John Stewart had become one of them. "It was a strange feeling. I was sort of numb at first," Stewart said. "I was a huge fan of Dave Guard's. He was my hero. So when I went to Frank Werber's house and we had our striped shirts for our first photo sessions, I caught a reflection in the big windows of his patio around the pool. There was me in the shirt and it just didn't seem right. Where was Dave? It was very surreal. But as soon as we started singing and got down to business, the dream became real."

Still, John believed he never fully acclimated – partly attributable, perhaps, to the fact that he was salaried rather than a financial partner in the Trio's corporate structure. "I was a duck in the wrong bathtub with the Trio because these were very fun loving, gregarious guys, and I was really a loner with a lot of dark corners," Stewart confided to us. "Playing music was a private thing I did in my room, and that's where the songs were born. There I was with these guys just having nothing but fun, and I felt as I usually did, the alien. I wrote about things that were from a sensitive point of view. There was no reason that I should have been in the Kingston Trio. There were guys with far more ability, but I think the reason I got in was I was good on stage, I was good at doing the lines between the songs, and I wrote songs."

Despite his self-doubts, Stewart did find his place with the Trio. He began feeling comfortable not only as a performer, but also in his personal life. In February 1962, he and Julia had a son, John Mikael, and then a year and a half later a second son, Jeremy. A daughter, Amy, followed. "After we recorded the *New Frontier* album, I gave a copy to JFK at the White House," Stewart told us. John F. Kennedy removed the PT boat pin from his tie and gave it to Stewart, who had written the title track, "The New Frontier," in tribute to the president's ambitious social program of that name.

Stewart enumerated other magical moments that for him that stood out in sharp focus against the blur of his six whirlwind years with the Kingston Trio. "The first gig at the Hollywood Bowl, with two nights sold out. Singing 'Where Have All The Flowers Gone' on the lawn outside the White House in front of [President] Lyndon Johnson, with the Washington Memorial shining across the Ellipse. Getting to know Scott Carpenter and John Glenn. Getting to know Bobby Kennedy and campaigning with him. Recording at Capitol Records. Getting to tour in every state except Alaska. Having more fun than a human being should be allowed. Getting to know the

Beach Boys and Judy Collins. The gigs at the hungry i. Rehearsing at Nick's on November 22 when John Kennedy was shot. Going on the Selma civil rights march."

The day Kennedy was assassinated, Stewart's shock and sadness motivated him to write "Song For a Friend." The day after Kennedy's funeral, the Kingston Trio recorded that memorial song for their album *Time To Think*, which Capitol Records released in December 1963. John, who began developing a strong social conscience during those years, stood on the courthouse steps in Montgomery, Alabama, in March 1965 with Martin Luther King Jr., Harry Belafonte, Peter Paul and Mary, Odetta and other public figures. The divisive Vietnam War was raging and strong opposition to the Johnson administration's military policies was mounting when the Trio performed "Where Have All the Flowers Gone" as part of their set at the White House. "You could have cut the air with a knife. A silence came over the crowd and we all had chills as we sang it. There was no doubt that Johnson heard the lyrics," Stewart said.

But the KT had many more joyous times than somber moments. "The recording sessions all had the ambience of a fraternity house," John reminisced. Nick was always wisecracking. It was nothing but fun. But when we got down to work it was really serious. We sat next to each other with three vocal mikes and three instrument mikes and were very attentive to detail because we really wanted to get it right. There was a six-pack of beer, but no one wanted to get drunk." John said the selections to record were always chosen democratically. "All of us had a say in the collective consciousness of the group. I'd bring in new songs that I'd written, and Nick and Bob would write dirty verses to them, and then we would all decide whether or not to do them."

The end of Stewart's time with the Kingston Trio also marked the end of his eight-year marriage to Julia, whom he divorced in 1968. "I had married the prettiest girl in high school, but I was on the road 280 days a year. Julia and I managed to have three kids, which is the greatest thing that happened. After I quit the Trio and was home all the time, it became painfully obvious that there never was a marriage," John said quietly. "She never liked my songs. I remember walking in the day I wrote 'Daydream Believer' and I played it for her and she said, 'Oh. Uh-huh, that's nice,'" John recalled. (Stewart subsequently performed an audition of the song for the Monkees' producer, Chip Douglas, who recorded the tune on a portable cassette machine and brought it to Colgems records, the Monkees' label. The Monkees' recording of 'Daydream Believer' earned RIAA gold record certification and held the No. 1 spot on the *Billboard* Hot 100 in late 1967, and Anne Murray's version became a top-20 hit in early 1980.) "The marriage was the result of my Catholic high school upbringing. My mother's an Irish Catholic and taught me you just didn't go screwing around. So what do you do when you're 19 and terminally horny? You get married. But as soon as I met Buffy, it was obvious that my marriage [to Julia] wasn't going to last," John said.

John met and united with Buffy Ford after a failed attempt to form a group with Henry Diltz, who was a member of the Modern Folk Quartet. When John left the Trio he decided to form a group to showcase his songs. "Even though I wanted to be a singer-songwriter, I didn't feel that I was a good enough singer and there was just enough cowardice there that I thought a group that I owned, a group with my very American point of view, could do my songs," John said. He envisioned a group that included female members, explaining that he longed for "the color of a girl's voice" after performing with only males for so long. "The songs I was writing, these American songs that were like plays, just cried for a female character." But after auditioning female singers from all over the country, John and Henry couldn't come to agreement. "Henry is one of the best rock photographers ever and one of my dearest friends, but it just wasn't working. He was committed to too many things."

Diltz recalled that John was more driven at the time than he was. "John was so serious, and I wanted to have fun," said Henry, remembering a gag he played that John didn't find funny. "I pretended I was going to give his guitar a hotfoot. I slid a match in underneath the strings, and then faked lighting another match. John was alarmed and jumped back. But I wasn't really going to light his guitar," Henry laughed. "John was a dear friend of mine, and remained so for as long as he lived."

Right after John decided he would form a duo with someone else, he met Buffy, who was singing in a theater in Fairfax, California, 10 miles from his Marin County home. Buffy was at the time with the Young Americans, a large ensemble that toured with Johnny Mathis. She was being courted by Jefferson Airplane, before Grace Slick joined. John asked Buffy if she would like to sing with him. "We didn't know how we would sound together, but the first song we tried, called 'Cody,' was perfect from the first note. She really had this great honest, innocent quality that was like the songs I was writing." John fell not only for Buffy's voice, but also for her heart. They would marry in 1975. Their wedding guests included astronaut John Glenn, who along with fellow astronaut Scott Carpenter had become friends of Stewart. Together John Stewart and Buffy Ford played the Troubadour, a premier folk club in Los Angeles. Working with Voyle Gilmore, who had produced the Kingston Trio's albums, John and Buffy recorded a critically acclaimed album called *Signals Through the Glass* for Capitol Records in 1968. "It sold about nine copies. Language records sold more than that one," John said sardonically.

In the spring of 1968, John and Buffy became involved with U.S. Senator Robert Kennedy's campaign for the Democratic presidential nomination. "While we were recording *Signals Through the Glass,* Bobby Kennedy called and asked us to be his campaign troubadours to warm up the crowd," John explained. He and Buffy agreed and went on the campaign trail to perform songs on stage before Kennedy took to the podium. Kennedy's assassination the night he won the California primary in June devastated Stewart. "At that point I was wondering what to do, when Nick Venet, an old friend who was a producer and A&R man at Capitol said, 'Let me hear your songs.' So I went in and played him what I was writing and he said, 'You've got to do this as a solo, and we're going to Nashville.'"

The resulting landmark album, *California Bloodlines,* earned laudatory reviews after its release in May 1969 and sold well. John's friend Henry Diltz shot the back cover photo of John standing alongside the boards of a red barn. Stewart wrote all 12 tracks for the album, which included "Never Goin' Back," released as a single by the Lovin' Spoonful in the summer of 1968; the episodic "Mother Country," celebrating the triumphs of the pioneering folk who helped build America, exemplified by an account of the last horseback ride of an aging captain of industry named E.A. Stuart, who was going blind; and "July, You're A Woman," a road song with references to the San Joaquin Valley traversed by the old U.S. 99. "I rode along 99 many times with my dad when I was a kid. Now I always drive Interstate 5, but about a year ago Buffy and I decided to take 99. The memories that brought back! You know, it's so Steinbeck," Stewart reminisced, referring to the role of the old highway in the migration of Dust Bowl refugees to the San Joaquin and Salinas valleys. "E.A. Stuart was the owner of Carnation Milk. My father worked for him as a horse trainer, and was there the day he rode that horse," John said. "You see, I've always considered myself more of a reporter than a songwriter, and that song was just a documentary." To promote the album, John went on a nationwide tour with a backup band composed of Henry Diltz on banjo, Chip Douglas on bass and preeminent session drummer Russ Kunkel.

155

Capitol also released a couple of singles, including one in August 1969 called "Armstrong," a song in tribute to the first step by astronaut Neil Armstrong on the surface of the moon. Some radio programmers, music reviewers and audiences misunderstood the intent of the song, perceiving it as a sarcastic condemnation of the American space program in the face of continuing poverty and racial strife. Stewart, however, said he wrote no sarcasm into the lyrics. "I wrote that song while watching them land on the moon. People just missed the point, which was that in spite of hunger and racial hatred, we were all one, for one moment, watching one of us walking on the moon," John explained. But his astronaut friends understood his motivations. "The astronauts aboard Apollo 13 [in April 1970] played Kingston Trio music in space, until serious mechanical problems forced an end to their mission," Buffy said.

True to his goals, Stewart remained a productive solo singer-song-writer on the strength of *California Bloodlines*. He followed that with a 1970 album called *Willard*, which Peter Asher produced right after he finished *Sweet Baby James* with James Taylor. The performers on *Willard* included Taylor as well as Carole King, who contributed to the album just before the release of her enormously popular *Tapestry* album. Unfortunately, the sales of *Willard* were disappointing, and Stewart jumped to Warner Bros. when an executive at that label expressed interest in him. He recorded two albums for Warner – *Lonesome Picker Rides Again* in the fall of 1971 and *Sunstorm* in the spring of 1972 – but both flopped. Poor promotion by the record company? "No. They just weren't very good albums," Stewart said candidly. "I'd lost my focus."

When John felt ready in early 1973, he signed with RCA Victor and went back to Nashville to record an album called *Cannons in the Rain*, produced by Fred Carter Jr., the session guitarist on Simon and Garfunkel's *Bridge Over Troubled Water* album. Buffy sang back-up vocals on that album, as she did on most of his others. *Cannons* was a stunningly good album, but didn't yield any hit singles. Despite the lagging sales of recordings, Stewart did well on the concert circuit. "That paid the rent and helped build the fan base," he said. Stewart followed that RCA album with another in 1974 called the *Phoenix Concerts*, recorded during a two-night stand in Phoenix's symphony hall. Once again, the critics loved it, but it didn't do well enough in sales, and neither did a follow-up album, *Wingless Angels*, released in April 1975. "After that I left RCA because I owed them more money in production costs than I made for them in sales."

Stewart took a respite from recording after he married Buffy, with whom he subsequently had another son, Luke. John said he knew what he needed to do when he signed with RSO Records in 1977. He achieved moderately good sales with his first outing, an album called *Fire in the Wind*. John said that RSO executive Al Cory, an old friend of his from the Capitol Records days, spoke frankly to him. "Al told me, 'you know it's the damndest thing, your albums sell 50,000 and then stop. That's the fan base. If you don't have a hit, I've gotta boot you off the label.' So I had my orders." With his next recording, Stewart struck gold with a top-10 album titled *Bombs Away Dream Babies* in 1979, on which Stevie Nicks and Lindsey Buckingham of Fleetwood Mac performed. It turned out that since his youth, Buckingham had been a fan of the Kingston Trio and had studied their guitar licks. Stewart, meanwhile, had admired Fleetwood Mac and Buckingham's artistry in particular. They quickly developed a close friendship. "Gold," a song from that album released as a single, hit the national charts in May 1979 and rose to No. 5. The album also yielded another top-30 single, "Midnight Wind." Stewart recorded one more album for RSO, *Dream Babies Go Hollywood* in 1980, before the expiration of his contract.

Unable to land a deal with another label, Stewart turned to new technology. "I started making my own records for my fan base, and collecting names and addresses. That's what I've been doing with the exception of a few excursions with labels," John told us in January 2000. Albums he issued following his departure from RSO have included the 1987 Cypress Records release *Punch the Big Guy*, of which John was particularly proud and which reviewers applauded. After the demise of Cypress in 1990, Shanachie Records reissued *Punch the Big Guy*. Rosanne Cash had a hit with "Runaway Train," one of John's compositions from the album. Stewart operated a label, called Homecoming, in partnership with bass player Dave Batti, with whom he began collaborating in 1984. "The studio is here in my house, and the office is Dave's den in Reseda, in Southern California. Labels come and go, but we won't go away," John promised. One Homecoming release was *Deep In The Neon – Live at McCabe's* in 1991. The following year, Shanachie released an album titled *Bullets in the Hour Glass*, for which Henry Diltz shot the cover photo.

In 1983, shortly before starting Homecoming Records, John had teamed with Nick Reynolds, Lindsey Buckingham and Gary Busey to record a seven-song mini-LP titled *Revenge of the Budgie*. It was designated a Nick Reynolds and John Stewart album, but Nick's vocals were largely omitted in the mixing process – as they also were on an early Homecoming 10-song cassette-only release, *The Trio Years*, which consisted of John's compositions that the Kingston Trio performed while John was a member. Ten years later, in 1993, Folk Era Records combined these on a CD titled *Chilly Winds*. The cover art for the CD was a watercolor sketch that John had made of the Trio of Nick, Bob and John. In October 1994, John performed at a club called the Turf Inn in Dalry, Scotland, and the gig, backed by the Scottish band Lies Damn Lies was recorded and released on a Folk Era CD titled *Bandera*. Buffy accompanied John on the trip and sang with him during another night at the Scottish club, and the performance was recorded for a 1996 Folk Era release titled *Live At The Turf Inn, Scotland* – the first John Stewart-Buffy Ford collaboration in nearly three decades. Four Buffy Ford solos were included among the 19 songs on the album. John also established another label, Neon Dreams Music, on which to record and release his solo recordings.

John wrote several books, which Crow Press published in the early 1990s. They included *Write From the Heart*, a handbook for songwriters; *American Sketches*, containing his artwork and lyrics of some of his songs; *Stories Behind the Songs, Volume 1*, explaining the symbolism in songs he wrote for his albums *Signals Through the Glass* and *California Bloodlines;* and *Stories Behind the Songs, Volume 2*, exploring the lyrics of songs on his *Willard* and *The Lonesome Picker Rides Again* albums.

With the notion of establishing a folk band, John and Buffy with other musicians signed a deal in 1997 with Appleseed Recordings, an independent label, and recorded *Darwin's Army*, an album of traditional folk songs played on acoustic instruments backed with drums – to give it a "rock and roll ethic," as Stewart called it. "It was a *killer* album, but the label absolutely dropped the ball. There was no promotion," Stewart said in exasperation. "So that was a huge disappointment."

At about that time, Buffy learned that she had a meningioma, a non-cancerous but damaging brain tumor, and underwent the first of several surgical procedures. The tumor apparently had been growing for 10 years before it was discovered. "Every doctor she went to thought she had a sinus infection because she had headaches in the sinus area. She was losing her hearing and getting eye twitches. One doctor finally said she needed an MRI scan, and there it was," John said. The tumor was in the portion of the brain that controls motor functions of the face as well as vision and hearing functions. Buffy said that she and John found only two doctors in the United States who had sufficient expertise at the time to operate on it.

"My doctors said that if the tumor had not been discovered, I would have been dead in two months," Buffy told us. The surgery caused paralysis on the left side of her face, and impeded her ability to walk. "Rehabilitation was very hard, but through faith, prayer and love I recovered." The following year a second benign tumor materialized. Buffy underwent Gamma Knife radiosurgery that suppressed the tumor to prevent additional growth. "I live with the brain tumor, and have periodic MRIs to monitor its size," she explained. The radiosurgery left her with trigeminal neuralgia, a chronic shock-like pain condition affecting the nerve that transmits sensation from the face to the brain. Buffy takes medication that helps diminish the intensity of the recurrent excruciating, often incapacitating, facial pain attacks.

"Since that treatment, Buffy has been experiencing blinding headaches. An MRI scan showed that the tumor had shrunk, so now it appears that the treatment damaged the nerves, which means she might have the headaches for the rest of her life," John said. He had stopped writing songs during that desperate period, but began again after the tumor appeared to be responding to treatment. And Buffy began performing with John again, despite double vision that has impaired her sense of balance. "It's therapeutic for both of us. But it's hard to do the show and make sure she's okay too," John said. Buffy compensates for the double vision by wearing an eye patch, and John was disturbed by some of the insensitive reactions from people. "During a sound check one guy asked her what was with the costume. He asked why she was dressed as a pirate." John's devotion to Buffy was unending. For more than three decades, they were a mutually supportive couple as Buffy helped John confront his own limitations. "I'm bipolar – manic depressive," he acknowledged. "I'm such an oddball, ya know. *I* don't even understand me."

John never learned to read music. "I never included that hindrance in my life," he said flatly. In the old days, he'd repeatedly play a song he composed until the chords were clearly etched in his memory. Eventually he used a tape recorder to make composing notations.

In the late 1990s, John and Buffy began recording together once again using their home studio, which they found more time to do after their son Luke was living on his own. During that period they released *Way Too Much Fun - Live at McCabe's,* an album that John digitally mixed on his home computer. John's younger brother Mike – who had success as the leader of the folk-rock group We Five that hit the charts in 1965 with "You Were On My Mind" and whose music production credits included Billy Joel's "Piano Man" – also turned to computing; he became a software engineer for Adobe Systems. John's album releases during his latter years also include *Rough Sketches from Route 66,* reflecting his enduring interest in life on the road. That 1997 album on the Folk Era label contained a song called "Johnny Flamingo on the Blue Dream Road," the title track for a musical about a wanderer on the Mother Road driving a "…'59 Cadillac with the top rolled down" in search of "an angel that I used to know."

As Buffy's condition stabilized, John was able to resume his focus and return to performing. Buffy and John subsequently staged the *Johnny Flamingo on the Blue Dream Road* musical four times. "I played the part of angel," Buffy said. In 2001 John received a lifetime achievement award at a World Folk Music Association tribute to his music at the Birchmere Music Hall in Alexandria, Virginia. Performers participating in the event included Rosanne Cash, Nanci Griffith, Noel Paul Stookey, Peter Tork – and the Kingston Trio. Buffy's medical torment had not ended, however. During the past decade she has contracted and prevailed over colorectal cancer, then breast cancer, for which she underwent a mastectomy, followed by hip replacement surgery.

"John was wonderful, incredible during all this. Unfortunately, I lost my medical insurance, which really put us in a difficult financial situation," Buffy told us. "John sold a lot of his instruments, and auctioned his original notations for 'Daydream Believer.' A lot of our fans sent money, and some sent water from Lourdes. I felt prayers come into my veins, like a river of peace."

As Buffy regained strength through her long ordeal, John became more optimistic, and resumed planning for the future. "I want to make digital movies. Docu-

John Stewart following a performance at the Palms Playhouse in Davis, California, March 9, 2001.
Photo by Amanda Domingues.

mentaries. Good people stories," he said. "And I want to keep writing music. Everything has been so up in the air with Buffy. For a couple of years, I wasn't interested in doing anything, so it's good to have some goals again."

Then John began developing medical problems of his own. On the day in 2000 when Buffy was diagnosed with colorectal cancer, John fell while riding a scooter. "He had a bump on his head big as a basketball," Buffy said. He thought he was all right, but later learned that the injury had caused formation of a clot in his brain. He took two other bad falls in following years. After he began to experience confusion, his physician broke stunning news to him in the summer of 2007. John had suffered frontal lobe damage in his brain, likely as a result of his falls and a series of small strokes that probably had occurred during his sleep, and he was in an early stage of Alzheimer's-like dementia.

He responded by writing a song called "I Can't Drive Anymore" about the mandatory loss of his driver's license due to his medical condition. He recorded it for the last of his more than 40 solo albums. The disease progressed slowly. "Although he lost the ability to write music, he could still sing and play. His doctor said that was so much a part of his memory bank that he would never lose that," Buffy said. "He would lose himself, he sometimes became confused and didn't know where he was, but he always knew who we were."

In mid-January 2008, the Stewarts traveled to San Diego to see a medical specialist for John and to visit with family members and Nick and Leslie Reynolds and other friends. "It was a beautiful week," Buffy told us in January 2011. The couple stayed at the Victorian-era Hotel Del Coronado, a favorite of John's just a few blocks from Nick and Leslie's home in the quaint little town of Coronado. In the hotel, John and Buffy chatted with an admiring maintenance man named Andrew, who was thrilled to know that John was staying there. "Coronado was like a second home to us. John and I nicknamed it 'tiny town.' He saw his children and grandchildren. Nick Reynolds' wife, Leslie, picked us up and brought us to her home. We considered Nick and Leslie part of our family. Nick at the time wasn't well; he was in a wheelchair. John and Nick sat there and held hands. It was the sweetest thing you could imagine."

As John and Buffy strolled on the hotel grounds the evening of January 17, a nightgown in the display window of a store captured John's attention. "The shop had just closed, but he started rapping on the window. The owner opened the door, and I explained that my husband wanted to buy that gown for me. The shop owner was very nice, said she understood, and let us inside," Buffy said. Inside the hotel after buying the gown, John spotted Andrew the maintenance worker, and in the elevator gave him a couple of CDs that he and Nick had signed for him. Andrew and John joyfully started singing some of John's tunes. "Then in our room, as I put on the gown, John began complaining of a headache. Within moments, he could no longer talk," Buffy said. She called 911, but by the time paramedics arrived John was unconscious.

The ambulance crew transported John to Scripps Mercy Hospital, where he had been born. Nick and Leslie Reynolds arrived as neurosurgeons showed John's MRI images to Buffy. The MRI revealed that John, who by then was comatose, had suffered a ruptured aneurysm. The blood vessel that had been blocked by the previously undiscovered clot had burst with catastrophic results. "His brain had been pushed to the right, and he would never be the same," Buffy said. Physicians determined that surgery would have been complex and likely would have left John unable to walk or speak. "All four of John's children arrived, and so did his band members. John's boyhood best friend, George Yanok, flew in from Nashville, and Chuck McDermott, another close friend of John's, traveled from Boston to be there. We were all with him, and everyone had a close private moment with John. It was almost like God choreographed his death."

John, who never regained consciousness, died on the morning of January 19. He was 68 years old. "For us to spend that last full day in Coronado with Nick and Leslie was a beautiful way to bring John's life to a close. Nick was like John's brother. They were so close to each other," Buffy said. "Leslie and I share an indelible bond created by the passing of these two beautiful souls within nine months of each other. A deep sorrow will always remain in our hearts over the loss of these two compassionate, magical men. To have them able to spend their last days together, and to have John's family and his dearest, closest friends by his side, is the sweetest, dearest thing I can imagine."

Only two months before John's death, Buffy convened a remarkable gathering of many of his musical friends, including Lindsey Buckingham; prolific recording session drummer Russ Kunkel; banjo and clarinet player Henry Diltz of the Modern Folk Quartet; and bass player Bryan Garofalo (who in addition to performing with John also worked with Cass Elliot, Jackson Browne, Dave Mason, B. B. King, Jackie DeShannon and others). She had called to inform them about John's dementia diagnosis and to invite them to a sing-along she planned as a treat for John. "They came and sang with John on that day, in late November 2007, and it was a wonderful surprise for him," Buffy said.

Fans – many of whom refer to themselves as "bloodliners" – may be pleased to learn that other Stewart recordings remain to be released. "Some demos that John had dismissed are in capable hands," Buffy said. Paul RyBolt, who had distributed many of John's CDs, is now managing Neon Dreams Music for Buffy. She also plans to re-publish John's songwriting guide, *Write from the Heart,* this time embellishing it with some of his artwork.

"My journey with John was a magical, unforgettable one. He's in the heavens; the face of heaven is Johnny. He's in the stars, wind, river, everywhere he wrote about. And in the heart of dreamers, and will be there forever," said Buffy, who now teaches private voice training lessons for singers. "He was the wisest man I've ever known; he was the other side of me. He will always live in me, and his light burns forever inside of me."

John was cremated, but his remains have not yet been buried. "He's on my altar, with my momma," Buffy said. "We eventually want to lay him to rest, so his fans can pay their respects, alongside a memorial bench engraved with lyrics of his songs."

Kingston Trio traveling exhibition

Leslie Reynolds and Buffy Ford Stewart are directing a campaign to develop a museum-quality Kingston Trio traveling exhibition to perpetuate the group's memory and to acquaint future generations with its music. Participants in the project include Lindsey Buckingham of Fleetwood Mac, Al Jardine of the Beach Boys, Timothy B. Schmit of the Eagles, Allan Shaw of Folk Era Records, historian Dave Samuelson, cinematographer Bester Cram, biographer William J. Bush, author Ron Cohen, author and documentarian Gus Russo, representatives of the Library of Congress and the American Oral History Association, and many others.

"All of us on the committee, and all fans of whom we are aware, are disturbed by the extent to which the Trio and its contributions to music have been overlooked," Allan Shaw said. "Contact has been made with various historical institutions and museums. We anticipate them playing a major role as development continues, and museums are expected to be among the major exhibitors of the traveling exhibit."

More information is available at **www.kingstontriolegacy.com** on the Web.

Chris Montez in the A&M Records studio, 1966. Courtesy of Chris Montez.

4

Let's Dance

Chris Montez

Chris Montez was a teenager and unknown as a performer outside
the Los Angeles area when his breakout single "Let's Dance" ascended
to the No. 4 position on the national charts in August 1962. On the
strength of that one record, he had achieved the dream that he had
envisioned four years earlier, when he had come face to face with his
idol from whom he had drawn inspiration – the late Ritchie Valens.
Montez modeled his singing style and persona after Valens as a
means of paying homage to his music and his memory.

Like many musically inclined adolescents of the era, Chris had
harmonized Everly Brothers songs with his brothers. But he said his
interest was only casual, explaining, "I had felt there were no opportunities for a Mexican in music, other than in a mariachi band. But
not in rock and roll." The success of Ritchie Valens, therefore, came
as a revelation for Chris. "He was my sole inspiration. I thought to
myself, my God, he's Mexican. That means *I* have a chance to do rock
'n' roll."

So as a junior at Hawthorne High School in the "South Bay" area
of Los Angeles, Chris practiced his guitar playing and began performing at parties with a local group called the Rhythm Dukes. With Chris
singing lead, the group had changed its name to Chris Montez and
the Invincibles by the fall of 1958, when Ritchie Valens was booked
for a performance at a night club in Hawthorne. Of course, Chris
bought a ticket, but the place was so packed that he found himself in
the "standing room only" section at the rear of the hall, awaiting the
appearance of his idol on stage. Rather than taking the stage from the
wings, however, Valens chose to make a dramatic entrance from the
rear of the club, and emerged from a door to the right of young Montez. Chris was stunned when he turned to his right and gazed at the
dimly lit figure standing right next to him, awaiting his cue. The star-
struck young man gasped, "You're Ritchie Valens, aren't you?" Valens
smiled and nodded. "I didn't know what to say to him," said Chris.

"I wanted to tell him how great I thought he was, but I couldn't express myself. I managed to tell him I wanted to be a singer like him, and he thanked me. Then the announcer introduced him, the spotlight hit him, and he ran up on stage." Chris was devastated by the death of Valens in a plane crash on a concert tour a few months later, in February 1959. But the tragedy strengthened Chris's resolve to become a performer.

He continued to sing following his graduation from high school in 1960. After Montez managed to save $30, he and his fellow musicians went to a small recording studio in Long Beach. There, they made a demo recording of two songs that Chris had written: "She's My Rockin' Baby" and "Forgive Me." The recordings emulated the rollicking, full-throttle style of Ritchie Valens. Chris had a vague notion of "shopping" it around to recording labels in the Los Angeles area. But before he had begun to do so, the phone rang at his family's modest home. Two young men who owned a fledgling publishing business named Tamerlane Music had heard the acetate recording of "She's My Rockin' Baby," and said they were interested in it. One of the men was musical arranger Billy Sherman; the other was producer Barry DeVorzon – who would go on to success as founder of Valiant Records (for which the Association recorded), leader of the singing group Barry and the Tamerlanes, and later as a renowned producer and arranger who scored a top-10 hit with the instrumental "Nadia's Theme (The Young and the Restless)" in 1976.

Sherman and DeVorzon, who had worked with singer Johnny Burnette, were more interested in Montez than in the two particular songs he had recorded. In the fall of 1960 they booked time at the Gold Star recording studio in Hollywood for him to record two tender ballads: "All You Had to Do (Was Tell Me)" – for which DeVorzon and Montez shared composing credits – and "Love Me." They brought the master tape to their friends at Indigo Records, an independent label at 3330 Barham Boulevard in Hollywood that had achieved a streak of success with the Innocents and with Kathy Young. She had been "discovered" at the old Pacific Ocean Park amusement pier in Santa Monica by Jim Lee, the label's A&R (artists and repertoire) supervisor, who produced her 1960 hit "A Thousand Stars." Lee, who previously had been a record promo man, liked "All You Had to Do (Was Tell Me)" and wanted to sign Chris, but Indigo's owners disagreed. However, the label had overextended itself financially. As its impending closure became apparent, Jim Lee decided to form his own label, and began looking for product to release. He thought of

Chris Montez as his first recording artist, and in late 1961 he called Sherman to ask about the status of the record.

"It's sitting here on the shelf, gathering dust," Sherman said, adding that he would be willing to let Lee have the master and release the record, as long as Tamerlane would retain the publishing rights. Lee phoned Montez, who agreed to the arrangement. Deciding to name his new recording company Monogram, Lee contracted with a pressing plant to produce a quantity of the records, which he released in early 1962. Applying his experience as a promo man, Lee managed to get airplay on Los Angeles radio stations. In mid-March, "All You Had to Do" peaked at No. 7 on KFWB, L.A.'s top-rated pop music station.

Encouraged by the success of that regional hit, 24-year-old Lee began looking for other material for Chris to record. He didn't have to look far, as it turned out. "One afternoon I was on the way home from my office on Hollywood Boulevard, and I became stuck in a traffic jam on La Brea Avenue," Lee recalls. "At the time I lived on Coliseum down in Baldwin Hills. And as I was sitting in traffic I started patting my leg, and the words just began to come out—'Hey, baby, won't you take a chance, say that you'll let me have this dance, let's dance'—and so forth. And I began writing the words down, with Chris in mind. When I got home I finished writing it. I called Chris, he came over, and we started rehearsing it." The song lyrics made reference to the popular dances of the day, including the twist, the stomp and the mashed potato. For the recording session, Lee hired seasoned studio musicians—drummer Jessie Sayles, organist Ray Johnson, bass player Ray Pullman, and lead guitarist Joel Scott Hill. From its opening bass drum salvo, the song crackled with the high-voltage energy of Valens' "Come On, Let's Go" and "La Bamba." But even beyond that, "Let's Dance" was a joyous celebration of what rock and roll was all about – rhythm and movement. "Let's Dance" was pure fun set to a solid, pulsating beat. Sparked by strong airplay in Los Angeles in the early summer of '62, "Let's Dance" whirled its way onto the national charts in early August and rose to the No. 4 position during its 16-week run.

Lee brought Montez back into the studio to record a follow-up single, "Some Kinda Fun" (a high-energy song that Chris wrote) as well as other tracks for an album, which was released as *Let's Dance and Have Some Kinda' Fun!!!* The album, consisting primarily of rock tunes and ballads, also included two songs in Spanish – "No, No, No" and "Chiquita Mia" (my little girl), which Chris wrote. As soon as

Montez came out of the studio, Lee sent him out on the road, doing concerts. Through much of '63, Montez was on tour with Sam Cooke, Jerry Butler, Clyde McPhatter, the Drifters, the Platters, and Smokey Robinson and the Miracles.

While "Some Kinda Fun" had achieved only modest sales in the United States, it was a huge hit in England. With Lee serving as his manager, Montez flew to the United Kingdom in March 1963 to head-line on a six-week concert tour with Tommy Roe, the Viscounts and popular British singer Helen Shapiro. There Chris was mobbed by screaming girls, who tore at his clothes. Lee hired publicist Andrew Loog Oldham, soon to be manager of the Rolling Stones, to handle publicity for Chris during the tour. One of his supporting acts on the tour was an up-and-coming British band that was beginning to build a strong following – a quartet called the Beatles. "Their song 'Love Me Do' was popular, and they'd play it every night," Chris recalled. "We became pretty good friends during that tour. I remember I had coats with a round-collar style called an English cut. One gray coat I owned had a round collar with a belt around the middle and everyone liked that. During the last days of the tour, Paul McCartney and John Len-non said, "Hey, Chris, I hope you don't mind that we're having our suits made in the same style as your jacket." Those jackets came to be known as Beatle jackets. Although as the warm-up act the Beatles played first in the lineup – preparing the audience for Tommy Roe and Chris Montez – a change took place near the close of the tour, in Liverpool, at Chris' behest. "This is their town," Montez magnanimous-ly told Lee. "They should close the show." But Chris holds the distinc-tion of being the last performer to headline in a show in which the Beatles appeared.

Chris continued touring in the United States, as Monogram released another single, "My Baby Loves to Dance," backed with "In an English Town." *Billboard* magazine gave it a favorable "pop spot-light" review on July 27, 1963, but the record was unable to crack the national top 100.

In 1964, two years after the collapse of Indigo Records left Kathy Young without a label, Jim Lee decided to pair her in a duet with Chris Montez by overdubbing – adding her voice to Montez's 1962 regional hit "All You Had to Do (Was Tell Me)." For the flip side, Lee overdubbed Young's voice on "You're the One," which was the B-side of Chris' "Let's Dance." The record label dubbed the duo "Chris and Kathy." While "All You Had to Do" received substantial airplay in Los Angeles, it went largely unnoticed elsewhere. A follow-up Chris and

168

Kathy single with two songs that Chris had written – "Shoot That Curl" (a surfing song) and "It Takes Two" – did not fare well – and neither did Montez's business relationship with Lee. After several singles, including one called "Monkey Fever," an album, and months of grueling touring, Chris had almost no money to show for it – so little that he was forced to sell the black Chevy Corvair that he had purchased when "Let's Dance" hit the charts. Believing that his royalty earnings should have been much greater than they were, Montez angrily left Monogram, which he said was misappropriating funds.

Jim Lee persisted but was unable to sustain himself in the recording industry. "I was very young. I had met with success early – maybe too early. I had no musical or business education. I hadn't even graduated from high school. I did it all on moxie," Lee said. Acknowledging that he was not equipped to weather the economics of the recording business, Lee immersed himself in education. He became a real estate agent in 1974, and went on to success as a broker and investor.

Chris' musical career stagnated following his departure from Monogram. Disenchanted with life as a performer, he also decided to advance his education, focusing on music composition. Enduring the taunts of acquaintances who ridiculed his decline as a pop star, Chris explained, "I didn't want to be looked upon as an uneducated Mexican." He enrolled in 1964 at El Camino College in Torrance, a city neighboring his hometown of Hawthorne. Chris could not have imagined that his exit from music was temporary, and that his star would rise bigger and brighter two years later.

But Chris' college education was likewise interrupted. He had the misfortune to encounter a professor whose methods of teaching the mathematical components of composition did not resonate clearly with Chris. The professor discouraged Chris from further studies in music. "As I look back on that experience now, I realize he was the worst instructor I ever had. Teachers are supposed to teach, not to discourage," he said. "But after hearing him say that, my spirits sank so low I didn't think I could get myself back up."

One day in the autumn of 1965 a saxophone player named Bob, whom Chris had befriended, invited him to ride along on an errand. Chris did not know his friend was delivering a demo tape to A&M Records, the independent label named for the initials of its two principal owners, Herb Alpert and Jerry Moss. In those days, A&M was seeking to expand its catalog beyond the offerings of the Tijuana Brass and the Baja Marimba Band. Although those two groups had established a strong following on adult-oriented "middle of the road" radio stations, Alpert and Moss had determined the need for the label to broaden its roster of artists. They met with success after signing the group We Five, which scored a top-10 hit with "You Were on My Mind." Encouraged, the label was seeking other performing acts. When Chris and Bob arrived at A&M's offices, Alpert greeted the pair, and they exchanged introductions. Extending his hand, Alpert asked, "Are you the Chris Montez who recorded 'Let's Dance'?" When Montez acknowledged that he was, Alpert asked if he would be interested in recording for A&M. Montez declined, explaining that he was burned out on the recording business and that he was attending college. "I was so destroyed mentally that I didn't want anything to do with the music world again," Chris explained. Alpert persisted and asked Montez to give it more thought.

After turning the idea over in his mind for a few weeks, Montez decided to accept Alpert's invitation. He had some songs in mind, and he began working with A&M staff producer Marshall Leib, who as a singer and guitarist had been a member of the Teddy Bears (who sang the 1958 hit "To Know Him Is To Love Him") and the Hollywood Argyles (who recorded the novelty hit "Alley Oop"). Chris began recording up-tempo pop tracks. After a couple of sessions, Leib called Chris aside and said, "You know, Herb doesn't like any of this stuff." Chris was stunned because he had been working on material that was in the Ritchie Valens-inspired rock vein. "He has an idea for you." Chris went to Alpert's office, closed the door, and was even more startled when Herb demonstrated his idea by playing and singing the opening bars of a Tony Hatch composition that Petula Clark had recorded for a four-song extended-play 45 RPM record released in the U.K. The song, subsequently issued as a track on her U.S. album *I Know a Place,* was "Call Me." On first impression, it was a sultry ballad that might have seemed more suited to a seasoned crooner like Peggy Lee than to an energetic rocker like Chris Montez. "You must be kidding. I want to do this later in life, but not now," Montez told Alpert. But Alpert heard something in the quality of Chris' voice that he wanted to develop. "He got me in the studio and stood next to me as I began singing 'Call Me,' and helped set me into that groove."

Alpert succeeded in keeping Montez in that groove through the ensuing recording session. The resulting track, released as a single, returned Chris to the national charts in January 1966. For Chris's follow-up single, Alpert dusted off a standard, "The More I See You," which crooner Dick Haymes had first sung in the 1945 motion picture *Diamond Horseshoe,* starring Betty Grable and Phil Silvers. For

Chris Montez, lightning had struck twice. After a four-year hiatus, he was once again a star - not at all in the Ritchie Valens mold that he had emulated, but re-shaped by Herb Alpert into a suave lounge singer. Gone were Chris's black jeans, guitar and pompadour hair style. For his debut A&M album, *The More I See You,* Chris was clad in a suit and tie, sported a natty modified Beatle-esque haircut, and was accompanied by three young women smiling approvingly. His fans, old and new, approved as well. And Montez was both surprised and grateful. "I had hits. It was like I was reborn," he said. "I told myself, 'now I get another chance - thank you, Lord.'"

Chris was even more astounded to learn that he was suddenly a sensation in Latin American countries, and particularly in Brazil. But his success there was not as surprising as it would seem. At the time Montez signed with A&M, the label had been moving toward Latin-flavored jazz, which became apparent with the addition of Sergio Mendes and Brasil '66 ("Mais Que Nada"), the Sandpipers ("Guanta-namera") and Antonio Carlos Jobim ("Wave") to its roster of artists. The instrumental backings of Chris' A&M recordings were steeped in the smooth Brazilian jazz style. In response to Chris' popularity in Brazil, A&M booked a concert tour for him there. The plane ride to Brazil seemed more like a dream than reality to Chris, who had gone from student to international star within six months. He lacked confidence in his knowledge of music, explaining "At that time I didn't have the musical education that I have now. But, on that flight to Brazil the captain was so thrilled we were on the plane, and persuaded the stewardess to ask me to sing a few bars over the PA system. And I did," said Chris, chuckling about the poor sound quality. "When I got off the plane in Rio, I saw a huge crowd. I figured that there must be some important people or some kind of event happening. It was like all these people were waiting for the Beatles - but they were waiting for me! There were all these banners that said 'Chris Montez,' and I was protected by guards. I thought, 'you must be kidding!'"

With Chris well-accepted as a crooner, Herb Alpert brought him into the studio to record "There Will Never Be Another You," another standard that Woody Herman first popularized in the 1942 film *Iceland.* Chris' version, released as a single in the summer of '66, took him to No. 33 on the national charts. The success of that single was nearly repeated just two months later by another single release, "Time After Time," which Frank Sinatra originally recorded for the 1947 motion picture *It Happened in Brooklyn,* in which Sinatra starred with Kathryn Grayson and Peter Lawford. The success of

Chris' single spawned an album titled *Time After Time*.

In March 1967, Chris was back on the singles charts with "Because of You," which had been a No. 1 hit for Tony Bennett in 1951. That single coincided with release of a fourth A&M album, *Watch What Happens*. But that album did not reach the charts, nor did three ensuing singles: "Foolin' Around," "The Face I Love," and George and Ira Gershwin's "Love Is Here to Stay." By 1968 Chris' popularity had waned, and his relaxed *Foolin' Around* album was his last pop release for A&M, which had become more interested in moving toward rock. Ironically, even though Chris Montez had first emerged as a rock performer, his crooning persona was firmly ingrained in the public consciousness. As A&M signed Procol Harum, Cat Stevens, Fairport Convention, Lee Michaels, Joe Cocker and other rock acts, Chris' business attorney advised him to look for another label. "Herb wanted me to stay with the company but at that time I felt I was getting lost in the shuffle, which was a mistake on my part. Herb offered me money to do another album, but I said, 'Nah, I'm going on. I'll get another contract.' Well, that didn't happen."

But Chris managed to capitalize on his international fame and continued to perform, primarily in Europe and South America. His success in those markets prompted release of bilingual Spanish and English-language material beginning on 1972 on CBS International, for which he had several hits in Germany, Austria, Holland, France and Spain. His song "Ay, No Digas (Oh, Don't Tell Me)," which he wrote, held the No. 1 spot in Austria for 16 weeks. Chris also recorded a strong interpretation of the Ritchie Valens hit "Come On, Let's Go" for CBS International.

As a CBS recording artist, Chris was invited in 1974 to participate in the Sopot International Song Festival in Sopot, Poland, one of the largest song contests in Europe. "They gave me list of five or six songs, and I had to choose two from among those. I also had to write a couple of original tunes especially for the performance. I called one of those 'La Luz de Amor' (the light of love)," Chris said. The contest was held in August in an amphitheater, where Chris performed with a 50-piece orchestra. The conductor was from Russia, and did not speak English. "We found someone there who could translate from Spanish to German, and then someone else to translate that to Russian, so I could communicate with the conductor," Chris said. By then he had grown his hair long and played a suave white Fender Stratocaster during the performance, for which the jury awarded him best artist of the show. "That was a wonderful experience in my life. I won about 18,000 zlotys, which was worth about $1,500, but I didn't enter for the money. It was an honor to be chosen a winner." Chris experienced another resurgence in popularity in the early '80s when A&M Discos, a label marketed to Latin American markets, released several of his recordings.

During the five decades since Chris recorded "Let's Dance," the song has experienced rejuvenation in media exposure. It composed the soundtrack for television commercials for JC Penney in 2008, and for the Bing search engine in 2011. Juice Newton and the Ramones each have recorded versions of Jim Lee's composition, and Tina Turner performed it on her 1988 *Live in Europe* CD. Jim Lee has remained in the residential real estate field since 1974. He owns a Coldwell Banker affiliate brokerage firm in Boulder Creek, near Santa Cruz, California. Over the years Lee continued writing songs. He recently began performing them under his full name, Jimmy Joe Lee, and posts them on YouTube.

Today, Chris Montez continues to tour in Europe, and he remains active on the U.S. oldies circuit. And he's particularly popular on a Hawthorne High School alumni Web site, where his youthful exploits and international fame alike are fondly remembered.

CHRIS MONTEZ U.S. HIT SINGLES ON THE NATIONAL CHARTS

Debut	Peak	Title	Label
8/62	4	Let's Dance	Monogram
12/62	43	Some Kinda Fun	Monogram
1/66	22	Call Me	A&M
4/66	16	The More I See You	A&M
8/66	33	There Will Never Be Another You	A&M
10/66	36	Time After Time	A&M
3/67	71	Because of You	A&M

Billboard's pop singles chart data is courtesy of Joel Whitburn's Record Research Inc. (www.recordresearch.com), Menomonee Falls, Wisconsin.

Epilogue: Chris Montez
Singer and guitarist

The energetic, jubilantly rhythmic style that characterized Chris Montez's early recordings came easily to him. It was only natural for Chris to emulate Ritchie Valens because both of them arose from comparable backgrounds. Although his household struggled with economic hardship throughout his youth, Chris, his four brothers, and four sisters shared a rich cultural heritage.

Chris and his siblings grew up knowing that they should not expect birthday or Christmas presents. To this day, Chris treats his birthday like any other day. The few possessions that Chris had as a child he earned by doing odd jobs around the neighborhood. As a boy, he saved enough money to buy an inexpensive acoustic guitar, which he would play as he and his brothers gathered around the kitchen table and harmonized Mexican ballads known as *rancheras.*

"Most of those tunes required only three chords, and that's how I formulated my style of strumming," says Chris. "We lived in a tiny house that wasn't more than a little shack. It had a little kitchen and a living room, and a room for my mother and father. At the back of the house my father, who worked as a laborer, built an extension with a pot-bellied stove, and that's where my brothers and sisters and I slept." It was the best that his hard-working, Spanish-speaking immigrant parents, Issac and Zoraida, were able to afford. "I didn't get to know my father too well, other than spending a few times with him. I remember

Chris Montez at his home on August 24, 2001. Photo by Jeff March.

174

getting up in the morning while he was getting ready to go to work, and I'd try to impress him by getting up early. I'd hear this sound of shhhhhh sizzling, and a thump, thump, thump rhythm, and it would be my mother rolling tortillas. That was what I always woke to in the morning. The coffee would be brewing, and she'd be making scrambled eggs and refried beans, and rolling tortillas and making tacos. I'd eat breakfast with my father, and then he would be out the door. But I remember one great thing about him," said Chris wistfully. "One day when I was 11 years old he took me to a warehouse where he had credit, and there I saw this English bicycle. It was maroon and it had three speeds, and he said, 'You like that?' And I said, 'That one, it's a beautiful one.' He said, 'Take that one.' I was in shock! We grew up never having presents. I said, 'You're kidding.' And he said, 'No. You can have that one.' So I rode it home. I guess he just wanted to buy me something, to let me know that he really cared about me. I'll always remember that about him."

Just a few months later, when Chris was 12, his father suffered a fatal heart attack in the family's home at 338 N. Grevillea Avenue, near Hawthorne Boulevard. "He died right there on the sofa in the little shack that we lived in. I saw him lying there, and my brother made me go into the other room while he was trying to revive my father," said Chris. "The last time I saw my father was when my brother said he had passed away. I kissed him on the cheek while he was lying there on the sofa. Everybody has a destiny, I guess, and that was his."

Born Ezequiel Christopher Montañez in Los Angeles on January 17, 1943, Chris was raised in Hawthorne, a working-class community in the southwestern area of the Los Angeles basin. His mother, who had married when she was only 14 years of age, had borne 18 children, but only nine had lived. Chris was the eighth of those surviving children.

Known throughout his youth as Zeke Montañez (mohn-tah-NYEZ), he endured ethnic taunts from his predominantly Anglo schoolmates. He attended Hawthorne High School, where the students included the Wilson brothers who formed the Beach Boys. Chris Montez and Brian Wilson were in the same science class. "Only a couple of other Mexican kids went to Hawthorne High at the time," he recalled. Zeke was excluded from the high school social groups – the surfers, the "hodads" (students who identified with surfers but didn't actually surf), snooty "sosh" kids who were involved in organized social activities, and greasers – guys who favored leather jackets, greased pompadour hairdos, hot rods and motorcycles. "I

remember always being called names – 'You Mexican' or 'Beaner.'"
Feeling like an outcast, Zeke began to lose motivation and his grades
declined. "No one had ever told me that I could go to college. I
thought that only people who could afford it or who had all A's on
their report cards could go. So I began hanging out with a rowdy
crowd of guys from other schools who accepted me. I got in trouble
a few times, and I spent one night in jail after getting into a fight.
Although I learned my lesson, that was a heavy scene at the time.
This is the first time I've spoken to anyone about that. Not even my
mother knew."

During those adolescent years, Zeke even felt shunned by his
Catholic church. "I had a strong love and fear of God because the
scriptures say that fearing God is wisdom." But during confession
one day, Zeke declared that he had become very interested in girls.
"In confession, the priest said to me, 'You know what they should
do to you? They should take you out of this church and stone you.' I
had wanted to be an altar boy. I wanted the recognition of being one
step above ordinary parishioners. But from that day on, I never went
to confession. In my private prayers, I said, 'Lord, I'll always believe
in you, but I'm never coming here again.' I went to catechism, but I
never learned scripture there."

Weary of the harassment he continued to endure from his
schoolmates, yet determined to graduate from high school, Montañez
resumed concentration on his studies and became more involved
with school activities. He decided to create a new image for himself,
and began by joining the Hawthorne High Cougars wrestling team.
"In my junior year, I started dressing real Ivy League. I cut my hair
short." While he still suffered the contempt of male students, his
good-natured personality, beaming smile and courtesy made him
popular among the girls. "The football players were always on my
case because I'd be flirting with the cheerleaders, who liked me.
Imagine that – the pretty girls with everything going for them liked
me. I was a charmer, ya know." It was at that time that Zeke started
playing weekends at dances with a band that first called itself the
Rhythm Dukes until his dynamic stage presence prompted the group
to change its name to Chris Montez and the Invincibles. "I still have
a poster with that name on it," says Chris. "I played guitar and sang.
And my whole persona became Ritchie Valens' style." Chris earned
enough money to buy a used green '51 DeSoto, which enabled him
to widen the geographic area in which he performed. Within months
of his graduation from high school in June 1960, he made the demo

176

tape that ultimately led to his recording contract with Monogram Records.

Although his fleeting success in the early '60s and his subsequent short-lived career as a student at El Camino College in Torrance were depressing, Chris's life had turned around after "Call Me" hit the charts on the A&M label in early 1966. He fell in love and married his first wife, Judith Cantor, a young woman of Jewish heritage. Together, they had three children: a daughter, Jennifer Jane Montañez and twin sons, Eric Boyd Montañez and Damon Boyd Montañez. For Chris, that was not only a blessing, but a dream come true. "I'll tell you a secret," he said. "When I was in junior high, I said to myself, 'Lord, if I ever become popular, I'd like to have a gold record, but there's something more that I'd rather have: If I ever get married, I'd love to be blessed with twin boys. To me, that was the ultimate. And there they were, and I couldn't believe it."

"Let's Dance" experienced a revival on the soundtrack of the 1978 motion picture *Animal House* starring John Belushi, Tom Hulce and Kevin Bacon. At that time, however, Chris Montez had begun a hiatus from performing, and enrolled in the Southern California Conservatory of Music in Sun Valley to study music composition. The comprehensive four-year program immersed him in music theory and studies of complex musical structures, including learning how to compose classical fugues. Upon earning his degree there, Chris decided to expand his understanding of jazz, the basis for many of his successful recordings at A&M Records. He enrolled in the Dick Grove School of Music in the San Fernando Valley. Grove was a jazz pianist, composer and arranger whose students included Linda Ronstadt, Michael Jackson and Barry Manilow. There, Chris took courses in improvisation to help him further explore and develop his own musical styles.

But while Chris was concentrating on musical training, his Latin American record sales were sputtering and his 10-year marriage to Judith faltered and ultimately failed. Divorced and despondent, Chris had to leave his home and his family behind. By the mid-1980s, the former international star was reduced to renting a room from some people he had met. At his apartment building, Chris befriended a building contractor who was interested in Chris' ability to speak Spanish and offered him a job. "I'll be here to pick you up at 6 a.m. tomorrow," he told Chris, unaware of who he was. He brought Chris to a construction site and put him in charge of supervising a crew of Spanish-speaking workers. That job led to another, doing television satellite dish installations. "For every satellite dish we put up, we'd each get $150," he recalled. By night, Chris began performing again, in local bars. "That wasn't for money as much as it was for practice, and to try to keep music in my system," he acknowledged. Chris put the practice to good use, and signed on with a show promoter who booked him as part of a small European concert tour in the late 1980s. And just like that, Chris Montez was back once more.

At the same time, Chris attained spiritual fulfillment as well. "I started studying scripture through a program called Learning the Bible in a Year, which teaches that in scripture God said in his own words, 'Confess to no man. When you want to confess, go by yourself and confess to me.' So that tells me there are a lot of hypocrites in life," says Montez, who now declares himself a Christian rather than a Catholic. I try to stay in touch with the Lord because I know he takes away obstacles. In my faith I have learned that if I let him take the helm of my life, I'm fine. It's when I try to take my own helm that I get into trouble."

Chris says he derived perhaps his most important philosophical guidance from the prophet Solomon, who said, "If you can eat, drink and be happy, these are the blessings of God." Chris is grateful that he's able to be both Zeke Montañez and Chris Montez. "I'm happy that I've been given the strength to continue in my life and that I'm not in a gold cage – I have the freedom to be Chris Montez when I want to, and I can be myself when I don't want to be Chris Montez. I feel the only time I'm Chris Montez is when I'm in front of the public, entertaining people. I love being Chris Montez. But when I'm not on stage, I'm just a regular guy who likes to be in touch with the realities of life. It gives me the perspective that money isn't everything – if you don't have your health, you have nothing. And if you don't have love in your life, you have nothing."

Once Chris' life was back on course, love came to him once again. While backstage at the Greek Theatre in Los Angeles, he met Colleen Bernhardt, a radio personality known as Chaz Kelly to listeners of KRTH Los Angeles. They began talking, then dating, before marrying on March 14, 1998. A year later, Colleen gave birth to their daughter, Ryan Taylor. Chris' ambitions for Ryan are simple and clear-cut: "To bring her up with love and with the guidance of the Lord." Chris' older daughter, meanwhile, has become a loan officer for a financial services company, and his twin sons are both graphic artists. Colleen has remained in radio, for the Westwood 1 network and several Dial Global satellite radio channels.

In the late 1990s Chris became a regular member of a recurring oldies concert ensemble known as the Rock and Roll Army Tour. As part of that touring group, he appeared with Gary Lewis and the Playboys, Mitch Ryder, Bryan Hyland, Tommy Roe, Billy J. Kramer, Dickey Lee and Len Barry.

He returned to recording as well, and finished an album of Spanish-language Tex-Mex ranchero music, hearkening back to the tunes he used to harmonize with his brothers as an adolescent in his family's kitchen. He also produced an album of Tejano-style Tex-Mex music called Puro Mexicano (pure Mexican), most of the songs for which he wrote. Production neared completion in the spring of 2011 on a rock and roll album called Chris Montez, U.K., which he recorded in England with the Brovers, a British group. He also has been at work recording, arranging and producing an album of Latin-flavored jazz standards, including new renditions of "Call Me," "I've Never Been in Love Before," "Green Dolphin Street" and "Have You Met Miss Jones?" He is contemplating creation of his own label to release his CDs.

In 2008, Frozen Pictures – owned by producers Burt Kearns and Brett Hudson (of the Hudson Brothers musical-comedy group) – began work on a documentary film, *El Viaje Musical de Ezekiel Montañez: The Chris Montez Story.* The first portion of the title translates to "the musical journey of Ezekiel Montañez." A rough cut of the film was a crowd-pleaser in May 2010 when it was screened at the Pacific Palisades Film Festival in California, where Montez appeared in person and sang an improvisational version of "Call Me." The documentary film is being prepared for theatrical release in 2011.

The film validates Chris' long-held aspiration. "I always wanted to be recognized as someone who prepared himself musically. That's what I set out to do."

For more information, visit **www.chrismontez.com**

The Spiral Starecase in 1969. From left, Bobby Raymond, Vinnie Parello,
Pat Upton, Harvey Kaye and Dick Lopes. Courtesy of Dick Lopes.

5

More Today Than Yesterday

The Spiral Starecase

In the course of their evolution, many bands changed their names before they gained widespread popularity. A British band called the Detours became the Who. The Tea Set adopted the name Pink Floyd. The Quarrymen transformed into the Beatles. The Pendletones became far better known as the Beach Boys. The Paramours evolved into the Righteous Brothers. The British band M&B 5 – named in reference to the Mitchells and Butlers brewing company – metamorphosed into the Moody Blues. And a band that had spent several years gaining acceptance as the Fydallions changed their appearance as they switched their name to the Spiral Starecase.

While the drug culture nurtured many of the recording artists of the late 1960s, it posed a growing threat to the livelihood of the Fydallions, which had been getting steady work in dance clubs throughout the Pacific Coast and the mountain states. Playing bright "cover" versions of top hits by other artists, the Fydallions drew a steady stream of dancing couples who kept the drinks flowing at the bar and the cash flowing for the bar owners.

But by 1967, dancing began to fall into disfavor as drug use displaced drinking among the bar crowd. Struggling against shriveling revenues, clubs replaced live bands with disc jockeys or jukeboxes. Some nightclubs filled their dance floors with seating and hired topless entertainers to boost drink consumption. Many clubs closed. The Fydallions – consisting of two guys from Sacramento, California, two from New York and one from Alabama – persevered on the club circuit.

Saxophonist Dick Lopes had inherited the Fydallions (pronounced fid-AL-yons) in 1963 when all the members – including its former leader – suddenly went their separate ways just two weeks before a previously scheduled gig in Sacramento, where Lopes was born and raised. Lopes, determined to fulfill the defunct band's agreement to appear at the Bowlers' Den lounge at South Bowl on Stockton Boulevard, managed to recruit a new group of musicians, starting with drummer and vocalist Stan Mustol and bass player Danny Hart. Dick and Stan spread the word in clubs and music stores that they were looking for a guitarist. "And here comes this young kid who could hit the high notes and blend just perfectly with our voices," Dick said. The "young kid," was Pat Upton who, despite his youthful looks, was two years older than Lopes. Upton was then a serviceman stationed at McClellan Air Force Base in the North Highlands area of Sacramento.

The members of the hastily reformed quartet complemented each other's musical skills and pleased patrons at the Bowlers' Den, which renewed the group's booking for several weeks. "We all sang, but at the time we considered Stan Mustol the lead singer," Lopes said. "Then Pat started developing, and he and I started doing rock and roll as Pat's voice began getting bigger and bigger."

But the real nighttime crowds in Sacramento were going to Parisi's, the Coral Reef, the Gilded Cage, the Trophy Room and other places eight miles northeast, on the Fulton Avenue "strip." During the early '60s, bands and clubs formed a self-contained ecosystem. Clubs provided bands with opportunities for work, and bands brought dancers into the clubs. "Clubs couldn't make it unless they had a band," said Lopes. "That was still the hard-liquor era before drug use became common. When dances like the monkey, the swim and the twist were popular, clubs held dance contests. And the dancers lived for those dance contests."

The Trophy Room had a reputation for hiring only out-of-town groups rather than local talent. Then the new owner of the Tropicana, a nearby club on Fulton that had been known for Latin entertainment, decided to bring in rock bands to appeal to a younger crowd. She got wind of the Fydallions, caught their act one evening at the Bowlers' Den, and hired the band to play at her club. The Tropicana launched dance contests, and the Fydallions got the crowds on the dance floor moving to popular dance-beat tunes of the era. "The Tropicana became the first club on the Fulton Avenue strip with a cover charge because we became so popular. Harry Martin, an entertainment reporter for KCRA-TV, interviewed us on camera. After that story appeared on TV we really packed the place," Lopes said. The Tropicana extended the band's booking to four months, before the Fydallions took to the road.

Because Upton was in his last few months on active duty with the U.S. Air Force and couldn't leave town, a guitarist named Danny

White temporarily accompanied the band on road trips away from Sacramento. "Danny was a much better guitar player than I was, but he didn't sing," Pat said.

The Fydallions began working longer gigs in clubs for stands of two or three months apiece. As the reputation of the Fydallions grew, the group found itself in demand by clubs throughout the West. Salt Lake City. Phoenix. Portland. Los Angeles. Fresno. Sacramento. Santa Maria.

Santa Maria is a small town not far from Vandenberg Air Force Base, a few miles inland from California's central coast. It was there that the Fydallions had their first shot at fame – and misfired. While the Fydallions were playing at a nightspot called the Hunters' Inn, two Columbia Records executives wandered in. They were in town supervising manufacturing of a new album at the label's pressing plant and shipping facility in Santa Maria. With Pat Upton on duty at McClellan Air Force Base at that moment, Dick, Stan and Danny Hart handled vocals. "We'd like our A&R people in L.A. to hear you," the two Columbia executives told Dick. The invitation, unfortunately, was premature. "I told the rest of the guys about it and they were all excited. And then they hounded me to get down there. I knew we weren't ready," Lopes confided. "We didn't have any original material. But the guys persisted and finally I gave in. We went down there and tried out, and Columbia rejected us. We needed Pat singing."

The Fydallions hit the road bound for Nevada upon Upton's discharge from the Air Force in 1964. Among their stops was a gig at Joe Mackie's Star Broiler, a Winnemucca gambling spot in which Dick had booked the band. As it turns out, the local police nearly booked a couple of the band members as well. Fydallions bassist Danny Hart and drummer Stan Mustol overextended themselves in gambling debts. And Pat made a mistake of his own. "My first daughter was three weeks old, we'd had two feet of snow, I had $8 in my pocket and while Dick went to the club manager to get our paycheck, I thought I'd play a little blackjack. Well, I lost it all in just a couple of minutes," Pat confessed. Meanwhile, Dick learned that the band's pay was being withheld as a result of bad checks that Hart and Mustol had written in an attempt to cover their gambling debts. Pat said, "Dick came out and told me, 'Hey man, we ain't getting paid.' And I was supposed to be getting pablum cereal for my daughter, Danielle. I learned about gambling right off." So did Hart and Mustol. The Fydallions made good on their debts, and stuck to the dance club circuit, working on their own and through agents to get bookings from California to Utah. Unsatisfied with Danny Hart, Dick let him go and began looking for a new bass player. Peggy Barnes, a hair stylist whom Dick had met (and later would marry) remembered that she knew another stylist named Dottie whose boyfriend was a bass player.

Lopes auditioned and hired the bassist, Bobby Raymond, whose daughter, Julie, was a toddler when the Fydallions hit the road in search of a recording contract. "Bobby had a beautiful singing voice," Lopes said. Drummer Stan Mustol, who had been the lead singer until Pat Upton moved into that role, decided to leave the group. Using Stan's departure as an opportunity to refine the sound of the group, Dick became the group's drummer, then hired electric piano player and guitarist Bob Desnoyers to play along with Bobby Raymond and Pat Upton – who began playing sax. "Shifting to drumming was a comfortable transition for me because I always had handled percussion with the group, playing timbales and shakers," Dick explained.

Seeking to become established in the Nevada casino circuit, Dick booked a gig for the Fydallions at the Golden Hotel and Casino on West Fourth Street in Reno. "We were performing in the afternoons, when new bands played. The casino bosses kept telling us to turn down the volume. Three girls named Trish, Gloria and Joanne who had heard about us came in to see us. All three of them danced, and Trish sang. They called themselves Trish Turner and the Topics, and they were the opening act in the Pearl Bailey show in Sparks," Dick said. "They didn't have anything booked after that, so I paid them to perform with the Fydallions in our next booking at the Tropicana back in Sacramento. They did their go-go dancing while we played. All of us rocked that place." The patrons at the Tropicana included Carol Fyffe, who worked for Tower Records founder Russ Solomon. "I remember the Fydallions and their girl backup group, Trish Turner and the Topics. I spent some great fun-filled times at the Tropicana," Carol said.

After a year pounding drumsticks, Dick returned to his primary role as saxophonist when he hired drummer Bill Boyd, making the Fydallions a five-piece band. "We came to know a lot of club owners and got a lot of jobs," said Lopes. At that time, the Fydallions played no original material, but rather established themselves as a credible "cover band." Specializing in dead-on replicas of current tunes, the Fydallions performed Motown hits by the Supremes, Martha and the Vandellas, Smokey Robinson and the Miracles, and Stevie Wonder, thanks to Pat's towering tenor delivery. "People liked us because we could play the popular songs that they wanted to hear. We played

184

all the songs in the top 30. Our versions of Stevie Wonder songs knocked people out because Pat had that range in his voice. We played a lot of Motown stuff."

Seeking an even bolder sound, Dick replaced Bob Desnoyers with Hammond B3 organist Harvey Kaye following a 1965 gig in Redwood City, south of San Francisco. Harvey had been playing in Northern California with his East Coast band, the Larks. After play-

The Fydallions with Trish Turner and the Topics, 1964.
Courtesy of Carol Fyffe.

ing an extended gig at the Embers in Redwood City, south of San Francisco, the members of the Larks told Kaye they wanted to return to New York, but Harvey disagreed, citing opportunities that he saw on the West Coast. At the time, the Fydallions were playing nearby, at the Fireside Club in San Mateo. Because the Embers' owner was familiar with the Fydallions from a previous engagement there, he called Lopes at the Fireside Club, and told him about Kaye. In short order, Kaye became a Fydallion. "He added a lot to our group because he played the big B3 Hammond organ, and we were able to do a lot more show material." With the rich sound of Kaye's organ backing them, Dick, Pat and Bobby harmonized and improvised. "While Harvey played the pedals, we could drop our instruments and get out among the crowd and do more show antics. By playing in clubs we worked our way into the Vegas scene, and that's where we wanted to be," Lopes explained. "Those were the big-paying jobs."

At a club date in Salt Lake City in July 1966, they met drummer Vinnie Parello, then a student at the University of Utah. Vinnie signed on with the Fydallions at the band's next gig, an engagement at the Trophy Room in Sacramento. With his addition, the lineup of the eventual Spiral Starecase was set. Grooming themselves for acceptance into the Vegas lounges, the nattily attired Fydallions wore vested suits, ties and top hats on stage. For the Fydallions, the road to Las Vegas ran through Los Angeles. At an L.A. gig, the group caught the attention of singer and arranger Fred Darian, who produced Dobie Gray's hit "The 'In' Crowd." The Fydallions inked a recording deal with Darian's label, Crusader Records, which had released Terry Stafford's 1964 hit "Suspicion." The Fydallions recorded several tracks, but no records were released, and the band's contract dissolved.

Then in the autumn of 1966, the group landed a steady gig at the 49er Club in El Monte, a San Gabriel Valley suburb in eastern Los Angeles County. There, the Fydallions attracted the attention of a fellow named Mike Greisman. The son of the club's owner, Greisman liked Pat's vocal work and, before long, signed on as the group's manager. The 49er Club drew top-name headliners, including the Righteous Brothers, Lou Rawls, and Ike and Tina Turner, as well as up-and-coming talent. That's what led Columbia Records A&R (artists and repertoire) staff member and producer Gary Usher to go there to watch the Fydallions perform, and this time the band was ready to audition for the label.

Usher, who first gained renown as a surf rock musician, had co-written the Beach Boys' hits "409" and "In My Room," and produced

186

recordings for the Hondells, then later for the Byrds and Chad and Jeremy. Although Columbia artists Simon and Garfunkel, Bob Dylan and Paul Revere and the Raiders were doing well on the charts, the Columbia catalog was laden with balladeers, including Andy Williams, Jim Nabors, John Davidson, Robert Goulet, Patti Page, and Ray Conniff and the Singers, and the label was seeking acts with appeal to younger audiences. Usher thought the Fydallions were musically promising, but he disliked their dapper clothes, their neatly trimmed hair and their name. "He called us up and told us, 'We don't like your hair, we don't like the way you dress, and we don't like your name,'" Lopes said. The band members agreed to trade their vested suits for mod-styled bell-bottoms, tie-dyed T-shirts and peace symbol medallion necklaces, and they began to let their locks grow. But they were undecided about a hipper name for the group until Lopes' brother-in-law thought a new twist on the title of the 1945 motion picture *The Spiral Staircase* would add just the right touch of intrigue. Adoption of the idiosyncratic spelling Spiral Starecase completed the metamorphosis. To reinforce the "stare" aspect of the band's new name, Harvey commissioned a large Naugahyde painting of an eyeball that he attached to the audience side of his organ.

Satisfied with the changes, Usher took the Spiral Starecase into Columbia Records' large Studio A at 6121 Sunset Boulevard in Hollywood, and produced two 45s. The band's first single was "Baby What I Mean," a bright, bouncy pop interpretation of a tune the Drifters had recorded two years earlier. The Starecase's version gained radio airplay in Upton's native Alabama, in Fort Wayne, Indiana, and in other spots around the country beginning in April 1968, leading to a gig in Lincoln, Nebraska. "And everything we released became a hit in Phoenix," noted Upton. But chart success in Phoenix wasn't sufficient to support the group. Another release brought them a mention in *Billboard* magazine, a radio programming and music industry trade journal. In July 1968, the college radio station at the University of Richmond in Virginia designated the Starecase's upbeat "Inside, Outside, Upside Down" as its top pick. The record didn't do well after all, but the mention in *Billboard* helped place the Spiral Starecase on the national radar.

Because the chemistry between Usher and the Starecase remained volatile, the band took a break from recording and headed to the showrooms of Las Vegas after being courted by a booking agent for one of the casino showrooms. The group had been signed to a lucrative gig, playing 12:30 to 5:30 a.m. in the lounge of the old

Thunderbird Hotel. From there, the Starecase made an easy leap to the Sky Room lounge at the Flamingo Hotel, which serendipitously had installed a spiral staircase leading to the newly constructed showroom. By night the Starecase performed, and by day Pat Upton began composing in his motel room. The band tested Upton's songs in their lounge shows. One song, inspired by a 19th-century French poem, generated particularly enthusiastic crowd reaction night after night. The song was "More Today Than Yesterday." The band returned to the Los Angeles area for a return engagement at the 49er Club, permitting resumption of recording in Columbia's Studio A.

When Gary Usher left Columbia Records, the label assigned Sonny Knight to produce Spiral Starecase recording sessions. Before Knight became a producer, he had been a disc jockey and music director for radio stations during a decade-long broadcasting career in the El Paso, Phoenix, Las Vegas and Denver markets, and he knew a hit when he heard one. Knight, who had first begun producing music sessions with Lee Hazlewood in Phoenix, worked as a producer for Vee-Jay Records in Los Angeles before joining Columbia Records. Knight called upon prolific musical conductor and arranger Al Capps, whose expansive recording session credits include arrangements for Brian Hyland, the Everly Brothers, the Nitty Gritty Dirt Band, Bobby Vee, the Limeliters, Sammy Davis Jr., Mason Williams, Mark Lindsay, Sonny and Cher, Johnny Mathis and numerous other performers.

"I liked the Spiral Starecase. They had a good sound, and they were packing the 49er Club. Everything about the band looked good to me," Knight told us in April 2011. "I thought they had good potential, and I was eager to try to make a hit record with them. I added horns because I had a concept for a jazz-rock feeling." Knight strongly credits Al Capps' arrangement work on the Starecase's recordings. "Al Capps is an artist, a genius in his own right. Al wrote the chart for 'More Today Than Yesterday,' working collaboratively with me and Pat Upton to make sure the keys were right. Al understood the sound I was looking for, and he got it for us," said Knight, who assembled a cadre of top-notch session musicians. Performers on the Spiral Starecase recordings included luminary drummer Hal Blaine, a member of a highly sought group of session musicians known informally as the "Wrecking Crew"; John Guerin, who had performed with Frank Sinatra, Thelonious Monk, Lou Rawls, Linda Ronstadt and Ella Fitzgerald, and was the drummer on the original *Hawaii Five-O* television theme song; rhythm guitar player Al Casey, who worked on sessions for Elvis Presley, Johnny Cash, Simon and Garfunkel, the Association,

188

the Beach Boys, The Monkees and other marquee names; "Wrecking Crew" guitarist James Burton, who played on Dale Hawkins' 1957 hit "Suzy Q," appeared weekly on TV alongside Ricky Nelson on *The Adventures of Ozzie and Harriet,* and later performed with Elvis Presley, Dean Martin, Bobby Darin, Merle Haggard, Buck Owens, Emmylou Harris and John Denver; and singer-guitarist Glen Campbell, another productive "Wrecking Crew" member. "They were a bunch of real fine studio guys. And when we were cutting 'More Today Than Yesterday,' they said, 'Man, you're in the groove, Sonny. You've got yourself a monster hit.' They just knew it was hot," Knight said. "We had two real good songs. 'Broken Hearted Man' could have been a No. 1 record as well, on its own, but we made it the B-side of the record, because I didn't want the Starecase to miss this shot." The group spent a week in the studio and recorded enough material for an album.

Columbia released "More Today Than Yesterday" as a single in the autumn of 1968, and sent promotional copies to radio stations – but no one appeared to notice. Weeks, then months passed without airplay. The Starecase members were becoming deflated. Determined to turn the record into the hit that he had promised, Knight took an unusual step for a record producer. He approached his boss, Jack Gold, Columbia's vice president of A&R (artists and repertoire). "I said, 'Jack, the promotion department is not doing a damned thing with this record, and I'm gonna lose a hit. Will you authorize me to do my own promotion to launch this record?' And he told me, 'You go for it.' So my staff began doing mailers and contacting radio stations, because it was obvious that the record had been lost in the stacks of music that the radio programmers receive," Knight explained. He switched hats, and began making calls, traveling and knocking on doors, market by market, assuming the role of a record promo man.

"You bet your ass, I did. I broke that record first in Sioux Falls, South Dakota," said Knight (who was known by that name on the air but whose birth name was Joseph Melendrez). "A friend of mine, Ray Ford, was programming a radio station in Sioux Falls. So I called him and asked, 'would you please test my record? I've got a hit and I'm losing it.' Ray said, 'I'll put it on our hitbound list to see what happens with it.' He called me back two weeks later and said, 'Your record is No. 1, man.'" On the strength of that success, Sonny called programmers at other radio stations in other markets to tell them about the public reaction in Sioux Falls. Knight and his staff members also called record stores to encourage them to order and stock the 45 in each market that began to generate airplay.

Finally, "More Today Than Yesterday" cracked its first major market – New Orleans. " I had personally gone to New Orleans, where I knew another radio station music director," said Knight. The March 15, 1969, edition of *Billboard* magazine listed "More Today Than Yesterday" as a "regional breakout" single in New Orleans – although it misspelled the group's name as "Spiral Staircase." But that mention in the important national trade production helped give the record the boost it needed. At the time, the soundtrack album and singles from the musical *Hair* topped the charts, and music fans were preparing to flock to Woodstock and other megalithic music festivals billing Jimi Hendrix, Janis Joplin, Cream, Joe Cocker, Canned Heat, Steppenwolf, Johnny Winter, Led Zeppelin, Vanilla Fudge, Jefferson Airplane, Ten Years After and other powerhouses of the psychedelic era.

Yet with a spirited, brassy love song with a driving Benny Goodman beat, the Spiral Starecase managed to break through, toppling the Fifth Dimension's "Aquarius/Let the Sunshine In" from the No. 1 spot in Los Angeles. The Spiral Starecase and Sonny Knight had their hit. Columbia sales reps hosted a press conference and party for radio programmers at the Coral Reef Motel on Fulton Avenue in Sacramento, the hometown of Lopes and Raymond. Johnny Hyde, who at the time was program director of Sacramento "top 40" hits station KROY, recalled that "We played 'More Today Than Yesterday' because it was one of the best 'top-of-the-hour' songs ever recorded." Powered by Pat Upton's soaring tenor and a driving brass delivery, "More Today Than Yesterday" made its debut on the *Billboard* "Hot 100" on April 5, 1969, cracked the top 40 on May 3, and peaked at No. 12 the following month. It became one of the most hummable hits of a year in which electronic feedback became accepted as an art form. "More Today Than Yesterday" quickly appeared on *Billboard's* list of best-selling sheet music.

On May 19, Columbia released the group's album, titled *More Today Than Yesterday,* with songs produced by Knight and arranged by Capps. The album's tracks included "Proud Mary," "For Once In My Life" and "This Guy's In Love With You," and it yielded two follow-up single releases that Upton composed – "No One For Me to Turn To" that summer, and "Judas to the Love We Knew," paired on a 45 with "She's Ready" at the close of the year. But the Starecase, distracted by management problems and squabbles over finances, was unable to duplicate the success of "More Today Than Yesterday," which came in at No. 50 on the *Billboard* magazine list of top songs of 1969 (beating Bob Dylan's "Lay, Lady, Lay," Donovan's "Atlantis," the Temptations' "Runaway Child, Running Wild" and Glen Campbell's "Galveston"). The song's popularity prompted Diana Ross, Sonny and Cher, Lena Horne, Patti Austin, Barbara McNair and other performers to record their own versions. Although the Spiral Starecase disbanded in 1970, it served as a launching pad for Upton's subsequent career as a soloist and as a member of Rick Nelson's touring band. Lopes was undecided about what to do after the breakup of the Starecase, but after nearly a year of pondering possibilities in Sacramento he decided to build a new Spiral Starecase. Bobby Raymond joined him there, and Dick recruited five other musicians, including a new guitarist, trumpet player and trombonist. But the seven-piece band played only one

The Spiral Starecase in 1969. From left, Dick Lopes, Bobby Raymond, Pat Upton, Vinnie Parello and Harvey Kaye. Courtesy of Dick Lopes.

191

eight-week engagement, at a club called the Climax on Del Paso Boulevard in North Sacramento, before differences of opinion drove the group members apart, and drove Dick to another career.

Sonny Knight – who later produced "But For Love," the first solo hit for former Crickets member Jerry Naylor, and brought country singer David Frizzell to Columbia – reflected on the Spiral Starecase's soaring success but loss of momentum. "We were lucky enough to have a great song, and we made 'More Today Than Yesterday' a hit record. It was a monster hit. It's true that I had told the Starecase that I would get them a hit record, but I did more than that. I got them a classic that sounds as good today as it did then. I was sorry that the band broke apart, and I wish we could have continued making recordings," said Knight, who subsequently produced the critically acclaimed debut album of the band Fresh Air. He later went on to a successful career in motion picture production management. (Knight's film credits include the 1986 ABC Sunday Night Movie *Club Med* with Linda Hamilton; the 1987 CBS production *Poker Alice* with Elizabeth Taylor, Tom Skerritt, George Hamilton and Richard Mulligan; the 1988 NBC film *Lovers, Partners & Spies*; and the 1991 RAI television film *Miliardi\Millions* with Billy Zane and Lauren Hutton.)

With Dick's approval, Harvey Kaye decided to resurrect the Spiral Starecase as a stage act in Las Vegas in 1972. Bobby Raymond came on board, and so did Vinnie Parello for a while. In 1984, however, Raymond caught a severe cold. The medication he had been taking was ineffective, so he went to his doctor, who prescribed another drug. Raymond continued taking the first medication, but when he supplemented it with the second drug the two medications interacted dangerously. His system's reaction triggered a fatal heart attack.

Under Kaye's management, the Starecase endured into the early 2000s. More than 22 years after its release, "More Today Than Yesterday" appeared on the soundtrack of the 1991 motion picture *My Girl*, starring Dan Aykroyd, Jamie Lee Curtis, Anna Chlumsky and Macaulay Culkin. A song so memorable that many fans can still sing the lyrics as well as the notes, "More Today Than Yesterday" may indeed be more popular today than it was yesterday.

U.S. HIT SINGLES BY THE
SPIRAL STARECASE

Debut	Peak	Title	Label
		Baby What I Mean	Columbia
		Inside, Outside, Upside Down	Columbia
4/69	12	More Today Than Yesterday	Columbia
8/69	52	No One for Me to Turn To	Columbia
2/70	72	She's Ready / Judas to the Love We Knew	Columbia

Billboard's pop singles chart data is courtesy of Joel Whitburn's Record Research Inc. (www.recordresearch.com), Menomonee Falls, Wisconsin.

Epilogue: Dick Lopes

Saxophonist and drummer

"You'll have that natural, flowing movement again. Klippers will make you look together. A head-shaking, kicky kind of haircut."

So said the 1973 radio commercial for a Sacramento, California, hair salon on the forefront of a new trend in hair design emphasizing blow-cut stylings. Decorated with wood-shingled walls and hanging ferns, Klippers helped transform the image of Rhodes and Liberty House department stores from square to hip. The driving force behind the salons was Richard Lopes, who only three years before he became known for blowing hair was better known as Dick Lopes, saxophonist for a band with one of the hottest-selling records in the country.

Lopes, leader of the Spiral Starecase, had no idea what he was going to do after the breakup of the group in 1970. His wife at the time, hair stylist Peggy Barnes Lopes, suggested he look into her profession. He enrolled in cosmetology school, went to work for a Sacramento hair salon, and found that his fresh cut-and-blow-dry approach was attracting a following. Once again, Lopes' star was rising. His new act caught the attention of a salon executive who happened to be an old fan of the Fydallions and Spiral Starecase lounge performances. "He used to come to some of the clubs where we played, and when he heard that I was out of the music business and had started styling hair under the name Richard Lopes, he came looking for me. He worked for a big company that installed and operated hair salons in department stores," Lopes said. The company contracted with Richard and Peggy to establish salons in the Rhodes department stores in Sacramento. Under Lopes' direction, the popularity of the salons grew, and he began training other stylists in the techniques he'd mastered.

Dick Lopes self portrait, Sacramento, California, 2011.

Pivotal to the mood of

Klippers was the rock music that Lopes carefully selected to create an atmosphere that invited younger clients. Other successes followed. The corporation that owned the stodgy Rhodes chain also operated elegant Liberty House stores. Disappointed with the prestige hair stylist operating the salon in a suburban Liberty House store east of Sacramento, the company appointed Lopes to operate that outlet as well. Before long, he was named director of all of the Liberty House salons throughout several Western states and Hawaii. Watching from afar, the international company that originally contracted with Lopes to operate Rhodes salons named him West Coast head stylist as well as director of education and promotion. And Lopes found himself on the road again, conducting training sessions in Portland, Seattle, San Francisco and other cities.

Feeling he'd been there and done that, Richard quit the company in 1975, and he and Peggy established their own salon called the Park Bench in Sacramento's Town and Country Village shopping center. They opened a second Sacramento-area Park Bench salon at the Birdcage Walk shopping mall in Citrus Heights, across Sunrise Boulevard from the first Liberty House salon that Richard had set up. His staff was composed entirely of former Liberty House stylists who followed him. "I had trained them and they were loyal to me," Lopes told us in 1997. Richard regained celebrity status in recurring appearances as a hair styling expert on a Sacramento television talk show. Business at the Park Bench topped $1 million during the first year of operation. One shop alone had 30 employees. "Our hair salons operated differently from today's salons, which now usually lease space to stylists. We paid each of our stylists a salary, plus a percentage of their business. People who did very well got up to 60 percent, and we supplied medical insurance and benefits. You could never afford to do it that way now," Lopes said. He continued operating the salons until the atmosphere that he created finally overcame him. "I realized that the hair business was not going to fulfill my needs as music had. We worked hard and made a lot of money, but I just got tired of it." The die for Richard's departure was sealed when he and Peggy divorced in 1979.

Sacramento is hometown to Richard Louis Lopes, born November 28, 1943, the second oldest among six siblings. Dick lived during the first few years of his childhood in downtown Sacramento, and attended William Land Elementary School. Dick's family struggled financially. His mother did seasonal work in the local canneries. His father worked for Southern Pacific Railroad, before becoming a truck driver and then a salesman for a pharmaceutical distributor.

Dick's first encounter with music came in the fifth grade, and school awards he received for performances in 1953 encouraged his further musical development in summer school. His family was not particularly musical. "They tell me that my father played some violin and a little bit of guitar, but that's about it," said Dick, whose family subsequently moved across the Sacramento River to working-class West Sacramento. Dick was an accomplished saxophonist by the time he entered James Marshall High School in West Sacramento in 1957. As a high school freshman, he joined a local band called the Unknowns, the members of which included a drummer, guitarist, bongo player Ray Vasquez and a bass guitarist, Troy Poole. When the kid who started the band moved away with his family a year later, Dick became leader of the band. "I earned money all through high school by playing dates with the band," Dick told us in February 2011.

After Dick's parents divorced, he moved with his mother to North Sacramento, where he attended Norte Del Rio High School, the name of which means "north of the river." Sacramento, California's capital, was established where the American River flows into the Sacramento River, which drains a predominant portion of the mountains and farmlands of interior Northern California. About 60 miles northeast of San Francisco Bay, Sacramento was a "government town" in the 1950s and '60s, when state agencies and the now-decommissioned Mather and McClellan air force bases and Sacramento Army Depot kept the local economy stable and life simple.

Ray Vasquez remained with the Unknowns even after Dick relocated the group to North Sacramento. Dick also recruited Stan Mustol, the first drummer with whom he had ever played. "The bongo player left the band because he got a job at the post office, and I also had to find a guitar player," recalled Dick, who quickly became a young entrepreneur. The band's active booking schedule didn't skip a beat. "We were doing dances for schools, for senior proms and balls. I used to do dances at the Palm Grove, a club above the old Fox Senator Theater on K Street in downtown Sacramento. I also did weekly dances in Roseville [a neighboring city] for high school kids. At first a guy was renting the hall and charging me, until I figured I could make more money by renting the hall on my own for a few hours. So I did that and charged kids a buck to get in."

Dick's classmates included a fellow sax player, Lee Greenwood – who went on to become a prominent country music singer. "He was a very talented sax player, but he was no country singer when I knew him," said Lopes. "He was one of the top musicians out of Norte Del Rio High. He had a group called the Apollos, went on and played Vegas and nearly joined the Rascals. Sometime after that I heard a rumor that he was dealing cards. I thought for certain he would quickly have a hit record, but it turned out that the Starecase beat him to it."

Young Dick initially was drawn to rhythm and blues hits in which saxophone defined the sound. As his music appreciation grew to encompass jazz, he discovered saxophonists Paul Desmond and Stan Getz. "I liked rhythm," Lopes explained. "I'm not a lyricist. I don't listen to the lyrics of a song as much as I do the music. I think that's what catches your ear when you first hear a song."

Despite discovery of his ability to earn money by playing music, Dick set his sights on becoming a drafting professional. After graduation from high school in 1961, he enrolled at Sacramento City College, but continued performing with the Unknowns and dating Carol Hager, whom he had met in high school. Their dating relationships developed into romance, and the couple married right after his graduation from high school, when he was only 18 years of age. His marriage brought the Unknowns to an end. "I hadn't planned on that but Carol and I got in the car, drove up to Reno and headed for a wedding chapel. I slipped," Dick laughed. He got a job in the shipping department at the California government printing plant, but found the job boring – especially after his co-workers told him to pack boxes more slowly because he was making them look bad. From there he took stockroom jobs with the Farmers' Markets and Bel Air Markets grocery store chains. "Those were the only salaried jobs I ever had. But then I realized what I really wanted was a ticket out of this town," Dick said. He decided to take his music in earnest.

In 1962 he joined the Fydallions, a band that bass player Steve Baptiste led at that time. "I guess I always wanted to be a musician. And music did get me out of this town. It got me to Eureka, where I did my first gig with the Fydallions." Eureka is an isolated town along the rugged far Northern California coast, 290 miles northwest of Sacramento, populated by loggers and fisherman. "So what. I didn't know where Eureka was, I'd never seen it before. But I didn't care." The band members were on their way to their next gig in Portland, Oregon, when Dick was involved in a head-on collision in his '61 Thunderbird. He was transported with serious abdominal injuries to a hospital in Sacramento. The band members continued to Portland without him. From there, the band played a gig in a nightclub in Los Angeles, then drove 470 miles north to Chico, where they performed at a dinner house and nightclub called Ricardo's. Dick, who had recovered sufficiently, rejoined the band there. The need to succeed took on added dimension for Dick as he and Carol started a family; their daughter Tamara was born in 1963.

Dick was thrilled to be back on the road and in the spotlight, but the other band members didn't share his sense of adventure. When the Fydallions returned from Chico to Sacramento in the autumn of '63, they had one more gig lined up there. The Bowlers' Den lounge at South Bowl off Stockton Boulevard in South Sacramento had decided to inaugurate live bands, and booked the Fydallions first. But band leader Steve Baptiste had been growing tired of life on the road and longed to return to his native San Diego. "Two weeks before we were going to open, Steve tells me he's gonna quit. And then everyone else quit," Dick said. Determined to keep the booking at the Bowlers' Den, he picked up the phone and began calling old friends. He reached drummer Stan Mustol, who by then was playing professionally with a band in Canada. Stan agreed to join the Fydallions, as did bass player Danny Hart, who had made somewhat of a name for himself in Sacramento.

"Stan Mustol did a lot of Louis Prima shuffle stuff. He had a very pleasing voice," Lopes recalled. "Stan could sing all of the standard tunes like 'Misty' and I used to sing all of the rough stuff – James Brown and Righteous Brothers tunes. Danny Hart liked Roy Hamilton, who sang 'Don't Let Go,' and we had a lot of swing stuff," Dick said. "The crowd at the South Bowl lounge was older than me, and they liked to swing. When I first met Pat Upton I asked him if he knew any of these songs. Turned out he didn't. He went out and bought sheet music before rehearsal." Pat turned in a convincing performance, and Dick hired him. Even though the four musicians had only one week to rehearse together, they clicked. Dick had salvaged the Fydallions and fulfilled the band's date at the Bowlers' Den.

"The Fydallions packed the place," Dick said. The band rotated through several other clubs throughout the region. All the while, Dick was underage. "I had a phony ID when I was playing because even though I was the group's leader, I was the youngest at 20 years old," Dick acknowledged. "I remember when one club owner took us aside and announced, 'I've learned that somebody in the group is underage.' To my surprise, the club owner turned to Pat Upton and asked to see his ID." Pat was 23 at the time. "You're kidding," she said.

"Everybody loved Pat and thought he was the baby of the group, but he was older than I was. The club owner had no idea I was the one who was underage," said Lopes. "Someone must have tipped her. An old girlfriend maybe," he smiled. Dick didn't let digressions like that distract him from the goal he'd by then forged. "My dream was to make a hit record." One important steppingstone toward that goal was the band's booking at the Tropicana nightclub in Sacramento, where they energized crowds throughout an extended four-month booking and attracted local TV news coverage.

Lopes began booking short road trips for the Fydallions, with Upton joining in as he was able to get leaves from his Air Force duties. But Dick's wife, Carol, strongly objected to the time he was spending away from home. The couple quarreled and separated when Carol was expecting their second daughter, Cari. They subsequently divorced. Dick soon began dating Peggy Barnes, whom he had met at the Tropicana during his separation. "She was on a date with this guy at the Tropicana, but I kinda crashed in and asked her for her number." Dick and Peggy began seeing each other and married shortly afterward. "And you know what? The guy that Peggy was with that evening began dating my ex-wife, Carol, and they married for a short time," Dick told us in March 2011. "And even weirder, it turned out that Peggy and Carol had been friends when they were kids. That's how small Sacramento was back then."

As the Fydallions underwent personnel changes, Lopes shifted from sax to drums for a little over a year. Around the nucleus of Dick and Pat, the quintet coalesced with the addition of bass player Bobby Raymond, organist Harvey Kaye and drummer Vinnie Parello. That was the configuration of the Fydallions in the autumn of 1966, when Columbia Records producer Gary Usher caught the group's act at the 49er Club in El Monte.

Usher, who had just finished producing the Byrds' *Younger Than Yesterday* album, was trying to strengthen the Columbia Records stable of rock groups. Usher wanted to get the Fydallions back in the studio – but not until they'd made a change. "You've got to get rid of that stupid Fydallions name," Usher said. Lopes agreed, but had no ideas for a new name. Dick shared his dilemma at a family get-together in February 1967 with Peggy, her sister Vicki, and Vicki's husband, Lonie Davenport. Then attending law school, Lonie came to the group's defense with an idea. After viewing the 1945 suspense motion picture *The Spiral Staircase*, he suggested a bit of a twist: the playful "stare" spelling. Lopes phoned Usher to ask what he thought of the new name. Usher said he loved it. But Lopes was suspicious. "I don't think he really cared about the group. He was mainly interested in Pat's voice," Dick asserted.

As the Starecase began recording for Columbia, they were booked to appear in Las Vegas – first at the Thunderbird Hotel, and then a gig at the Sky Room at the Flamingo Hotel in 1966. "The Sky Room was one of the first big dance rooms, where many of the big stars, such as Liza Minnelli, came to dance after finishing their respective gigs for the night. We played there for months. We did very well in Vegas," Lopes said. He was so happy to be working in Vegas that he'd all but dismissed the notion of recording. But Usher had urged Upton to try a hand at songwriting, which he began doing in his motel room. When Lopes expressed his displeasure about working with Usher and hinted that RCA Records had shown some interest in the group, Columbia assigned producer Sonny Knight to work with the Starecase. Lopes liked the choice because Knight said the magic words: "I can get you a hit record." Knight, who had been a radio disc jockey and music director, knew the ingredients necessary to gain radio airplay. As soon as the Starecase fulfilled their contract at the Flamingo, they accepted a return engagement at the 49er Club, closer to Columbia's recording facilities.

When the band members went into the studio, they brought five of Pat's songs along. The band relied on Sonny to pick their next single. He chose an Upton-penned tune: "More Today Than Yesterday." Then the band went to work, starting in Los Angeles. And it paid off. "We did every stinkin' local TV show in that city," said Lopes. "L.A. was the market that made the Spiral Starecase. We were No. 30 and all of a sudden we climbed to No. 2, and then we took 'Aquarius' off the charts."

For the remainder of 1969, the Starecase was in high demand. The group signed a management contract with the William Morris Agency. Their bookings changed from dance bars to national TV shows hosted by Della Reese, Barbara McNair and other performers. The band appeared on youth-oriented *American Bandstand* as well as the premier adult talent showcase, the *Tonight Show* with Johnny Carson. "*The Joey Bishop Show* had us on three times. Joey Bishop didn't like a lot of the groups at the time in part because of their dress. But ever since our gigs in Vegas, we wore hand-tailored outfits," Lopes said, gesturing as if to straighten his lapels. "We were the first group to give a concert on the plaza at Wall Street, sponsored by Chase Manhattan Bank. We did the *Mike Douglas Show* in Philadelphia." The Starecase was a remarkably adaptable act, sharing the stage with performers as varied as Creedence Clearwater Revival, Carol Channing and the Osmond Brothers.

A couple of more Starecase singles charted after "More Today Than Yesterday," but the group's meteoric rise was short-lived. The group went back on the road, touring the college circuit by bus. The Starecase played the last date of that final three-month concert tour in Chico, within about 80 miles of Sacramento, its place of origin.

Although he saw it coming, Lopes was emotionally unprepared for the breakup of the group in 1970. "I went into a state of depression. I didn't know what I was going to do. I only knew that I was tired of taking care of guys who were older than I was," Lopes said. "Musicians can be very undependable. I just couldn't keep the band together because everything was just pulling it apart. So I came back here and sat around for a while before finally going into the hair business."

Dick's nine-year hiatus from entertainment ended in 1979, when he walked away from hairstyling. Hoping to channel his enduring interest in music and his emerging fascination with computer technology, Lopes enrolled in the University Extension adult education program at the University of California, Davis, where he completed a certificate program in multimedia production. "I was there when 16-track recording was new. I was there when recording engineers were still turning knobs. Now 40 or 80 tracks and digital processing are common." Embracing the new technology, Lopes invested in equipment in the early '80s. He launched Spiral Productions and Associates, his own video production firm specializing in corporate presentations and television commercials. His clients included state governmental agencies, corporations and advertising agencies. Although he hired subcontractors for some functions, he typically did the studio production work himself because he trusts his own judgment more than he does the judgment of other producers. "Clients aren't going to go for the psychedelic sunburst. These are conservative people, and working with them requires mature judgment," said Lopes. "I know how to produce. I was always the guy who chose the songs to play based on the audience. That's the kind of guy I remained."

Dick became a married guy again in 1987, five years after meeting Brenda Milner at TGI Friday's, a popular Sacramento-area bar and restaurant. A native of eastern Montana, Brenda rose through the ranks of a pharmaceutical company before Pete Wilson, who was then California's governor, appointed her state deputy secretary of trade and investment. That marriage ended in divorce in 2000, about the time Dick decided to shift from video production to information technology consulting. He renamed his business StareCase Communications, in which he builds and maintains computer networks and develops websites for small-business clients. One of those clients is Salon 663 Arden, a Sacramento hairdressing salon in which his ex-wife Peggy is a partner. At the insistence of clients he has known for years, he styles hair there one day each week. He also prepares marketing materials for his eldest daughter Tamara's business, Capital Corporate Locators, which helps businesses find and lease furnished apartments in the Sacramento area for visiting guests, consultants and clients.

Dick has been a granddad since 1989, when Tamara gave birth to a daughter. His younger daughter, Cari, who is a paralegal in Washington state, has a son, born in 1990, and a daughter three years younger. Reflecting on his life, Dick said, "I think the biggest mistake anyone can make in life is lack of education." That, he indicated, limited his own success. "My father was gone, and I didn't know anything about business." As a result, he was an easy mark for opportunists. "If you're going to go into business for yourself, you've got to learn who you can trust, because you'll have to rely on someone, whether it's your wife, brother or friend. The hardest thing is to know when to trust people." And, for Dick, waiting for results can be difficult as well. "I'm not a very patient person," he acknowledged.

Lopes holds a surprisingly objective view of his years in music. "When I was a sax player, I strived for my own distinctive sound. But I wasn't a technical musician. I wasn't an explosive musician. People simply liked my horn playing. I entertained them. We sang, we danced, we did whatever it took to survive." He has resumed dabbling in music with the notion of resurrecting the "dinner club" concept of soothing live background performances. Working with a guitarist who also plays bass, Dick is composing and producing MIDI (musical instrument digital interface) control tracks for electronic instruments that he and other entertainers could use in supper club engagements. He has reserved an Internet domain name, www.dinnerwithmusic.com, through which to market his concept. "I'm still not done. I know guys who are looking at retiring, but I don't see myself retiring. I still have a lot of energy to do other things."

For more information, call **StareCase Communications, 916-412-8151**

202

Epilogue: Pat Upton
Lead singer and guitarist

On New Year's Eve 1985, a private Douglas DC-3 aircraft bearing the registry N711Y attempted to land in a field near De Kalb, Texas, after smoke filled the plane's passenger compartment and cockpit. As the plane neared ground, it sheared through some power lines, hit a power pole, flipped and smashed into a grove of trees, where it came to rest with one wing ripped off. Of the nine people on board, seven perished, including singer Rick Nelson, his girlfriend, Helen Blair, and members of his Stone Canyon Band. The group members were en route to Dallas, where they were scheduled to perform in concert. Only the pilot and co-pilot survived, by kicking out the cockpit windows and escaping.

The televised news reports of the crash the following morning stunned, then angered, Pat Upton. He had been with Nelson the night before, when the Stone Canyon Band played Upton's Alabama night club. Initial accounts suggested that the smoke resulted from cocaine free-basing aboard the aircraft by Nelson and others. "I knew that couldn't be true," said Upton, "particularly because they hadn't even positively identified Rick or the contents of the plane, yet they had already accused him of freebasing. That just angered me so much. I couldn't believe they were saying that because they didn't have a clue. I knew both pilots and, in fact, about 1994 I saw the copilot in Minneapolis and he told me what happened. They were flying along and the heater warning light went on. So they shut the heater off and in a few minutes, everyone started complaining about being cold, so the pilot turned it back on. The light

Pat Upton in the early 1990s. Photo by Buddy Taylor.

came back on so he turned the heater off again and went back to try to fix it. He thought he had but when he turned the heater on for the third time, that was it. The plane caught fire in midair. They later found out that a replacement part that wasn't built for that plane was used in the heating system." Although the Federal Aviation Administration and the National Transportation Safety Board later agreed with that account, the erroneous freebasing assertion still clouds Rick Nelson's public perception. That disturbs Upton, who sang and toured with Nelson from 1979 until 1983. That was a pretty remarkable ascendancy for Upton, a self-described hillbilly who was pulling duty as a "grease monkey" in the Air Force when Rick Nelson already had achieved national television and recording stardom.

Patrick N. Upton was born August 5, 1940, and raised in Geraldine, a farming town of fewer than 1,000 residents in the Sand Mountain region of northeast Alabama. Singing came naturally to Pat, who grew up in a family of Southern Methodists. "As far back as I can remember, we sang in church. My grandparents sang and my grandmother played piano. Our family had a lot of good singers and piano players," Pat said. As teenagers, Pat and his brother formed a gospel quartet whose performances won banners and trophies in Future Farmers of America competitions. Their renown extended 50 miles east to Rome, Georgia, where they appeared two or three times on a local television program. After graduation from Geraldine High School in 1959, Pat stayed around Geraldine for a while, a bit aimless until one Sunday morning. "After attending Sunday school I decided to skip preaching and went to the local cafe in Geraldine. A friend of mine also skipped preaching and as we were punching up Duane Eddy tunes on the jukebox, he told me that he had just bought an electric guitar. We went over to his house so I could see it, and it just mesmerized me," said Upton. Pat quickly bought himself a guitar, then enlisted for a four-year stint in the Air Force, just as Elvis Presley was being discharged from the Army.

It was the spring of 1960. Frankie Avalon, the Everly Brothers, Connie Francis, Brenda Lee and the Kingston Trio were atop the pop charts. An American U-2 reconnaissance plane was shot down in the Soviet Union as Upton headed to tech school at Lackland Air Force Base in Amarillo, Texas. Upton was transferred to Hamilton Air Force Base at the northern shore of San Francisco Bay before his assignment to McClellan Air Force Base in Sacramento. His duty at McClellan: "I was a hydraulic specialist, a grease monkey," said Upton, who married his first wife, Marge, in 1963. In his off-duty hours, he'd strum his guitar as he listened to records by the Ventures, Freddy King and other performers of the era. When a musical competition at the air force base in 1963 drew only one entrant – a jazz trio – a McClellan worker encouraged Upton to start a band. With a couple of buddies from the base, he did. They learned four songs, won the contest on the base and advanced to a worldwide competition at Edwards Air Force Base in Southern California before elimination by a band from Nashville. Upton's instrumental group was short-lived. "We were together only for a few months to prepare for that contest," he said. "We played a few times and if we made gas money, we were happy." Upton was preparing to retire his band when he and the other group members stopped by the Sacramento pizza parlor where Dick Lopes and the Fydallions were playing. Dick, who was searching for a new guitarist, invited Pat to sit in with the Fydallions. Dick liked Pat's guitar playing, but was even more impressed by his voice, and hired him. "I just wanted to play, but Dick kinda had to make me sing," Pat grinned. Dick began to groom Pat for stardom. "Dick was always into clothes and he was a sharp dresser. He made me look good," said Pat. Shortly after Pat's discharge from the Air Force in 1964, he and Marge celebrated the birth of their first child, daughter Danielle. Pat spent much of the time during Danielle's infancy on the road with the Fydallions.

After the Fydallions became the Spiral Starecase and signed with Columbia Records, the band members had attained the opportunity they sought but soon found themselves under pressure to create a hit recording. "When we began having trouble finding tunes to record, Gary Usher asked me to consider writing," Upton said. "Well, I'd had an idea for a song kickin' around in my mind for a year or so. A girl I'd met at the 49er Club had told me about a French poem that she liked. She thought it might make a good song." The verse – which French poet Rosemonde Gérard wrote in 1889 to her husband, writer Edmond Rostand – was, "Car, vois-tu, chaque jour je t'aime advantage / Aujourd'hui plus qu'hier et bien moins que demain." Titled "L'Eternelle Chanson," its English translation is: "For, you see, each day I love you more / Today more than yesterday, and less than tomorrow." Pat agreed that sentiment could be the basis for a good song, but in the absence of a melody, the idea remained dormant.

"After we had worked in Vegas for almost a year, a musician friend named Mike and I were jamming. He showed me a guitar fingering chord pattern that I liked, and I wanted to find a way to use it," Pat told us in February 2011. The chords and the lyrics came together when Pat least expected it. He contracted an inner ear infection and was feeling lousy one day. "I was in the motel room, and every time I tried to stand up, I'd throw up, but I was OK when I was sitting down." Passing the time and waiting for his medication to take effect, he sat on the edge of his bed and began strumming his guitar. Pat played the chords that Mike had shown him. "When I got to the chorus I realized that French poem fit, and the words just fell into place," Pat said. The song, "More Today Than Yesterday," was Pat's first complete musical composition. "But the first time we played it, we didn't really like it." The band members experimented until they discovered just the right arrangement. Reassigned to Columbia producer Sonny Knight, the band recorded it in the autumn of 1968, along with another Upton composition, "Broken Hearted Man," a bright tempo-shifting tune that Columbia initially considered for the "A" side of a single release. Wavering, the label ultimately chose to make "More Today Than Yesterday" the "A" side of the band's next single. Upton wrote five songs that were recorded for the Starecase's first album.

Few realized the personal agony that Upton underwent about the time he wrote "Broken Hearted Man." His five-year marriage to Marge was succumbing to strain, and ultimately crumbled as their son Patrick was born in 1969. At the same time, reaction to the release of "More Today Than Yesterday" was delayed, and the Starecase's recording career appeared stalled. "The record was out for three or four months before anything happened," recalled Upton. "A disc jockey in Sioux Falls, South Dakota, played "More Today Than Yesterday" and started giving reports to *Billboard* magazine. We were actually in the process of breaking up. We recorded it while we were working in Vegas and we learned that our manager was pocketing money for the sound system we had bought instead of paying the bill. But when the record started to become a hit we decided to stay together." Upton recalls one phone call in particular that seemed to cement the group's success. "We got a call from KRLA saying, 'You just went to No. 1.' That was when I first felt that we had done it." KRLA Pasadena, a leading pop music station in the Los Angeles market and a national trendsetter in the broadcast industry, was a launch pad for national talent, with an air staff that included Casey Kasem, Bob Eubanks and Shadoe Stevens.

The Spiral Starecase mounted a hurriedly assembled concert tour. Granted custody of his two kids, Pat struggled to balance his career with the demands of single fatherhood. "Our first concert was in a theater-in-the-round in Woodland Hills, California, near Los Angeles.

We worked there with Three Dog Night. I didn't know how we did. I didn't have the confidence to know."

Upton's reservations were unfounded. The Starecase played to appreciative crowds across the country on that tour. However, internal strife compounded by unsustained popularity led to the group's dissolution. "I had no use or respect for our manager, and I felt that I needed to get away from the band," Upton explained. "I tried to do a solo act, but that didn't work because I didn't have focus or direction." In July 1971 Upton signed a record production contract with Moonchild Productions, which Jerry Fuller launched after leaving his A&R management position with Columbia Records. Upton then signed a deal in March 1972 with Playboy Records, which paired him with producer Tim O'Brien. Neither of those collaborations was productive. "During those years I made a lot of bad choices," said Upton, in reference to disadvantageous contractual arrangements he accepted. "I wrote songs, but didn't get royalty money until years later." Upton blames poor accounting and paperwork. "Columbia to this day says it doesn't know how many records of ours sold," Upton told us in 1997. "A couple of months ago Casey Kasem played 'More Today Than Yesterday' on his national program and said, 'This song's popularity today denotes far more popularity than when it charted.' Things like that happened a lot in that business."

One good choice that he made during those years was matrimonial. Pat remarried in 1972. He and his second wife, Lynn, had two daughters of their own: Jennifer, born in 1974, and Nicole, born in 1977. During his brief solo career attempt in that era, Upton signed with RCA and began working with Jim Ed Norman, producer of many of Ann Murray's hits. The most tangible product of that association was a Pat Upton single called "This Time," which RCA released in 1975. "It didn't do anything. When we recorded it with all of the instruments it lost all the spontaneity that the demo had." After Norman went to Warner Brothers, he asked Pat if he would like to record for that label. "He wanted to bring Anne Murray and me over there as production artists. I turned him down, and I've kicked myself a million times. That was probably the biggest mistake I ever made," said Upton. "It was because of a managerial problem I was having. I didn't want to get my manager involved in it so I didn't do it, which was stupid."

But opportunity knocked another time. In 1975 Upton met a manager named Greg McDonald, who knew Colonel Tom Parker, Elvis Presley's manager. Elvis' admirers included Rick Nelson, who met McDonald through his association with Parker. Upton and Nelson met, leading to some vocal work by Upton on Rick Nelson's album *Playing to Win*. In 1981, after McDonald had become Nelson's manager, Nelson asked Upton to join his Stone Canyon Band for a six-month concert tour to promote the *Playing to Win* album. Upton agreed, and remained with Nelson's band for four years.

During his time with Nelson's band, Upton and his family had been living in Los Angeles. After leaving Nelson's band, Pat decided to return to Alabama, withdraw from the music business and spend some time just sorting things out and working on his golf game. Finally Upton, who had spent his early years with the Fydallions playing in dance clubs and bars, decided he wanted a nightspot of his own. He found a spot in Guntersville, a town not far from Geraldine on the Tennessee River downstream from Chattanooga. There in 1985, he and a business partner named John Brannum leased a building that a tire store had vacated. "It was in an alley, behind an appliance store that also had become vacant. "I also leased the appliance store's space, and the owner gave me permission to cut a doorway between the two stores," Upton said. Pat and John converted the properties into a 200-seat nightclub that they named PJ's Alley. Pat formed his own band to play there. In late December 1985, about five months after PJ's opened, Greg McDonald called. "I'm in Orlando with Rick Nelson and the band, and we've got a few days off before our next gig in Dallas," McDonald told him. Wishing to avoid flying from Orlando to Los Angeles and back to Dallas two days later, Greg asked Pat, "What if we came and played at your place for the door [cover charges]?" Upton agreed. "Rick came and played," said Upton. "He made expenses and a little extra. The night after playing my club they were on their way to Dallas when their plane crashed."

Upton continued operating the bar for two more years, when business began to decline. "Then they changed all of the alcohol laws and drunk driving became such a severe crime, it no longer was a good business to be in," he said. He sold the place and, when oldies concert promoter Donnie Brooks called, Pat agreed to return to the stage. A recording artist who had two chart hits of his own in 1960, Brooks booked Upton to sing in a steady procession of state fairs, music festivals and oldies tribute shows, appearing at various times with Bobby Day, Al Wilson, Jewel Akens, Mitch Ryder, Tiny Tim, Gary Lewis and the Playboys, Cub Coda of Brownsville Station, Chuck Berry, Little Anthony and the Imperials, the Swingin' Medallions, Mark Lindsay of Paul Revere and the Raiders, Len Barry and others. "I worked with all kinds of people throughout the years. Tiny Tim was a very eccentric guy, but he was truly an expert on music from the early 1900s up until the 1940s," Upton said. "I told him about my father being sick and passing away and he asked, 'How old was he?' I said, 'He was born in 1911.' Tiny asked, 'Do you know what the No. 1 song was in 1911?' He then told me it was written by so-and-so and he went into this song. I always just called him Tiny, even though he was better than 6 feet tall. He never asked me to call him anything else."

Although Pat still writes music and he continues to perform on a limited basis, he stays close to home these days. In 1997, to help defray the college expenses of his two younger daughters, as well as his golf hobby, he took a part-time job at a Guntersville golf course. "I had never punched a clock before, but for that job I had to get up at 6:30 in the morning. Actually that was the first job I ever held," Upton laughed. "I fixed carts, changed the cups and picked up golf balls – whatever was needed." But it wasn't as much fun as playing golf, and it wasn't what Upton truly loved – entertaining. So he left that job behind after a few months and returned to the stage.

In 2002 he received a call from an entertainment promoter in the Philippine Islands, where the Spiral Starecase had an enthusiastic and loyal following. "Every song we did on that first album was a hit in the Philippines," Upton told us. He was booked for a show on Valentine's Day 2003 at the Hard Rock Café in Manila. The place was jammed with Spiral Starecase fans. Upton returned to Manila for a series of three sold-out performances at the Aliw Theater, the Manila Hotel and the Waterfront Hotel Cebu in January 2006. In July 2008 Pat appeared in a double bill with the Lettermen at 16,000-seat Araneta Coliseum in Quezon City, the Philippines' premier entertainment venue.

Upton is pretty content these days. He plays golf when he can and entertains the notion of playing in a celebrity golf tour. "Some guys who are shooting 16 over par are making $6,000 to $8,000 per tournament. I'm a three handicap and I know I can beat them. I don't know if I have the status to be chosen for participation, but I would certainly do it if asked." But Upton is unlike some of the flamboyant personalities who populate the golf circuit. "I'm just a hillbilly," he says in his soft drawl. "I try to be a good person. I'm just me."

In recent years, he's done several shows with singer and guitarist Terry Sylvester (formerly of the Swinging Blue Jeans and the Hollies) and singer Sonny Geraci (who had played with the Outsiders and Climax). Nowadays, Pat is collaborating in writing pop songs with

Steppenwolf guitarist Larry Byrom. They have recorded some demos together through which to market their compositions.

Pat's oldest daughter, Danielle, whose pablum money he lost gambling in Winnemucca while on the road with the Fydallions in 1964, is doing fine in Burbank, California, where she lives with her husband and two daughters of her own. She is a food writer and posts recipes and cooking ideas on her blog, "Cooking for My Peace of Mind." Upton's son Patrick Jr., nicknamed "Spud," is doing much better these days than he was in 1993, when the Gulf War veteran broke his neck in an automobile accident after returning to the United States. Taking after his father, Spud got a job in 1997 singing and strumming guitar at the Burbank Bar and Grill. He now does film editing and owns a recording studio not far from his parents' home. Pat's daughter Jennifer, who graduated from Jacksonville University in Alabama in 1997 with a degree in mass communication, is married and has children. She is an office manager for a medical prosthetics company near Birmingham. And daughter Nicole, who also is married and has a family, designs bedding fabrics. "My beautiful wife, Lynn, is a residential interior decorator and is very good at it," says Pat, who speaks adoringly of her.

Upton says he and Columbia achieved some degree of restitution 10 years after he left the Spiral Starecase. "I got a new manager who helped me get my copyright back and got many things straightened out. In the early days, royalties weren't much. But in the later years, after I moved back to Alabama in 1983, I reached 'millionaire' status at the BMI Awards. That's accorded when you reach over a million plays in broadcast performance, and that's done well for me," Upton said. "Performance-wise, this song could easily make $40,000 to $50,000 per year."

True to its title, "More Today Than Yesterday" has taken on added depth for Upton. "I didn't really write 'More Today Than Yesterday' for anyone in particular at the time," he said. "But when I sing it to Lynn today, I really mean it."

For booking information, email **pupton@localaccess.net**

Epilogue: Vinnie Parello

Drummer

"Paging Vinnie Panariello. You have a call on line three."

Panariello strode briskly past the gleaming Volvos on the showroom floor, grabbed a phone in an unoccupied sales cubicle and punched up line three.

When Vinnie answered that phone, he ended the authors' search for the "lost" member of the Spiral Starecase in 1997. Neither Dick Lopes, Pat Upton nor Harvey Kaye had known Vinnie's exact whereabouts following his retreat from music years before. Harvey recalled that Vinnie had been with a men's clothier in Las Vegas. Pat heard that he was doing something in automotive sales. So did Dick. Maybe in Southern California. Maybe Volvos. The World Wide Web was in its infancy and not yet useful as a search tool. As far as Dick, Pat and Harvey knew, Vinnie had dropped out of show business years ago. But the way Vinnie sees it, he still was in show business. For nearly three decades beginning in 1979, his stage was the showroom floor. And

Vinnie Panariello, March 19, 2011. Photo by Cory Panariello.

211

he's been going by his birth name, Panariello, rather than the truncated stage name Parello by which he was known during his years in music.

"The car business is just like show business," said Vinnie, who by the late 1990s had become manager of Volvo of Orange County in Southern California. "I try to explain this to the sales people. I tell them that people walking through the door expect to see a performance, just like they do when they go to see *Phantom of the Opera*. They expect you to show them the car and give them a sales presentation. And I tell them that even though you might feel like crap during your break, when the lights go on, you're performing. That's what it's all about. I can sit at my desk all pissed off about something, but if someone walks in and wants information, you become a showman. There are a lot of parallels. On stage when people see that you're happy it's contagious."

But Vinnie's career in music left him somewhat scarred, both emotionally and physically. Playing a round of golf, he gingerly rubbed his wrist. Another golfer noticed the scar. "How'd you get that?" asked the golfer with a quizzical bob of the head. "Drumming," Vinnie answered simply. The damage was done in the mid-1980s, when Vinnie picked up the sticks after a long absence. He'd go out into the garage, where he had set up his drums, and pound furiously. "I shouldn't have," he said. "I didn't warm up properly and I began to feel a tingling, but I kept it up. Then I bought a house, worked a lot on it and my hands became worse. When I would raise my hands up, they would go numb. When I became unable to write or shave, I finally decided to have surgery. My doctor told me that the condition could have led to permanent nerve damage." Following successful surgery for carpal tunnel syndrome on his right wrist in 1996, Vinnie underwent corrective surgery on his left wrist the following year.

Drumming has been an essential part of his life since the age of 9. "I found a drum in a garbage pail near my house at Coney Island," Vinnie recalled. "Across the street, there was a guy named Joe who was a drummer. I guess he just got fed up with it and threw it out. So I started banging on it and got addicted to drumming. After that I started taking lessons. My family had a grocery store, V. Panariello & Sons, on West 16th Street, and I used to deliver orders for them. With the tips I made, my Dad chipped in to buy a set of drums." Then Vinnie discovered Buddy Rich and big-band jazz at Birdland, a cavernous jazz club in Manhattan on Broadway near 52nd Street named in honor of legendary alto saxophonist Charlie "Bird" Parker, who often headlined there. "When I was 12 or 13, I was able to get into Birdland and sit in an area called the 'peanut gallery.' You couldn't drink but you could listen and get an education. Birdland was the Mecca for jazz."

Born in the Coney Island section of Brooklyn, New York, on August 24, 1943, Vincent Louis Panariello grew up during the Truman and Eisenhower years in an apartment above the grocery store on West 16th Street, one block from the Coney Island Steeplechase amusement area. "It was a fun area to grow up in. You could walk around any time of day or night," Vinnie said. Neighbors took care of each other. Friendships were close and lasting. "One of the guys I hung around with on the corner back then lives out here in California. I've known him for over 50 years. My father owned some property and we were his landlords for about 35 years. Some of those guys had an amazing gift for laughter and they didn't even realize it. They were just naturally funny."

Vinnie had a happy youth as the youngest in a family of five kids. He excelled in sports at school, and made all-city and all-metropolitan in football playing guard. Weighing scholarship offers, he was packed and ready to go to the University of Indiana until a friend, Leo Hershman, persuaded him to accept an offer from the University of Utah. "Leo was a great football player at UCLA – one of the best. He was friends with all of the coaches at Utah." They included Vinnie's freshman coach, George Seifert, who went on to guide the San Francisco 49ers to two Super Bowl victories during an eight-year reign as head coach. Off the football field, Vinnie majored in sociology and earned a teaching credential. On weekends he'd begun playing with a jazz trio at the Brighton Resort ski area. During the week he was student-teaching in Salt Lake City when he learned something about himself: "I'm a good teacher, but I'm a better drummer. Teaching is a good proving ground. It makes you aware of just what you do or don't want to do."

One thing he didn't want to do was return to New York, despite the urging of his parents. His father, Vincent "Jimmy" Panariello – an immigrant from Naples, Italy, and his mother, Antoinette – a native New Yorker – had built the family wholesale and retail grocery business into a thriving enterprise. They wanted Vinnie to be a part of it. "Graduating from college and having my Mom and Dad fly in from New York to see it was one of the highlights of my life. My mom was an angel, and just seeing them there was something I will never forget," he said nostalgically. But Vinnie wanted to test his own wings.

213

With his degree and teaching credential in hand, Vinnie decided to see how far music could take him. The jazz trio won a steady gig in Salt Lake City at a club called the Copa, laying down sultry jazz standards by Erroll Garner, Dave Brubeck and Bill Evans. One evening he heard about a band that was playing down the street at the Black Hawk Club. A friend told him the band leader was looking for a new drummer. The group was the Fydallions. On stage that night were Dick Lopes, Bobby Raymond, Harvey Kaye, Pat Upton and drummer Bill Boyd.

"They had the place packed, and they did it seven nights a week," said Vinnie. "They were doing top 40 music, but they were performing it a little different from everyone else because of Pat's unique vocal style. They were doing songs by the Supremes and Dusty Springfield, which many groups couldn't do because they didn't have the range. It was phenomenal. And the girls loved that stuff." Vinnie was impressed. And before long, he was a Fydallion – on July 19, 1966, to be specific. That's the date he traveled to Sacramento to join the group following his successful tryout in Salt Lake City. That's when he became Vinnie Parello. "My first gig with them was at the Trophy Room on Fulton Avenue in Sacramento. It was a great club, where a lot of bands played on their way to make a name for themselves. But I don't think there was a better club group around than the Fydallions. Every place we played, we were a hit. Since the girls liked us, the guys followed. It's a simple business. If you get girls into the club, you're gonna get guys."

Panariello said the Starecase became renowned for replicating current pop hits on stage. "Dick was on top of all the new releases. He'd hear a song, study the arrangement, we'd go into rehearsal and we'd be playing it note for note on stage before most people had heard it on the radio," he said. "Dick was the type of guy who would strive to get the original sound from the records, although that came to be a detriment in years to come because we were great at playing everyone else's songs but had some difficulty creating our own."

Vinnie felt comfortable in Sacramento. "I ran into a lot of people there from back East, people from my neighborhood who used to come to the club. They knew my brother, my oldest sister, my brother in law." With Sacramento as a base, the Fydallions did gigs in Stockton, Modesto, San Francisco. Then a date that Vinnie still remembers: "January 1, 1967. I'll never forget it. We worked at a place called the 49er in the L.A. area and we met this guy Michael Greisman, who became our manager. He wasn't one of my favorite guys," Panariello

214

admitted. It was at the 49er Club that the group hooked up with Columbia A&R man Gary Usher, but not much came of that association right away. The group returned to the road. Next stop: a lounge called the Crazy Horse in Scottsdale, Arizona. From there, the band's fortunes took a dramatic turn upward with a booking at the Thunderbird Hotel in Las Vegas. "We knocked 'em dead. From 2 to 6 a.m. you couldn't get into the place," Vinnie told us in September 1997. From there the guys became the house band at the newly opened Sky Room at the Flamingo Hotel, where they remained for nearly a year. "That's when Pat wrote 'More Today Than Yesterday," Vinnie recalled. "It was slow getting started, but after it broke onto the chart in Sioux Falls, South Dakota, other radio stations in other markets jumped on it and it spread all over the place. The next thing we knew we were on tour. And then we broke up," said Vinnie, who attributed the group's dissolution to squabbles over management. "As hard as it was to get up there, it was easy to fall back."

On a concert tour the fall of 1969, even before the group's last single charted, Vinnie parted company with Dick Lopes in an airport passenger terminal in Seattle. They haven't seen each other since. Vinnie had accepted an offer from a musician named Paul Cisneros to join a group called Brown Dust. "Paul was a phenomenal performer. He played trumpet and sang. But you know, there are a lot of good singers out there. The chemistry has to be right." It was. Vinnie and Paul, now a businessman in San Diego, began a friendship that endures to this day. Married briefly, then divorced, Vinnie left for Hawaii with Brown Dust, an ensemble of five musicians and two dancers who spent about a year playing clubs and hotels in Honolulu, on Kauai and on Maui. Harvey Kaye and Bobby Raymond also joined the group for a short period. "Brown Dust was a helluva group. Visually those guys would destroy an audience," Vinnie said.

Vinnie remained with Brown Dust for two years, then played with a group called Tightrope for about eight months. In early 1972 he happened to run across Harvey Kaye and Pat Upton playing at a club called the King's Table in the suburban San Gabriel Valley section east of Los Angeles. Vinnie joined them, and they played local clubs as a trio for a while until Pat went on to pursue a solo career. Harvey and Vinnie decided to launch a new "show group" called Tootsie, encompassing comedy and dance routines as well as music. They worked the clubs in Southern California and Arizona before returning to Vegas with a booking at the original MGM Grand Hotel and Casino, now called Bally's Las Vegas. The return to Las Vegas

215

marked a resurrection of sorts. There, Harvey changed the band's name to the Spiral Starecase after he had obtained permission from Dick Lopes, who was by then knuckle-deep in the hair styling business. From there, Vinnie rejoined with Pat Upton, playing together at a few clubs including a six-month stand at Howard Manor in Palm Springs.

When that gig came to a close in 1976, Vinnie was ready to return to New York. There he joined his brother-in-law Mario Stefano's trucking business, which delivered papers for the *New York Times*. Vinnie was placed in charge of truck dispatching and office management. But by no means did he set music aside. As soon as he arrived in New York he looked up a couple of his old music teachers and began "wood shedding" – locking himself in a room to intensively study drumming theory and technique. "It was rewarding because I learned so much more. The old teacher I had, a guy named Charlie Tappan who has since passed away, was probably one of the best teachers in the world." Tappan worked at the Henry Adler Music Store on West 46th Street near Broadway, which had a school upstairs. His roll-up-your-sleeves approach took Vinnie to new levels of proficiency and precision. "I went from 'pretty good' to exceptional," said Vinnie, who practiced every night and 10 to 12 hours each weekend during his missionary training. "I didn't even date for two years. It was a personal thing. I didn't know if I wanted to start playing professionally again. I just wanted to finish what I had started."

A visit from Harvey Kaye helped Vinnie determine his future. Playing a gig in New Jersey, Harvey stopped to see Vinnie at the music store where he was studying. "Harvey had gone in to buy some equipment because he was working down the road. He told me that work was getting more difficult to find because a lot of clubs had closed. Disco was coming in, and I saw the writing on the wall for live bands. Playing was always great, but musicians sometimes forget that it's a business and it has to be run like a business," Vinnie observed. "And anytime you build a business you need to determine what you hope to get out of the business. You have to ask yourself if you can comfortably retire from that business." For Vinnie, the answer to that question was a resounding "no."

In 1978 Vinnie remarried and determined he would start fresh. With his new wife, Cory, he went to California, certain that he needed to leave New York but uncertain of what he'd do next. He called an old friend, a hair stylist named Vivi Avila he knew from the dapper Spiral Starecase days. Vinnie told Vivi about his career dilemma.

Vinnie mentioned Pete Valenzuela, a mutual acquaintance who had been a bartender at one of the clubs in which the Starecase had played. Vivi said, "You ought to call Pete. He's selling Volkswagens in Montebello." The showroom of Colome Motors was only a few miles from El Monte, where the Starecase had played at the 49er Club many years before. Pete, the dealership's manager, hired Vinnie as a car salesman. He achieved success quickly, but his family once again exerted pull. Vinnie moved back to New York with Cory, who gave birth to their first child, Bianca, on April 26, 1979. After a year's stay in New York, they moved back to Southern California. Vinnie returned to Colome Motors, which Pete had left to join Volvo of Orange County. "You've got to come over here," Pete told Vinnie. He did, remaining with that Volvo dealership until 1992. "That was when the California economy went in the dumper," Vinnie said. Formerly brisk automotive sales dwindled to a trickle.

Vinnie's family called again. "My nephew Louie had a gigantic retail men's clothing business in New York called Garage Clothing. He said he was going to open a store in Vegas, and asked if I would like to run it. I said, 'yeah, that sounds good.' So I went there and opened it, and it did great." The store's clientele included Tom Jones, Rip Taylor and other mainstays of the Vegas club and lounge scene. "I liked the clothing business a lot. I met a lot of people, including a lot of entertainers. Vegas is a crazy town. The worst and the best are in Las Vegas. Everything was wonderful until we had a misunderstanding, and I left there in February 1995." Vinnie returned to Volvo of Orange County, this time as manager. His return was short-lived, however. Once again, economic hard times took their toll, and a reduction in force left Vinnie without a job as the dealership's owner took over the management position. By this time a seasoned automobile sales professional, Panariello quickly found work at Circle Imports, a dealership in nearby Long Beach, selling Volvo, Volkswagen, Porsche and Audi automobiles. He and Cory bought a home in the community of Walnut. On October 1, 1997, Circle Imports purchased Volvo of Orange County and appointed Vinnie general sales manager. The company demolished its old Garden Grove building and moved into a new facility in the Santa Ana Auto Mall. Vinnie and Cory bought a vacation condo in the desert community of Palm Springs, about 100 miles east.

Cory, meanwhile, was manager of a personnel agency. Cory's daughter Gina from her first marriage is herself married and has a child. Now grown, Vinnie and Cory's daughter Bianca studied communication in college. After Vinnie's parents died, his brother Danny continued to run the family business in New York until his death in 1989. His sister Anita has retired and moved to Florida, and his sister Marie lives in Poughkeepsie, New York, where she works part-time in food distribution for Target stores. Vinnie's oldest sister, Josephine, nicknamed Jeppy, has remained in Brooklyn. Vinnie feels a twinge of regret about the painful disagreement he had with his family at Garage Clothing. "I wish I could go back and make amends with my family," he said quietly. He also candidly admits that he made a wrong turn when he pursued pop music. "If I had it to do over again, I wouldn't have gone into rock. I would have stayed in the jazz scene for the artistic satisfaction. I've always derived more enjoyment from jazz."

That reflects how he viewed the greatest success the Starecase achieved. "Even today, people know 'More Today Than Yesterday' and still think it's a great song," said Vinnie. "It's a classic. Yet it is a very simple swing song. It's really a Bennie Goodman beat – simple, but very infectious." As the incision on his left wrist began to heal, Vinnie gingerly picked up his clubs and returned to the golf course in the summer of 1997. "I was playing golf with a guy by the name of Al Sanada. It turns out that Al has a band and he uses some of the greatest guys in Hollywood, including the trumpet guys from the *Tonight Show*." Sanada asked if Vinnie would like to play with his band. With that, he resumed practicing his drumming, but far less strenuously.

Vinnie remained with Volvo of Orange County until 2006, when the faltering economy began taking a heavy toll on new car sales. "Work was becoming more of a grind, and I decided it was time to move on," Vinnie told us in January 2011. He and Cory put their Walnut home up for sale, moved into the Palm Springs condo temporarily, and then decided to remain in the resort area. They bought a home in nearby Indio, and retain the Palm Springs condo as a rental property. Vinnie now works as a representative for Retail Consulting Group, helping negotiate agreements between car dealerships and owners of cars that have been declared "lemons." He plays golf regularly, shooting in the high 80s. He also enjoys helping a friend sell golf equipment on weekends, and drums in his garage using practice pads with the notion of playing some gigs occasionally.

"I know I can't push it because I don't want to end up with problems again," said Vinnie. "But if I do decide to play, I want to be as good as I can be. If I can do it, I will."

218

Epilogue: Harvey Kaye

Keyboard player

August 22, 1938 – August 17, 2008

If you ever asked Harvey Kaye what he did in the Air Force, he invariably would have told you he flew a Remington SL21. "What kind of plane is that?" people wondered. "It's not a plane," Harvey would grin. "It's a typewriter."

Keyboardist Harvey Kaye, who supplemented his military pay by playing in a band he and other Air Force recruits formed, always kept a practical perspective of the music business. A personnel administrator during his Air Force stint, Sgt. Kaye obtained his bachelor's degree in business administration from the University of Maryland through an on-base teaching program. Kaye had a specific goal in mind. "Music has always been my first love, but that college program really taught me how to apply business practices to a music career. Through business administration you learn about sales, and what I've done to this day involves selling music," Harvey told us in 1997.

Harvey had his first realization about the sales implications of music at the age of 11, when his father's boss visited their home for

Candy and Harvey Kaye at the Sahara Hotel in Las Vegas, August 21, 2001. Photo by Jeff March.

219

dinner one evening. On his father's request, young Harvey played a song on the piano for their houseguest, who responded by giving Harvey a five-dollar bill. "I realized that for four minutes' work I'd been paid $5, which was worth a lot back then. That spurred me to go into music professionally."

Born Harvey Kaplan on August 22, 1938, the young pianist grew up 30 miles north of New York city in the town of Haverstraw, which had a population of about 5,000. Harvey first began taking lessons from an instructor named Professor Cuzzo at the age of 5. "I hated it because all I did was play exercises for four or five years. I asked him, 'When are you going to let me play a song?' He said, 'I'll let you know when.' All I could play was exercises from sonatas by Mendelssohn, Beethoven and Bach. About six years after I started lessons, he put a new song in front of me. It was 'Malagueña,' and it was 14 pages long. I played it right through the first time and he just smiled at me and said, 'That's why. You had to practice first – to get your hands in shape and to understand music.' He was an excellent teacher and I never knew why he was doing what he did until then."

When the professor died, an uncle of Harvey's recommended a friend who played piano and organ professionally and taught lessons. The new teacher gave Harvey an opportunity to develop his own style with an expanding repertoire of music. As a teenager under his tutelage, Harvey took an interest in the organ. Harvey enlisted in the Air Force upon graduation from high school in 1956, and formed a musical group called the Sound Barriers at George Air Force Base in Victorville, California. The group earned more on two weekend dates than Kaye received in his monthly Air Force check. After transferring to England for a three-year tour of duty in 1957, Harvey joined what he called a "hillbilly band," playing the kind of country music upon which the early rock classics were based. "I was stationed outside of London and that's what I did to make money. We played all over, including many of the English countryside towns on the weekends." Music took on increasingly greater importance for Harvey. When it came time for him to re-enlist, his captain told him, "I think you have a lack of motivation toward the military service."

Discharged in 1960, Harvey returned to the states. Coming from a family in the clothing business, Harvey took a job in the E. J. Korvette department store in Nanuet, New York. Within a year he was named manager of the men's haberdashery department. "There I was, working all week for about $100," said Harvey. About that time a friend of his told him about a band at a local Italian restaurant that was looking for an organ player. Harvey thought he'd audition. "I didn't own an organ, but there was an organ on stage. I didn't really know how to play that particular organ, so I just pulled all of the stops out to get it as loud as I could and started to play." The restaurant owner liked Harvey's playing but not his name, asserting, "Kaplan isn't good for the stage."

Harvey asked, "What should I call myself?"

"Well, think of Joey Dee, Molly Bee, Sammy Kaye. Spell it like Sammy Kaye because he's very successful," suggested the restaurateur.

"Let me ask you a question," replied Harvey. "If I call myself Kaye instead of Kaplan, can I get the job?"

"Absolutely."

"Call me Kaye," he said.

The name stuck. "Somewhere along the line years later I legally changed it. Now I'm not sure why. But I got that job and once again, I was making more on the weekends than I was during the week." Harvey got more than the job. He got the band, which was renamed Harvey Kaye and the Larks – a five-man ensemble with guitarist, bassist, drummer, saxophone player and Harvey on keyboards. They were soon joined by a female vocalist named Cammie, and bookings kept the group busy three days a week. "We would play rock and roll on Friday and Saturday nights as the Larks. On Sundays we all wore tuxedos, called ourselves the Harvey Kaye Orchestra, and we played standards and dance music for the older people."

After doing that for a while, Harvey and the other group members decided they were good enough to play Manhattan. They traveled the 20 miles to New York City and headed for the Peppermint Lounge, 128 West 45th Street, at that time the epicenter of the twist dance craze. The headlining act was Joey Dee and the Starliters, who had hit the top of the charts with the organ-powered "Peppermint Twist." In the window of the Peppermint Lounge was a promotional photo of Joey Dee, on which was imprinted the name of Dee's manager. Harvey called the manager and said, "I'm looking for someone to manage my rock and roll band." After an initial meeting, the manager signed Harvey Kaye and the Larks and booked them in the Peppermint Lounge, at the Wagon Wheel and at Trudy Heller's in Greenwich Village. "We were doing really well, we thought. The whole band was making about $600 per week, and we gave 20 percent of that to our manager. But we were really happy." When his manager booked the group into a club called the Embers in Redwood City, California, south of San Francisco, Harvey said, "God, we've never been there before." Cammie declined to travel, but the five guys in the band piled into a 1960 Ford Econoline van and drove straight through from Greenwich Village to Redwood City.

Their brand of heavy funk music played well at the Embers. "Groups from New York were very powerful. We had a strong sound, because we had the Hammond B3 organ," explained Harvey, who emulated legendary jazz organists Jimmy Smith, Jack McDuff and Jimmy McGriff. "A lot of the California groups were playing surf music and they used Farfisa organs." With the Embers as home base, Harvey Kaye and the Larks embarked on a West Coast tour in 1965. Harvey saw opportunity in California. The other band members wanted to return to New York. The breakup was fortuitous. The Fydallions were playing at the Fireside Club, not far from the Embers. "They had a Farfisa organ player with them who didn't quite get it," Harvey observed. Uncertain about the Fydallions, whom he'd not heard, he was entertaining an offer to join Bill Haley and the Comets, who also played at the Embers. "Bill Haley offered me a job playing B3 with them. I asked where the band played and Bill told me that they spent a lot of time in Mexico because he had a home there. I wasn't particularly fond of leaving the country after almost three years in London. So I went to the Fireside Club that night and listened to the Fydallions play. Pat Upton was with the group then, and he was the only guy I'd ever met who could sing in a girl's key. He could do songs that no other groups could do because of the range of his voice. Dick Lopes, who was the sax player, also played timbales, giving the band a double-percussion sound. They also had a good bass player who also happened to be a very good singer. The drummer was adequate, but the Farfisa player had to go," Harvey told us in August 1997. "The Farfisa was a little electric organ made in Italy. They were looking for that funky type of big sound that I could offer. The Hammond B3 has a tone generator in it that can produce orchestral sound. At the first rehearsal we looked at each other and said, 'that's it!' We weren't the greatest musicians, but there was something that clicked between the five of us that gave us this special sound that we hadn't heard ever before."

Harvey joined the group, which took to the road, working clubs throughout the West. The Fydallions had played the Black Hawk Club in Salt Lake City, but in the summer of '66 they returned with Harvey's Hammond. "We knocked out songs by the Supremes and all of these girl groups and the harmony was happening. We packed the place night after night. That's when we met Vinnie Parello." A guitarist whom Harvey had met when he was with the Larks introduced Vinnie to Harvey. He told Harvey, "You've got to hear this guy play drums." Vinnie stopped by and sat in with the Fydallions. The two New Yorkers, Harvey and Vinnie, struck up an easy friendship. After that date in Salt Lake City, the Fydallions – with the addition of Vinnie – played Sacramento in Northern California before landing an extended gig at the 49er Club in El Monte, a suburb in the eastern portion of metropolitan Los Angeles. "We would work from 9 p.m. to 2 a.m., and at about 2:30 Ike and Tina Turner would come on, working for $1 a head at the door. The Righteous Brothers would drop by and sit in. We got so popular that they painted our picture on the wall."

The Fydallions' popularity attracted the attention of Columbia Records producer Gary Usher. "He never said much but he knew exactly what he wanted," Harvey recalled. "He listened to us just one night and then he came up and said to me, 'I like the way Pat sings and the way you play the B3.' He told us we needed to grow our hair longer, dress more casually, and dump the Fydallions name because it didn't mean anything. He told the group to come the next night, our night off, to Studio A at Columbia Records and bring our song list with us. One of the tunes we did in the studio was 'Baby What I Mean' by the Drifters, which he really liked. The next day he brought in a studio horn section to play on top of that and added background harmony to Pat's lead."

The group made some unfortunate misjudgments about material to record, however. "We turned down 'Celebrate,' which later became a hit by Three Dog Night. We turned down a suggestion to remake Ben E. King's 'I, Who have Nothing,' which Tom Jones made a hit again. We turned down the old Temptations tune 'Get Ready,' which Rare Earth later recorded. We thought we knew what we were doing," Harvey said. When the first couple of releases failed to generate much national chart action, the group's impatience led to tension with Usher. Before they began working with new producer Sonny Knight, they headed to Las Vegas for an extended stay. That was a bright time in the spotlight for the group.

"Ladies and gentlemen, the Thunderbird Hotel is proud to present Columbia recording artists the *Spiral Starecase*." Harvey fondly remembered that booming announcement that introduced them on stage night after night. Soon after entertainment director Bill Miller caught the group's act, they opened at the Flamingo Hotel's new Sky Room. "Bill Miller loved us, and it wasn't just for our music. We

223

dressed better than anybody. All of our clothes were custom made," Kaye explained. "We looked really sharp on stage." The Flamingo is on the Las Vegas "Strip," directly across Las Vegas Boulevard from Caesar's Palace, where Frank Sinatra and other top-name entertainers headlined. "Frank Sinatra came to see our show. So did José Feliciano, who came up and sang with us. Frank didn't sing with us, but we were just glad he was there because he was always handing out $100 bills to the guys. We met a lot of really nice people there."

During that era Pat Upton began to compose songs, beginning with 'More Today Than Yesterday,' in his room at the Bali Hai motel. "We played 'More Today Than Yesterday' in the Flamingo Sky Room to see if people would dance to it. Every time we played it people would ask, 'Hey, who did that song?' And we knew then we had a hit on our hands," Harvey told us. "We took it to Los Angeles and Al Capps rearranged it." For the recording session, Capps and producer Sonny Knight brought in top-notch performers who worked steadily as studio musicians, including Glen Campbell to lend guitar licks.

Again, disappointment followed as the latest release by the Starecase languished; frustratingly, radio stations ignored the record – until one station began playing it. Word reached the Starecase at the 49er Club in El Monte that "More Today Than Yesterday" had finally broken into the top 40 in Sioux Falls, South Dakota. Radio stations in other markets around the nation quickly jumped onto the record. In rapid succession in the late spring of 1969, "More Today Than Yesterday" hit the *Billboard* "Hot 100," the William Morris Agency signed the group, and a national tour was hurriedly assembled. "We hired a horn section to tour with us because we had used horns in the studio. Now we had this monstrous hit but a terrible concert show because we were just a dance band. Here we are working the same bill with Creedence Clearwater, which had lots of top hits, and we had one," Harvey said. Still, the band polished its concert act and managed to stretch that tour out to nearly a year. "But during that year things started getting a little funny. People were talking to Pat about his leaving the group and going on his own. We were having disagreements with our manager. We had lost confidence and trust in him. I finally quit." Upton departed a few month later, and he and Harvey began to talk. They discussed assembling a new group, played a few club dates in Southern California that at times included Vinnie Parello, but the project never really fully materialized and Upton set off in pursuit of a solo career.

Left alone with the name Spiral Starecase, which he acquired after the band dissolved in 1970, Harvey remained intent on building a new show group. Because Vinnie was playing in Hawaii with a group called Brown Dust, Harvey contacted Vince Dina, a drummer and vocalist who was a friend of Pat's. Harvey dubbed the new group Tootsie. "I didn't want to use the Spiral Starecase name until I had a band that I believed was worthy of the name," Kaye explained.

Tootsie was managed by Lenny Martin, whose stable of artists included Tony Bennett. "In the old *Vegas* television series, you would see the Tropicana Hotel sign that read, 'Lenny Martin presents....' Lenny got bookings for us all over the country for about a year and a half. Finally one day I flew back to Vegas from Boston, I had lunch with Lenny at the Sahara, and I said, 'Lenny, we're ready to call the group the Spiral Starecase.' And Lenny said, 'OK, let's do it.' We were working on the road, playing dinner theaters and hotels from 1972 until 1984 as a show group. Because Vince was such a great singer I put him in the front and hired another drummer. For awhile, Bobby Raymond came to work with me, and Vinnie was with me, so for a time three out of the five original Starecase members were performing. But Vinnie decided to get off the road, and changes in the group had diminished the quality, so by 1984 I was ready to retire the name Spiral Starecase until it could be presented right again."

By that time, Dick Lopes was operating his own video production company, Pat Upton was preparing to open a nightclub and Vinnie was selling cars. That was also the year that bassist Bobby Raymond died following an illness. Harvey decided to apply what he'd learned about booking gigs. Leaving Las Vegas, he returned to New York and got into the talent management business. In 1991, after the Spiral Starecase had been in dormancy for seven years, Harvey moved back to Las Vegas and phoned Vince Dina. "Let's bring the Starecase back," Harvey said. Vince was willing. True to his principals, Harvey determined that the resurrected Starecase must comprise a potent complement of musicians. "So we took three or four years to put it back together. That's how long it takes to find the right people."

While he judiciously began to assemble a new incarnation of the Starecase, he began another labor of love: management of the singing career of his daughter, Brenda Kaye Starr. "When she had her 1987 hit 'I Still Believe,' she was like a Puerto Rican Debbie Gibson," said Harvey. Born in October 1966 when the Starecase was playing the 49er Club, Brenda developed a new following in the late 1990s under the name Brenda K. Starr when she began to record salsa music in

Spanish, which she speaks fluently. The strategy turned to gold as she hit the top of the Latin music charts with "Herida," a song about emotional hurt on which Mariah Carey sang backup. "Notice that some of Mariah Carey's albums say, 'Special thanks to Brenda Kaye.' Mariah and Brenda are very good friends, and Mariah is the godmother to Brenda's oldest daughter, Kayla," Harvey explained. Brenda became the star act of Harvey's Las Vegas talent management company called SMASH – Super Management Association Strictly Hits. Harvey's son, Harvey Jr., is two years older than Brenda, for whom he was road manager for many years. Meanwhile Harvey's wife, Candace, operates her own company called SMASH Productions, a video production firm that began with work for Harvey before branching out to include other clients. "That's how I produce my groups and sell them. We've got a nice little dual business thing going. It's very successful," Harvey explained in 1997.

Harvey had met Candy in 1974, after being divorced from his first wife. He was on tour with the Starecase in Erie, Pennsylvania, where Candy worked as a computer technician for GTE. "We were appearing in a place called Gatsby's, and it looked like it was straight out of a John Travolta movie with an illuminated floor," Harvey grinned. "Candy came in and started talking to Vince. I told her, 'You don't want to fool around with him, because I think he's got a wife. Fool around with me.' We hit it off really well and every time I came back to Pennsylvania, we would spend time together. After a while I asked Candy to quit her job to be with me. She gave up a lot to just to be on the road," Harvey acknowledged. They married in 1980, and Harvey put Candy in the act as a dancer. "But we realized that when no one else could solve problems with lighting or the sound equipment, Candy could. She had an absolute knack for that. So I fired her as a dancer and put her in charge of keeping everything else in shape. She's very organized and began to do my books and keep everything in line for me. She was invaluable to me. Still is to this day," Harvey said. "The only reason I'm organized is because she's organized. I'm good at selling and promoting and she's good at keeping track of everything, every little detail. She's more analytical and I'm more impulsive. We have a beautiful home in the northwest part of Vegas and we have a couple of Rottweilers and a little dachshund, a couple of canaries, and we're very happy together."

By the late '90s the magnetic pull of New York had diminished its attraction for Harvey because most of his family members were by then living in Las Vegas. His brother Steven was a meat cutter for

Vons markets there. Harvey's parents moved to Vegas in 1967, when the Starecase headlined at the Flamingo Sky Room. His father, a tailor, died in 1992, but his mother, who worked in retail sales, remained in Vegas. Harvey's sister, Brenda Guarino, lives a few hours away in Gilbert, near Phoenix, Arizona, where she's a representative for Jafra Cosmetics.

"Right now the Starecase is probably sounding the best it ever has," Harvey asserted in 1997. "I've got a six-piece group out there working in major lounges. They're working solidly and begging for time off." But Harvey, who stepped down from performing with the group, had even grander plans in mind for the Starecase. "I called Pat and asked him to come back and sing with the Spiral Starecase. Pat told me it would be too hard to find a group. I never told him that I already had a group of musicians who know all of the songs. Finally I told him I thought I could find the group that can do the job, and I sent him a video of the Starecase. Then he became interested." Harvey proposed to fly Pat out only for special performances of the Starecase. "And I'll have a Hammond B3 for me. It's only a matter of time before Pat joins me again," Harvey said confidently. "My pet project is the Spiral Starecase for sentimental reasons. I'm really happy that the name is out there right now and that it's presented so well."

That reunion, unfortunately, did not occur. Harvey and Dick Lopes had seen each other from time to time. Harvey recalled one occasion in February 1997 when Dick attended a computer industry exposition at the Las Vegas Convention Center. "We had a couple of drinks together at the Stardust Hotel. I didn't even recognize him at first," Harvey admitted. "He had been this tall skinny guy when we played together and now he looked like a business executive. Dick was an experience to be involved with on the road. He was crazy back then. We had to hold him down every night. Dick and I talked about the new Starecase project and he seemed to support it completely. I promised him that as long as there's life in me that name will never die. And I also promised him that whoever is performing as the Starecase through me will put on a class act. I remember Dick came up to North Shore at Lake Tahoe in 1980 when we were appearing in the main showroom at the Cal Neva Club. Dick sat in the front row, and I thought he was going to cry out of pride when we did 'More Today Than Yesterday.' We have a deep feeling for this group." Pausing to reflect, Harvey in 1997 surmised, "I think Dick is beyond wanting to play and tour. But Pat never got done singing. And I never got done playing."

While remaining the lifeblood of the Spiral Starecase, in late 2001 Harvey began a new endeavor for which his outgoing personality was well-suited – selling vacation time-share units for Eldorado Resorts Corporation, which had developed two resort properties in Las Vegas. While Candy ran SMASH Productions, Harvey quickly became Eldorado Resorts' top-selling sales representative, a distinction that he held for six consecutive years.

"Harvey enjoyed working there. The company's office had a friendly, upbeat attitude," Candy told us in December 2010. "Harvey had told his colleagues that every time 'More Today Than Yesterday' played on the radio, he made about 5 cents in royalties. So when the song would come on the music system in the office, the other salespeople would stand up and cheer, telling Harvey, 'you just made another nickel.'"

While Harvey's colleagues knew about his entertainment background he didn't tell his customers about his involvement with the Spiral Starecase until after a sale was completed, because he believed he should focus on the customers and their needs. After a sale was complete, he gave the customer an autographed copy of a Spiral Starecase CD.

In July 2008 Harvey decided he wanted to undergo Lap-Band gastric surgery. Although he wasn't obese, he had high blood pressure, sleep apnea and mild diabetes. "Lap-Band surgery was believed to be helpful for those conditions," Candy explained. Harvey told his doctor, 'I want to live a long life with my wife.' Harvey failed a pre-surgical stress test, however, and the diagnostician told him he should consult a cardiologist because several blockages were detected, and he probably would need stents inserted. Even so, the cardiologist who examined Harvey concluded he didn't need stents or angioplasty, and sent Harvey home without further treatment. Three weeks later Candy had to attend the funeral of a friend in New York City. On the Friday morning when Candy's flight to New York was scheduled, Harvey mentioned that he had indigestion, but assured Candy he would be all right and told her to go to the funeral. When she phoned him from New York on Saturday, he said that the indigestion had mostly disappeared, but that his chest muscles had become sore. That Sunday morning, August 17, Candy called home but Harvey did not answer the phone. She tried calling him again Sunday evening, but still was unable to reach him. Concerned, Candy called her sister, who also lived in Las Vegas, and asked her to check on Harvey.

"My sister went to our house and found Harvey, dressed for work, dead on the floor," Candy said. "He apparently had collapsed there on Sunday morning while getting ready to go to work. I arrived home on Monday morning after flying all night from the East Coast. We didn't hold a funeral for him. Instead, we held a celebration of life, and many people from the music and entertainment industry came to honor him, including members of Joey Dee and the Starliters and the Brooklyn Bridge."

Candy, stunned, continued running SMASH Productions, eventually eliminating talent management and focusing on video production for clients. About a year and a half after Harvey's death, managers at Eldorado Resorts persuaded Candy to join that company as a sales representative. "I'm not as good at sales as Harvey was, but few other people were," she said.

Harvey's son, Harvey Jr., had suspended working with Brenda K. Starr in September 2005 to assist with Hurricane Katrina relief by driving demolition and reconstruction workers in and out of devastated areas. He now works as a truck driver in Florida. Debbie, Harvey's oldest daughter, lives in Petaluma, California, with her husband Morty Wiggins, who had been a partner of the late rock music entrepreneur Bill Graham in concert promotion and artist management, as well as an A&M Records executive. Wiggins remains well connected in the music industry.

Throughout his life, Harvey Kaye remained resolute that the Spiral Starecase never would have dissolved in the first place if not for management problems and lack of self-confidence. "If we had the foresight back then, we would have taken charge and organized a cooperative type of group in which we all had a say, kind of like the Grateful Dead did," Harvey mused. "If we would have done that, this group could have been an icon today. We didn't realize how good we were."

For more information, visit **www.smashproductions.com/ home.html**

Shadows bass player Dick Dunkirk and Bobby Vee in the early 1960s. Photo by ann Grenier.

6

Take Good Care Of My Baby

Bobby Vee

As a 15-year-old high school kid who had grown up in Fargo, North Dakota, Robert Thomas Velline was accustomed to the brutal winters that gripped the Northern Plains. But the news he heard the afternoon of February 3, 1959, chilled him to the bone. Jubilant that he held a ticket for that evening's Winter Dance Party in Moorhead, Minnesota – a stone's throw from Fargo – young Velline learned of the deaths of the show headliners: Buddy Holly, Ritchie Valens and the Big Bopper. Enroute to Moorhead following their performance the evening before at the Surf Ballroom in Clearlake Iowa, they perished with their 20-year-old pilot Roger Peterson, in a light plane crash on the snow-covered Iowa countryside. The tragedy ultimately put Velline unexpectedly on a course toward international stardom in a music career that gave him more hit singles than Holly, Valens and the Big Bopper combined.

The Moorhead Winter Dance Party was to feature Dion and the Belmonts and Frankie Sardo, along with Valens, the Big Bopper and a new group of Holly's Crickets that included Waylon Jennings, a friend of Holly's. It was one of the first packaged rock and roll tours to come through the Midwest, and Bobby Velline had a ticket and was excited about going to see one of his favorite groups – Buddy Holly and the Crickets. "There weren't many rock and roll acts that ventured that far out into the prairie," says Bobby, "and so it was pretty exciting to have this huge rock and roll show."

Fargo radio station KFGO and DJ Charlie Boone had organized the promotion of the show. When the bus arrived in Moorhead on February 3 with Dion and the Belmonts, the Crickets and Frankie Sardo on board, the station decided to go on with the show as scheduled despite the demise of the three headliners. "It was an odd decision, in view of the fact that three of the four major stars had perished," says Bobby, "but they asked for local talent to help fill in the evening so Jim Stillman, our bass player at the time, called the radio station and was told to have the band backstage at 7 p.m. There was no interview or anything. They just said, 'Come on down.'"

The group of local guys who went on stage that night didn't have a name. "This had been the most consistent group of guys who had been showing up for the little jam sessions. It wasn't like we were trying to start a career or anything. We were just there trying to help put out the fire. When those kinds of events happen, people come to the occasion with whatever they can bring. And we were just trying to help them get through the night and help people get through this tragedy, ourselves included, because I was a huge, huge Buddy Holly fan. We climbed on stage, knees knockin', and when Charlie said, 'What's the name of the band?' we didn't have a name, so I quickly replied, 'The Shadows.'"

Bobby didn't sing any Buddy Holly tunes that night, although it's been said that he did. "We sang some old rock and roll, some Elvis tunes, Jerry Lee Lewis and Little Richard. We were on for about 15 minutes, and it was a frightening experience for me," says Bobby. "I was only 15 years old and the audience was in shock. Some of them had just arrived at the venue and hadn't heard about the plane crash until they were in line. So it was quite an emotional evening. I do remember a point in that little set we did where I actually came back to Earth and I started hearing what we were doing and I was thinking to myself, 'You know, it sounds pretty good.'"

By the end of the evening, a local talent agent named Bing Bengtssen introduced himself to the Shadows and offered to book them. "It hadn't occurred to us that we could do anything beyond that concert, but we called him and he started booking dates for us. By June of that same year, we went into Minneapolis and recorded our first record. We put it out as Bobby Vee and the Shadows."

The group's first recording, a song written by Bobby called "Suzie Baby" was released by Soma Record Co., a small independent label based in Minneapolis. "It was a package deal. We paid $500, went in the studio, and they gave us three hours of recording time and a thousand records. So we cut two instrumentals and two vocals: 'Suzie Baby' was on the 'A' side and 'Flyin' High' [written by Bobby's brother Bill] was the instrumental that we chose for the 'B' side."

Bobby Vee and the Shadows began promoting "Suzie Baby" themselves in June 1959 by delivering it to radio stations around the Midwest. "Soma had initially recorded a lot of polka music, and we used to kid that we were the only band on the label that didn't wear lederhosen [leather shorts worn by men and boys, especially in Bavaria].

It was probably true. But when it started taking off, the record company got involved in it and started cranking out the records, and we sold probably 20,000 records in the upper Midwest."

While enjoying the regional success of their first hit "Suzie Baby" in 1959, the Shadows decided to add a piano player – someone who could play like Jerry Lee Lewis. Bobby recalls, "One day my brother Bill came home and said he had met a guy at Sam's Recordland named Elston Gunnn (with 3 n's), who claimed he played piano and had come off a tour with Conway Twitty. Bill auditioned him at the KFGO studios, and found that he rocked pretty good. So we bought him a shirt to match our stage attire, and his first dance with us was in Gwinner, North Dakota. All I remember is an old crusty piano that hadn't been tuned, ever! And in the middle of 'Lotta Lovin'" I heard the piano go silent. So I looked over to find Elston Gunnn dancing next to me as he broke into a background vocal part. The next night was more of the same. He was good spirited about the fact that none of us had the money to buy a piano for him, and none of us had hard feelings as he made his exit for the University of Minnesota. That's basically the Bob Zimmerman (AKA Elston Gunnn; AKA Bob Dylan) story as it relates to the Shadows. What I remember most is his energy and spirit. A rock 'n' roll contender even back then."

By the end of the summer of 1959, "Suzie Baby" had reached No. 1 on all the local stations in the upper Midwest. Major record companies, including Columbia, MGM and RCA, were calling with interest in this new young singer, Bobby Vee. In the fall of 1959, A&R man Snuff Garrett of Liberty Records persuaded the group to sign with that label, which was based on Sunset Boulevard in Hollywood. In January of 1960 Bobby flew to California, took an apartment in Hollywood and began his recording career with the label – an association that would span well over a decade.

Garrett had been a disc jockey in Lubbock, Texas, when local talents Buddy Holly and the Crickets were coming into their own. He had also become good friends with Holly and the members of the Crickets – drummer Jerry Allison, bass player Joe B. Mauldin and guitarist Sonny Curtis. Shortly after Holly died, Garrett joined Liberty Records, and he had been looking for new talent when "Suzie Baby" crossed his desk. "They had Eddie Cochran on the label, and they had signed Johnny Burnette. Snuff loved our record and he thought it reminded him of Buddy Holly and the Crickets. So he was interested in signing me to the label. Well, the original Crickets by then had also moved to California, and Snuff had also signed them to the label. And so here I was at the tender age of 16 working with some of my heroes: Jerry Allison and Tommy Allsup, who was on that 'Winter Dance Party' tour playing guitar for Buddy Holly. Tommy had been doing a lot of studio work, and he played lead guitar on 'Rubber Ball' and a lot of my records. So there was this nucleus of people who had Buddy Holly connections."

By 1961 Bobby Vee was touring extensively while his friend Bob Dylan was beginning to make a name for himself by performing in the coffee houses and folk clubs in New York's Greenwich Village. In his 2004 book *Chronicles: Volume One* (Simon & Schuster UK Ltd.), Dylan fondly recalls the similarities of their backgrounds. He wrote, "We had the same musical history and came from the same place at the same point in time. He [Bobby] had gotten out of the Midwest, too, and had made it to Hollywood."

Dylan describes how he took the D train to the Brooklyn Paramount theater where Vee was appearing with the Shirelles, Danny and the Juniors, Jackie Wilson, Ben E. King, Maxine Brown and others. After the show, the two got together as old friends and talked about what they were doing musically. "I wouldn't see Bobby Vee again for another 30 years," wrote Dylan, "and though things would be a lot different, I'd always thought of him as a brother."

That same year, Bobby's group changed its name from the Shadows to the Strangers after an English singer by the name of Cliff Richard, who had a band called the Drifters, changed its name to the Shadows. The change was to avoid confusion with the American rhythm and blues vocal group the Drifters, who laid claim to the name by virtue of their string of hits including "There Goes My Baby," "This Magic Moment," and "Save The Last Dance For Me." Bobby recalls, "Cliff Richard and his band were already huge in England and when they toured America it looked like they were going to be huge everywhere, so we thought, while this whole thing is young let's just pick another name, so we changed our name to the Strangers."

In 1962 Bobby recorded an album with the Crickets called *Bobby Vee Meets the Crickets*. "That completed another Buddy Holly loop," says Bobby. The album was successful in America and it also did very well internationally, climbing to No. 2 in England. Following the album's success there, Bobby and the Crickets toured Great Britain in the fall of 1962. By 1963, Bobby had amassed 10 top 40 hits in England, sharing the charts for 40 weeks with the Beatles.

During the following 30 years, Bobby Vee would garner 38 *Billboard* Hot 100 singles, an RIAA-certified gold record and 14

234

top 40 hits. He has recorded more than 25 albums, including a gold album from England for his 1981 *Singles Album* release. And *Billboard* magazine called him "One of the top 10 most consistent chart makers ever." Bobby retains strong name recognition and devotion from his fans, performing around 100 dates a year for appreciative crowds in the United States and abroad.

For more information, visit **www.bobbyvee.net** and **www.rockhousepro.com**

BOBBY VEE U.S. HIT SINGLES ON THE NATIONAL CHARTS

Debut	Peak	Gold	Label	
8/59	77		Suzie Baby	Liberty
4/60	93		What Do You Want?	Liberty
8/60	6		Devil or Angel	Liberty
9/60	81		Since I Met You Baby	Liberty
11/60	6		Rubber Ball	Liberty
2/61	33		Stayin' In	Liberty
2/61	61		More Than I Can Say	Liberty
5/61	63		How Many Tears	Liberty
8/61	1		Take Good Care of My Baby	Liberty
11/61	2		Run to Him	Liberty
11/61	53		Walkin' With My Angel	Liberty
2/62	15		Please Don't Ask About Barbara	Liberty
2/62	92		I Can't Say Goodbye	Liberty
5/62	15		Sharing You	Liberty
9/62	20		Punish Her	Liberty
9/62	99		Someday (When I'm Gone From You)*	Liberty
12/62	3		The Night Has a Thousand Eyes	Liberty
3/63	13		Charms	Liberty
6/63	34		Be True to Yourself	Liberty
6/63	85		A Letter From Betty	Liberty

* Bobby Vee and the Crickets

continued

Debut	Peak	Gold	Title	Label
11/63	55		Yesterday and You (Armen's Theme)	Liberty
12/63	99		Never Love a Robin	Liberty
1/64	83		Stranger in Your Arms	Liberty
2/64	52		I'll Make You Mine**	Liberty
5/64	63		Hickory, Dick and Doc	Liberty
12/64	84		(There'll Come a Day When) Ev'ry Little Bit Hurts	Liberty
12/64	97		Pretend You Don't See Her	Liberty
2/65	99		Cross My Heart	Liberty
5/65	85		Keep On Trying	Liberty
7/66	52		Look at Me Girl	Liberty
7/67	3	Δ	Come Back When You Grow Up	Liberty
11/67	37		Beautiful People	Liberty
2/68	46		Maybe Just Today	Liberty
4/68	35		My Girl/Hey Girl	Liberty
8/68	83		Do What You Gotta Do	Liberty
12/68	98		I'm Into Lookin' For Someone to Love Me	Liberty
8/69	92		Let's Call it a Day Girl	Liberty
11/70	88		Sweet Sweetheart	Liberty

Δ symbol: RIAA certified gold record (Recording Industry Association of America)

Billboard's pop singles chart data is courtesy of Joel Whitburn's Record Research Inc. (www.recordresearch.com), Menomonee Falls, Wisconsin.

** Bobby Vee with the Eligibles

EPILOGUE: Bobby Vee

Guitarist and singer

The youngest of three boys, Robert Thomas Velline was born on April 30, 1943, in Fargo, North Dakota. Bobby recalls as a 4-year-old hovering close to the radio thoroughly enthralled by musical guests appearing on the *Arthur Godfrey Show*. Music was an integral part of family life as Bobby's father, Sidney Velline, a short-order cook in a restaurant in Fargo, played violin and piano for enjoyment. Bobby's uncle was a professional musician who played the saxophone, and his mother, Saima (pronounced Syma), a homemaker, had a beautiful singing voice. Bobby's two older brothers, Bill and Sidney Jr., both played guitar.

Bobby and his brother Bill Velline.
Courtesy of Bobby Vee.

While growing up, Bobby enjoyed a variety of musical styles, but his earliest interest was country music. "There were only a couple of radio stations in Fargo at that time, and one of them played Hank Williams and Hank Snow and everybody named Hank. And the another station played some of the pop music of the day – Frankie Laine, Johnny Ray, Kay Starr, Peggy Lee and people like that. But when I was a young teenager, I made the transition from country music into rockabilly and rock and roll. The first time I heard Elvis on the radio was on a country station. We give him credit for country roots, but no one would call him a country artist. But that was his entrance into the music business, with 'That's All Right,' and I just thought it was really good country music."

All three Velline boys played instruments in high school – Bobby played the saxophone, Sydney Jr. played trumpet, and Bill played trombone. "But when rock and roll started coming along, we put down payments on guitars, and eventually we all played guitar and had our own little Louisiana Hayride right up in North Dakota," recalls Bobby. "My brother Bill kinda sang like Johnny Cash, and he was a great guitar player. He didn't use a guitar pick. He plucked the strings with his thumbnail and first two fingernails on his right hand, sort of like Mark Knopfler of Dire Straits. He pulled on the strings. Others have done it this way but it was really heartfelt the way Bill picked. Diehard guitar fans ask about him often."

Bobby yielded more seriously to the allure of music in the spring of 1958, when his brother Bill had a garage band and would take him along to jam sessions. "Nobody sang, they just played the music of all these Gene Vincent and Eddie Cochran songs, and Elvis songs, and they would get lost in the music. Different guys would show up. Bill knew that I sang because we used to go to all the country shows together that would come through the area, and he would say, 'Bobby, how's the bridge go on this?' And I would sing it to him. And that's how I became a singer in the band."

The group that soon transpired consisted of Bobby on vocals and his brother Bill on guitar, Bob Korum on drums and Jim Stillman on bass. They rehearsed wherever they could – in garages and basements and occasionally in one of the music rooms at Moorhead State College (now Minnesota State University Moorhead). "The college students would come around and listen while we were playing. We hadn't played professionally. And we had never played any music with the thought of ever playing it again, so we would just blast through all these rock and roll songs that we knew."

A sophomore in high school when he filled in on the Buddy Holly show, Bobby finished the school year but didn't return for his junior year. "I didn't know what to do, and I didn't know who to ask. Even my parents didn't know what I should do. They looked at it realistically. I was 16 years old and had a No. 1 record in the upper Midwest. And they loved music. And we always got high marks for playing in the band or singing songs or writing songs or poems. So they were excited about it, too, and it was hard for them to be objective. So I went to my school counselor and told him what was going on, and I really wanted him to talk me out of leaving school. And he said, 'Wow! A No. 1 record. Man, that's gotta be exciting.' And I said, 'Well, it really is exciting, and I'm signing a record contract with a company in Los Angeles.' He said, 'You've gotta be kidding. Unbelievable. That's great!' Instead of talking me out of it, he was getting all excited about it, and he said, 'Let me ask you a question. If this whole thing didn't work, would you come back to school?' And I hadn't thought about that as an option, and I said, 'Well, yeah.' He said, 'Well, then, let's do

238

this. Let me set you up with some correspondence courses at the college here. You can study on your own.' And he did. So I'd be out there on the road, rockin' away, and I'd come back to my room and be doing algebra. And that got me through '60 and '61, when I was a senior. And my career got so busy that I ended up not finishing. I was a few credits away from getting my high school diploma. But it was a great experience."

While AM radio, local television record hop shows, soda shop jukeboxes, and touring provided outlets to promote the rock and roll hits of the day, enterprising record companies and movie producers discovered a powerful new platform for exposure via the drive-in movie screens. The drive-in movie phenomenon, which began during the 1950s, provided an ideal forum to bring both the sounds and images of rock and roll to the masses. After teenagers responded in huge numbers to motion pictures starring Elvis Presley and the beach party flicks with Frankie Avalon and Annette Funicello, MGM hit upon a stunning strategy – showcasing its stable of recording artists including Connie Francis, Herman's Hermits, Sam the Sham and the Pharaohs, and others in lighthearted movies cranked out by its motion picture division. "A lot of those movies became that vehicle, sort of the MTV of the day," says Bobby, who appeared in four films beginning in 1962. "Even going back into the '50s, Alan Freed was making movies – *Rock, Rock, Rock* and *Don't Knock the Rock* and *Rock Around the Clock* – and they really made it possible for some of the people in the outlying areas, like me living in Fargo, to see what Eddie Cochran looked like, and Gene Vincent, and some of these guys, even though they were all terrible movies."

Bobby played a lead role in the 1967 Paramount Pictures film *C'mon, Let's Live a Little* about a country boy who went away to college and fell in love with the dean's daughter, played by Jackie DeShannon, another Liberty recording artist. "I studied acting with Agnes Moorehead, who played Samantha's mother, Endora, in the television series *Bewitched*, for a couple of years. Then I studied with Jeff Corey, who was blacklisted as a communist during the whole McCarthy thing. He was a great instructor. When Jeff was finally able to get back into acting, he turned his class over to Leonard Nimoy (before the TV series *Star Trek* aired), and I studied with Leonard for about a year and a half."

Bobby claims in the beginning he was a shy kid – not a candidate for show business. "Bill and I were just country guys, and he hated all of the glitz and all of the stuff that goes along with the business. But acting was a way for me to learn how to move my body, and how to look at people, how to sing to them, and how to present myself. It was a great, great learning experience for me."

Body movement was a key component of Agnes Moorehead's acting class, which engaged in fencing for body movement, and stage blocking for positioning on stage. "I learned a lot about performing in those classes, about singing to the back of the room and gesturing and those kinds of things that seem phony and foreign until they become part of you and it's part of performing. So it's like learning anything else: the basic skill has to be there. It really increased my comfort level a lot, and just made me a lot more comfortable with myself as a person," says Bobby. "But I never really saw myself as an actor. And I also realized very quickly that people spend a lifetime trying to have an acting career, and people spend a lifetime trying to develop a singing career, and there aren't very many people that cross over. I was so into music, I didn't really have the time to devote to the acting career."

In 1963 Bobby participated in two Dick Clark Caravan of Stars tours. "Dick actually traveled on the bus with us on the first tour, then of course he quickly realized he could have five tours out at the same time rather than one, and then he would kind of skip around from tour to tour," says Bobby, who recalls traveling with artists such as Del Shannon, Bryan Hyland, Little Anthony and the Imperials, Peter Noone and Herman's Hermits, Little Eva, and the Dovells. "We were on the bus and off the bus and on the bus and off the bus, and into a hotel, on the bus, into the show, on the bus, into the hotel. It was like 30 days of that. The only comfort we had was each other. And I made some fast friends on those tours. You can imagine, a bunch of teenage guys, and all of us traveling all around the country together."

Bobby was on a Dick Clark tour in Dallas on November 22, 1963, when John F. Kennedy was shot. On that fateful day, Bobby was staying at the Sheraton Hotel. When he visited Dallas in January 2000, the memories of that day 36 years prior came back in haunting fashion. "I was talking on the phone to a buddy in Dallas and I said, 'Where is the Sheraton Hotel? I stayed at the Sheraton when I was here on the Dick Clark tour, when Kennedy was killed.' And he said, 'Where are you staying?' I said 'At the Adam's Mark Hotel.' He told me the Adam's Mark had been the Sheraton. And I thought it was one of those *Twilight Zone* things. And the Texas School Book Depository building was not far from there. And all those memories came back to me."

Dick Clark is a longtime friend of Bobby's. "Dick Clark is a wonderful man, he really is, and a very astute businessman. Dick has been part of my family's life, too. When we lived in Los Angeles we used to get together with him frequently. When my youngest son Robbie called Dick and told him he wanted to come out to the American Music Awards in January 2000, Dick and his wife, Kari, welcomed him. My son brought a couple of friends with him, and they got him seats in the 12th row in the middle. As soon as he got there, the security people took him back to see Dick and Kari. And they treated him so nice. It was such a nice feeling for me because we've got a lot of time invested in this business, and there are some people that we can call on that I think of as friends, and Dick is certainly one of them."

Bobby and his wife, Karen Bergen [pronounced with a soft "g"], first met in Minnesota when they were 16 years old. They dated, then married in 1963, when they were both almost 21. The couple bought a house in Bel Air, California, where they lived until 1981, when they moved back to the Midwest. "We never really left the Midwest. I always had a lake cabin in Minnesota, and we'd come back in the summertime and spend the summers, and then go back to California. So it was a real easy transition for me." says Bobby.

Bobby Vee in 2000.

Bobby and Karen have three sons, a daughter and five grandchildren. Jeff, the oldest, was born in January 1965; Tom was born in 1966; Robbie was born in 1967, and daughter Jennifer was born in 1972. Bobby's three sons are members of a band called the Vees. "The Vees started working with me on my shows in 1994, and they're great players. When they were young and I was out doing shows in the summertime, I'd take them along, usually one at a time, and so they got to meet a lot of the people – Del Shannon, Gene Pitney and certainly Dick Clark," says Bobby. "People ask me how my sons all managed to be interested in the music business, and I just throw up my hands and say I had nothing to do with it. We always had a lot of music around the house, a lot of musical instruments, but they worked all that stuff out in their own personal sandbox. I wouldn't want to try to manage that, and I didn't. And it's the best band I've ever had. And they're so respectful of the people that we work with, and the other acts that we do shows with. They know the time period, they love the time period, and they're playing the music the way it's supposed to be played. It's just a great, great time for me."

Although Bobby and Karen's daughter, Jennifer, also has a nice singing voice, she has no interest in being part of the music scene. A professional graphic designer, Jennifer graduated from Minneapolis College of Art and Design, and went to work for a marketing company before starting her own business called Sassafrass Design.

During the early '70s Bobby and Karen traveled to Sydney, Australia, where Bobby was performing at a Hilton Hotel. "At that time it was Carole King and *Tapestry* and James Taylor, and disco and all that stuff. It was *not* oldies radio. There really wasn't such a thing. I was going out and rehearsing with bands, and then I would perform. It became so boring for me, and I realized that I sort of hit the wall when I was down there, and I thought, 'God, this is just tough. I'm not having any fun, I've got to do something else.'"

Still signed with Liberty Records, which had been absorbed by the United Artists label, Bobby returned to Los Angeles, went into the studio and recorded *Nothing Like a Sunny Day* under the name Robert Thomas Velline. "It took me back to my 'Suzie Baby' days, and I made a real important re-connection with my own spirit and my heart. The songs I wrote were a reflection of all the things that I like about music. It was a little bit country and a little pop and a little bit rock and roll. And it's because it was so different, we labored over whether we should put it out as a Bobby Vee album or put it out as a Robert Thomas Velline album. So we put it out and got wonderful reviews on it. Didn't sell any, but what it did for me was to reconnect me with the things that I love about music rather than the things that I dread about music. So it's a place that belongs to me, that I can go to, that keeps me on track and keeps my values in order."

Bobby has endured the death of his parents and both brothers. His father died in 1985 and his mother died 10 years later. His brother Sidney Jr. (two years Bobby's senior) died tragically in a house fire in 1989, which also took the life of Bobby's 9-year-old nephew, Ronnie. His brother Bill (five years his senior) died in 1997, leaving his wife and two adult children from a previous marriage.

A member of the Shadows until 1963, Bill had a difficult time coping with life on the road. "I tried to drag him along as a tour manager after he quit the band and he made a decision. We were out in Buffalo, New York, and he said, 'I'm going home.' I would have been around 19 or somewhere around there. I said, 'Geez, Bill, we've got 10 more dates left on this tour.' And he said, 'I know, but I've gotta go

home.' And so we called his girlfriend, wife-to-be, and she came out
to Buffalo and joined us and finished the tour. And I thought, I could
understand that, missing your loved one, even at that young age. But
that was it. He didn't ever want to go out on the road again, and later
went into radio and sales and promotions. Bill was my mentor and
hero," says Bobby. "He taught me how to play guitar and encouraged
me to be myself and do my best."

Bobby's brother Sidney was considered the rebel in the family,
until later years when he began to take responsibility for his life circumstances. "It was joyful to see him with his children. And we had
such a good relationship, so it was difficult when he died at the age
of 49," Bobby said.

In 1981 Bobby and Karen wanted to get more involved in their
new community in Minnesota and helped to organize a fund-raiser
for Cathedral High School, which their children attended. "Karen
suggested that it would be fun if they would do a sock hop, like
a '50s kind of thing, and they liked that idea. It was a smoke-free,
alcohol-free event that went on for 24 years and raised over $1 mil-
lion for the Catholic schools. It was a place where families could
come together and dance like the ballroom days of early rock and
roll. Adults and kids alike came dressed up in costumes and wearing
poodle skirts and ducktails, and grandparents out there dancing with
their grandkids. It was a great family event that all could afford in
support of a great cause."

Past shows have included the Coasters, the Shirelles, Chubby
Checker and Bo Diddley. "Dick Clark's wife graduated from high
school in St. Cloud, and she was the homecoming queen at Tech
High School," says Bobby. "So I called Dick and I said, 'How'd you like
to bring the queen back to the hop?' And he liked the idea and said,
'Kari would love that. It would really be fun for her.' So they came in
a couple of days early, and we took them around town, and everybody said, 'Wow! Dick Clark!' He donated his time, and he was so gra-
cious. He signed autographs for two hours. He's just amazing."

Karen has been a licensed social worker (MSW) and therapist
since 1983. She has her own practice and works with people with
addictions. "She is the grounding factor in the family. She is a woman
of options. I can tell her what's going on, and she can say, 'Well, what
about this?' She'll always come up with more options."

Bobby and his sons have a record label called Rockhouse Productions (www.rockhousepro.com). "It *was* in our home, and it started
out as the family sandbox, and it has become a commercial entity. So

we bought an old bank building in St. Joseph, Minnesota, and put a studio in there. And I'm loving having the studio in a separate place. I think of it as a sort of creative workshop. We've got a lot of really talented musicians, and some good writers, and they come in and demo their songs, and some of them come in and do albums. We also have a video production company that's doing lots of different things."

Semi-retired, Bobby spends part of his time in Tucson, Arizona, where his longtime producer and lifelong friend Snuff Garrett also lives. He and Karen also own seven acres on a spring-fed lake in Minnesota, where they enjoy water sports during the summer months. For pleasure and relaxation one of the things Bobby loves to do is paint. He enjoys working with oils and with acrylics. He continues to write music. "I basically do it for myself, although my youngest son Robbie is spending a lot of time in Nashville. He's been writing with Wayne Carson, the guy who wrote the Willie Nelson hit 'Always on My Mind,' and 'The Letter' for the Boxtops. But I basically work on my own projects."

Throughout the 1990s, Bobby performed from the United Kingdom to Australia, and all points in between. Sir Andrew Lloyd Webber invited Bobby to perform at the opening of his musical *By Jeeves.* In 1996, Bobby was a guest performer at Web-

Tommy, Bobby and Jeff Vee at the Surf Ballroom in Clearlake, Iowa, February 2009. Photo by Craig Kienast.

ber's Sydmonton Festival, a summer arts festival held periodically at his Hampshire country house where a variety of exclusive previews are presented to a private audience of people from theater, television and film in order to gauge the future potential of his works. Performances take place in a deconsecrated church on the grounds (www.

andrewlloydwebber.com/about/sydmonton-festival/).

On three separate occasions, Paul McCartney invited Bobby to be part of his annual Buddy Holly commemoration event, performing in both New York and London, where McCartney joined Bobby, the Crickets and Carl Perkins for an all-star finale.

What kind of music does Bobby listen to today? "I tend to hit the scan button and when it stops, if I like what I hear, that's what I listen to on the radio. I find myself listening to more country music, which is very pop-ish, and I also have enjoyed plugging into some of the things that I missed years ago – some of those great doo-wop groups, the Nutmegs and the Spaniels and the Orioles, and the list goes on and on. It's a time period that I, growing up in the upper Midwest with country music, missed out on. There's a lot of good stuff to listen to."

Fans of Bobby Vee's music would likely agree.

CD RELEASES – 2000-2011

- 1990 to 2006 – All Bobby Vee LPs reissued on CD by Beat Goes On records
- 2000 – *Down The Line,* a tribute to Buddy Holly, released and received critical acclaim worldwide. Bobby's ballad version of "Tell Me How" was adapted by the London Symphony Orchestra and re-recorded at Abbey Road Studios.
- 2002 – *I Wouldn't Change A Thing,* a collection of old favorites and self-penned tunes featuring a song written with Sir Tim Rice called "Whatever Happened to Peggy Sue"
- 2003 – *Up North December,* a Christmas CD with new versions of old favorites and several self-penned holiday songs co-written with Bobby's family
- 2006 – *The Singles Collection – Box Set*
- 2008 – *The Very Best of Bobby Vee*, a brand-new hits collection that the British Phonographic Industry certified silver in the UK
- 2011 – *Rarities: Rare and Unreleased Gems From the Capitol Vaults* – 61 track double CD released in January

---

The Zombies in 1965. From left, Chris White, Hugh Grundy (seated), Rod Argent, Colin Blunstone, Paul Atkinson. Courtesy of Hugh Grundy.

7

Time of the Season

The Zombies

In the early days of rock and roll, New York's "Tin Pan Alley" was the gristmill of songwriters who composed the hits that pop stars recorded. That convention was challenged by the Beatles, who not only unleashed the British invasion but also validated the concept of the self-contained band performing songs that the members had written themselves. The Beatles were the first Britons to hit the top of the American charts with their own material. The Zombies were the very next.

The Zombies were five serious young men whose musical interests were rooted in jazz, blues and classical music. The quintet's music was distinguished by the pleading, breathy vocals of singer Colin Blunstone and the haunting compositions of keyboard player Rod Argent and bassist Chris White.

Argent formed the Zombies in 1961 with Blunstone, guitarist Paul Atkinson, bass player Paul Arnold and drummer Hugh Grundy. All five were students from St. Albans, Hertfordshire, England, about 20 kilometers (a dozen miles) beyond the northern reaches of London. The musicianship of Argent's elder cousin Jim Rodford inspired Rod to form a band. Paul Arnold and Rod were neighbors and had known each other since their primary school years (ages 7 to 11). "I first heard Rod play the piano at a recital in school when we were 10 years old," Arnold recalled. Paul and Rod subsequently enrolled in separate grammar schools (for students between the ages of 11 and 18). Paul attended government-supported St. Albans Grammar School, while Rod entered fee-charging St. Albans School, a "public school" – akin to an American college preparatory private school. At 11 years of age, in his first year at St. Albans Grammar School, Paul Arnold met classmate Colin Blunstone, with whom he shared an interest in athletics.

Rod, who was not quite 16 at the time, began assembling his band by recruiting the two Pauls. Rod had heard Paul Atkinson, who had just turned 15, playing guitar in a student folk music club. Asked to join the band, Paul Arnold, 16, set about building a bass guitar as a school project and asked Paul Atkinson to help with the frets. Arnold also approached Colin Blunstone, who was then going on 16. "We sat in alphabetical order in St. Albans Grammar School, and 'Arnold' was in front of 'Blunstone.' Paul knew I had a guitar, and one day he turned around in his chair and said, 'one of my neighbors is starting a band,'" Colin recalled. Arnold told Argent, "I've got a good mate at school called Colin Blunstone who plays guitar and sings a bit. I'll bring him along." In search of a drummer, Rod went to see the school "Army cadets" marching band. "As it was marching past, I picked the guy who seemed to have the best sense of rhythm – Hugh, who also attended St. Albans School," Rod said. Hugh had just turned 16. "And that was the band! It was a chance in a million that it all worked."

Few diversions existed for teenagers in the early 1960s in St. Albans, which had two movie theaters – both of which closed by 11 p.m. – and only two black-and-white television channels. "There was no point staying home and watching TV, because there was nothing on for teenagers," Atkinson told us in 1999. "We had no choice but to either play sports or form a band for something to do." Colin, who would become the lead singer, was at first reluctant to join the band. "I was involved in a lot of sports in school, and most of my nights and weekends were taken up with sports. My first reaction after Paul asked me was, 'Oh, my God, what have I got myself involved in?' I went along for the first rehearsal and it was really good fun," Colin said.

For the band's first rehearsal, Jim Rodford drove to the boys' homes and picked them up in a van into which he had loaded musical instruments and amplification equipment that belonged to his own group, the Bluetones. Of all the band members, only Paul Arnold knew Colin, and Paul was not in the van when it drove up to the Blacksmith Arms Pub, where they had agreed to meet Colin. Colin had a few days earlier broken his nose in a rugby match. "Are you Colin Blunstone? Are you joining our band?" the voices from inside the van asked. "Yes," he said as he climbed into the van. "I got into this car of strangers and, as we drove off to rehearsal, I think they were all a little nervous about me because I had two black eyes and strapping across my nose," Blunstone grinned. "I think they thought I was pretty rough and tough. Once the black eyes were gone, they realized I wasn't quite as tough as they thought I was."

Initially, Rod was cast in the role of lead singer and Colin was designated the band's rhythm guitar player. Colin recalls that the band practiced "Malagueña" at that first rehearsal. During a break, Rod headed for an old piano in the corner of the room and started banging out B. Bumble and the Stingers' searing boogie-woogie number "Nut Rocker." Blunstone thought it was odd that Rod was not playing keyboards in the band. After a few weeks, the roles of Argent and Blunstone were reshuffled into their proper alignment: Argent on keyboards and Blunstone as vocalist, although Colin did continue to play rhythm guitar on occasion.

During its first few weeks, the band played as the Sundowners and as the Mustangs before settling on the name Zombies, which Arnold suggested. "We wanted to find a name that no one else had thought of. We thought that surely no one would be so foolhardy to call themselves the Zombies. As you can guess, we were getting a little desperate," Blunstone laughed.

Playing in small youth clubs in the St. Albans area, the Zombies set out to build a following. Rod recalled, "At the time there were no electric pianos, so I played whatever piano was available, bashing away as I normally did. I'd run my thumb up and down the keys like Jerry Lee Lewis, and I did it so often that my thumb would often start bleeding. Imagine this sweaty guy with blood coming out of his fingers."

After a year or so, the band underwent its first and only personnel change. Bass player Paul Arnold, born in Blackpool in December 1944, planned to become a physician. Accepted to medical school at St. Andrews University, he found he was unable to devote sufficient attention to the Zombies as schoolwork began to consume more of his time. "I didn't tell the group I was going to quit until I found my replacement, Chris White," Arnold said. Chris, a student at the local art school, had been a schoolmate of Paul Arnold's older brother, Terry, at St. Albans Grammar School. Paul asked Terry to introduce Chris to the band. Chris, who was two years older than the other band members, brought the band an additional dimension as a composing collaborator for Rod Argent.

When Paul Arnold departed, Terry left his bank job to become the Zombies' first manager; he eventually became the band's tour manager when the band hired another manager. Initially, the band's gigs were confined to "drinking men's" clubs, church youth clubs and other polite social venues in "Herts," as Hertfordshire is colloquially known. The band members got their first taste of popularity after Colin Blunstone introduced the band to his school's rugby and alumni club, which presented periodic dinner dances in the evenings following rugby matches. "The club would struggle to get 20 people to go to these dinner dances. We were allowed to play an interval once, and it went down so well that they asked us back to play for a full dance, and it really took off," said Colin. "We started playing at other rugby clubs as well and they all were just packed out. That's when we started to think that there was something to build on."

Hugh Grundy recalls those gigs with fondness. "Those were exciting days. Very good days, they were," said Grundy. From late 1962 until early 1964, the Zombies confined themselves to playing in clubs within a 30-mile radius of St. Albans. They were earning from £5 to £15 per gig. "That was a substantial amount of money for an 18-year-old in those days," Atkinson said. "It was enough to enable us to buy equipment and sorely lacking instruments. We'd save up and buy an amplifier or guitar or one drum, one at a time, until we had a whole drum kit." That money enabled Argent to buy a Hohner Pianet electric piano, which contributed strongly to the distinctive sound that the band evolved.

While Rod had been accepted by a university, he obtained a one-year deferral for his entrance in order to concentrate on the band. All of the band members excelled academically – so much so that they would later be recognized for collectively posting the highest exam scores of any emerging British rock band of that era. During Rod's school hiatus, the band entered a musical talent contest in Hertfordshire called the Herts Beat competition, sponsored by the *Evening News* newspaper. One of the prizes was a demo recording session. Hugh recalled his apprehension about the first performance. "I can distinctly remember we were all very, very nervous. I was experiencing paralyzing fear and an overabundant use of the toilet," Hugh chuckled. "That nervousness was dissipated from then on, because I thought, 'Well, we've done that, and there can be nothing more nerve-wracking." The band members' subsequent self-confidence served them well. In the competition, spanning several Saturdays in April 1964 at the 2,000-seat Watford Town Hall, the Zombies progressed to the finals.

"On the day of the final, to my amazement, the place was packed," recalled Rod. "Coach loads of Zombies fans had come from outlying villages in an organized campaign. We knew nothing about any of this. Suddenly we were on stage and it felt like to us what it must have felt like for the Beatles, who seemed to be conquering the world at that time. There were all these screams, and banners saying 'Zombies.' It was extraordinary because it was completely unexpected. That moment is still a highlight for me." The busloads of fans energized the Zombies' performance and likely were influential in the decision to award the band the recording session prize.

The session that the band won took place at a small home studio in the town of Rickmansworth operated by a former disk jockey named Jack Jackson, whose English-language pop music broadcasts on Radio Luxembourg had been a favorite of British teenagers. At Jackson's studio, the Zombies recorded two tracks: Rod Argent's "It's Alright With Me" and George and Ira Gershwin's "Summertime."

After the competition the band received offers from several record labels. Chris White sought advice on the contracts from his uncle Ted White, a musical arranger for the BBC. Upon Ted's suggestion, the boys contacted a friend of his named Ken Jones. A songwriter and producer, Jones examined the offers, and advised them about their good points and bad points. "When we asked if he could do anything for us, he offered us a deal that had all of the good points!" said Chris.

With the help of Jones, the Zombies began generating interest and receiving offers from additional record labels. They chose Decca Records, with which they signed a three-year contract. Jones encouraged the band members to prepare original material for their first session, on June 12, at the Decca studios in the West Hampstead section of London. They brought four songs, including a composition by Chris White called "You Make Me Feel Good," along with the second tune that Rod had ever composed – "She's Not There." The band

The Zombies in early 1964. From left, Hugh Grundy, Chris White, Colin Blunstone, Paul Atkinson and Rod Argent. Courtesy of Hugh Grundy.

251

recorded four-track masters, working with the same technical crew in the same studio complex in which the Rolling Stones, the Moody Blues, Marianne Faithfull, the Bachelors, Tom Jones, Lulu, Them and other Decca acts recorded. The Zombies found that recording required discipline to which they had to adjust. "Recording was completely different from performing for an audience," Atkinson said. "On stage you're providing entertainment, but in the studio you're focusing your attention on getting a perfect take. That took some getting used to." Atkinson observed that the strain of trying to achieve perfection can be stifling. "I think we did our best when we weren't really trying so hard, but we were simply playing naturally. Our best recordings were those when we were playing for ourselves and not for the producer."

Decca released "She's Not There" in July 1964. Driven by a persistent bass line, the song climbed impressively to No. 12 in the United Kingdom in late summer, but did even better in the United States after its release on the Parrot label, a division of London Records. "She's Not There" hit the American charts in early October '64 and ultimately attained the No. 2 position on the *Billboard Hot 100* and No. 1 in *Cashbox* magazine – making the Zombies only the second British band after the Beatles to score that high on the American charts with their own composition.

Argent identifies blues artists John Lee Hooker and Muddy Waters as influential in his life at the time he wrote "She's Not There." He says the song was inspired by a John Lee Hooker song called "No One Told Me," the title of which became the opening words of "She's Not There." From that phrase, Argent built his composition. "I started messing around with chords and with a vocal line and built it from there," he explained. "There were a couple of chord sequences I liked very much. Particularly what attracted me was in the bit that goes, 'it's too late to say you're sorry,' when the chord changes go from a major chord to a minor chord, but the bass doesn't play the root of the chord. The bass plays the major third and when the chord changes, it plays the minor third." Argent says the bass line was written rather than improvised. "The bass line and the drum segments were intrinsic parts of the song. That's how I started. Some parts were improvised, but the bass and drums were not. Pat Metheny, who I met years later, said he loved 'She's Not There' when he first heard it because of all of the modal influences on it. I wondered what he meant, because I thought there was nothing modal about it. So I went back and played it and only then did I realize that the way I approached the chord sequences was in a modal way, but I had done it without thinking. I guess it was because I had listened so much to Miles Davis' *Kind of Blue* album. I applied things in that way because of what I had been listening to. But in the end, that mixture turned into something that was really original. I don't think 'She's Not There' sounds like anything else," Argent observed.

Based on the international success of "She's Not There," Decca rushed the Zombies back into the company's West Hampstead studio in late November 1964 to record their first album, *Begin Here*. Blunstone fully assumed the role of lead vocalist and no longer played guitar on any Zombies recording sessions; he sang on all but one track of the debut album. "Because the success of 'She's Not There' took everyone a bit by surprise, that first album was recorded very quickly – in, oh, I should think, three or four evenings," Blunstone recalled. "We'd go into the studio for an evening and we'd come out with four finished tracks. After I had gone home one evening they realized they had time to do one more track. It was 'I Got My Mojo Working,' which Rod sang."

As soon as recording for the album was completed, the Zombies boarded a plane to New York. Entrepreneurial WINS radio disk jockey Murray "the K" Kaufman had booked the Zombies for a 10-day engagement at the Brooklyn Fox Theatre at 10 Flatbush Avenue beginning a few days before Christmas 1964. Unfamiliar with airline meal accommodations, Blunstone's mother packed sandwiches and an apple for Colin to take on the flight. While aboard the airliner Colin did eat his sandwiches but not the apple. When the airliner touched down in New York, the Zombies were escorted to the U.S. Customs check-in point. There an inspector opened Colin's lunch bag. "He took the apple that my dear old mother had packed for me and ate it in front of me, with no explanation that bringing fruit into the country is not permitted," said Blunstone. From there he was taken to an immigration office. "There were policemen with guns, and I had never seen a gun before. A guy showed me his badge, led me off to a telephone booth and then put his hand inside his jacket." He pulled out a picture of his daughter and showed it to Blunstone. "Listen," said the immigration officer. "I'm going to call my daughter. Will you say 'hello' to her?" the officer asked. "Because he hadn't explained what he was doing until that moment, I was a nervous wreck by the time I left the airport."

The Zombies, from modest backgrounds and with little money to their names, were picked up by a trio of Cadillac limousines awaiting their arrival at the airport in New York. After their less-than-hospitable treatment by federal agents, the boys thought that New York City had rolled out the red carpet for them. "Then about three days later, we got the bill for the limousines," said Blunstone.

Appearing on stage at the Murray the K Holiday Revue at the Fox with a score of other acts – including Chuck Jackson, Ben E. King, Dick and Dee Dee, the Drifters, the Vibrations, the Nashville Teens, Patti LaBelle and the Blue Belles, and the Hullaballoos – the Zombies did five shows each day, typically singing only a few songs at each performance. "Still, we had to remain at the theater all day. We'd get there about 10 in the morning and we'd leave about 9 or 10 at night," Blunstone remembers. "We couldn't leave the building before then because it was surrounded by thousands of people. We had to wait until everyone left." And then the five Zombies boarded the subway to return to their rooms at the St. George Hotel at Clark and Hicks streets in a section of Brooklyn Heights populated by rooming houses. "The hotel was a bizarre place. We were the only people under 65 there; everyone else seemed ancient because it was somewhat of a retirement home. It wasn't very grand at all. People would never understand that we were just about broke when we came to America. That part of Brooklyn was a pretty rough and tough area, and they wouldn't believe that we'd walk to the subway and ride it back to the hotel because we didn't have much money," Blunstone said.

Parrot Records released most of the songs from *Begin Here* in the United States on an album titled simply *The Zombies* in January 1965 – two months before the British release was issued. "She's Not There" had remained on the charts for nearly four months, until late January, when it surrendered to the second single by the band, "Tell Her No." Striking No. 6 on the charts, "Tell Her No" appeared to establish the Zombies as consistent hit makers, and they went out on the road, touring the United States for six solid weeks with the Dick Clark Caravan of Stars. Teenage fans packed the Rotunda of the Las Vegas Convention Center the evening of May 16, 1965, when Dick Clark's Caravan rolled into town. Joining the Zombies on that tour were headliners Del Shannon (whose hits included "Runaway" and "Hats Off to Larry,") and the Shangri-Las ("Leader of the Pack," "Give Him a Great Big Kiss"), along with Dee Dee Sharp ("Mashed Potato Time," "Do the Bird"), Jewel Akens ("The Birds and The Bees"), the Ikettes ("I'm Blue," "Peaches 'n' Cream"), Tommy Roe ("Sheila," "Everybody"), the Ad-Libs ("The Boy From New York City"), Mike Clifford ("Close to Cathy"), the Larks ("The Jerk"), the Velvelettes ("Needle in a Haystack") and Jimmy Soul ("If You Wanna Be Happy"). A few hours preceding the show, disk jockey Jeff Colson of KENO, the radio station sponsoring the concert, played a practical joke on one of the members of his fan club. Putting on a convincing English accent, he phoned her number. "Hello, I've been asked to ring you up. This is Colin Blunstone of the Zombies," said Colson in his mock English accent. The girl's shrieks from the other end of the phone could be heard across the room. [Jeff March, co-author of this book, sat in the front row of that concert as a guest of KENO radio, and was with Jeff Colson when he made that phone call.]

Driven to a frenzy during the show, swarms of shrieking teen-age girls pursued the Zombies as they burst from a stage door and dashed for the tour bus at the evening's end. "We came running out of the theater toward the coach, which was parked a bit far away," recalled Grundy. "As we darted out the stage door, all of the audience poured out the front door and came running around the back, and girls were chasing after us. I could feel them catching up to me. We all had fairly long hair, and one of the girls managed to grab hold of my hair and threw me off balance, and down I went. I hit my head on the pavement and laid there stunned with all of these girls tearing up to me. It could have been a pushy moment but fortunately, the tour manager, Fat Frankie, saw me and he scooped me up off the pavement and threw me on the coach," Hugh said. Chris White recalled, "Blimey, I'll always remember that show. That was a great tour. Las Vegas was a shock to us English people, who hadn't really known America. Police officers there stopped Rod and Colin later for walking. Being English, we walk most places. And with long hair, they probably looked to the police like down-and-outs." Colin added, "I remember that concert really well. Rod and I always remember Las Vegas – there was sand blowing in off the desert on the streets where we were walking. It really did seem like a quite small town in a desert." That spring of 1965, the Zombies were as tremendously popular with American pop fans as any band could be.

Paul Arnold maintained his friendship with the band members. "I kept in touch with them during vacation times from medical school," he told us in April 2011. "I remember going with them to Oxford University, among other places. They all had sports cars, whereas I had to be content with my minivan."

Even though subsequent singles, including Rod Argent's anguished tempo-shifting pop aria "She's Coming Home," were just as musically intricate and lyrically compelling as their first two hits, radio audiences and record buyers didn't embrace them as strongly.

"To be honest, 'She's Coming Home' was less memorable than some of our other songs. Its production was too complex for the time. You couldn't dance to it. The other songs of the time were much simpler. 'She's Coming Home' wasn't hummable, and that's what makes a hit," asserted Atkinson – who played guitar but did no singing with the Zombies. "I'm really not surprised that it wasn't such a big hit, but I was surprised that other ones, such as 'Whenever You're Ready' and 'Indication,' were not. We were all convinced that they were hit singles, and I do believe that they failed because of lack of promotion."

Still, the Zombies continued performing through 1966 and into 1967. Typical was a show in which they shared billing with the Who at a college concert in Brighton, England. Chris White had purchased a starting pistol for stage theatrics. After the sound check was done, the members of both bands were hanging around in the large dressing room they all shared. Chris displayed the starting pistol to the band members. "When Keith Moon saw it, his eyes lit up," recalled Chris. Moon reached into a sack and pulled out a gas mask, as well as his own pistol – which unknown to the others, contained tear gas. Paul Atkinson also vividly remembers the incident. "Keith had seen the gas mask and tear gas in a store, and he bought them," said Atkinson. "It was just shortly before we were to go on stage, and Keith, laughing hysterically, shut the dressing room door, locked it with all of us in the room, put the key in his pocket, and fired the tear gas gun. We all attacked him and said, 'You mad fool, open the door!' He said, 'Nope,' and he was the only one with a gas mask. So we're all down on the floor on our knees and finally we broke the door down after about 10 minutes. As we burst out the promoter was saying, 'On stage! On stage!' So we all ran on stage, crying our reddened eyes out, and the audience didn't know what was going on. That was Keith Moon's idea of a good time."

The Zombies weathered that, but disenchantment started during a concert series in the Philippines, which attracted enthusiastic crowds but was mired in political and financial complications that hit a sour note with the band members. "We played for 10 nights just outside Manila," Blunstone recalled. "The Beatles had just been there and had a lot of trouble because of their supposed refusal to go to meet Philippine President Ferdinand Marcos. It was just a mixup; I don't think they ever knew they were invited to go to see him. But that created a lot of friction and the Beatles were practically expelled from the country. So who's the next British band to go over there? Us! But we played in this huge indoor auditorium to crowds of thousands for 10 days, and it was very exciting." The band was paid only £75 per night, split among the five guys. When the option for more appearances came up at the end of the 10-performance run, the band members asked for more money. The arena concert promoters refused, so the Zombies accepted more lucrative bookings at two of the larger, more prominent clubs in Manila. Unknown to the Zombies, those club bookings ignited tempers – and more; within 48 hours of performances by the Zombies there, the two clubs were destroyed by fire. The band members subsequently learned that their managers in London had been paid £2,000 per night for the arena appearances that netted the band only £75. Paul Atkinson's older brother, Keith, an accountant, observed apparent improprieties in the band's financial records. "I used to do the Zombies' accounts and always questioned whether the per-gig fee shown in the contracts was the entire story," Keith told us in May 2011. "In the early Zombies days all the parents were really worried about whether they were filing all the necessary tax returns, so I ended up keeping things financial on track."

The Zombies returned from that tour to find that their recording of "Goin' Out Of My Head" had been issued as a single with production values that they found disappointing. Disagreements arose over the progression of the band. Blunstone, for one, felt the band was falling into somewhat of a rut. "When we recorded 'She's Not There' I just sang it naturally. I think there was a lot of compression put on my voice which helped create that breathy sound," he said. "But we all felt that Ken Jones, who had done a wonderful job producing our early tracks, was forever trying to re-create that sound. He felt that we should capitalize on an individualistic sound that we'd established. But as time went by, we wanted to move on and do something new." That opportunity soon presented itself.

After the expiration of the Decca contract, the future of the Zombies seemed uncertain and individual band members began to think about other pursuits. The band parted company not only with producer Ken Jones, but also with their manager and their agent. But the Zombies remained together and signed in 1967 with CBS, which asked them to record an album and agreed to grant the band creative control of the production. That album was *Odessey and Oracle*, which would prove to be both an enduring masterwork as well as the band's swan song. Although the album designer's misspelling of the word "odyssey" was unintentional, the "odessey" spelling did fortuitously reflect the poetic content of the album's 12 intricately melodious tracks about imperfect love and haunting memories, all of which Argent and White composed. The band recorded *Odessey and Oracle* over a six-month period beginning in June 1967 at the EMI Abbey Road Studios (where the Beatles only weeks before had completed recording their *Sgt. Pepper's Lonely Hearts Club Band* album) and at Olympic Studios.

"At the time we were recording *Odessey and Oracle* it was already obvious to me that everyone wanted to break up. Nevertheless it was an album we wanted to record because both Chris and I wanted to produce an album ourselves before we stopped," Argent said. Because the modest budget CBS allocated for their session in the summer of 1967 did not provide for auxiliary session musicians, the Zombies turned to technology – the Mellotron, the same device that helped the Moody Blues soar to artistic heights by simulating orchestral sounds. *Odessey and Oracle* was a work of sophistication and complexity in which delicately melodic baroque and evocative medieval elements were woven with interlaced harmonies on a foundation of psychedelia-tinged rock. Reviewers praised the album following its U.K. release in April 1968. Supporters included highly popular BBC disk jockey Kenny Everett, on whose program the Zombies appeared as guests numerous times. Playing tracks from the album, Everett warned his listeners, "the Zombies say that if this is not a hit, they're going to break up. Please go buy it because we don't want them to break up."

Among those who did buy and embrace the album was blues great Al Kooper of Blood Sweat and Tears, who happened to be in London. CBS Records failed, however, to recognize the musical genius of *Odessey and Oracle,* and only after Kooper prevailed upon CBS President Clive Davis did the label finally release the album in the United States in June 1968. "In fact, Al Kooper even wrote the sleeve notes for the American release," Blunstone noted. Even at that, CBS issued the American release on Date, its subsidiary label for which the ballad-singing Arbors and the R&B duo Peaches and Herb recorded. "Because we didn't have a manager and we didn't have an agent, there was not a lot of interest in live performances of the Zombies, not a lot of interest in our album, and it was a very disheartening time," recalled Colin Blunstone. "Although Rod and Chris had still managed to maintain their enthusiasm, Paul and I were getting disheartened and we weren't being as enthusiastic and positive as you need to be in situations like that," Blunstone admitted. "We were rehearsing one afternoon and, as I remember it, Paul said he thought it would be best if he left the band. Rod said, 'If Paul wants to leave, I think the band should stop.' I said nothing. I just kept my head down. I went for a long walk afterwards, and that was it."

In obligatory fashion, Date listlessly released two singles, but inadequate promotion doomed them to commercial failure. Meanwhile, a group called the People scored a top-20 hit with a Chris White song called "I Love You" that the Zombies had released on the "B" side of a single. After progressive rock stations began playing a particular album cut from *Odessey and Oracle,* Date Records released it in late 1968 as the third single from the album, and it received enthusiastic mention in a disk jockey "tip sheet" that reviewed new releases. Unaware that the Zombies had disbanded, disc jockeys at AM "top 40" stations began playing that third single, "Time of the Season," which soared to the top of the charts during the first weeks of 1969 and went on to sell nearly 2 million records. The label suddenly wanted more Zombies product and asked the band members to re-group and return to the studio. But by then Rod Argent and Chris White had formed a new band called Argent, and were in the United States in the midst of negotiating a record contract, and Colin Blunstone had become a soloist. "Rod and I had been working on the *Argent* album when CBS asked if we would record another Zombies album," White recalled. "Because the Zombies had split up, Rod and I decided to record a few new tracks and we also with the help of Colin found some unfinished or unused tracks and added new vocals and arrangements to them." The label released one of the new tracks, "Imagine the Swan" as a single, but the album never was issued.

Ultimately, all of the Zombies members had accomplished what each of them had set out to do – even Paul Arnold, who had left the band to become a physician. After interning in orthopedics, he passed part 1 of a fellowship in the Royal College of Surgeons, the first step toward becoming an orthopedic surgeon. Arnold was named an assistant professor at the University of Alberta in Edmonton, Canada, and began orthopedic research. He became a fellow of the American College of Angiology (the study of blood and lymphatic vessels) in 1976, and supplemented his academic salary by working part-time as a family physician. Finding that work appealing, he decided against pursuing a career as an orthopedic surgeon and, over a period of years, opened five family medicine clinics in the Edmonton area, where he has lived ever since. In 1980 Paul married Caroline McNeil, of Novia Scotia, and the couple had two children, Mark and Melissa. After 18 years of marriage, they separated and divorced. Paul subsequently married Ankur Gulati, a Canadian from New Delhi,

India. They have two children: Amar (born in 1999) and Aryan (born in 2009). In recent years he has scaled back his practice to two All Well Primary Care Centre clinics, but he also operates an investment holding company, which has properties in Edmonton, in Victoria and Vancouver (British Columbia) and in London and Bedford (U.K.).

The Zombies remained dormant for 22 years, until 1990, when Colin, Chris and Hugh gathered to resurrect the Zombies' name and recorded an album titled *New World.* Joining them for the sessions was keyboard player and guitarist Sebastian Santa Maria, who filled in for Rod Argent and Paul Atkinson (although Rod and Paul did perform on a few tracks). The Essential label released *New World* in the U.K., and RCA issued it in Europe. Following the release of the album, the band members once again went their separate ways. (*New World* was unavailable in the United States until 2003, when music archivist Alec Palao produced a reissue of the album for the Big Beat label of Ace Records Ltd. (http://www.acerecords.co.uk/), as a follow-up to the '60s Zombies catalogue reissues with which he had been involved.)

"The band came back together as friends and associates in 1997 during the course of my assembly of the *Zombie Heaven* four-CD box set for Big Beat, which documents the band's entire 1960s career and included 42 previously unreleased tracks," Palao told us. The 119 tracks of the ambitious project included nearly every song the band had ever recorded, along with some demo recordings and radio pro-motional spots. "The launch party for the box set at the Jazz Café in London in November 1997 was the first time all five Zombies had been in the same room for almost three decades, and they played two songs – the first Zombies performance in 30 years." Chris White praised Palao's work. "It's a masterpiece in the art of compilation of tracks. He remastered it from the original tracks, so it's an excellent piece of work," White asserted.

Enthusiastic fan reaction to release of the box set prompted Colin, who had been touring as a solo performer, to resume perform-ing with Rod in May 1999. "At first it was as Colin Blunstone and Rod Argent, but after they started to regularly visit the U.S. from 2001 on, they found they were getting booked as the Zombies, and thus assumed the name for touring," Palao said. He coordinated Big Beat packaging and release of a succession of Zombies album reissues: the *Odessey and Oracle 30th Anniversary Edition* in 1998; an expanded version of *Begin Here* containing 22 tracks in 1999; *Singles Collec-tion: As & Bs 1964-1969,* containing both sides of all 14 Zombies U.K. singles, in 2000; and two years later, *The Decca Stereo Anthol-*

ogy, a two-CD set containing stereophonic remixes of many songs previously mixed and issued only in monaural.

Argent and Blunstone released a collaborative album in 2002 titled *Out of the Shadows.* They followed that two years later with a new Zombies album titled *As Far As I Can See,* released on the Go! Entertainment label in the U.K. and Rhino Handmade in the United States. The recording was a family affair, with Rod's cousin Jim Rodford (who had played with the Mike Cotton Sound in the 1960s, Argent in the 1970s, and then with the Kinks) on bass and Jim's son Steve Rodford on drums, along with session guitarist Keith Airey. Rod co-wrote one of the album's songs, "Wings Against the Sun," with his son, Mark.

All five Zombies gathered in January 2004 for a memorable performance in Los Angeles in response to somber circumstances. Paul Atkinson was gravely ill with kidney failure and inoperable spinal cancer. Though gaunt and weak, Paul managed to take to the stage and perform once more, in the company of appreciative musical colleagues and friends. He succumbed to his illness that April 1.

The following year, Argent and Blunstone appeared on stage, and their performance was captured and released on Zombies DVD and CD packages, titled *Live At The Bloomsbury Theatre, London,* released in the U.K. in February 2005, and in the United States two years later. In 2007, the Big Beat U.K. label released *Into the Afterlife,* a compilation of post-*Odessey and Oracle* recordings by Argent, Blunstone and White, including demo tracks, alternate mixes and other experimental recordings.

Argent and Blunstone staged a monumental musical event in 2008 – a more encompassing Zombies reunion to present the first-ever concert performances of *Odessey And Oracle,* the group's masterpiece that was not released on record until the group had dissolved. Rod, Colin, Hugh, Chris and guitarist Keith Airey (in place of the late Paul Atkinson) appeared on stage at Shepherd's Bush Empire Theatre in London on three successive nights, March 7 to 9, 2008, to commemorate the 40th anniversary of the release of the album. "We also had Darian Sahanaja of Brian Wilson's touring band with us to replicate the double-tracked Mellotron parts that Rod couldn't play at the same time as the other keyboards," Chris explained. "My wife, Vivienne, also appeared on stage to help create the layered harmonies and the horns for 'This Will be Our Year.'" The performances attracted fellow entertainers as well as record-buying fans. *New Musical Express (NME)* reported that singer-composer Robert Plant of Led Zeppelin, Paul Weller of the Jam and Style Council, and lyricist Sir Timothy Rice were among the members of the audience. The *Odessey and Oracle 40th Anniversary Concert* was recorded and released in CD and DVD formats for appreciative Zombies fans. Argent and Blunstone subsequently collaborated in an album titled *The Zombies and Beyond,* which was released in 2008. The following year the same lineup that had coalesced for the *Odessey and Oracle* 40th anniversary concerts mounted a U.K. concert tour, performing in Glasgow, Manchester, Bristol and the Apollo in London.

Mojo the Music Magazine named the Zombies to its Mojo Honours List in June 2008, when the British publication presented the group with a "Classic Album Award" for *Odessey and Oracle.* Rod Argent accepted an award from BMI (Broadcast Music Inc.) in October 2010 recognizing that "Time of the Season" had achieved a lofty distinction – surpassing 6 million logged radio plays in the United States. In late 2010, Ace Records' Big Beat label released a group of six vinyl EP (extended-play) $33^1/3$ RPM records, titled *Zombies R&B, Zombies à Go Go, At Work (N' Play), Zombies '66, Time of the Season,* and *Zombies at the BBC.*

The Foo Fighters paid tribute to the Zombies in April 2011 when they released a vinyl album called *Medium Rare,* consisting of tunes originally recorded by Cream, Gerry Rafferty, Pink Floyd, Paul McCartney and Wings and other bands. *Medium Rare* – the band's tribute to Record Store Day celebrating independently owned record stores – included the Zombies' *Odessey and Oracle* song "This Will Be Our Year," which Chris White wrote. "I gather that [Foo Fighters founder] David Grohl is a great fan of the Zombies. He told us some time back that they'd record it," White told us.

In May 2011 Argent and Blunstone completed and released a new Zombies album called *Breathe Out, Breathe In* on the Red House Records label. "It's turned out great, and I'm very excited about it. I think it's the best thing I've been involved in for many years," Rod said. "Its release coincided with the 50th anniversary of when we first got together and began rehearsing, around Easter 1961." The anniversary might have gone by unnoticed were it not for an incidental discussion. "It was only by chance in a conversation, when Rod and I were trying to work out how long ago something happened, that suddenly it dawned on us it had been 50 years that the band first got together," Colin said. "We thought that was an anniversary that was worth celebrating." Argent and Blunstone took to the road with guitarist Tom Toomey, bass player Jim Rodford and drummer Steve Rodford for a series of commemorative concerts in Greece and the U.K. The anniversary tour culminated in a May 27 appearance at Shepherd's Bush Empire Theatre, where Hugh and Chris joined them on stage. The Zombies continue periodic touring in the U.K. and North America.

Colin Blunstone is not at all bashful about expressing his admiration for the musical talents and arranging skills of Rod Argent, and his fondness for the time during which the Zombies were together – back in the old days, and during their recent collaborations. "Most of the song arrangements came from Rod. For a 19-year-old, he was a pretty sophisticated musician, and it was obvious to everyone that it was best to take his lead in all musical things," said Blunstone. "Because we were together for seven years, including three years on the road, and it was all through our teen years, we actually grew up together. Now bands will do a four- or five-week tour and that's it – they go off and do different things. We played non-stop for three years. For most of that time, we were traveling in the back of a van. It wasn't as grand as you might think. We got to know each other pretty well, I can tell you," Blunstone laughs. "We had our heated moments, but you don't forget a period of your life like that."

For more information, visit **http://thezombies.net.**

THE ZOMBIES U.S. HIT SINGLES ON THE NATIONAL CHARTS

Debut	Peak	Gold	Title	Label
10/64	2		She's Not There	Parrot
1/65	6		Tell Her No	Parrot
4/65	58		She's Coming Home	Parrot
6/65	95		I Want You Back Again	Parrot
2/69	3	Δ	Time of the Season	Date

Δ symbol: RIAA certified gold record (Recording Industry Association of America)

Billboard's pop singles chart data is courtesy of Joel Whitburn's Record Research Inc. (www.recordresearch.com), Menomonee Falls, Wisconsin.

Epilogue: Rod Argent

Keyboard player, singer and composer

Nearly 40 years after he first took to a stage, Rod Argent said he felt like he was just starting out. And he was very pleased about that. Argent was referring to his then-renewed collaboration with Colin Blunstone, the lead singer of the Zombies. After three decades of pursuing separate paths, Argent and Blunstone were side by side once more in 1999, collaborating in recording and producing a new album, and talking of performing on stage together. Although the music of the Zombies was tinged with blues and jazz influences, the reunion came about at a time when Argent had begun pursuing his enduring interest in classical music.

Rod always had enjoyed listening to classical music, but he had not played classical piano until the mid-1990s, when he began a self-imposed program of classical training. In October 1999 he appeared with the Cornish Sinfonia, an orchestra in Cornwall, with which he performed Bach's G-minor keyboard concerto. He recorded *Classically Speaking,* a classical album as a solo pianist that he made available through his Web site (www.rodargent.com). On the recording

Rod Argent in January 2011.
Photo by Keith Curtis.

he performed works by Frédéric Chopin, Maurice Ravel, Johann Sebastian Bach and Edvard Grieg as well as some of his own compositions in the same vein. "As far as I can work out, it's the only time that a guy from the rock and roll side of the business has actually done a purist classical album," Argent said with obvious pride.

As he was working on that album, he received a call from Blunstone, who said he was going to be performing at clubs in Argent's area. "I'm doing six gigs," Blunstone told Argent. "Do you fancy just for a laugh doing them with me?" Argent unhesitatingly agreed. "So we did these gigs, and it was fantastic. We got great audience response and from that, we decided to do an album together. It was the first time that Colin had done an album of my songs since the Zombies split up," Rod said. He

264

considers the recording a progression from the Zombies. "It has many of the same elements because of the chords that I naturally write and because of the way Colin naturally sings." Their friendship spans five decades and was built upon the common bond of music. Born only 10 days apart, they lived in separate towns, attended separate schools and met when Rod's formation of a band drew them together.

Rod and his younger sister Rosslyn were raised in a working-class household in St. Albans, which was founded before the Romans conquered England in A.D. 43. Rod's father, Les, worked for a living as an engineer machining parts in the De Havilland aircraft factory, which manufactured military aircraft and in 1952 introduced the world's first commercial jet-powered passenger airliner, the De Havilland Comet. But Les also had been the leader of two semi-professional dance bands, the Les Argent Quartet and Les Argent and the Rhythm Kings. Rodney Terence Argent was born in St. Albans on June 14, 1945, less than six weeks after the surrender of Nazi Germany brought an end to World War II in Europe. The modest Argent household had a piano, and Rod became intrigued by music at a young age. Sitting in the barbershop with his father waiting for a haircut, 4-year-old Rod would spontaneously start singing popular songs of the day. Rod began two years of piano lessons at age 7, when he took a liking to the 19th-century romantic classics of Tchaikovsky, Brahms, Dvořák and Grieg – typically, the music heard most often at home.

After learning the rudiments of reading music, Rod continued learning and practicing piano on his own, and in 1956 at age 11 joined the esteemed choir at the Cathedral and Abbey Church of St. Alban, Great Britain's oldest continually used house of Christian worship. That's when he was first exposed to the music of Elvis Presley. "Elvis completely turned me around," said Rod. "For six months or so, I didn't want to hear anything else except the most raw rock and roll I could get my hands on. I remember listening to 'Hound Dog,' 'Lawdy Miss Clawdy,' 'That's All Right,' and 'Mystery Train.' And I heard modern jazz for the first time. That was a really great time to hear it because that's when Miles Davis was bringing out *Kind of Blue* and the things he had done with Gil Evans, and I loved that as well. So I was listening to all of those. I didn't see why you shouldn't love Elvis and at the same time listen to the Bartók String Quartet."

In those days, the availability of pop music in the United Kingdom was very limited. "Only one or two radio shows a week played pop music. It was very hard to hear, but that made it even more important. In actual fact, the first time I heard those songs was down the road at my cousin Jim Rodford's house," Argent said. Jim, four years older than Rod, was a member of the Bluetones, one of the very first rock groups in the area and the only one with an electric guitar. Rodford played "tea-chest bass," an improvised single-stringed broom handle instrument common among skiffle groups. The first time Rod heard the Bluetones perform was a pivotal moment in his life. "I was about 12, and I just thought it was brilliant. I realized that's what I wanted to do. I wanted to be a part of it. I remember watching the Bluetones and thinking, 'If I could be sitting behind the piano, playing and being part of it, I'd be completely happy.' I really felt at home with music. It was a very powerful attraction for me," Rod said.

Despite the modest family income of Les and Phyllis Argent, scholarships enabled their son Rod to attend St. Albans School – a public school that imposed fees, the English equivalent to private school in America. They're called public schools in Britain because they became the first schools several hundred years ago to educate people who weren't in the clergy. "A public school in England is quite an elitist place," Rod explained. "The majority of kids who went there had to pay to go. My parents were from a very working-class family, so even though I got scholarships to this school, they still had to make financial sacrifices to pay for the uniforms, books and other things." Rod admittedly struggled in school. "I excelled at very few things. In the lower subjects – geography, physics and chemistry, science, math – I was bottom of the class. It was appalling. But there was one subject in which I excelled – English literature and language." School administrators categorized students according to three "forms," or performance levels, labeled A, B and C. "Because I did so badly in a lot of subjects, by the second year I was put down to the C form," said Argent. "But in English, I came in at the top, even though I was in the C form." At age 16 students were asked to choose between an arts- or sciences-oriented curriculum. "Once I got into the arts side, I did a lot better. In fact, I became quite good at two or three other subjects, including history." The school curriculum did not, however, include music, which Rod pursued independently through the Zombies.

By age 18, Rod performed well enough on the A-level (advanced level) exams to qualify for admission to a university. But Rod said he deliberately applied to the university too late to enroll for the 1963–64 academic year in order to concentrate on the professional development of the band. "I remember saying to my Mom and Dad, 'I think I'm going to write to the university and ask if I can defer coming for a bit because I want to have a chance to turn professional with this band.' My mother and father asked, 'Are you sure you're making the right decision and this is what you want to do?' I told them I was absolutely certain and they said, 'OK, go for it!' And they supported me 100 percent," Rod said.

Rod and the other band members rehearsed diligently and performed regularly, and a little more than a year later their recording of "She's Not There" became an international hit record. Rod remembers that the band members were in the process of recording their second single when they heard the news of their success. "We were recording what became our second release in the United States when our American publisher, Al Gallico, phoned us at the session to tell us, 'Hey, you guys, you're No. 1 in *Cashbox*,'" said Rod. The charts in *Billboard* and *Cashbox* magazines monitored popularity of recordings. "The thought of actually being No. 1 in America was absolutely inconceivable. It was just like a dream."

That dream ended when reality set in after a protracted period with no hits. "I didn't want the Zombies to disband, and I wanted to stay in music, as did Chris. But it was becoming pretty clear that both Colin and Paul had had enough. We were only professionally together for three years, although at the time it seemed much longer than that. A year had passed since we'd had a hit anywhere. Chris and I both wrote and my songwriting royalties were pretty good, so I wasn't in a financially bad situation, but Colin and Paul were feeling the pinch, and they wanted to get out," Rod explained. "When Colin made it very clear that he was going to leave, I realized there would be no point in keeping the band going without him, and I realized it was time to move on."

Rod decided to put together a new band, in which he persisted despite calls for the re-formation of the Zombies after the unanticipated success of "Time of the Season." Rod said that letting go of the Zombies wasn't traumatic because he had his eye on the future. "I was saturated by music. I wanted to be a part of it and wanted to see where it led. I loved the chance of being able to continue to write, to set out with a new outfit with different ingredients," said Rod. "I didn't want to look back, really." For the first time, Rod left his native St. Albans and moved to London. Together, he and Chris formed Nexus Productions and recruited a group of musicians. Rod named the new band Argent.

During its initial rehearsal phase, the band Argent consisted of Rod on keyboards, guitarist Rick Birkett, Zombies drummer Hugh Grundy, and Rod's cousin Jim Rodford on bass. The band solidified after Grundy was replaced by drummer Bob Henrit, and Birkett was replaced by Russ Ballard, who emerged as lead vocalist. Henrit and Ballard had previously played with Adam Faith's band the Roulettes and with the Unit 4+2, the band that recorded the hit "Concrete and Clay." After the breakup of the Zombies, Rod Argent and Chris White decided to share songwriting credits for all Argent compositions, and they collaborated in all production as well.

In late 1969, Epic released the band's self-titled debut album. Included on the album was "Liar," a tune written by Ballard that Three Dog Night would record and drive into the top 10 as a single in July 1971. By then Argent had released a second album, *Ring of Hands,* which like the debut album was given supportive reviews but received little airplay and consequently did not sell well. The band hit its stride, however, with its third album, *All Together Now,* a 1972 release that Rod produced. The standardbearing track on that album was "Hold Your Head Up," which became a top-five single on both sides of the Atlantic in the early summer of 1972. The following year a fourth Argent album, *In Deep,* yielded the anthemic hit "God Gave Rock 'n' Roll to You," which the band Kiss also recorded in 1992. In 1974 Argent recorded a fifth album, *Nexus,* which was the last with Ballard, who struck out on his own on the basis of his songwriting talents. Singer-guitarist John Verity and guitarist John Grimaldi subsequently joined Argent. During the remainder of 1974 and 1975 Argent released three more albums: *Encore: Live in Concert; Circus;* and *Counterpoints.* But the dynamics of the band changed and it appeared to lose musical direction as it experimented with somewhat inaccessible art-rock recordings before its dissolution in 1975.

Rod now thinks that he kept Argent active longer than he should have. "I think we should have called it a day when Russell left," said Rod. "But there was so much still good about the band that we held it together. I think things do have their natural cycles and, in retrospect, I think that would have been a good time to finish Argent." He remains very proud of that band, and particularly of its first two pre-hit albums, *Argent* and *Ring of Hands.* "I can play *Ring of Hands* now and think, 'God, that's a great album.' Without question, I can say that those were my two favorite albums that we did, but they never sold because they came before the hits," Rod noted.

When Argent broke up, Rodford and Henrit joined the Kinks but Rod Argent decided after 12 years on the road to relax for a year. Rod, who with Chris White had produced Colin Blunstone's first three solo albums – *One Year* in 1971, *Ennismore* in 1972 and *Journey* in 1974 – turned to session work. That one-year hiatus from stage performing stretched into a much longer period as Rod played on sessions with Andrew Lloyd Webber and recorded albums with the Who and with Roger Daltrey before moving on to television, for which he wrote numerous program theme songs and scored a series of television films, often in collaboration with Peter Van Hooke. Rod also wrote the themes for two World Cup soccer championships.

The departure from touring also enabled Rod to devote time to his family. While at work on the third Argent album in 1972, Rod married Cathy Lawrence, and they settled in St. Albans. Rod and Cathy met as a result of the relationship of fellow Zombie Paul Atkinson with an American choreographer named Molly Molloy, who married Atkinson. Cathy was the lead dancer in a jazz dance troupe that Molloy directed. Rod and Cathy had two children: Mark, who was born in 1974, and Elesa, born the following year. In 1976 the Argent family moved farther north, into an early 19th-century Georgian-styled home in the countryside of the county of Bedfordshire, where the Argent household remains today.

Rod built a recording studio at his home and in 1987 formed a business partnership with Peter Van Hooke, who for many years played drums for Van Morrison, and later for and Mike + the Mechanics. The two began producing recording sessions, among the first of which was the 1988 debut album by singer Tanita Tikaram, a European sensation who inherited her exotic appearance from her Malaysian mother and the Indian-Fijian heritage of her father, a British Army officer who was stationed in Germany when Tanita was born. Although Tanita is virtually unknown in the United States, her debut album *Ancient Heart,* which Argent and Van Hooke produced, was a massive hit for the WEA label throughout Europe, selling more than 4 million copies. "We recorded and mixed that in the studio here at my house," Rod said. He and Van Hooke also produced her second album, *The Sweet Keeper* (released in 1990) and the following year co-produced the third, *Everybody's Angel,* with Tikaram. Argent and Van Hooke also produced an album, *Painted Desert Serenade,* by California singer-pianist-composer Joshua Kadison. The album included two American hit singles for SBK Records: "Jessie," which reached No. 26 in 1993 on the *Billboard Hot 100,* and "Beautiful in My Eyes," which hit No. 19 and remained on the charts for 15 weeks in 1994. Consumers bought 2.5 million albums. Their production credits also included the 1991 MCA album *Late Night Grande Hotel* by Texas folksinger Nanci Griffith, and a 1996 Latin American album called *On Nights Like This* by the late singer Soraya, which scored big sales in Latin America and Germany.

Rod and Peter continued producing virtually non-stop for 10

years, until Argent decided that he wanted to resume concentration on his own projects. "While I enjoyed parts of production, I found that if you do two projects a year, that represents six or seven months of the year totally taken up."

After nearly four decades, Rod and Cathy remain married. The former dancer moved on to choreography before returning to school, and has become a psychotherapist. Their daughter Elesa Argent, who obtained her Ph.D. degree in sports management, is a senior lecturer at London Metropolitan University. She was elected in 2010 as the only female member of the executive board for the International Federation of American Football, and she plans to marry in 2011.

The creative skills of Rod's son, Mark, include writing poetry. Rod plans to set some of Mark's compositions to music. Rosslyn, Rod's sister, has remained in London, where after pausing to raise her daughter she has resumed her career as a successful graphic artist even as Rod has resurrected two interests of his own stemming from his youth: classical music and his collaboration with Colin Blunstone.

Despite Rod's sojourn into classical performance with his 1999 solo piano album *Classically Speaking,* he says he has no designs on introducing the classics to new audiences. Rather, he views classical music as a means through which to refine his musical skills. "I've always loved classical music and never stopped listening to it. I think that each musical form informs the others. I think you become a better rock player because you play classical music, and you become a better classical player because you're playing rock music, and similarly with jazz," Argent explained.

Argent remains intrigued by the figurative open door into the next room. He has no specific strategy, he preferring to remain observant and opportunistic. "I'd like to see what opens up and follow it. It's great working with Colin again," he said. "Between the Argent hits, the Zombies hits, and the individual hits that Colin's had, especially in Europe, you're talking about 10 smash hits. The creative potential of that is exciting to me. At the same time, I'd like to follow the classical thing as far as I can to develop that area, and I'd like to play some jazz rather than just listening to it. All of that is fantastic to me. I plan to develop those personal areas rather than just involve myself in supporting other people's work. I feel like I'm just starting out."

For more information, visit **www.rodargent.com** and **http://thezombies.net**

Epilogue: Colin Blunstone

Lead singer

Neil MacArthur. After 25 years as Colin Blunstone in real life and on stage, the former lead singer of the Zombies had to become accustomed to his new name. Suddenly, overnight, he was Neil MacArthur. Not by his choice.

The name change was the suggestion of Mike Hurst, the producer of the early Cat Stevens records, including "Matthew and Son," "I Love My Dog" and "I'm Gonna Get Me a Gun." Following a one-year hiatus from music after the dissolution of the Zombies, Blunstone sought to return to performing. Hurst offered that opportunity – as long as Colin would change his name to Neil MacArthur, because Mike thought it offered more commercial appeal. Colin recorded three singles for the Deram label, hitting the charts with a new arrangement of "She's Not There" under the Neil MacArthur alias. "When I look back now, I can't imagine why I would take that path other than the knowledge he had produced wonderful records for Cat Stevens. I was also quite flattered that someone was interested in recording me."

When Hurst approached him in early 1969, a year after the dissolution of the Zombies, Blunstone was working in the insurance business. "After the Zombies broke up, I took the first job I was offered," said Blunstone. "I went to work in a big underwriting department in London for nearly a year, just as I had done when I first got out of school."

Colin Blunstone in 2000. Photo by Susi Blunstone.

Indeed, when Colin left school at the age of 18, before the Zombies achieved stardom, he went to work in the insurance trade in the financial district of London. Although he didn't adopt the bowler hat and dark umbrella that was the style of many of his contemporaries, he did wear a three-piece suit at the insurance brokerage where he worked. "It was a very proper job," he smiled. On the weekends, he continued playing with the Zombies.

Colin was interested in attending art college because he did well on the A-level art exam at St. Albans Grammar School, but his father, Arthur Blunstone, wouldn't hear of it. "Although my father would let me be in a rock and roll band, he wouldn't let me go to art school. He said I would just chase girls and drink beer. He's probably right," Colin laughed.

Arthur Blunstone was well-accustomed to Colin's love of music. "I think quite a few of the people who lived near me thought I was completely mad because I would walk along the road singing at the top of my voice," Colin chuckled. "Even from a early age, I was very interested in music."

Colin Edward Michael Blunstone, born June 24, 1945, grew up in a small town called Hatfield in Hertfordshire County. He was the only child of Arthur and Dorothy Blunstone, who had relocated to Hatfield after their home at London's edge was destroyed by German bombing during World War II. "When my dad came out of the air raid shelter, there were five time bombs around the house. He was allowed at his own risk to go in and pull out whatever valuables he could. Then my parents waited at a safe distance for the house to blow up."

When Arthur and Dorothy relocated to Hatfield, they did what most other adults there did – they both went to work at the De Havilland aircraft manufacturing plant. Although Arthur had an engineering background, Dorothy had been a dancer in her youth. "When I was young my mom didn't work at all, but later she fancied getting out of the house," said Colin, explaining why she chose to work in the factory.

Colin himself had no career ambitions while in school. "I cannot believe how little thought I gave it. I must have thought that school would go on forever," admitted Colin, who was a passionate rugby and basketball player as well as a sprinter. "I was mad on sports and that's the only thing I thought about." The idea of a career in pro sports crossed his mind, but he dismissed it. "I would have loved to have played sports professionally, but in all honesty, I didn't think I was good enough," Blunstone said. "I never got the chance to find out one way or another because of the music business. For a time I did try to do both. I would play rugby and get beaten up and then get in the car and drive 100 miles or so to play a date with the Zombies. But I did that only a few times because I was absolutely exhausted after the gig, and then I'd have to drive back home."

Colin recalls that the parents of all of the Zombies were supportive when they recorded "She's Not There," even though they had no sense of how popular the record would become. "I remember when we let our parents know that we wanted to go on the road and become a professional band. Travel was very unusual for young boys in bands in those days. We didn't have freeways, and it took us all day to get anywhere," Colin explained. "Only Paul Atkinson's parents were reluctant, but in the end they came around. I was amazed when my parents said, 'Well, give it a go.' I think they felt that I would only do it for a year or so. Perhaps they thought it would be good to get it out of my system before I get on with a proper job."

That is what it appeared Blunstone did at age 22 when he returned to the insurance field following the demise of the Zombies. "I felt I needed a rest from the music business," explained Blunstone. At that point, he didn't know if the break would be temporary or permanent. "Because Rod and Chris were prolific songwriters, they were in a different financial situation than the other three members of the band. They were, in fact, quite comfortably off, whereas the three of us were close to being broke." By day, Blunstone labored in the restrained environment of the insurance office. But by night, he resumed recording on his own, at home, for creative enjoyment. So Blunstone's singing voice was still in tune when Mike Hurst approached him after "Time of the Season" reactivated interest in the Zombies. "I had hoped that perhaps I could get back into the business, but I didn't think the opportunity would come until Mike Hurst encouraged me to re-record 'She's Not There.' The first record I did was a small hit in the United Kingdom, and that was it – I was back in the music business again, as Neil MacArthur." So he remained for a year until one day Chris White abruptly asked, "Why don't you just drop this Neil MacArthur thing and record with Rod and me again?" The three approached Epic Records, with whom Colin had signed a contract in 1971 as a solo artist. White and Argent produced Blunstone's first album for the label, titled *One Year,* which yielded a British hit single, "Say You Don't Mind." Rod and Chris composed three of the songs on the album, and Colin wrote four. All the members of the new band Argent participated in the recording sessions. Colin promoted the album by forming a backup band of his own and touring with the Electric Light Orchestra.

Ennismore, Colin Blunstone's second solo album, which Rod and Chris produced in 1972, contained another track that became a

European hit: "I Don't Believe In Miracles," written by Russ Ballard of Argent. White and Argent also produced Colin's third album, *Journey*, in 1974. Although Rod was then on the road with his band Argent, he still managed to play keyboards and contribute some vocal work to the album, as he had done with the previous two. The King's Singers formal choral music sextet also performed on three of *Journey's* tracks: "Wonderful," "Beginning," and "Keep the Curtains Closed Today."

After touring relentlessly throughout the United Kingdom during the early 1970s, Blunstone withdrew from live performances as he dabbled in recording radio jingles and commercials. In 1975 Blunstone signed with Elton John's Rocket label and moved to California to record three more albums: *Planes* in 1976, *Never Even Thought* in 1978 and *Late Nights in Soho*, a 1979 release that Rod Argent produced.

As a soloist, Colin had amassed more hit singles in the United Kingdom than the Zombies had. That proved frustrating to him upon his return to the United Kingdom in 1980, when an ongoing contractual dispute with Epic Records prevented him from recording as a soloist for that or any other label. He did, however, perform as a guest on several album releases by the Alan Parsons Project, as well as on Dave Stewart's 1981 recording of the 1966 Jimmy Ruffin hit "What Becomes of the Broken Hearted." He also sang on the *Tarot Suite* album by Mike Batt and on an album titled *Exiled* by Mitchell/Coe Mysteries. In 1982 he performed again with the Alan Parsons Project, singing the international hit "Old and Wise" for the *Eye in the Sky* album.

In 1984 Blunstone participated in the formation of a new band called Keats, in which he was joined by guitarist Ian Bairnson, drummer Stuart Elliott, keyboard player Pete Bardens, and bass player David Paton. Although the band recorded an album that was released that August, the individual members were unable to follow through because they all had other conflicting commitments with other bands. Disappointed, Blunstone recorded another tune, "Dancing on a High Wire," for the Alan Parsons Project album *Ammonia Avenue*, before disappearing once again from public view. He also did some recording for television in the U.K., including compositions for made-for-television movies and two theme songs for ITV's broadcasts of World Cup football games.

In 1987 Colin married Susi Wing, a flight attendant whom he met through a mutual friend. Together they raised their daughter, Rosy, who was born in 1988. For an extended period, Colin did little but sing backup and make guest appearances with other groups. But in

1991 he stepped forward for the Castle label to record *Colin Blunstone Sings His Greatest Hits,* a collection of re-recorded versions of tunes that he made famous as a member of the Zombies and as a soloist. All of the Zombies except Paul Atkinson, who was unavailable due to work, performed on the album, which was produced by Chris White. In 1995 Colin recorded another album, *Echo Bridge* on the Permanent Records label – which unfortunately proved to be anything but permanent when it went out of business. Colin was given renewed visibility in 1997 when Mike Batt called once again. Batt was producing the soundtrack for the British motion picture *A Merry War* (adapted from the 1936 George Orwell novel *Keep the Aspidistra Flying*), starring Richard E. Grant and Helena Bonham Carter. He enlisted Blunstone to sing "Tiger in the Night" for the film's soundtrack. His evocative interpretation of the hauntingly beautiful ballad, sung over the film's closing credits, was a powerful reminder of Blunstone's vocal talents. It was then that he decided to resume his concert career, after a two-decade absence from public performing.

He recorded another album, *The Light Inside,* which Mystic Records released in 1998. It was well received, and generated sufficient fan response to prompt two brief concert tours in the United Kingdom during 1999; Colin performed during the latter portion of the year on a bill with Paul Jones and Alan Price from the Animals. On the basis of a sell-out show at the Borderline Club in London and a successful two-week engagement at the Cafe Royal, Colin began making plans for a new recording and an additional series of appearances with a backup band. And that's when his serendipitous May 1999 on-stage reunion with Rod Argent occurred. They discovered that their stage symmetry had not diminished through all those years. "It was brilliant, as if we'd played together the night before rather than 32 years before," Blunstone said exuberantly.

By the following September, Colin was back in the studio working with Rod on *Out of the Shadows,* a duo album of contemporary ballads. At the same time, Blunstone, who recorded more than 30 singles during the solo phase of his career, began refining his songwriting skills.

The concert tour on which he and Rod Argent performed in the spring of 2000 brought together more than just the two old friends. Their band included Rod's cousin Jim Rodford of the band Argent and Jim's son, Steve Rodford, on drums. "It was quite a little St. Albans Mafia, really," quipped Blunstone, who now lives with Susi in the home they own in Woking, in the county of Surrey, southwest of London. He is determined to remain a performer for good. In February 2009 he released a well-received solo album titled *The Ghost of You and Me,* on his own Ennismore label. On the recording, he lends the characteristically ethereal tones of his voice to themes of longing and love. "The album has done fairly well in sales. One has to take into account the record industry is going through a very strange phase, in which very few records are selling in huge quantities. But the title track had really good airplay in this country," Colin said. "To get on the BBC playlist is no mean achievement, but 'The Ghost of You and Me' was on the playlist for seven or eight weeks. Obviously that gave the album a lot of profile. It hasn't sold in huge quantities, but I'm not sure anyone was really expecting that."

Something else he wasn't expecting was a career decision by his daughter, Rosy, of whom he is very proud. Rosy – who, like Colin, is an only child – completed her degree work in history at the University of St. Andrews in Scotland with the intention of becoming a solicitor – the British term for a lawyer. Then she abruptly changed her plans. "About a year ago she decided that the legal profession wasn't for her, and she wanted to go into medicine instead," Colin told us in March 2011. No one in either Colin's or Susi's family had been in the medical profession. "Her decision came right out of the blue. We were really surprised. She'll be starting in the autumn at Barts and The London School of Medicine and Dentistry, which was a big surprise for us. It's a very, very old establishment, with a distinguished history. Because in her earlier education she took a lot of science exams, she is able to go to medical school. We're very happy that she's found what she wants to do, and she's been successful in her application to medical school. So it's been an interesting and exciting journey for her, and we're very thrilled for her."

Colin continues touring with his own backup band, consisting of keyboard player Pete Billington, drummer Pat Illingworth, guitarist Tom Toomey and bass player Chris Childs. "I also am totally committed to the Zombies project Rod and I are working on. But it permits room to recommence my solo career, and it's shown me that there is a way ahead," Colin said. He added that he cares deeply about the songs he writes and his performances. "My driving force is to make wonderful records. That's what I'm in the business for. Fame and money often come together, but that's never been the main objective for me. It's always been to make the best records and give the best performances I possibly can," Colin said. "Sometimes you can be disappointed in what happens, but regardless of how things worked out, you did do your best. I hope people realize that I'm a serious artist who has always done my best."

Encouraged by the enthusiastic response to the May 2011 release of the Zombies album *Breathe Out, Breathe In* and the corresponding European and U.K. tour, Colin began work on another solo album, which is not yet titled, and is tentatively scheduled for release in February 2012.

"That's the plan we're working towards. We would be looking to get the album finished by the end of October. We've got a lot of live work scheduled, so that might be quite a tall order," Colin said. "I could hazard some guesses about what the title of the album might be, but they would just be the titles of some of the songs. So we'll have to wait and see. I think titles for albums sort of emerge over a period of time. It becomes apparent, while you're recording, what the title's going to be." Blunstone is recording the album with producer Jon Sweet, who also produced *The Ghost of You and Me.*

"Most of the recording will be done in Jon Sweet's studio on the south coast in a place called Bournemouth, although we are recording basic tracks in The Grange Recording Studio in Norfolk, in the country northeast of London. It's a really lovely residential studio, so we can go there and stay. We just thought it would be a good idea to get away and have some time when we're not going to be interrupted by phones and things like that," Colin said.

"I remember saying years ago that I'd love to find an audience for myself that doesn't depend upon having hit records," said Blunstone. "I'd like to continue being a performer who can attract audiences large enough to finance touring, which is quite an expensive business." But Blunstone admits he'd also like to win acceptance as a songwriter. "It's also a real thrill to write a song and see it go through the processes of recording, and then have a bit of recognition from your peers and from the reviewers – bless them – and also from the public. That would be perfection."

For more information, visit **www.colinblunstone.co.uk**

Epilogue: Paul Atkinson

Guitarist

March 19, 1946 – April 1, 2004

As a prominent part of the "British invasion" that swept youth culture in a creative new direction, the Zombies captivated young people who embraced the band's music as their own, in large part because it was so different from the "square" standards that their parents enjoyed. In later life, Zombies lead guitarist Paul Atkinson had a markedly different role: preservationist of many of those still-beloved pop and jazz standards by Frank Sinatra, Nat "King" Cole, Dean Martin, Peggy Lee, Bobby Darin and other crooners and jazz greats. They're part of the vast catalog of EMI/Capitol, the same label for which the Beatles, the Beach Boys, Peter and Gordon, the Kingston Trio, Lou Rawls, Pink Floyd, Megadeth, George Thorogood and the Destroyers, Tina Turner, the Steve Miller Band, Heart, and Bob Seger and the Silver Bullet Band subsequently recorded.

In November 1998, Paul Atkinson became the vice president of catalog A&R (artists and repertoire) for Capitol Records, based in Hollywood, California. There, he was in charge of catalog opera-

Paul Atkinson at Capitol Records studio control room, June 19, 2000.
Photo by Jeff March.

tions, encompassing all recordings in the company's extensive vaults dating from its founding in 1942. Atkinson decided which albums were maintained in Capitol's active catalog, which of the older titles should be reissued, which should be repacked into "themed" compilations or "greatest hits" offerings of "box sets," double or triple CDs, and which should be discontinued. He developed comprehensive "catalog plans" to freshen the offerings of the label's most prominent artists such as Nat "King" Cole – who alone astonishingly recorded 1,600 songs for Capitol.

"Such recordings need to be re-mastered, re-packaged and marketed properly, in different ways from brand-new albums," Atkinson told us in 2000. "Even though an artist may not be recording any new records for the label, many artists are still actively touring and performing, and it's our job to keep their audience aware of their legacy on Capitol and to make sure those recordings are available to them." Older recordings often require signal processing to reduce ambient noise and pops, as well as remixing to produce new stereo masters, functions in which Atkinson participated. "We can make a 40-year-old recording sound extremely fresh with a lot more presence than the old mix had."

Atkinson was particularly pleased with one of his first projects for Capitol, a remastered release of the Beach Boys' landmark 1966 album *Pet Sounds*. "It marked the first time a stereo mix of *Pet Sounds* had been available on a single disk. It originally was mixed in mono by Brian Wilson," Atkinson explained. "Most of the Beach Boys' singles were mixed in mono. Most of the Beatles singles were in mono. You have to remember in those days the focus was on monaural AM radio. The idea was to get your record to sound as good as it possibly could on AM radio. So Brian Wilson would mix the Beach Boys' tracks and George Martin mixed the Beatles' recordings to sound as good as they possibly could in mono. As an afterthought the record company would tell a producer, 'By the way, we'd also like a stereo mix.' George Martin is on record as saying that they probably expended 10 or 20 times as much time and effort doing the mono Beatles mixes as they did those in stereo, and that was probably true until *Sgt. Pepper's Lonely Hearts Club Band*."

In the days before multitrack recording techniques became common, music sessions often were recorded on only three tracks. In a Sinatra session, the vocals were typically recorded on one monaural track, and two microphones recorded the orchestra on the remaining two tracks. For the original monaural releases, the three tracks were mixed down and "dubbed" (duplicated) onto a single-track tape. Depending upon the positioning of the microphones in the studio, those original master tapes can be used to produce a new mix with stereophonic qualities. Atkinson was directly involved in the remixing process, with an eye to product marketing. "As an A&R manager, I have one foot in the studio and one foot in the office," he said. Actually, A&R work is a bit more complex than that, as the fulcrum upon which a balance among musicians, producers, record company merchandisers and financial personnel must be achieved. It's a role about which no one had greater understanding than Atkinson, who had worked steadily in pop music A&R positions since 1971 – devoting the vast majority of that time to signing artists and making records. His success in the field would have amazed people who criticized rock and roll during the early 1960s, when the Zombies were formed.

"Adults in the U.K. ordinarily regarded rock and roll, particularly the American variety, as trash. They viewed it as very ephemeral, and believing that it was going to be gone in a year or two, discouraged young people from wasting their time with it," Atkinson said. But in the absence of any other career goals, pop music had become a consuming interest in the life of Atkinson as a teenager.

Paul Ashley Warren Atkinson was born March 19, 1946, in a small Hertfordshire County village called Cuffley, about 20 miles from St. Albans. Paul's interest in music was not shared by his brother, Keith, three years his elder, who eventually became a chartered accountant – roughly equivalent to a certified public accountant in the United States. And their parents had "not the slightest" musical inclinations, according to Paul. His father, Stanley Atkinson, was a stockbroker, and his mother, Clyde, was a teacher in a technical-oriented college, known as a secondary modern college, in St. Albans. There she taught courses in English, languages and secretarial skills.

Paul doesn't know why, but his father bought him a recorder flute for his 10th birthday. Before then, Paul had shown no exceptional interest in music. But he taught himself to play that simple wind instrument. That prompted his mother to buy a violin for him and enroll him in violin lessons – which he disliked intensely. In his school, he joined an after-school music club as he developed an interest in skiffle music, a boogie woogie-influenced style popular just before the advent of rock and roll. "Even though I really didn't like the violin, I liked music, and I met a lot of friends there who had other instruments," Atkinson explained. "One guy who had a guitar was interested in my violin, and we did a swap. So I came home with a guitar, much to my mother's disgust, and I fell in love with it. She bought me guitar lessons for a couple of years and by the time I was 13, I was playing pretty well." His fellow students at St. Albans School included Hugh Grundy and Rod Argent. Paul's brother Keith noted that the roster of "Albanian" alumni since the school's founding in the 10th century includes theoretical physicist and cosmologist Stephen Hawking; film director Mike Newell (whose motion pictures include *Four Weddings and a Funeral*); Academy Award-winning lyricist Sir Tim Rice; and Nicholas Breakspear, who in the year 1154 became Pope Adrian IV, the only Englishman to attain the papacy.

Although Paul was interested in music, he thought he might like diplomatic service, a field in which several of his relatives were employed. He contemplated studying anthropology in college – simply to give himself three or four more years to decide what kind of career to pursue. "Very few of my friends knew what they wanted to do, and going to college just postponed the decision for them," Atkinson chuckled.

College acceptance required passage of two "A-levels" (advanced-level examinations). Upon the urging of his parents, Paul took three A-level exams, in English, French and German literature, while at St. Albans School. Paul passed all three, and consequently was accepted by three colleges, including Newcastle University, in which he enrolled.

The Zombies' victory at the Herts Beat competition presented Paul with an unanticipated dilemma. "None of us had really imagined music as a career. We thought of it as great fun. We were getting quite well known around our local area, but we hadn't considered performing beyond grammar school. We thought we'd just go off to college," said Atkinson. "The others had decided to postpone college for a year, but the time for my decision was approaching in the summer of 1964 because at age 18, I was the youngest. Of course, my parents wanted me to go to college, and I was prepared to go. But if I went to college, the band was going to replace me, so I had to persuade my parents to go along with it because we were all under age and had to have our parents sign for us. I managed to convince them. Otherwise, I would have gone to college and the band would have replaced me, and I would have missed all of this." The college dean agreed to hold Paul's slot open for a year. By then, the Zombies were on the British and American charts, and Atkinson told the dean he wouldn't be returning to Newcastle University. "Instead, I went to the college of rock and roll," he joked.

The Murray the K Holiday Revue series in which the Zombies performed in December 1964 proved to be more consequential for Paul than for the other members of the band. The performers on the bill at the Brooklyn Fox Theatre included the Shangri-Las, Ben E. King, Dick and Dee Dee, the Shirelles, Dionne Warwick, the Nashville Teens, Chuck Jackson, the Drifters, the Vibrations, Patti LaBelle and the Blue Belles, and the Hullaballoos. On December 21, the day before opening day, crews of technicians were busily setting up amplifiers, speakers, and electrical and microphone cabling as performers began arriving. At the side of the stage stood two young women; they were dancers that Murray the K had hired. The five Zombies lined up at the back of the ornate 4,000-seat theater and surveyed the frenzied activity on the stage. Paul Atkinson, noticing Colin Blunstone's gaze, asked, "who are you looking at?" Gesturing, Colin answered, "that girl over there – the one with the great legs." He had pointed to a young dancer named Molly Molloy. Paul stiffened and said, "Well, you'll have to pick another one. She's mine. In fact, I'm going to marry that girl."

Molly was a classically trained ballet dancer who was raised in Massachusetts, but had moved to Manhattan to train at the High School of Performing Arts and the Metropolitan Opera Ballet School. Molly's agent had sent her to audition for Murray the K Kaufman, but she was unfamiliar with the Zombies' music or any other performers on the bill. Clutching her dance clothes, she found Kaufman's cramped office in a building near Columbus Circle in Manhattan. "Murray the K was quite a character, who sure knew how to get bands together for practically nothing," Molly told us in April 2011. When she arrived for the audition, Kaufman was talking on a phone with a long coiled extension cord. He gestured for Molly to come in and sit down. "He was circling me while he was on the phone, then when he finished the call he asked if I could dance. He hadn't even looked at my résumé or photos, but when I answered 'yes,' he told me I was hired. He told me that the rehearsal for the gig would be held the day before the opening. I wore a miniskirt but took my dance clothes to the rehearsal, where I was expecting to see a director and choreographer. There was no choreographer, no director, no changing room – just Murray the K running around the theater, and the most glamorous rock and roll people," Molly said. Murray the K told the two dancers that the clothes they already were wearing were fine, and showed them where to stand on stage. "When I point to you, start dancing," he told them.

The Holiday Review encompassed five shows per day for a

10-day run – a total of 50 shows. Fans continually mobbed the streets outside the magnificent old theater, which was housed in a 12-story office building. The theater's rehearsal hall was eight floors above street level. Performances began each day at 9 a.m., and continued into the late evening. "We ate our meals there, we did not move from that building anytime during the day because of the screaming throngs outside. It was like being incarcerated, but it was great fun. I was totally enthralled by everybody and everyone," Molly said. Paul continued to admire Molly from afar, but did not approach her. "The Zombies had exquisite manners, and Paul was way too shy," she explained. About December 30 she stepped into an elevator packed with performers and production workers. By ones and twos, people exited on various floors. "Then Paul and I realized we were left alone on the elevator. Paul was stammering as he said, 'um … I was wondering if … that is … would you and your friend like to go out for a bite to eat with the lads and me later?" Because it was already getting late in the evening, Molly declined and went home to her mother. But on New Year's Eve, following the last show, the Zombies were eager to celebrate. "I thought they were all adorable, and I agreed to go with them. We all piled into cars, and Paul and I were in the same car," Molly said. "We wound up going to two parties." When Paul and Molly parted later that night, they agreed to remain in touch with each other.

In March 1965, Molly went on a vacation trip to England, where she stayed with friends and met Paul and the Zombies. When tours brought the Zombies near New York, Paul called on Molly. She moved in late 1966 to England, where she began teaching dance. Her students included Cathy Lawrence, whom she introduced to Rod Argent; Cathy and Rod would marry in 1972. Molloy, who gained renown as a premier choreographer and artistic director, remains a luminary of musical theater in New York, London, Paris and Las Vegas.

The relationship between Paul and Molly flourished, and the couple married in October 1967. "At Paul and Molly's wedding, practically the entire *Ready, Steady, Go!* TV team showed up," said Paul's brother, Keith, who for many years was vice president of finance for United International Pictures (worldwide distributor for Paramount, Universal, MGM and UA). Keith subsequently became chief executive officer of a U.K. publicly listed company, Lonrho Africa PLC, based in Nairobi, Kenya, until his retirement in 2001. "I had no music talent at all, but have had a lifetime love of theatre and have been an amateur actor and theatrical producer for more than 40 years, so clearly Paul and I shared an artistic creative gene."

Molly said she was not apprehensive about marrying a rock musician. "I was young and in love. And in my business – dance – security is not the name of the game," she told us. "I had great confidence in Paul, who had an excellent sense for judging musical talent. He once said to me, 'what I truly envy about you and Rod is your creativity.'"

After "graduating" from the "college of rock and roll" upon the breakup of the Zombies at the close of 1967, Atkinson was persuaded by a friend to join him in the nascent computer programming field. By then, the couple was living near northern London, and Molly was teaching 60 classes a week and choreographing for BBC shows, which allowed Paul financial flexibility to explore career options. He joined a new company called Computers in Business as a computer operator and programming trainee, working in the COBOL and FORTRAN programming languages. During his time with the Zombies he had mused about what he might do subsequently. He was certain his work would involve music, but he wasn't certain how. Computers in Business seemed remote from the music industry, until he was assigned to a project involving a joint venture with the BBC and *Record Retailer Magazine,* the precursor to *Music Week.* They had contracted with Computers in Business to computerize the data in the *Record Retailer* music charts, and Atkinson was assigned to assist on the project. He worked with an ICL (International Computers Ltd.) mainframe computer that filled a climate-controlled 25-by-30-foot room, but that was primitive by modern personal computer standards. After Atkinson began work on the project, his office phone rang at 1 o'clock one morning. On the line was Colin Blunstone, who by then was recording as a soloist under the name Neil MacArthur. His first hit, a remake of "She's Not There," was headed up the charts. "Paul, where am I on the chart?" Colin asked, knowing that Paul had access to the newest, unreleased chart data. "Number 22," Paul responded. "Oh, NO!!" Colin was hoping to make an appearance on the highly rated British television program *Top of the Pops.* Only recording artists with a record in the top 20 were invited to perform on the show. Paul encouraged Colin to remain optimistic. Colin called again the following week. "You made it," Paul told him. "You're in the top 20."

Even though the programming project was associated with music, it was too unrelated for Atkinson. Bored, he decided to try talent management, working with two bands. Neither of the bands achieved success, but the record deals that Atkinson had negotiated for them with small record labels brought him into contact with

Charisma Records, which in those days before its acquisition by Virgin was a small, independent label for which several bands including Genesis recorded. He had met Dick James, owner of DJM Records – Elton John's first label – as well as publisher for Elton John and the Beatles. There Atkinson met Elton John and Bernie Taupin, with whom he remained friends for years.

Paul and Molly celebrated the birth of a son named Matt in October 1971. Working for DJM as a talent scout, Paul discovered a gifted performer among the London cast of the musical *Hair* – songwriter and singer Joan Armatrading. When James declined to sign Armatrading to a recording contract, Atkinson quit and in 1972 accepted an invitation to join CBS Records UK, for which the Zombies had recorded. Paul felt he was beginning to hit his stride.

Paul scored a major coup when the Swedish group ABBA agreed to sign a recording contract with a modest advance of only $1,000. ABBA would generate more than $75 million in revenue for CBS during the following half-dozen years. In the spring of 1974 Molly was able to fulfill her ambition of forming her own dance company in Paris – Molly Molloy Dance Theatre. Unfortunately, the competing demands of long-distance careers tugged Paul and Molly in separate directions and, late that year, tore them apart. "The breakup wasn't because we didn't love each other. Paul was the love of my life," she asserted. "Would we have done it differently if we were older and wiser? Maybe, but that's the road we didn't follow." During the ensuing three decades, Molly would attain stratospheric renown in choreography and artistic direction for musical theater, cabaret, and television and motion picture productions throughout the United States, Europe and the U.K.

At the London office of CBS Records, Paul subsequently met Helen Coward. She was from Trinidad and started as an assistant in the art and A&R departments at CBS, then in 1974 joined the public relations staff at Island Records, where she worked with Bob Marley and Toots and the Maytals. Atkinson's insight in the signing of ABBA, as well as his guidance of the launch of the Philadelphia International subsidiary label for CBS in England, brought him an address change and a substantial promotion.

In 1976 CBS Records International placed him in charge of worldwide A&R activities, with administrative headquarters in Manhattan. Paul moved to New York and Helen accompanied him. The couple married in 1980. At CBS, Atkinson soon was given A&R responsibility for a large portion of the Columbia Records roster of artists, including Paul McCartney, Aerosmith and Pink Floyd, with whom he worked on production of *The Wall*. He also signed Judas Priest and Patty Smyth, among others. On November 7, 1980, Paul and Helen celebrated the birth of a son, James.

Atkinson remained with Columbia until 1982, when he agreed to become senior vice president of A&R at RCA Records in Los Angeles. On August 4, 1986, Paul and Helen celebrated the birth of their daughter, Lucy. During that era, Paul bolstered the roster of the label by signing Bruce Hornsby and the Range, whom he discovered playing at a music club in Los Angeles. Atkinson was executive producer of Hornsby's debut album, *The Way it Is*, which earned a Recording Industry Association of America platinum award for selling 3 million copies. Hornsby was named best new artist at the Grammy Awards ceremony in 1987. Atkinson also worked with the Eurythmics, and was instrumental in developing five No. 1 hits for RCA during one 18-month period.

In 1990 Atkinson answered the call of MCA Records, where he was hired as executive vice president of A&R. There he worked with his old friend Elton John, as well as with Tom Petty, B.B. King, Meatloaf and Lyle Lovett. The entrepreneurial bug bit Atkinson after three years, and he left MCA to establish an on-line music production company based in San Diego. In addition to producing and manufacturing records, the company also created CD-ROMs and entered into the then-new field of website development. After five years of operating that enterprise and dealing with the uncertainties of the newly emerging Internet music business, he accepted his position with Capitol Records, where he decided which recordings from the label's vaults to resurrect, remix and repackage.

"I base those decisions on my own ears and on historical sales performance," Atkinson had said in 2000 in his office high above Vine Street in the cylindrical Capitol Records tower. He also carefully monitored musical trends. "After a revival of swing music, we've brought out a lot of titles by swing music performers that had been dormant for decades. The Louis Prima song 'Jump, Jive, an' Wail' was used in television commercials for the Gap stores. Louis Prima sales went through the roof because of the revival of swing music. Since we re-released his records, they sold hundreds of thousands." At Capitol, Atkinson was reunited with the recordings of the band Pink Floyd, which previously left Capitol to join Sony Music, the parent organization of Columbia Records. When Capitol acquired all the Pink Floyd masters, Atkinson oversaw the entire Pink Floyd catalog of recordings. He also was the compilation producer of a Nat "King" Cole boxed set on EMI/Capitol Records called *The Classic Singles,* encompassing 101 songs that had been recorded between 1942 and 1964.

"After being involved in A&R for 26 years, this is a great transition for me," Atkinson said. "I grew up with many of the artists in the Capitol-EMI catalog, including Gene Vincent, Fats Domino and Eddie Cochran. And some, like the Beach Boys and the Beatles, I had met in the '60s." Surrounded by shelves of CDs, as well as Zombies gold record plaques and photographs of the pop greats of bygone years, Atkinson reflected further. "It's a real pleasure to find myself in a position where I can re-release and restore many of these classic records. In many cases, they have earned great respect, which had eluded them when first released. I'm very fortunate to have a long and fulfilling career in the music business, and my role as a member of the Zombies is what started it all," he told us when we visited him at Capitol Records.

The Atkinsons had easily adapted to Southern California. "Paul had a passion for the outdoors, and spent every weekend he could cycling his way up the Santa Monica Mountains, often with our children in tow," Helen told us. Her longtime interest in fashion prompted her to accept a position managing a women's clothing boutique

Paul, James, Helen and Lucy Atkinson in 1999. Photo by Matt Kellard.

near the couple's home in Pacific Palisades.

Paul subsequently left Capitol to consult with Warner Strategic Marketing on the Frank Sinatra Reprise catalogue, and also worked with several independent labels on talent acquisition. Since 1997, however, Paul had been battling illness. He had developed a non-alcohol-related liver problem, for which he had undergone two liver transplants, and dialysis was performed on him regularly as a result of kidney failure. In 2003, he was diagnosed with inoperable spinal cancer.

Paul's last job was at Rhino Entertainment, for which he was a consultant. "By that time his health was failing. He really put up a big fight for his life, but honestly, some days he could barely get out of bed," Helen said. "Whilst with Rhino, he worked on the Sinatra catalog. There were other projects in the works, but he did not live long enough to complete them."

On January 27, 2004, music industry co-workers and friends staged a benefit tribute in his honor at the House of Blues Los Angeles, on Sunset Boulevard in West Hollywood. Ticket sales supported a family trust that had been established to help defray Atkinson's monumental medical expenses. At the event, he was honored with the Recording Academy President's Award for his accomplishments during nearly four decades in the music business as an artist and A&R executive. The highlight of the evening was a performance by all of the original Zombies – their first time together on American soil in more than 30 years. Brian Wilson, Bruce Hornsby, Richard Page of Mr. Mister, Patty Smyth, and Mickey Thomas of Starship also performed in tribute to Paul. His family members there that evening included his brother, Keith.

"It was like being at a memorial concert with the deceased in attendance and enjoying it. Paul was terribly ill, gaunt and exhausted, but rising brilliantly to the occasion. He said to me afterwards that going on stage to play guitar with the Zombies after a 30-year gap was terrifying," Keith told us. "James, Lucy and Helen were there – so proud of what all these celebrities were saying about Paul. The artistes all praised his integrity 'in a business sometimes short of that virtue,' and said that the fact that he himself had been an artiste meant he understood their concerns. Brian Wilson played for a magnificent 30 minutes 'for you Paul.'"

Keith admired Paul's talent for recognizing and developing the potential of other performers. "Paul enjoyed the fame and what went with it, and he was very happy to go along with the Zombies' success until he needed to earn a serious income. The writers earned royalties at a much higher level than the performers, so he broke away fairly early," Keith observed. "I think Paul developed a real talent to earn the trust of performers – they signed up to the labels he represented because they liked him. His success with ABBA was a classic example, but Paul McCartney, Brian Wilson, Johnny Mathis and the Sinatra estate all entrusted their musical catalogue to Paul. He was one of these rather understated, modest, talented people that rise to the top through sheer ability, talent and likeability."

A little over two months after the House of Blues benefit concert, just before midnight on April 1, 2004, Paul Atkinson died in his sleep at the UCLA Santa Monica Medical Center, a few miles from his Pacific Palisades home. He was only 58 years of age.

"Paul was a kind, gentle and thoughtful soul," Helen told us in April 2011. "He loved rock, and having worked as a musician, and then as a record executive, he always kept the artists' interest at heart. After all, he had been there." Paul's son James agreed. "My dad was a humble rock and roll fan who was brave enough to follow his dream. He was a soft-spoken guy, not at all a mercurial type, but I think my sister and I learned from his example," said James, who is a video editor in Los Angeles with expertise in special effects. He has worked for Comedy Central, HBO, Disney and *Time* magazine.

Five months after Paul's death, his daughter, Lucy, moved to London. She gained acceptance to the Brighton Institute of Modern Music, an affiliate of Sussex University, with the intention of pursuing a music career. She graduated in 2009 with a foundation degree in professional musicianship. "I sing and rap in a live dubstep [electronic dance music] act, and have gigged around the country along with some European venues, too," Lucy told us in April 2011. She also works as a session singer and in radio

Paul Atkinson in 2000. Photo by Henry Diltz.

voiceover production. "I have quite a distinct and husky voice." She has some online demo tracks at www.onthesly.co.uk/onthesly.html on the Web. Lucy and the members of her band have begun working with a producer to help polish their sound.

"A nice memory I have with me and my Dad is when he came down to one of my singing lessons in L.A. He was really ill at the time but was determined to come down," Lucy recalled. "He listened intently, and afterwards when I asked for his honest opinion he told me that he thought I had a great studio voice. I wish he would have gotten to see me performing now. I miss him so much and find it such an honor that people are still listening to the Zombies today. I still get a lot of street cred whenever anyone finds out who my Dad was."

Paul and Molly's son, Matt, works in information technology, as Paul had for a while. Matt and his wife, Sam, have a daughter named Kiara. Molly told us, "Paul and I repaired our relationship, we repaired our life. Helen and I are dear, dear friends. So it's a happy ending in that regard. We belong to an exclusive club of two."

Following Paul's death, Helen was recruited by a friend of hers who owns a television commercial casting agency. Although she doesn't think of herself as an actress, she has since appeared in numerous TV commercials. "Working in commercials and managing the apparel store happen to be things that I enjoy. They keep me busy," Helen explained.

Paul's fellow Zombies had admired him professionally and cherished him as a friend. "He was a really successful record executive. I think he did amazingly well. He was involved in so many successful projects. It just makes it doubly tragic that he should die so young," Colin Blunstone told us. "He really cared about music. At CBS in London, he used to listen to all the material that other CBS offices perhaps in Europe were issuing. Of course, there would be lots of records that wouldn't have a lot of relevance in the U.K. market, but he was very dedicated." That dedication, Blunstone said, led to Atkinson's signing of ABBA to CBS in the U.K. "In the U.K., ABBA have been huge, absolutely huge, and Paul signed them. He was a lovely bloke."

Helen said, "I consider myself lucky to have met someone like him. A truly British bloke and the girl from Trinidad. It worked! I am also fortunate that James and Lucy, our children, have inherited his creative genes. They are both pursuing careers in the entertainment field. They say the good die young. I miss him terribly."

290

Epilogue: Hugh Grundy

Drummer

In late 1948, in the De Havilland factory in Hatfield that had turned out scores of Tiger Moth training planes and Mosquito fighter aircraft during World War II, aircraft inspector and metallurgist Ted Grundy was at work on a test bench. Grundy and a friend were using woodworking tools during their off-hours to make a drum. That Christmas, Ted and his wife, Aileen, gave the drum to their only child, Hugh, who was then 3 years of age. It was a gift that would shape the course of young Hugh's life.

"If not for that drum kit, I wouldn't be here today," Hugh Grundy told us in August 1999, during a pause as he served customers in The Vine, the English public house of which he and his wife, Tracy, were proprietors at the time. It's an old-world "community pub" in a village called Buckden in Cambridgeshire, just off England's main A1 highway, about 60 miles north of London. As the end of a typical workday approached, a few customers already were seated at small tables softly illuminated by candlelight. In the kitchen, Tracy and the cook were preparing "roasters" – on that particular evening, roast lamb – as well as bangers and mash (plump sausages and mashed potatoes). As Grundy wiped down the bar with a cloth, the front door opened, tearing the velvet darkness with a burst of golden light from the rays of the setting sun. The polished brass fittings on the bar glinted in the slab of light. One of The Vine's regular customers sauntered in, paused to acclimate to the dim interior of the timbered pub, then headed for the bar.

Hugh Grundy in 2000. Photo by Alec Lewis (courtesy of Hugh Grundy).

"Hey, mate, you look in top form this evening," Grundy said cheerfully. "The usual?" he asked. With a wide grin, the grizzled patron replied, "Indeed! Why change at this stage of the game?" Grundy drew a pint of ale from a tap and with a flourish placed it on the bar. Other individuals and couples began trickling in. An hour later, many of them were dancing to the music of a live band, and before the set was over, Grundy was coaxed onto the stage to pick up his drumsticks once more. "I always got up on that stage. It was a prerequisite. If the artists wanted to play, they had to accept the fact that I was going to play the last 20 minutes or so," Grundy chuckled. "I was the house drummer. I just couldn't give it up. Once it's in your blood, it's in your blood." Music has remained in Hugh's blood throughout his lifetime, even during those years when he was far from it, driving a delivery van and, more recently, chauffeuring military personnel.

Hugh Birch Grundy was born in Winchester in Hampshire County on March 6, 1945, and his household moved to Hatfield when he was still an infant. As a child he sang in the church choir, but he took a greater interest in drumming. "That little handmade toy drum drove my parents mad for quite a little while," laughed Hugh. "Birch was my father's mother's maiden name, so that's how I got that name. Used to hate it as a kid, but don't mind it now." As a teenager at St. Albans School, Hugh joined the "Army cadets" marching band, initially as a bugler. He found himself at the rear with the other horn players during school marching processions. Realizing that "the drummers were at the front and they didn't have to do all of that blowing," Grundy gained approval to switch to drumming, which was taught there in the highly disciplined and structured military style. He devoured the instruction. "I realized that I truly enjoyed drumming, and I had a natural aptitude for it," he said. That fortuitous change brought him into contact with Rod Argent, a parade spectator who was impressed by Hugh's energetic drumming and invited him to join the band he was forming.

Although Hugh's father, Ted, played the violin for enjoyment and did not object to Hugh's initial involvement in the Zombies, he encouraged his son to pursue a career in the banking business. Hugh did so with Barclays Bank for about a year after his graduation at age 18 from St. Albans School. But by night, he continued performing with the Zombies as they gradually made a bigger name for themselves within the Hertfordshire region. When the Zombies began their recording career and achieved success on the charts, Ted and Aileen were supportive – to the extent that Aileen, a secretary at the police headquarters in Welwyn Garden City, was instrumental in establishing a Zombies fan club. "My mom ran the fan club for quite some time. My mother replied to many of the fan letters that arrived, and I replied to many of them myself. It was lovely, actually. I didn't find that burdensome at all. I've still got all of those clippings, pictures, and one or two bits of memorabilia among the scrapbooks for me," Hugh said.

Among his memories he counts a booking at the Brooklyn Fox Theatre on Flatbush Avenue during which he was asked to handle motorcycle sound effects. Sharing the bill with the Zombies were the Shangri-Las, whose hit "Leader of the Pack" was punctuated by the roaring engine of a motorcycle. "To re-create the sound effects that were on the recording, the promoter brought in a motorcycle. Nobody could get it started except me, so I got the job," Hugh laughed. "When the Shangri-Las were performing, I was backstage with the motorcycle. When they performed the song, I started up the motorcycle, and at the right moment in the song I revved it up, just like it is on the record."

Hugh remains very fond of his days with the Zombies. "When you put five people together who mix well not only as friends, but as musicians, that is something special. The Zombies resulted from a magic mixture of five people. A lucky, magic mixture," Grundy said. He accepted the breakup of the band as a reflection of changing tastes – not of the band members, but of the public. "People had moved on to other things."

Grundy moved on also. After coasting for nearly a year, grabbing gigs here and there sitting in with other bands, he decided to get a job. He headed to the Zombies' last label, CBS Records. He introduced himself, saying "I used to be the drummer for the Zombies." He asked if the label might have a job for him. He was hired in late 1968, and assigned to the promotion department initially, then transferred to A&R. He remained at CBS Records for nearly five years, during which time he was instrumental in persuading the label to release Redbone's "The Witch Queen of New Orleans," which became a hit in the U.K. One day he received a tape from an unknown band. Grundy listened to it and was impressed, telling the label, "This is going to be huge." The band was Queen. The label disagreed with Grundy's assessment. He wasn't terribly disappointed, therefore, when his position was eliminated as a result of a management change. But during his years at CBS Records he had married a young woman named Terry Webster and together they had a daughter, Louise, in 1973.

Friends at a St.Albans food and beverage supply outlet owned by General Foods invited Grundy to work for them. Hugh agreed, accepting a job as a driver delivering packaged foods, tea, coffee and coffee-making machines to businesses. The "tea lady" in each company then brought the refreshments to individual employees. "The tea lady would visit offices with a tea trolley on which she would have beverages and packaged foods. Tea ladies were employees of those companies. The tea lady also helped in the company canteen at lunch times," explained Grundy. "Quite a few companies still have a tea lady." The Grundys had another daughter, Haley, in 1976, but Terry and Hugh dissolved their nine-year marriage before the end of the decade.

While working for General Foods, Hugh moonlighted in the late '70s with the King Fishers, a local dance band. He developed a friendship with the band's new keyboard player, a young woman named Tracy Sturgeon. By day, Tracy worked in the vehicle registration department of the Ford Motor Co. After performing two years with the band, Tracy sold her car and with other savings, took a vacation trip to San Francisco. "She was on Fisherman's Wharf one day and she heard 'She's Not There' over the radio in a restaurant there. She wrote me a letter, which I still have," said Hugh. "From that point on, I knew there was something special. I then set about to chase her until she caught me," he chuckled. They married in September 1983, and two years later celebrated the birth of a daughter, Helen. They had a second daughter, Caroline, in 1987.

In 1991, Hugh and Tracy both joined Suits You, a St.Albans chain of menswear shops. "Tracy looked after the 'formal hire' men's wear – tails, top hats and dinner jackets that people would rent – and I dealt with the transport side, delivering to the shops," said Hugh. In 1994, he and Tracy idly brought up the notion of running a pub. The idea appealed to them and they began to give it serious consideration. They tested the waters at the Builders Arms, a pub in Potters Bar, a village south of Hatfield. While trainees there, they enrolled in a pub management training course. After completing the course and determining that they could work together, they became managers of the Rose and Crown, a pub in the little village of Stevenage in northern Hertfordshire. After substantially increasing the business at the Rose and Crown, they stepped up in April 1998 to their own pub, The Vine, which they operated in partnership with the Whitbread Beer Co. "We were under their roof and it was their beverage we sold, but it was actually our business and we did the hours we wanted," Grundy explained. "I wouldn't say we were making a fortune, but business was good."

The Grundys lived in Buckden above the white brick pub. "We had a flat with three bedrooms, a bathroom and our lounge [living room], and we used the pub's kitchen downstairs. We didn't have to worry about traffic anymore. It was like running a family house, but instead of just having your own children come home from school, we had all of the public coming into our lounge downstairs. We always liked entertaining at home. There would always be children and parents around and we'd barbecue, and the pub was an extension of that, really." Hugh credits Tracy as the "driving force" behind the business. "I did the mundane things, like clearing the drains and fitting the light bulbs and serving drinks. I just looked good behind the bar," he laughed. "Rod played at my pub now and again, which was lovely, really lovely. Rod was and still is the most wonderfully gifted keyboard player. We've had some great old evenings."

Among the regular patrons at The Vine was a former Royal Air Force pilot who flew combat missions during World War II. "He was a lovely old guy with a wonderful sense of humor and good stories. But he didn't talk much about his days flying a Mosquito bomber. He was a very brave man who used to fly solo missions into Germany. He flew fast and low and dropped his bombs before the German aircraft were able to get off the ground," Grundy said reverently. "I learned this from another retired gentleman who regularly came in. He used to be a Lancaster bomber pilot, and not many of them came back, I have to say. Lovely guy. That's the sort of people we got in the pub."

The stories of aerobatic feats and bravery have stirred an ancient yearning within Hugh. "Because my father was an aircraft inspector, that is also an interest and a love of mine. I don't have a private pilot's license, but one day I may have," he said wistfully.

Although The Vine succeeded financially, it fell short of an important expectation. They had imagined that living and working at the pub, rather than working in a distant job, would enable them to spend more time at home with their children at the end of each school day. "Unfortunately, it worked out that we spent less time with the children as we got busier and busier. And Tracy and I were getting a bit tetchy with each other because of the stresses of it, so we thought we'd call it a day while we were at the top of the game," Hugh said. "We had done well at what we had set out to do, so we thought, 'enough's enough.'" They sold the business in December 2000 and, upon the encouragement of a Royal Air Force employee who was a patron of The Vine, Hugh applied for a job as a chauffeur for the RAF in early 2001.

"I got in touch with the person he recommended in the mechanical transport section. He said, 'well, you're lucky. At the moment we've got somebody off long-term sick. We'll take you on temporary, and we'll see how we go.' I stayed there until my retirement," Hugh said. "I drove all sorts of personnel, from lowly corporals to air vice marshals and above. I drove an officer of every rank, sometime or another, to either airports or to other RAF bases. I had a coach license, so I was able to drive busloads of people to other bases."

Hugh retired from his RAF job at the end of March 2011. "That is, I'm retiring from regular paid work," he added. "But I don't mean to say I'm not going to do anything. I shall be looking for something to keep me occupied because I wouldn't want to just sit around at home doing nothing." Hugh and Tracy live in a home in Kimbolton, a village about seven miles west of Buckden. "It's a wee bit more in the country," said Hugh, who still periodically visits The Vine with Tracy.

Hugh's eldest daughter, Louise, lives in Wales, where she is a graphic designer. "She's had great success with children's stories on apps for mobile phones. I'm very proud of her," Hugh said. "My next daughter, Haley, is now mother to my two grandchildren, which absolutely thrills me to bits. And at one time she was director of a market research company. She'd done that well, and we're very proud of her. I'm proud of them all, for goodness' sake. Helen has been a beautician, and she worked on cruise ships for a while, and thoroughly enjoyed that. But she's living near home now, and we see her quite regularly. And Caroline is going to finish her degree next year in health and nutrition at the University of London.

Music remains a vibrant force in Hugh's life. "I'm playing with a local band now, which is great fun. There's no pressures on it as such. I get the [drum] kit out, we go to either a pub or a local club and we have a great time, playing rock and roll covers, and it's fantastic. I love it," Hugh told us in March 2011. His drum kit consists of a bass, four tom-toms, and a snare. "I've also got a rack, and mikes affixed to the rack, and six cymbals, high hats and one or two other bits. It does look lovely when it's set up." Hugh's wrists remain limber, not afflicted by pain that some drummers have experienced later in life. "What bothers me is dragging the kit out the garage and then setting up and taking it all back down again and putting it back into the garage at the end of the evening. Sometimes you say to yourself, well, wouldn't it be better to be a flute player? Believe it or not, I can get it in my estate car [station wagon] easily. But a while ago I had to take it somewhere when my car was unavailable, so I took it in me wife's car. She's got a Ford Fiesta. I had to put it in, take it out, put it in several times before I got it right, and then there was no room for anybody else, just for me to drive."

Now that Hugh has retired, he and Tracy have bought a vacation home at Minorca, a Spanish island in the Mediterranean Sea. They plan to remain in England during the winter, but spend much of the remainder of the year at Minorca. "Tracy's brother-in-law has lived there for the past five years. I don't think we'll live there permanent because in the wintertime it's a little bit isolated, a little bit bleak, and there's not many people about. But it's glorious in the summertime. It's just heaven. We sit out on our terrace and we look at the sea. There's a few islands and rocks, and if the sea is rough it crashes around. It's fantastic. It's really small, but we love it. Absolutely love it. It's a popular holiday island, I have to say, and it does get quite crowded in summer. But we have our own place, so you can just disappear inside and you're alone."

Hugh was thrilled to participate in a reception at the Jazz Café in London in 1997 commemorating the release of *Zombie Heaven,* a comprehensive four-CD digitally remastered box set issued on Ace Records' Big Beat label. "Everybody in the music business who knew us from those times past attended. That was the first time all five of us had been together in one room since the group broke up, and the talk of the evening was, 'Are they going to play?' It was quite heady, actually, and it was filmed for VH1," Grundy said. "We did perform 'She's Not There' and 'Time of the Season,' and it went down an absolute storm. The place just erupted, and it was marvelous."

Epilogue: Chris White

Bass player and composer

A year before the formation of the Zombies, Rod Argent answered a knock at his door. A teenage boy standing there introduced himself. "My name is Chris White and I'm forming a dance band," he announced. "I heard you're a pretty good pianist. Would you like to join?" Though that would have appeared to be the beginning of a long musical collaboration, Rod declined. "No, thanks," said Rod. "That's not the sort of music I'm interested in."

Two years would pass before Rod and Chris were re-introduced. When Paul Arnold was preparing to leave the Zombies to study medicine, he began quietly scouting for a new bass player with the help of his brother, Terry. Paul and Terry thought of Chris White, who had attended St. Albans Grammar School as they did. White was by then attending the St. Albans School of Art (now part of the University of Hertfordshire), in pursuit of a four-year fine arts degree. Terry Arnold had remained friends with Chris, and introduced him to the band. Chris fit in instantly at his first rehearsal with the Zombies. It was the beginning of a songwriting collaboration through which Rod and Chris would create a body of work that is still revered by pop music aficionados today.

Chris was planning to become an art teacher, and was accepted for his final year of teacher training when he left college to play with the Zombies full time. Although he never returned to art college, he has

Chris White in 2000.
Photo by Tony New.

remained committed to the performing arts, encompassing not only musicianship and songwriting, but also recording production and musical theater. Chris is flexible if anything. He is a musical composer as well as a lyricist who wrote Argent's top-five single "Hold Your Head Up." He has written lyrics for other musical composers, and he has composed music in collaboration with lyricists. But he has a particular affinity for record production, which he regards as "a straight defendant of the song." He is starkly honest about his attraction to music and production. "I can't do anything else," he shrugs.

298

Christopher Taylor White, born in Barnet, Hertfordshire, on March 7, 1943, had done sufficiently well in his "11-plus" exam at age 11 in primary school to gain admittance to arts-oriented St. Albans Grammar School, rather than a trade-oriented secondary school. He lived in nearby Markyate, where his parents, Harold and Nan, owned the village general store that stocked groceries, hardware, paints and furniture. As youngsters, Chris and his sister worked in the store. "That's why I didn't become a store owner. It's very hard work," said Chris. "I remember my dad de-boning his own bacon and cutting it in slices." For enjoyment, Harold played double bass in dance bands that performed the music of Glenn Miller and other swing bands, and he gave Chris his initial musical training. After first learning to play guitar, Chris played bass during his teenage years with local skiffle groups, and formed a couple of his own short-lived bands. He also gained experience playing in local big bands, orchestras and jazz bands.

He brought that experience with him not only to the Zombies, but also to Argent, the band that he helped Rod Argent form in 1969. Chris lived modestly during the late '60s, rooming in the North Finchley sector of Greater London with friends he had known since his art college days. Although White did not appear on stage with Argent, his name was on the CBS recording contract, and he had a key role in musical arrangements and rehearsals. "Argent was a great group to work with. We used the same production principles as we did with the Zombies – working the songs through before we went into the studio," said White, who became the band's producer. Chris and Rod also produced Colin Blunstone's first three solo albums.

During the Argent era, Chris had become a family man, raising his sons with his wife, Lyn, whom he had married in 1970. After Argent disbanded, White decided to concentrate on songwriting. He subsequently sought a change of scenery as well, and the young family moved in 1979 to Spain, where they had previously vacationed. They settled 20 miles southwest of Barcelona, in the small coastal town of Sitges where a colony of musical composers had aggregated. Although Chris found the environment creatively stimulating, the marriage did not survive. In 1984 the family members returned to England – Lynn and the boys to Ealing, west of London, and Chris to an apartment at Sloane Square in central London that he shared with some writer friends, including the late Duncan Browne, who wrote songs for David Bowie and Colin Blunstone.

Chris immersed himself in production, working on two albums with organist Matthew Fisher, who formerly was with the band Procol Harum. Chris produced the first demos for Dire Straits, before that band landed a recording contract. He did production work for American composer and guitarist Michael Fennelly, formerly with the West Coast quintet Crabby Appleton, which scored a 1970 hit called "Go Back." He did production work for several English recording artists at a popular recording studio in Montreux, Switzerland.

In 1989 Chris became involved with development of a musical theater production called *Once Upon a Dream,* on which he has been collaborating with playwright Patrick Williams. Arlene Phillips, whose theatrical credits include the Andrew Lloyd Webber musical *Starlight Express,* expressed interest in choreographing the dance-based stage musical. *Once Upon a Dream* became an unfulfilled passion for White, who learned firsthand the difficulties of bringing a musical to the stage. Despite interest from several producers in New York and California, the production is still awaiting its first performance as those involved in its creation continue to seek financial backing and performance venues. "I'm absolutely determined to get it on before I die," White said. "The theater musical business is far more difficult than film or the music industry. You've got to hit the right person at just the right time and the right place."

Shortly after beginning work on *Once Upon a Dream*, Chris met artist and musician Vivienne Mair Boucherat, who at the time was working on two musical interpretations of artist Richard Long's work, used in an exhibition of his work. "We started writing together on the first night, and we decided to be together from then on," said White. The couple married in 1996 and settled in London.

Despite his advice to the contrary, Chris' sons were drawn to the performing arts. Matthew, born in 1972, became a record producer, sound-recording engineer, writer and computing programmer who has worked with Genesis, Tom Jones, Pink Floyd, Pulp, the Manic Street Preachers, Robbie Williams, Kylie Minogue, Danii Minogue, David Gray and Mick Hucknall, lead singer of Simply Red. He also has collaborated with producers, including David Bascombe, Steve Power and Gil Norton. Matthew engineered *Out of the Shadows,* the album that Rod Argent and Colin Blunstone recorded together in 2000 at Rod's studio. In partnership with Chris and Viv, Matthew also operated a small production company, Sunfish Music Ltd., which helped develop the careers of new artists. Most recently he has become director of user experience at Omnifone Ltd., a London digital music downloading company that contracts with electronic device manufacturers, mobile phone network operators and Internet service providers. "Omnifone is the world's leading independent digital music provider of unlimited and a la carte music services. We have global music rights for multiple platforms and currently are live in 21 countries. Recently we were very proud to announce that we have been working for two years with Sony, the world's largest consumer electronics manufacturer, to build and power their new online global multi-platform music service, Q Music Unlimited, currently available on TVs, Blu-ray players, games consoles and all PCs," Matthew explained.

"My middle son Jamie, who has a very good voice, decided to go into music after university," said Chris, who produced and performed on Jamie's first CD recording, *Featherhead*. Jamie released that recording in 2008 under his stage name, JJ White. Jamie, a guitarist as well as a singer, now is in a band called Et Tu Brucé, which in early 2011 recorded an album of their own songs. "It is very good, and that's not just my opinion. Their live gigs go down very well – live is very important in the Internet age," Chris observed. "Jamie and his wife, Clare, have also made me a first-time grandfather with 2-year-old Jackson," he proudly told us in March 2011.

Sacha, born in 1979, is finishing work to obtain his Ph.D. degree in plant and environmental science at the University of Warwick in Coventry. He has presented lectures in the subject at several conferences around the world. "But he still retains a very active interest in current music," Chris added.

Vivienne has her own art studio and works in several media, and her distinguishing creations include individual handmade slides, installations and collage. "She works with large prints and layered prints sourced from her 'magnified hand-made micro collages' which are constructed on 35 mm slide cases and then enlarged," Chris explained. Vivienne has exhibited her artwork at the new Tate Modern Gallery and at The Mall Gallery in Central London. She also is a songwriter, instrumental arranger and a singer with the London Bulgarian Choir, which has backed several bands at the Roundhouse in London and the Glastonbury Festival. "I love the Bulgarian music," Chris said. "It's absolutely energetic and exciting. A builder friend of ours who is a heavy metal fan was staying with us because he was doing some work on our house. We took him along to a London Bulgarian Choir performance, and we didn't think he was going to enjoy it but he said, 'that's the most exciting thing I've seen since Led Zeppelin at Knebworth [Music Festival].' So we're involved very closely with them and helping them out, because it's only an amateur choir, but it's wonderful."

The Whites have produced music for films and animation in their digital studio and, in November 1998, won an international song contest with the theme of world peace and harmony, sponsored by the International Federation of Festival Organizations (Federation Internationale des Organisations de Festivals or "FIDOF") of Sherman Oaks, California. Chris' songwriting collaborators include his nephew Andy Nye, a well-regarded keyboard player who has worked with Michael Schenker, the German heavy-metal guitarist who formed the Scorpions, as well as with singer Sheena Easton and Scottish rock band musician Barbara Dixon, who had several hit records and performed in musical theater in the west end of London. Nye is the son of Chris's older sister Daphne, who died in 1980.

Chris, Matthew and Viv collaborated on writing, recording and producing an album for singer Bianca Kinane, who records under the name of Bianca K. In late spring 2011 they were creating a website to publicize her as-yet untitled album. "Bianca has a fantastic voice and a great personality," Chris said. On hearing the album, Academy Award and Golden Globe lyricist Sir Tim Rice said it was "a bit like Enya meeting Roxy with Sibelius lending a hand." Multiple-hit songwriter and musician Russ Ballard, previously a member of the bands Unit 4 + 2 and Argent, wrote, "I found the music moving, atmospheric, and obviously a labour of love."

Meanwhile, Chris and Viv wrote a couple of songs for an animated 3-D film that will be a joint Chinese-Spanish-Italian-German and French production. They may be commissioned to compose all the background music for the production. "I don't know what it's going to be called, but it's about a black sheep who wants to go to the moon," Chris said. Chris and Viv previously worked with the film's French director on other animated features. Chris marvels at changes that have taken place in the music industry during the past four decades. "I see live music being more to the forefront now. Bands used to tour to promote an album; now they put out an album to promote a tour."

In his home studio in South London, Chris works with the latest digital equipment – sequencers and other gadgetry. He is a perfectionist, often laboring two to three days in mixing an individual song. "Sometimes I wish for the old days where you recorded a take in a half an hour. But songs that were done that way are of an era. Nowadays performers are judged by the quality of the sound and the tightness of the arrangement. But I do sometimes wish for the spontaneity of it all," White said. "We did, of course, rehearse for a week with each song before each session to get it tight as if we were recording it."

Precision in the studio was a necessity in those days, when the Zombies were recorded on four-track equipment – even the last *Odessey and Oracle* sessions at the Abbey Road studios. "Bass, drums and guitar were recorded on one mono track, keyboard on another. We'd lay the instrumental tracks down first, and then the lead vocal and harmony on the other two tracks. We all played together, and if someone made a mistake, we'd have to do the whole thing again," White explained. "Later, when Rod and I did Argent, it went all of the sudden to eight-track, then 16, then 24 during the time we were recording. There were advantages to that, but most of the advantages went to the studios, which started earning more money."

As simplistic as the recording techniques of the '60s were, they enabled artistic improvisation that newer technological approaches can stifle. "Thrown together as we were at a young age, the Zombies worked with a total blank canvas, and everybody's interest was melded into it," observed White. "Our sound was distinctive because of the keyboard lead, the fact that Rod was such an excellent keyboard innovator, and Colin's voice, as well as our arrangements." He believes that assessment is validated by the newfound respect being given to the band. "In the '60s, we were just one of many groups. Now interest in the Zombies seems greater than when we were together. In fact, I think we're earning more money now through the sales of records, because we've been getting great press in America, and rave reviews on the CD box set. And Tom Petty has said he learned to play his guitar by hearing the bass line from 'She's Not There,' and Billy Joel and other performers have talked about being influenced by the Zombies. But the most fascinating is the groups of 18- and 19-year-olds coming to small gigs and telling me that their favorite album is *Odessey and Oracle*. That was recorded more than 40 years ago, and they're listening to it and raving about it. It's quite fascinating, really."

Despite his impressive musical legacy, Chris is content to concentrate on writing and production rather than on performing. But he allows that he does enjoy occasional forays into the spotlight.

"I don't consider myself a jobbing musician," Chris told us in March 2011. "I really, really enjoyed the Zombies' reunion in 2008, and the following year. It was great being on stage with the guys again. It was just like yesterday. And it was really nice to do the *Odessey and Oracle* 40th anniversary performance. We had never done it live before then because at the time it was released, nobody wanted the album. Since then we received the Mojo Award for the classic album of the '60s. It has become a cult thing now." Chris said he treasures the connections he has made with people as a result of his own work and his participation in the Zombies.

"Having our work recognized that way was a pleasure. Really, though, the most important thing about working with music is that you connect. Many young groups have been quoting the Zombies as an influence on them. We went to see the Fleet Foxes recently at the Roundhouse in London, and the first thing they did was give me a hug and tell me 'thanks for the music.' That was a pleasure," Chris said. "At the anniversary concerts in 2008, I learned that singer-songwriter Paul Weller, whom I'd never met before, is a fantastic fan and advocate of *Odessey and Oracle.* He came backstage for all three nights. He was originally with the Jam. He's a stalwart of English music, and he's called the 'modfather of rock.' When I introduced myself he gave me a great big hug and he said, 'Chris White, you're the reason I started writing songs,' which I thought was one of the things you really treasure, you know?"

White is unable to speculate what his life might have been like if he'd completed that last year of teacher training at art college rather than remaining with the Zombies. "I've taught my kids that they should never say, 'if only.' You are what you are today because of the route you've taken," White asserts. "It's absolutely impossible to imagine what I'd be now if I hadn't been in the Zombies, because all of my connections and all of the routes I took were through the friends I made jointly and individually in the Zombies. I can't imagine knowing any of them had I not been in the Zombies."

He has another important piece of advice for his sons: "Be honest with yourself. Look at the recurring patterns in your life if something keeps going wrong. Keep centered, and if an opportunity comes up, take it. Don't play the safe route. There's no such thing. Every day is a new challenge. I think the second coming was Bill Hicks, the comedian who died in 1994 at age 32. He said, 'It's just a ride.' Life is just a ride, so hold on, and get it right, and be truthful to yourself. I learned not to do things for money, because if you try to write a hit song, it never works out. But if you write a good song and even if it's not a hit, you're still left with a good song. Of course, you can't always play to those rules. Sometimes you have to pay the bills, but where you can, do it for the music."

For more information, visit **www.biancakmusic.com**

Index

Index

Index